SOCIOLOGICAL
INQUIRY

SOCIOLOGICAL INQUIRY

A HUMANISTIC PERSPECTIVE

edited by

Kooros M. Mahmoudi
Bradley W. Parlin

Indiana University

K|H

KENDALL/HUNT PUBLISHING COMPANY
DUBUQUE, IOWA

Library of Congress Catalog Card Number: 73-84129

ISBN 0—8403—0786—1

Printed in the United States of America.

To
Nellie and Susan

It can be said that the first wisdom of sociology is this—things are not what they seem.

Peter Berger

CONTENTS

PART IV
STRATIFICATION

PART V
WORK AND ORGANIZATIONS

PART VI
DEVIANCE

PART VII
POPULATION AND ECOLOGY

PART VIII
THE FUTURE OF MASS SOCIETY

Preface

A book of readings in general sociology cannot hope to provide a comprehensive coverage of all the literature of the discipline and maintain a well defined perspective. A major shortcoming of many of the readers in introductory sociology is the "shotgun" approach, which seems to characterize the selection of articles for the volumes. In short, they lack well defined perspectives.

It is the editors' belief that a reader should exhibit a sensitivity for continuity. Something of sociological substance should tie the selected readings together. Even a cursory glance at the proliferation of introductory readers on the market suggests two basic themes: "lifeless empiricism," which purports to represent "typical" sociological research on the one hand, and "pop" sociology on the other. Neither of these perspectives provides the student with anything but a conglomeration of unrelated readings.

The stimulus for this endeavor was primarily to present the introductory student with readable, high-quality articles from the scholarly journals of the discipline oriented around two important themes within the discipline. First, the authors take a *humanistic* perspective in their analysis of social phenomenon. Second, the impact of *social structure* upon the individual is a fundamental premise.

Another important difference between this reader and most others we have reviewed is that it makes no pretext of being "value-free." With all due respect to the great German sociologist, Max Weber, the editors believe that value freedom in science is neither attainable nor necessarily desirable. The implications and consequences of social research for the human beings whose activities comprise the subject matter of our discipline, we feel, should be a central concern to the social scientist. Hopefully, our selection of articles and organization of the contents are consistent with the above orientations.

Finally, the editors would like to acknowledge the thoughtful comments and criticisms of two colleagues, Professors Warren Lucas and Marty Zusman. We would also like to thank Kathy Haller, Jane Nusbaumer, and Debbie Winkler for the extensive and enthusiastic research and secretarial assistance rendered in the preparation of this project.

Part I

SOCIOLOGICAL INQUIRY

"One way of looking at the history of the human group is that it has been a continuing struggle against the veneration of 'crap.' Our intellectual history is a chronicle of the anguish and suffering of men who tried to help their contemporaries see that some part of their fondest beliefs were misconceptions, faulty assumptions, superstitions, and even outright lies. The mileposts along the road of our intellectual development signal those points at which some person developed a new perspective, a new meaning, or a new metaphor. We have in mind a new education that would set out to cultivate just such people—experts at 'crap detecting.'"

Neil Postman and Charles Weingartner

Introduction to Part I
(Sociological Inquiry)

Sociological inquiry is a form of explanation which seeks to understand and explain the relationships between social structure and human behavior. Of prime concern to the sociologist is the way in which elements of social structure affect the behavior of groups. Sociological inquiry, because of its structural perspective, is often difficult for the student to grasp. Students, by and large, come to the classroom rather poorly equipped to understand the structural position. This is because individuals in American society are socialized at home, in elementary and secondary schools, and through the political system to think largely in terms of individual explanation.

1

To demonstrate or exemplify sociological reasoning, it might be best to first provide an example of the antithesis of sociological inquiry. The most common forms of explanation in our society might be nominally deemed "individual explanations."

Individual explanations of human behavior generally interpret the relative success or failure of actors within a social system in terms of some attribute peculiar to the individual. This form of individual explanation is what one sociologist has called "Blaming the Victim." An extreme, but rather humorous, example of Blaming the Victim is related by William Ryan.

> Twenty years ago, Zero Mostel used to do a sketch in which he impersonated a Dixiecrat senator conducting an investigation of the origins of World War II. At the climax of the sketch, the senator boomed out, in an excruciating mixture of triumph and suspicion, "What was Pearl Harbor doing in the Pacific?"*

Another example of Blaming the Victim occurs when a student's failure to perform well in school is attributed to some flaw in the student's personality. He was too lazy, stupid, arrogant, antagonistic, etc. This form of explanation is often myopic. The sociologists would look, not necessarily at personality attributes of the student, but rather at the structural circumstances which might account for his failure. Questions in which the sociologist would be most interested might include:

1. How might the racial orientation of the school's bureaucracy account for the likelihood of success or failure of some students?
2. To what extent does the competitive character of the school system create levels of frustration which might lead some students to simply "give up" and "drop out?"

In short, the sociologist is most interested in the way in which structure affects human behavior.

Another important feature of sociology is that it is at the same time an art and a science. Individual sociologists often cling more closely to one or the other of these two orientations. Some tend to emphasize the art of sociology, while others emphasize the science of sociology. The editors have attempted to maintain a balance between the arts/sciences dichotomy of arts and sciences.

The articles by Professors Redfield and O'Neill emphasize the way in which sociology is an art. If a sociologist is to truly understand human behavior, he must always remember that as a human being he is part of the drama he is investigating. The sociologist must

*William Ryan, *Blaming the Victim* (New York: Vintage Books, 1971) p. 3.

not become totally dependent upon the complex methods and techniques of social science investigation. If the research findings of sociology are to be of any value, the sociologist must exercise his imagination as an artist, for meaningful research results begin with imaginative and often critical ideas about the human condition. It is in this sense that the sociologist and the artist have a common identity.

Professor Zusman's article emphasizes the way in which sociology is a science. Although meaningful research begins with artful questions about human behavior, the goal of sociology is explanation and prediction. To explain and predict human behavior, the sociologist uses the methods and techniques of science. A central feature of the scientific perspective lies in the notion of skepticism. A sociologist must always be skeptical of accepted dictums concerning human behavior. Not only is the sociologist skeptical of so-called "common sense" explanations of human behavior, but he is also skeptical of the research findings of his own colleagues. Skepticism, then, is the cornerstone of science. Skepticism, as a perspective means, simply that the sociologist, like any scientist, approaches reality critically. His job is not to reinforce or support popular beliefs, mythologies, or theories. A responsible sociologist seeks to better understand social phenomena through critical analysis.

1. THE ART OF SOCIAL SCIENCE[1]

Robert Redfield

A dozen years ago I was a member of a committee of social scientists on social science method charged to appraise some outstanding published works of social science research. Our task was to find some good publications of social science research and then to discover in what their methodological virtue consisted. The first part of our task we passed on to the communities of social scientists themselves. We asked economists to name some outstanding work in their field, sociologists to pick a work in sociology, etc. We limited the choice to publications by living social scientists. Of the books or monographs that received the greatest number of nominations, three were then subjected to analysis and discussion. I participated in the study of the methodological virtues of *The Polish Peasant* by Thomas and Znaniecki and of Webb's *The Great Plains*. These were books

Reprinted from *The American Journal of Sociology*, Vol. LIV, No. 3, November 1948, pp. 181-190, by permission of the publisher, The University of Chicago Press.

nominated by sociologists and historians, respectively, as outstanding in merit.

A curious thing happened. Herbert Blumer, who analyzed *The Polish Peasant* for the committee, came to the conclusion that the method in that book was really unsuccessful because the general propositions set forth in the work could not be established by the particular facts adduced. The committee had to agree. Yet it remained with the impression that this was a very distinguished and important work. Webb's history of cultural transformation in the American West fared no better at the hands of the young historian who analyzed that work. He pointed out many undeniable failures of the author of *The Great Plains* to use and to interpret fully some of the evidence. And yet again a majority of the committee persisted in the impression that Webb's book was truly stimulating, original, and praiseworthy.

Of course one does not conclude from this experience that the failure of facts to support hypotheses, in whole or in part, is a virtue in social science or is to be recommended. No doubt these books would have been more highly praised had these defects been proved to be absent. But does not the experience suggest that there is something in social science which is good, perhaps essential, apart from success with formal method; that these works have virtues not wholly dependent on the degree of success demonstrated in performing specified and formalized operations on restricted and precisely identified data?

I recall a comment I heard made by a distinguished social scientist whom I shall call A, about another distinguished social scientist whom I shall call B. A said of B: "He is very successful in spite of his method." Now, A was one who laid great stress on the obedience of the research worker to precise methods of operation with limited data, whereas B was much less so concerned. Yet A admired B, and the success he recognized in B was not worldly success but success in advancing our understanding and our control of man in society. Perhaps A felt that B's success was troubling to A's own views as to the importance of formal method. But A, a generous and able man, recognized something of virtue in B as a great student of man in society—a something other than methodological excellence.

What is that something? In attempting an answer here, I do not propose a separation between two ways of working in the scientific study of society. Nor do I deny that social science is dependent upon formal method. I seek rather to direct attention to an aspect of fruitful work in social science which is called for, in addition to formal method, if social science is to be most productive.

Let us here try to find out something about the nature of this nonformal aspect of social science through a consideration of three books about society that have long been recognized as important, influential, and meritorious: De Tocqueville's *Democracy in America,* Sumner's *Folkways,* and Veblen's *The Theory of the Leisure Class.* For from almost fifty to a hundred years these books have interested and have influenced many kinds of social scientists. Veblen and Sumner were economists, but the books they wrote are important for sociologists, anthropologists, historians, and other kinds of social scientists. De Tocqueville's book is a work interesting to political scientists as well as to historians of America, but it is quite as much a work in sociology, for De Tocqueville was concerned not so much in reporting what went on in the United States in 1830 as he was in defining a sort of natural societal type: the democratic society, including in the type not merely its political institutions but also its moral, familial, and "cultural" institutions and attitudes, treated as a single whole.

None of these books tells very much about research method, in the sense of teaching special procedures of operation with certain kinds of data. There is nothing in any of them about kinship genealogies, or sampling, or guided interviews, or margins of error. There is nowhere in them any procedure, any kind of operation upon facts to reach conclusions which might not occur to any intelligent and generally educated person. Sumner made notes on the customs of exotic peoples as he read about them. Veblen's methods, as represented in *The Theory of the Leisure Class,* are no more formal than Sumner's. The factual substance of De Tocqueville's book is the record of his own observations as he traveled about America looking at what there was about him and talking to the people he met. If these books have merit, it is not by reason of any inventions or devices of method, for they exhibit none. Yet these are books which have for many years profoundly affected the course of social science and have contributed to our understanding of man in society. They might be even more important if they also made contributions to or through formal method, but, as they do not, something may be learned from them about that part of the study of society which is not formal method.

Perhaps these are not works of research. Perhaps for some "research" always means special procedures of operation which have to be learned or means analysis of some small set of facts or very limited problem. If this is your view of research, I shall not dispute it. Then the three books are not works of research. But what is there in them that is admired and that is valuable in the study of man in society that is not dependent upon formal method?

If these three classic books are not books in social science, what are they? They are surely not novels, or journalism, or yet belles-lettres. That they have qualities of literary style is true—and is not to be deplored—even Sumner's book impresses with the effective iteration of its terse, stark sentences. But the value of these books for the student of society lies not in any appeal they make to aesthetic sensibilities but for the illumination they throw upon man's nature or upon the nature of society. It is true that great novels do that too. But there are, of course, important differences between the books named, on the one hand, and, let us say, *War and Peace* and *The Remembrance of Things Past*, on the other. These last are works for social scientists to know about and to learn from, but they are not works of social science. They are not because neither Proust's book nor Tolstoi's is a generalized description of the nature of society stated at some remove from the personal experiences of the writer. De Tocqueville made his own observations, but he stated his results objectively in generalized and analytical terms making comparisons with other observations and conclusions easy. Tolstoi wrote about a real Russia during the real Napoleonic Wars, but his Pierres and Natashas are imagined, individual, personal, intimate, and ungeneralized. It is not difficult to distinguish the great analyses of society, as objectively studied and presented in generalized conclusion, from the works of personal record and of freely creative imagination.

Are the three books "objective" descriptions of society? In varying degree, but all three to some degree. Probably De Tocqueville, who of the three writers was least a professional social scientist, impresses one most with an air of severe detachment, of willingness to look at this social being, a democratic society, without blame or praise. De Tocqueville's work seems as objective as a social scientist might wish. Sumner, too, is describing, not evaluating, yet there is in the *Folkways* an undertone of patient scorn for the irrationality of man, for man's obedience to whatever folly his tradition may decree. Veblen seems the least objective. Below the forms of scientific analysis lies, urbanely and ironically disguised, the condemnation of a moralist. As a recent writer on Veblen has put it, he used "the realistic paraphernalia of scholarship" to attack the morality of capitalistic society.[2] Nevertheless, even Veblen's book presents a fresh description of a part of modern society, and the description is not that of a creative artist but of one who is responsible to facts studied and facts verifiable.

The three books are works which are not novels, which do not have much to say about formal procedures of research, and which, nevertheless, throw light upon man in society through the more or less objective presentation of generalized conclusions from the study of particular societies. In these respects they correspond with what is by at least some people called "scientific." What did the authors do that constitutes their contribution to the understanding of man in society?

It is surely not that these writers have been proved to be invariably right. Indeed, in each case there are points in which in the later days they have been found wrong. Veblen's account overemphasizes competitiveness in terms of consumption and accepts a good deal of what was then current as to race and as to stages of social evolution which is not inacceptable today. Sumner's conception of the mores, immensely stimulating as it was, exaggerates the helplessness of men before tradition and is especially inadequate as a concept for understanding modern societies—as Myrdal has recently shown. And, although De Tocqueville's account of early American society is perceptive and revealing to a degree that is almost miraculous, there is certainly confusion in it between what is necessarily democratic and what is characteristic of the frontier and between what must be characteristic of any democracy and what happened to be in the Anglo-American tradition.

In three respects these books, which have nothing to teach about formal method, make great contributions to the understanding of man in society.

In the first place, each is an expression of some perception of human nature. In each case the writer has looked at people in a society, or in many societies, and has directly apprehended something about their ways of thinking and feeling which are characteristic of the human race under those particular circumstances. His central concern has not been some second- or third-hand index or sign of human nature, some check marks on a schedule or some numbered quantities of anything. He has looked at people with the vision of his own humanity.

Not all of what is called social science is concerned with human nature. The study of population is not concerned with it until matters of population policy are reached. Marginal analysis in economics is concerned with such a slender sliver of human nature, so artificially severed from the rest, that it, too, is unrepresentative of studies of human nature. And this is also of necessity true of much of the archeology of the North American Indian.

These last-mentioned kinds of investigation, worthy as they are, are the special or marginal cases that mark the outskirts of the study of man in society. The essential nature of man in society is his human nature and the expressions of that human nature in particular institutions. To find out the nature and significance of human nature there is no substitute for the human nature of the student himself. He must use his own humanity to understand humanity. To understand alien institutions, he .must try to see in them the correspondences and the divergences they exhibit in relation to the institutions with which he is more closely familiar. To understand an alien culture, it is not, first of all, necessary to learn how to interview or how to make schedules for a house-to-house canvass, useful as these skills are. It is first needful to have experienced some culture—some culture which will serve as the touchstone in apprehending this new one.

One aspect of the great merit of the three works mentioned lies in the central attention directed by Sumner, Veblen, and De Tocqueville to the humanity of their subject matter and in the success each had in apprehending the particular facet of that humanity as it was shaped and conditioned by the surrounding circumstances. Sumner, looking especially at small, long-isolated societies or at the later little-changing societies derived from primitive conditions, saw the resulting creation, in each individual there born and reared, of motives and designs of life that were there, in the customs of that society, before him. He saw in human nature the extraordinary malleability of human nature and the precedence of custom over habit. Veblen looked freshly at the behavior of consumers, saw them as people who actually do buy and consume, in their families and their communities, and recognized theretofore insufficiently recognized aspects of human nature in society. De Tocqueville touched Americans in their age of self-confidence and in a great number of true perceptions saw what their behavior meant to them and why. Just compare his success in using his own humanity with imagination, and yet with detachment, with Mrs. Trollope's failure to achieve understanding of these same people.

It is at this point that the methods of the social sciences—now using "method" in its broadest sense to include all the ways of thinking and even feeling about subject matter—approach the methods of the creative artist. Like the novelist, the scientific student of society must project the sympathetic understanding which he has of people with motives, desires, and moral judgments into the subject he is treating. Neither the one nor the other can get along without this gift, this means of understanding. But whereas the novelist may let his imagination run freely, once it is stimulated by personal experience and reading, the scientific student must constantly return to the particular men, the particular societies, he has chosen to investigate, test his insights by these, and report these particular facts with such specificity that his successor may repeat the testing. In spite of this all-important difference, the territories of the humanities and of the scientific study of man in society are in part the same. The subject matter of both is, centrally, man as a human being. Human beings are not the subject matter of physics and chemistry. So it would be error to build a social science upon the image of physics or chemistry. Social science is neither the same as the humanities nor the same as the physical sciences. It is a way of learning about man in society which uses the precise procedures and the objectivity characteristic of physics as far as these will helpfully go in studying human beings but no further; and which uses, indispensably, that personal direct apprehension of the human qualities of behavior and of institutions which is shared by the novelist.

A second observation may be made about the three books chosen. Each brings forward significant generalizations. In the case of Veblen's book, the general conceptions that are known by the phrases "pecuniary emulation," "vicarious consumption," etc., are, like the concepts in *Folkways*, names for new insights into persistent and widely inclusive aspects of man's nature in society. In reading these books, we catch a glimpse of the eternal in the light of the ephemeral. We see ourselves as exemplifications of patterns in nature. Social science is concerned with uniformities. The uniformities are exaggerated; they transcend the particularity of real experience and historic event; they claim more than each fact by itself would allow; they say: "If it were really like this, this would be the pattern." De Tocqueville, too, offers such patterns that go beyond the particular facts. Indeed, the case of De Tocqueville is particularly plain in this connection, for so interested is he in presenting a system of coherent generalizations as to the necessary nature of democratic society that in many passages he makes no reference at all to what he saw in the United States but derives one generalization as to the democratic society he conceives from some other generalization already brought forward. He is not, therefore, to be rejected as a contributor to the scientific understanding of society, for these deductions are tied to generalizations that in turn rest upon many particular observations of many particular men and events. The concept, like the novel, is a work of creative imagination but a work more closely and publicly bound to particular facts of observation and record.

Like the apprehension of the humanly significant, the making of the generalization is a work of imagination. Sumner did not find out that there is such a thing as the mores by learning and applying some method of research. He discovered it by watching the people around him and by using the observations recorded by other men and then by making a leap of thought across many diversities to apprehend the degree of uniformity that deserves the term "mores." In the reaching of a significant generalization as to man in society there is an exercise of a gift of apprehension so personal and so subtly creative that it cannot be expected to result merely from application of some formal method of research.

The three books show thinkers about man in society who have had some new and generalized apprehension of human nature or of human institutions. They have succeeded in communicating this apprehension in such a way as to show it to be both important and true. It is true in the sense that there are facts accessible that support it. It is not, of course, all the truth, and it may be that some other apprehension will come to appear "more true," that is, even more illuminating, as applied to some set of circumstances.

There is another quality in the thinking and the creating of the three writers that deserves recognition by itself: the freshness and independence of viewpoint with which each looked at his subject matter. One feels, in reading any one of the three books, how the writer saw what he saw with his own eyes, as if the previous views of it were suspect, just because they were previous. One feels in the case of each writer a discontent with the way some aspect of man in society was then being regarded, a clearheaded willfulness to take another look for himself. There is a disposition to make the thing looked at a true part of the viewer's own being, to go beyond obedience to the existing writings on the subject. De Tocqueville was dissatisfied with the views of democracy current in his time: the passionate condemnations or the equally passionate espousals. He would go to the country where the angel or the monster was actually in course of development, and he would, he resolved coolly, look for neither monster nor angel; he would look at what he should find, and grasp it, in its whole and natural condition, as one would look at a newly arrived class of animal. He could weigh the good and the bad, then, after he had come to understand the natural circumstances that would produce the creature. Sumner's book is in one way a reaffirmation of a viewpoint then current and in another way a reaction against it. As the folkways come about by no man's planning but through the accidental interactions of men and the competition of alternative solutions, they are consistent with that conception of unrestrained individualistic competition which Sumner supported in the economic sphere. On the other hand, the *Folkways* reads as a reaction against the Age of Reason. It seems to say that men do not, after all, solve their problems by rational calculation of utilities. Looked at anew, the ways of men appear not reasonable but unreasonable and determined by pre-existing customs and moral judgments which make the calculation of utilities seem absurd. From this point of view the book is an act of rebellion. An economist looks for himself at the whole human scene and says, too emphatically, no doubt, what needs to be said to correct the preceding vision. Something not so different could be said about the fresh look that Veblen took.

It may be objected that the qualities in these three works are qualities one may expect to find only in an occasional book written by some unusual mind. These books have passed beyond social science, or they fall short of it; and the humbler toiler in the vineyard cannot expect to learn from them anything that would help him in tending the vines of his more limited hypotheses or in pressing the wine of his more restricted conclusions.

Yet all three of the qualities found in these works may be emulated by the student of any human aspect of man in society. It is not only in good major works that there is found that human sympathy which is needful in apprehending a human reality. The exercise of this capacity is demanded in every study of a community; it is exacted in every consideration of an institution in which men with motives and desires like our own fulfill the roles and offices that make it up; it is required in every interview. One may be taught how to pursue a course of questioning, how to map a neighborhood, or how to tabulate and treat statistically the votes cast in an election; but to know how to do these things is not to be assured of meaningful conclusions. Besides these skills, one needs also the ability to enter imaginatively, boldly, and, at the same time, self-critically into that little fraction of the human comedy with which one has become scientifically concerned. One must become a part of the human relations one studies, while holding one's self also a little to one side, so as to suspend judgment as to the worth of one's first insight. Then one looks at the scene again; perhaps, guided by something one has known or read of human beings in some comparable situation, in some other place or age, one may get a second insight that better withstands reexamination and the test of particular observations. This procedure, call it method, non-method, or what you will, is an essential part of most of social science, great and small.

As for the exercise of the ability to see the general in the particular, is this not also demanded of anyone who takes a scientific attitude toward anything in human nature or society? We are not freed from the obligation to look for what may be widely true by the narrowness, in time and space, of the facts before us. Surely Sumner did not wait to conceive of the mores until he had piled up those five hundred pages of examples. Malinowski provided a clearer understanding of the nature of myth, in its resemblance to and its difference from folk tale, from the view he had of the stories told and the ways they were told in a small community in the South Seas. Webb, a historian rather than one of those students of society who more easily announce generalizations thought to be widely applicable, does not, in his *The Great Plains*, announce any; but the value of the work lies for many in the fact that it is easily read as an exemplification of the tendency of institutions adjusted to one environment to undergo change when imported into a new and of the effects of changes in technology upon human relations. The social scientist is always called upon to use his imagination as to the general that may lie within the immediate particulars. The formal method may lead him to these generalizations; after he has added up the cases, or completed the tests, he may for the first time see some correspondences that suggest a generalization. But it happens at least as often that he sees the generalization long before the formal methods have been carried out; the exercise of the formal method may then test the worth of his insight. And a significant generalization may appear without formal method. The conceptions of marginal utility in economics and of the marginal man in sociology perhaps illustrate the development of a concept, on the one hand, with close dependence upon formal method and, on the other, without such dependence. In the latter case Park was struck by resemblances in the conduct of particular men and women whom he met, American Negroes, mission-educated Orientals, and second-generation immigrants: humane insight, guided by scientific imagination, then created the concept.

The third quality of good social science in its less formal aspects is freshness of vision. It is the looking at what one is studying as if the world's comprehension of it depended solely on one's own look. In taking such a look, one does not ignore the views that other man have taken of the subject matter or of similar subject matter. But these earlier views are challenged. Maybe, one says, it is not as my teachers told me I should find it. I will look for myself. One has perhaps heard something about folk society. But at this particular society with which I am concerned I will look for myself. Perhaps there is no folk society there. Perhaps there is something else, much nearer the truth.

It is difficult for teachers who have expounded their own views of some aspect of man in society to teach their successors to take some other view of it. Perhaps it cannot be taught. Yet somehow each generation of social scientists must rear a following generation of rebels. Now rebellion is not well inculcated in the teaching of formal procedure. Indeed, an exclusive emphasis on formal procedure may cause atrophy of the scientific imagination. To train a man to perform a technique may result in making him satisfied with mastery of the technique. Having learned so much about field procedure, or statistics, or the situations in which interviews are held and recorded, or the criticism of documents, the new social scientist may come to feel that he has accomplished all the learning he needs. He may rest content in proficiency. Proficiency is excellent, but it must be combined with an imaginative dissatisfaction. In little investigations as in large ones, the situation studied demands a whole look and a free look.

It is equally doubtful whether one can give instruction in the exercise of humane insight or in recognizing the general in the particular when the generality is not thrust upon the student by a marked statistical predominance. These are qualities of the social science investigator that perhaps depend upon the accidents of natural endowment. Humane insight is a gift. The concept is a work of creative imagination; apprehension is a gift. In stressing the necessity, in good social science, for the investigator to think and to speculate independently and freely, in emphasizing the reliance of good social science upon the personal and human qualities of the investigator, one seems to be talking not about a science but about an art and to be saying that social science is also an art. It is an art in that the social scientist creates imaginatively out of his own human qualities brought into connection with the facts before him. It is an art in degree much greater than that in which physics and chemistry are arts, for the student of the atom or of the element is not required, when he confronts his subject matter, to become a person among persons, a creature of tradition and attitude in a community that exists in tradition and in attitude. With half his being the social scientist approaches his subject matter with a detachment he shares with the physicist. With the other half he approaches it with a human sympathy which he shares with the novelist. And it is an art to a greater degree than is physics or chemistry for the further reason that the relationships among the parts of a person or of a society are, as compared with physical relationships, much less susceptible of definitions, clear and machine precise. In spite of the great advances in formal method in social science, much of the understanding of persisting and general relationships depends upon a grasp that is intuitive and that is independent of or not fully dependent on some formal method. In advancing social science, we invent and practice techniques, and we also cultivate a humanistic art.

The nature of social science is double. In the circle of learning, its place adjoins the natural sciences, on the one hand, and the humanities, on the other. It is not a result of exceptional political ambition that political scientists and anthropologists are to be found included both in the Social Science Research Council and in the American Council of Learned Societies; it is a recognition of the double nature of social science. On the one hand, the student of society is called upon to apprehend the significant general characteristics of human beings with something of the same human insight which is practiced by a novelist or a dramatist. On the other hand, he is obliged to make his observations and his inferences as precise and as testable, and his generalizations as explicit and as compendent, as the examples of the natural sciences suggest and as his own different materials allow.

It is the example of the natural sciences which social scientists have on the whole striven to imitate. In the short history of social science its practitioners have turned their admiring gazes toward their neighbors on the scientific side. They have looked that way, perhaps, because the natural sciences were the current success. They have looked that way, surely, because when the students of human nature in society came to think of themselves as representing one or more disciplines, with professors and places in universities and in national councils, social science was not very scientific: it was speculative and imprecise. To achieve identity, it had to grow away from the making of personally conceived systems of abstract thought. It had to learn to build, a brick at a time, and to develop procedures that would make the building public and subject to testing.

But now the invention and the teaching of special procedures have received too exclusive an emphasis in the doing of social science and in the making of social scientists. In places the invention and the teaching of special procedures have gone ahead of the possibility of finding out anything very significant with their aid. It is certainly desirable to be precise, but it is quite as needful to be precise about something worth knowing. It is good to teach men and women who are to be social scientists how to use the instruments of observation and analysis that have been developed in their disciplines. But it is not good to neglect that other equally important side of social science.

To identify social science very closely with the physical sciences is to take one view of the education of social scientists: to think of that education chiefly in terms of formal method and formal knowledge of society already achieved and to be taught. Then programs for making social scientists will be made up of training in techniques and the opportunity to take part in some kind of research in which the procedures are already determined and the problems set by some established master. Then the holder of a fellowship will go to a school, where a way of working is well known and well fixed, and he will acquire the procedural competences taught at that school.

If this is all we do for young students of society, we are likely to have proficient technicians, but we are not likely to have great social scientists or to have many books written that are as illuminating and as influential as those by Sumner, Veblen, and De Tocqueville.

It would be well to give some attention to the humanistic aspect of social science. Part of the preparation of good social scientists is humanistic education. As what is called general education, or liberal education, is largely humanistic, it follows that the social scientist has two interests in liberal education. Like the physicist, like everybody else, the social scientist needs liberal education in his role as a citizen. But, in addition, he needs liberal humanistic education in his role as a social scientist.

The art of social science cannot be inculcated, but, like other arts, it can be encouraged to develop. The exercise of that art can be favored by humanistic education. If the social scientist is to apprehend, deeply and widely and correctly, persons and societies and cultures, then he needs experience, direct or vicarious, with persons, societies, and cultures. This experience is partly had through acquaintance with history, literature, biography, and ethnography. And if philosophy gives some experience in the art of formulating and in thinking about widely inclusive generalizations, then the social scientist needs acquaintance with philosophy. There is no longer any need to be fearful about philosophy. The time when young social science was struggling to make itself something different from philosophy is past. Now social science is something different. Now social scientists need to learn from philosophy, not to become philosophers, but to become better social scientists. The acquaintance with literature, biography, ethnography, and philosophy which is gained in that general education given in high schools and colleges is probably not rich enough or deep enough for some of those who are to become social scientists. The opportunities for advanced education given to some who appear to have exceptional gifts as students of man in society may well consist of the study of Chinese or East Indian culture, or of the novel in Western literature, or of the history of democracy.

The humanistic aspect of social science is the aspect of it that is today not well appreciated. Social science is essentially scientific in that its propositions describe, in general terms, natural phenomena; in that it returns again and again to special experience to verify and to modify these propositions. It tells what is, not what ought to be. It investigates nature. It strives for objectivity, accuracy, compendency. It employs hypotheses and formal evidence; it values negative cases; and, when it finds a hypothesis to be unsupported by the facts, it drops it for some other which is. But these are all aspects of social science so well known that it is tedious to list them again. What is less familiar, but equally true, is that to create the hypothesis, to reach the conclusion, to get, often, the very first real datum as to what are A's motives or what is the meaning of this odd custom or that too-familiar institution, requires on the part of one who studies persons and societies, and not rocks or proteins, a truly humanistic and freely imaginative insight into people, their conventions and interests and motives, and that this requirement in the social scientist calls for gifts and for a kind of education different from that required of any physicist and very similar to what is called for in a creative artist.

If this be seen, it may also be seen that the function of social science in our society is a double function. Social science is customarily explained and justified by reason of what social science contributes to the solution of particular problems that arise in the management of our society, as a help in getting particular things done. As social scientists we take satisfaction in the fact that today, as compared with thirty years ago, social scientists are employed because their employers think that their social science is applicable to some practical necessity. Some knowledge of techniques developed in social science may be used: to select taxicab drivers that are not likely to have accidents; to give vocational guidance; to discover why one business enterprise has labor troubles while a similar enterprise does not; to make more effective some governmental program carried into farming communities; to help the War Relocation Authority carry out its difficult task with Japanese-Americans.

All these contributions to efficiency and adjustment may be claimed with justice by social scientists. What is also to be claimed, and is less commonly stressed, is that social science contributes to that general understanding of the world around us which, as we say, "liberalizes," or "enriches." The relation of social science to humanistic learning is reciprocal. Social scientists need humanistic learning the better to be social scientists. And the understanding of society, personality, and human nature which is achieved by scientific methods returns to enrich that humanistic understanding without which none can become human and with which some few may become wise. Because its subject matter is humanity, the contribution of social science to general, liberal education is greater than is the contribution of those sciences with subject matter that is physical. In this respect also, creative artist and social scientist find themselves side by side. The artist may reveal something of universal human or social nature. So too may the social scientist. No one has ever applied, as a key to a lock, Sumner's *Folkways* or Tawney's *Religion and the Rise of Capitalism* or James's *The Varieties of Religious Experience*. These are not the works of social science that can be directly consulted and applied when a government office or a business concern has an immediate problem. But they are the books of lasting influence. Besides what influence they have upon those social scientists who come to work in the government office, or the business concern, in so far as they are read and understood and thought about by men and women who are not social scientists, or even as they are communicated indirectly by those who have read them to others, they are part of humanistic education, in the broad sense. Releasing us from our imprisonment in the particular, we are freed by seeing how we are exemplifications of the general. For how many young people has not Sumner's book, or Veblen's book, or some work by Freud, come as a swift widening of the doors of vision, truly a liberation, a seeing of one's self, perhaps for the first time, as sharing the experiences, the nature, of many other men and women? So I say that social science, as practiced, is something of an art and that, as its best works are communicated, it has something of the personal and social values of all the arts.

[1]A lecture delivered at the University of Chicago in May, 1948.

[2]Daniel Aaron, "Thorstein Veblen—Moralist," *Antioch Review*, VII, No. 3 (fall, 1947), 390.

2.   SOCIOLOGY AS A SKIN TRADE

John O'Neill

Sociology owes its fortune to the fact that nothing occupies man like himself. We are amazed as much by the misfortunes of others as by our own good fortune. Every need of ours involves someone else. The great tissue of human involvement which is woven out of our inability to live without the love and labor of others arouses a constant wonder in us. It is the framework of everything that is relevant to us.

Sociology is the study of people. It is a human pastime with pretensions to science. Sociology can be done in armchairs or buses, at sidewalk cafés or at university. Sociology belongs to familiar scenes, to neighborhoods, gangs and slums. In everyday life sociology belongs to the cunning of the salesman, and the hustler or to the proverbial barman and taxi-driver. This is an embarrassment to sociology once it aspires to science, affluence, and organization. Sociology when practiced seriously is a profession, like the priesthood or prostitution. Sociologists generally profess not to like priests, though they are often more friendly to them than to social workers. This is a matter of professional pride. For some reason, sociologists prefer prostitutes to priests or policemen and have become their natural protectors. This is a matter of professional jealousy; it belongs to the battle for souls, or clients, as they are called nowadays. To the extent that sociological alibis give more comfort than confessions of sin, the world belongs to sociology and is rid of priests. No one notices that the sociologist, the policeman and the prostitute then

Reprinted from *Sociological Inquiry* (Winter, 1970), by permission of the author and the publisher, Alpha Kappa Delta-National Sociology Honor Society.

proceed to divide the world between them in a three-penny opera of science and beggary.

Sociology has a natural fascination for young people painfully conscious of themselves and others. Sociology stirs the seriousness of youth and awakens its sense of justice and awkward curiosity. At the same time, the complexity of social problems threatens to overwhelm young minds and to exhaust their natural idealism. For this reason youth is sometimes apathetic and even cynical. Many young people arrive at the university vaguely aware that they have been deprived of the natural protection of the home and family. They sense that home, school, and church lie on the social consciousness like those backward regions which are forced to send away their children to the city in search of jobs and excitement. In this sense all of today's youth, white and black, is seething in the ghettos, suburbs and colonies of the corporate business world. For young people the university has become the vital way-station in the civil rights movement which is essentially a youth movement, mindless of color. Yet these events take the sociological profession by surprise. It is not comfortable at sit-ins, teach-ins and ride-ins.

Today's youth is remarkable for its solidarity. It has a sense of community which resists commitment to the universal-achievement values of organizational society. Admittedly, the young community is as likely to choose pot as politics in order to express its own values. But whether marching or smoking, youth experiences a libidinal solidarity which challenges the repressive competitiveness of the market and ideological politics. Youth is a force for demystification. For this reason it delights in marches and demonstrations for the sake of their literal and palpable embodiment of arguments which cannot be captured in slogans or official replies. They remind us when marching against the Vietnam war of the evident truth that war is wrong because it separates lovers and kills young people who have no joy in regimentation. They remind old men that they operate a system which blows children to bits and is willing to starve and imprison others. They tell us that our children are the flowers of the earth and yet we set policemen to trample them.

It can hardly be doubted that today's youth would like to do something about the world. Indeed, students are interested in sociology because it is already part of their world and sociology has already insinuated itself into their civic consciousness. They do not need to be reassured in the opening chapters of their introductory texts that sociology is a science. Only sociologists worry about that in moments of professional anxiety. Whatever the reason, sociology is there in the world, ringing in everyday vocabulary, and enshrined in university calendars. Students, then, come to sociology expecting it to be relevant to their everyday lives. The major scenes of war, race, poverty, science, and bureaucracy are familiar to them. They already use a vernacular sociology created out of their experience with the system and confrontation. Yet, in the classroom today's students meet a quite alien scheme of relevances dictated by scientism, value-neutralism and professional sociologism.

So far the point of these introductory remarks is to convey how involved contemporary youth is with people. I want to emphasize that their concern with people is not just a charitable one, nor is it purely political. It is a libidinal and expressive concern which is partly religious, potentially political, but above all sociable. It is a belief that things go better with people than against them. It is a conviction which is troublesome to their elders. Strangely, it also is a belief from which they must be cooled out if they are to settle in as sociologists.

Students, however sullen-looking and apparently self-obsessed, come to sociology because they believe it is concerned with people and that it contributes to the understanding and practical improvement of human relations. They expect with the aid of some sociological training to find themselves in a position to "work with people." Now nothing is more likely to throw the sociological profession into turmoil than the persistence of this popular belief that sociology involves working with people. Students who will still believe this are called radicals and activists. They are regarded as throwbacks from the days when the academic establishment did not distinguish sex, socialism, and sociology. Sociology's status as a science was won very painfully and depends very much upon the segregation of those whose sympathies are with social work, or political and community action. Now there are signs that this conception of the professional role belongs more to the generation which worked its way up with sociology than to the contemporary generation of students who do not have the same status qualms about science or affluence. For it is not the professionally alienated or poorer sociology students who retain the activist and populist conception of sociology. The truth which the older generation of social science professionals must confront is the return of bad times and the inescapable involvement of sociology with the ills of society. Curiously enough, whereas the older professionals saw the priest as the specter of bad times, nowadays the young sociologist regards the older technicians and professionals as the high-priests of the bureaucratization of spirit and imagination to which they attribute much of our social malaise.

Working with people creates a bewildering variety of practices which I shall call skin trades. People need haircuts, massage, dentistry, wigs and glasses, sociology and surgery, as well as love and advice. A vast number of people are involved in trades which fit out, adorn, repair, amuse, cajole, confine and incarcerate other people. A special aura attaches to working with people. The work of the priest, judge, doctor, and missionary is regarded as holy. The work of the prostitute, the pickpocket, and undertaker is considered profane. In reality, these trades are all involved in dirty work with people. Alternatively, with the exception of the pickpocket, all of these trades may be regarded as holy occupations because of the sublimity of their purpose, to restore and make whole the person.

Working with people is a precarious undertaking and thus the skin trades are especially marked with the ambivalent aura of sacredness and profanity which surrounds the human body. For this reason, every society defines rituals of approach and avoidance to govern contacts between people, between the sexes and between trades. The vast symbiosis of social life is naturally represented as a body in which the spiritual functions are relieved for prayer and thought through the excremental services of the lower-orders. In this scheme of things, the skin trades have been traditionally low-caste, their services being required in order to keep the higher castes free from bodily impurities and thus holy. The lower castes cut hair, wash clothes, clean latrines and dress corpses. In the dutiful performance of these tasks, the lower castes exchange the possibility of mobility in this life for the certainty of it in the next life. This social division of labor is again expressed in the concentration of the skin trades in a locality of the city, for example, around ports, railway stations and markets. With their teeming produce and swarming crowds, these areas symbolize the metabolism of social life. They are also the scenes of bar-fights, prostitution, hustling, miscegeny and missionary work. Ports, markets, and railway centers are the body orifices of society. As such they arouse the anxiety of the forces of law and order housed in the symbolic center of the social organism. Once sociology enters the house of government it too becomes anxious about margins, disorder and deviations.

Sociology is best thought of as a skin trade. This does not mean that sociology is not a profession and a science. It merely implies that sociology is obliged to claim the status of a science and a profession because that is the dilemma of the skin trades in the modern world. It suggests, too, that some of the scientific equipment of the sociologist, like that of the dentist, cosmetician, and pharmacist may be more related to status management than the real nature of his task. Consider the dentist's dilemma. As a mouth-miner he is employed in a dark hole filling cavities, stopping odors, uprooting and removing debris. To save face as a professional it is essential for him to spend more time on the surface than in mouth-mining. Thus the office decor, receptionist, nurse, and para-surgical front of the dentist's suite furnishes the necessary choreography of his professional activity. It enables him to reconstruct his mouth-work in the frame of the professional-client relationship.

Much of the sociological apparatus functions, I suggest, to support a ritual of decontamination between the scientist and his subject. It is essential that the sociologist view his subject only with professional eyes and that he resist the look in the eyes of the sick, the poor and the aimless who turn his questions back upon him. In this way the erotic symbiosis of talk is reduced to the interview schedule or attitude survey in which the client comes clean before the professional *voyeur*. As the sociological apparatus increases in size and complexity it has to be housed in offices and institutes and its services can only be afforded by wealthy clients. This has the disadvantage of shutting sociology out of crowd scenes, disasters and riots. It also demands standards or decorum from the sociologist which make it difficult for him to pass in the underworld of crime, sex, race and poverty. The professional sociologist is curiously caught in his own caste.

In my view sociology is a symbiotic science. Its promise is to give back to the people what it takes from them. This is true of all culture but sociolgy more than any other discipline promises to make this a practical truth. This is not to say that sociology does not need the other sciences. On the contrary, it presupposes other physical and social sciences. But it has its own task in the need to articulate the connections between individual experience and the transvaluation of human sensibilities worked by the institutional settings of technology, science and politics.

But, in its aspiration to become a science and to bestow professional status upon its members, sociology has uncritically assumed all the trappings of science. It has lodged itself in the bureaucratic organizations which are the institutional expression of the process of rationalization that as made the fortune of modern science and technology. The same processes of rationalization control the selection and organization of data collected for the sake of client projects parasitic upon the public life and concerns of the people. The apprentice sociologist is as much exploited by these projects as the people they are intended to benefit. He learns the collection and manipulation of data chosen as much for their machine-culinary properties as for any relevance to practical social or theoretical concerns. However, in exchange for domesticating his imagination with trivial generalizations or with the more frequent correlations which litter the sociological journals, the apprentice sociologist is assured of his acceptance to the sociological profession. He is all the more converted when he contemplates the power of professional method and organization which can produce an instant sociology of the Berkeley Free Speech Movement or of Watts, or of crime and violence in the streets, of poverty, or of affluence.

The most profound shock which the apprentice sociologist experiences occurs when he is confronted with the professional neutering of his sense of relevance and concern. This is achieved in a number of ways. Every freshman learns the distinction between facts and values. The effect of this distinction is to convince him that the classroom is a laboratory which can only be contaminated by his everyday knowledge of class, race, war, poverty, sex and the body. To put it another way, many students come to sociology because its questions are raised for them in their everyday contact with one another, with the ghetto, the police, the military and the administration. They have met "the system" in their high schools, in their fights with university administrators, the city-fathers and the sublime indifference of most people. They are not content with the abstract problem of how organizations handle uncertainty. They would like to know which in particular are the most powerful corporations. What is life like in these institutions? What is the ethnic composition of their labor force? What percentage of their production is destined for military purposes? What do their activities in colonial countries mean for the lives of those people? In short, they would like to know which organizations determine the distribution of comfort and security for some and poverty and danger for others. They know they cannot get answers to these questions from a sociology which relies on statistical data never intended to probe the consequences of organizational rationality.

These questions are often dismissed as the concerns of activists. This is short-sighted. Such questions really call upon sociology to reexamine its own sense of the relevance of things. They remind the professional sociologist that his own "isms"—careerism, scientism and opportunism—are showing through. They challenge the optimistic assumption of middle-range theory that somehow the data will pile itself up into the big answer to the big question with which no one meanwhile need concern himself.

There is no single road to sociological disenchantment. The fact-value distinction is only one of the devices for altering the student's sense of relevance. Another favorite is the method of "sociological vertigo." The strategy in this case is to confound the ethnocentrism of young students with a bewildering tour of the most exotic sociological and anthropological scenes. The purpose here seems to be to convince the sociology student that everything might be some other way—a terror usually reserved for students in introductory philosophy courses.

Nowadays such "trips" are losing their power to convert students who live their lives experimentally and at short notice. In any case, once they discover that the sociologist's "high" is on functionalism or social determinism and that he never understood what *they* meant by individualism and community, they turn off on the paid-piper. For the striking thing is that so many young students have thought through for themselves what it means to encounter other people as they are and to know them without needing the way in to be marked esoterically or the way out to be anything else than the time-in-between-people.

Each time one meets a class of sociology students one knows that sociology cannot escape into itself. This is possible only if we allow our jargon to turn meaning away from language and the world toward which it carries us. Yet sociology must speak in its own voice and according to its own experience. Much of what I have said may seem highly critical of professional sociology. If it were nothing more, then it would not serve young sociologists. What I mean to do is to awaken the sense of some of the root metaphors which apply to sociology as a "trade," a "craft" or a "field." These metaphors remind us of the care and sweat in doing sociology. At the same time, they remind us that sociology is only a way of earning a living and cannot presume to contribute more than others to the public good. It means that when we teach we take others into our care and in turn we must lend ourselves to what they need in order to grow and to become themselves. Young people are looking for work. We must show them the fields and how we care for them so that they will want to share the work. There is no way of legislating what sociologists should do even though we may be clear about what is urgent and important in their task. The practicing sociologist must answer for himself and to his colleagues and to the rest of men.

In calling sociology a skin trade I want to restore its symbiotic connections with the body-politic and to situate it in relation to the exchange of organic needs and the utopian celebration of libidinal community which surpasses all understanding. This means that the rhetoric of scientism in sociology as well as its humanism must be tested against the commonsense relevances of everyday life. It is a reminder that society is richer than sociology and that for all our science the world is still the mystery and passion of being with our fellow men.

3. SCIENTIFIC EXPLANATION IN PERSPECTIVE

Marty E. Zusman

"Here then is the difficulty to which no other science presents anything analogous. To cut himself off in thought from all his relationships of race and country, and citizenship—to get rid of all those interests, prejudices, likings, superstitions, generated in him by the life of his own society and his own time—to look on all the changes societies have undergone and are undergoing, with reference to nationality, or creed, or personal welfare; is what the average man cannot do at all, and what the exceptional man can do very imperfectly."[1]

Herbert Spencer

The goals of science, it has sometimes been said, are threefold: to understand, to explain, and to predict. When we say "to understand" we are suggesting the act of discovery by which we come to be aware of new relationships. We discover with the tools of science the concrete empirical world. This is the world of data which is observable by all. Inflation, crime, disease or inequality can be noted by anyone who has the knowledge to seek them out. However, it is only the first goal of science to discover that crime is highest in the central cities. The second goal is to explain why. This explanation must also be empirical. Crime is not highest because of unknown or unmeasurable factors. A causal relationship must be demonstrated to explain the data. Lastly, the final goal of science is to build upon past relationships and knowledge to predict future occurrences. This does not mean to predict with perfect accuracy, but only with a high degree of probability. If crime is related to poverty, then we may predict higher rates of crime in any area in which we find higher rates of poverty.

While the explicit goals are threefold, there is an implicit goal of science which is far more important and yet too often overlooked. That goal is the scientific consciousness. It is the in-depth application of the knowledge of science. In the world of non-science we live our lives without ever considering what it is that encompasses reality. We do not live one life, but two. Like chameleons who change color as they move from light to dark, so too do we change positions as we move from the scientific frame of reference to our non-science lives. Above all else we forget that what we discover by science is fact and what we live in our lives is belief. We fail to develop the scientific consciousness by which we incorporate into our lives the facts and skeptical approach of science. This should be above all else a goal of science, to develop in society a scientific consciousness.

To develop a scientific consciousness is to replace all of the myths, beliefs, and attitudes that form our inner selves with the empirical reality of scientific data. It is to learn all over again how to explain the world as if we had never learned of its existence. In reality we have not. We do not know the real world, but only the world of beliefs which we have been taught. To develop the scientific consciousness we must learn to question everything around us; not only what is said to us, but also what we say ourselves. We must learn to be skeptical. How often have we heard, said and believed that opposites attract, that welfare recipients are lazy or that we are in a sexual revolution? Are we aware of the empirical reality that underlies such statements making them in actuality correct or incorrect? No, most of us are not. Our entire lives have led us to observe and understand only a small part of the world which lies before us. In actuality, we learn that which is peculiar to our individual, personal backgrounds. It was for the most part our parents; we have now inherited their prejudices, their views, their religion and their politics. It is our new explanation of the world which we protect and refuse to change. If what is said to us by science or others fits our explanation then we unquestionably accept it. And if what is said to us does not fit our beliefs we reject it without ever considering its possibility, for we lack a scientific consciousness. If you disagree with me, if you say I am wrong, then let me ask you of that being to whom you have sometimes prayed. If you are white, can that being not be black; and if you are black, can it not be white? What is its race? What is its sex? What has blindly led you to accept that which you accept? Is the lord not yellow? Is she not thin? Are you not a product of your times who accepts explanations because you are more human than scientist? Yes, so are we all products of our times. Yet to be a sociologist is to develop a scientific consciousness. You must replace your myths, beliefs, and attitudes that form your inner selves with facts. You must learn a new understanding and explanation of a complex world. You must learn a new, refreshing and sometimes difficult approach to the world in which we live: the scientific approach.

I.

What is the purpose of that thing we call science? The ultimate purpose of science is explanation. When we explain any aspect of reality, that explanation must satisfy the intellectual skepticism of the individuals to whom we speak. When we were young and were told that the tooth fairy paid money for our teeth, or that Santa Claus brought our gifts, or even that the stork brought babies, we were not skeptical; we believed. Today we are told that heroin is a killer, that the population is exploding, or that women are being discriminated against and we are not skeptical, we believe.

It is for that very reason that sociology is unique among the disciplines. It studies the obvious with a scientific skepticism. It does *not* believe; it questions to ascertain the facts. For example, consider the following findings from a study by Lazarsfeld concerning the adjustment of servicemen to military life during the second World War:

1. Better educated men showed more psychoneurotic symptoms than those with less education. (The mental instability of the intellectual as compared to the more impassive psychology of the man-in-the-street has often been commented upon.)
2. Men from rural backgrounds were usually in better spirits during their Army life than soldiers from city backgrounds. (After all, they are more accustomed to hardships.)
3. Southern soldiers were better able to stand the climate in hot South Sea Islands than Northern soldiers. (Of course, Southerners are more accustomed to hot weather.)
4. As long as the fighting continued, men were more eager to be returned to the States than they were after the German surrender. (You cannot blame people for not wanting to be killed.)[2]

Why be skeptical, you might ask, for aren't the findings of science merely common sense? The answer is no, and this is the first belief you must part with. For in actuality the above findings are the opposite of the actual results. Better educated men showed fewer symptoms; men from city backgrounds were in better spirits; Northern soldiers better stood the climate of the South Sea Islands; and men were more eager to return to the States after the surrender. These are the facts that build science and we never know what they may be until we apply the methods of science to understand, explain and predict.

The purpose of science, then, is to develop an explanation which makes its users skeptical and its data accurate. As such, scientific explanation is made of three components: (1) theory, (2) statements of prediction and (3) verification of those predictions.

Theory is both the beginning point of science and its logical conclusion. It is most often a model that helps us explain relationships and make predictions. Theoretical models of Freud, Piaget, Mead, Durkheim, Marx, Weber and numerous others who have influenced sociology help us to develop general explanations of similar occurrences. A theory that explains the relationship between patterns of socialization in the family and success should be able to help us predict which individuals in society should achieve the greatest rewards.

Often we begin with a problem. We are curious why students sit in the same seats time after time until they all but own them or why people say "how are you" when they really don't care. Even as we seek data to answer these questions, we are concerned with the larger realities which constitute social life. For example, we may begin by being curious as to why so many firstborn children attend college. An explanation may lie in the relationship between family interaction and sibling position. In explaining that relationship, we may be able to make predictions about future differences between firstborn and laterborn in our society. Sometimes conceptualized as sets of statements which have been tested, theory makes predictions which await the gathering of data for verification. Ultimately, theory is an explanation based on fact. It begins with an understanding of relationships that predict occurrences which can be verified with data. Science is a process which eventuates with an explanation based on empirical data. Whatever you may say, or whatever others may have said, if the scientific approach has been followed you are in the position of demonstrating truth or falsity with empirical fact.

It is this very process which has made the discipline of sociology a science. If you say to me that working mothers cause delinquency, I will say to you, Where is your data? I will say that because I am a scientific skeptic and because all of the data which exist within this discipline show that it is lack of supervision and not working mothers *per se* that leads to delinquency.[3] And if you say to me that our country is one where hard work pays off, again I must ask you if you have not simply been a product of your times, who accepts explanation because you fail to be a scientific skeptic. Where are your data? Are you willing to look for data which could find you right or wrong? Are you willing to not only entertain the idea that you are wrong, but change your system of viewing the world if data show you otherwise? If you are not, you have no place in science. For if you believe that hard work pays off equally for everyone, you are wrong. Given the same education, hard work pays off for whites, but not equally for blacks (Table 1). In fact, 1969 was the first year in American history when the average income for black males with a high school education was higher than for white males with an elementary school education.

Table 1. Median Income of Men 25 to 54 years old, by Educational Attainment

Education	Median Income, 1969		
	Negro	White	All Races
Elementary: Total less than 8 years	$3,291	$4,529	$4,285
8 years	2,973	3,613	3,429
	4,293	5,460	5,345
High School: Total	4,748	7,890	7,578
1 to 3 years	5,222	7,309	7,079
4 years	6,144	8,631	8,434
College: 1 or more years	8,567	12,437	12,255

SOURCE: U.S. Bureau of the Census[4]

Four extra years of hard work to attain $2,500 less per year than a man with the same education who by accident of birth had white skin. And if you then still say to me that things are getting better, I will have to say to you, Where is your scientific skepticism? Have you sought out evidence to verify your position? Because if you did you would find that the gap between blacks and whites in most areas appears to be widening.[5] The only explanation acceptable is one that satisfies that third criteria: empirically verifying one's predictions.

II.

Verifying does not necessarily mean quantification. It does mean however that you must be able to gather your data in such form as to make them replicable. That is to say, whatever you discover, any other individual must also be able to apply the scientific method and find the same results. Otherwise there can be no real science. This part of the scientific enterprise consists of research methods which are, simply, data collection techniques. Every individual who follows the scientific approach is capable of gathering the data for himself to determine if he is correct; to test his ideas and beliefs. While there are numerous non-science approaches from tradition to common sense, they are characterized by one overwhelming factor. The individual who proposes them never seeks evidence which might prove him wrong. He relies upon his beliefs. In sociology beliefs are unacceptable and empirical evidence must always be obtained. This is accomplished using a variety of research methods. Among the most important is the use of (1) official statistics and documents, (2) observation and (3) survey research techniques.

We live in an age where a massive statistical cross section of the population is compiled by official sources daily. Evidence to demonstrate the differences in income, education, housing conditions and countless thousands of other relationships is available to anyone who wants to seek it out. Instead of debating whether or not a "brain drain" exists whereby foreign intellectuals are migrating to the United States leaving European countries with a lack of scientific expertise, we can check the United Nations Demographic Yearbook or its shortened summary, the Statistical Yearbook. Instead of debating whether more males or females are born each year, or how long males or females, blacks or whites survive, we can check our own official statistics which demonstrate (Table 2) that before age one death is greatest for black males, then black females, white males and white females in that order. Similarly, we can understand from official statistics that life expectancy is longest for white females and shortest for black males (Table 3). An explanation is called for and no matter what it may be, it will be empirically validated scientifically before it enters that body of knowledge we call science.

Table 2.   Death Rates per 1000 for Ages 0-1 in the United States by Race and Sex (1968).

Racial Category	Sex Male	Female
White	21.8	16.3
Non-white	37.7	31.1

SOURCE: U.S. Public Health Service.

Table 3.   Life Expectancy in Years for the United States by Race and Sex (1968)

Racial Category	Sex	
	Male	Female
White	67.5	74.9
Non-white	60.1	67.5

SOURCE: U.S. Public Health Service.

Every ten years the United States Bureau of the Census produces a Statistical Abstract of the United States. Every three months from nearly 16,000 households data is gathered on Americans for the Quarterly Household Survey. And almost every month, based on nearly 35,000 households, the census publishes the Current Population Survey to keep more accurate tabs on changes in the American population. As if this isn't sufficient almost every act of our lives is monitored by some statistical agency. When we buy a car, get married, enter a hospital, attend any school, and when we eventually die, official records and documents will be maintained. Whether we use these official statistics or numerous others issued from the Bureau of Labor Statistics or the U.S. Department of Health, Education, and Welfare, one thing is for sure, we have the ability to answer the skeptic who disbelieves.

While official statistics are highly useful, they are only one source for data collection. Another important method of data collection is observation. All science and particularly sociology relies upon observation. It is essential if we are to understand the reality that surrounds us that we learn to carefully observe and record phenomena. Certainly we are all observant. The problem is that we are all selective in our observation. What do you observe in your sociology classroom? Some of you observe the esthetic surroundings: the walls, the windows, the lighting, the noise in the hall, or your own feelings which come from the slow pacing of the professor who walks quietly but consistently back and forth before the class. Others of you may record different observations. You may note the spatial arrangements of the chairs and podium, the fact that the professor seems to talk more to the front of the room than the back, or the general monotony of his facial expression or verbal tone. Observation is a technique which must be rigorously practiced to gain any data which are sociologically relevant. If you observed the above, you have observed little that is useful for the study of sociology. Did you observe the racial composition of the class? Did you note the distribution of age and sex? Did you note differences in power which occurred between various statuses and the role relationships which were maintained by various formal and informal patterns of communication? Probably not, although you could have observed these factors if you understood their importance. Observation is an important method of gathering data which helps us verify our ideas or beliefs by learning to accurately observe phenomena.

A third method of data collection is survey research. Almost all of the data gathered in sociology are gathered by two survey research methods, the mailed questionnaire and the personal interview.[6] The term mailed questionnaire refers to a data collection method whereby a questionnaire is mailed to a respondent who reads and responds to each item and then mails it back to the researcher. The personal interview on the other hand is a much more versatile data-gathering method with many variations. The basic interview procedure involves an interviewer who asks the respondent numerous questions and records the interviewee's replies. Unlike observation, the use of surveys gets at only self-reports. Respondents are asked about their attitudes, beliefs, and behavior. The data which are used reflect not the actual behavior of the respondent, but his self-report of that behavior. All surveys gather their data by asking numerous questions which relate to the subject under investigation. Some information can hardly be obtained without the use of surveys. Criminal or sexual behavior, for example, are not clearly reflected in official statistics or by observation. Yet, while different research methods are applicable to different theoretical problems, more often the choice of a research technique is based upon known methodology.

III.

Methodology is in part the analysis of research methods. It is the means by which we assess and improve the methods of gathering data so that we might produce higher quality data. Each research method has particular problems which limit its utility. It is important to understand the advantages and disadvantages of research methods to fully understand the limitations of sociological explanation. Official statistics on crime, for example, are sometimes used to obtain increased funds for police departments at which time the higher the crime, the greater the need. On the other hand, for political reasons it is sometimes necessary to demonstrate that crime is decreasing. At these times the gathering and recording of what is called a crime changes to produce fewer statistics of actual crime. Similarly, official statistics have the problem of not measuring actual crime, but instead reflect differential arrest among the lower class.[7] The accuracy of official statistics has not been accepted by scientific skeptics. Studies of undetected delinquency have demonstrated the over-representation of lower-class delinquents which biases the official statistics.[8] This is not to suggest that all official statistics are compounded with this particular problem or are of no use. It is only that as scientific skeptics our explanations lean heavily upon analyzing the methods by which data are gathered. The limitations of sociological data gathered by official statistics are of constant concern.

Similarly, data gathered by the method of observation also have particular disadvantages which lower the reliability and validity of the data. While there are numerous problems, four stand out as most important. First among these is the problem of understanding new situations which often contain unfamiliar actions. If we wish to explain the emotional feelings of Indians in American society one method would be to go and live with them for the purpose of gathering such data by observation. New and unfamiliar situations might lead us to erroneous assumptions about their feelings. Secondly, a basic problem is that as humans our feelings interact with the scientific enterprise which often leads to distrust of some respondents and overidentification with others. Third, in these new situations we will find it difficult to determine what we should be observing and to put these observations in such form as to make them measurable. How shall we standardize expressions of emotion which we see around us to gain a measure of intensity? All of these problems lead, lastly, to the problem of replication. It is very difficult for another researcher to find the same results since, at every stage of the method, they may be led to observe a different reality. Thus, a white, a black and an Indian all doing participant observation of Indians will have tremendous problems in gathering similar observations (reliability) and observations that truly measure emotional feelings (validity).

The most commonly used methods of survey research also have their disadvantages. One major disadvantage of the personal interview is that, like participant observation, the interviewer has an effect upon the data he is gathering. In answering questions the respondent alters his answers in terms of the various characteristics of the interviewer. The interviewer's age, race, sex, manner of speaking and dress may alter responses. If the interviewer has a certain bias he may unintentionally ask questions in a tone and manner that pressures the respondent to answer in a way other than he believes. In fact, personal questions and threatening questions may lead a respondent to evade an answer or refuse to respond for fear that his verbal reply would not remain anonymous. If the respondent is asked, "Do you like your present job?" he may fear that an answer of "no" might incriminate him or ultimately cost him his job. For these reasons, well-trained interviewers are needed to assure that responses are as reliable and valid as possible. Interviewers are taught to be brief, polite and careful in both the asking and recording of responses. For example, questions can only be repeated. They cannot be explained, since in the explanation may be a cue as to the interviewer's feelings which might alter the response of the respondent. Similarly, the interviewer may not show emotion other than mild approval. He may not lead a respondent, argue with a respondent or laugh at a respondent's replies. If he asks the respondent to strongly agree, agree, disagree, or strongly disagree with the statement "I can understand why blacks are sometimes driven to violence," and the respondent answers "Hell no, they ought to walk," he must not laugh, but repeat the question, note the response and continue.

On the other hand, data gathered by mail questionnaire also have disadvantages. The respondent is not in any way controlled. He may answer questions in any order, have friends help him respond, misinterpret what is wanted, refuse to put in his own handwriting answers which he feels might incriminate him, or just refuse to respond. Mail questionnaires have a high rate of non-response which can limit their usefulness. When a respondent refuses to respond, no interpretation is possible of why he didn't respond. It may be that the survey was uninteresting, that he lacked the time to respond, or simply that he felt his answers were just not needed. The loss of too many respondents and the sociologist must either contact non-respondents or ignore his data.

The point of methodology is to understand the advantages and disadvantages of the various methods so that data can be improved. Sociological explanation is premised on a constant vigil and skepticism of all data. The understanding of the disadvantages of the methods have led to numerous techniques to minimize or eliminate those aspects which lessen the quality of the data which eventuate in sociological explanation.

IV.

The final result of sociology is that the sociologist has become his own most vociferous critic and developed a scientific consciousness. Our intellectual satisfaction is stimulated by the knowledge that even the best methods known to the science have disadvantages. We have gained a healthy respect for our data-gathering methods and explanations. The entire belief in science has led us to see the world in a new way ,as complex and never perfect. If the data have been gathered by the best techniques and methods of the science we still do not unquestionably accept them. We look for their limitations and within their limitations we use them. It is the best answer available. At least we know for sure that if the data are correct others may also replicate and discover the same findings.

The advantage of scientific explanation is that it works. It leads us beyond our times, beyond our social realities, beyond our belief systems. It leads to an explanation of reality that can satisfy any skeptic who asks the question where are your data, how were they gathered, how accurate are they. If he disbelieves the data, he is capable of finding out the same information simply by learning the science and applying it. Science is, of course, only as good as those who are capable of doing it and the methods which exist. While the advantages of the scientific explanation are not fully known, one thing is clear: like acupuncture of the East and anesthesiology of the West, all we can really say about scientific explanation is that it works. It allows us to understand, explain and predict.

NOTES

1. Herbert Spencer, *The Study of Society* (New York:Appleton-Century Crofts, 1877), p. 74.
2. Paul Lazarsfeld, "The American Soldier," *Public Opinion Quarterly*, Fall, 1949, pp. 379-80.
3. Elenor E. Maccoby, "Effects Upon Children of Their Mothers' Outside Employment" in Norman W. Bell and Ezra F. Vogel eds. *A Modern Introduction to the Family*. New York: The Free Press, 1960, p. 523.
4. New York Times Family Almanac, 1972, p. 402.
5. See Drake, St. C. "The Social and Economic Status of the Negro in the United States" in Parsons and K.B. Clark (Eds.), *The Negro American*. Boston:Houghton Mifflin, 1966, p. 3-46; Fein, R. "An Economic and Social Profile of the American Negro," pp. 102-133. Moynehan, D.P. "Employment Income and the Ordeal of the Negro Family," pp. 102-133.
6. Brown, Julia, and Brian G. Gilmartin. 1969. "Sociology Today: Lacunae, Emphasis and Surfeits." *American Sociologist* 4:283-91.
7. Joseph W. Eaton and Kenneth Polk, Measuring Delinquency: *A Study of Probation Department Referrals* (Pittsburgh: University of Pittsburgh Press), 1961, p. 4.
8. La Mar Empey and Maynard L. Erickson, "Hidden Delinquency and Social Status," *Social Forces*, June 1966, pp. 546-54 and Martin Gold, "Undetected Delinquent Behavior," *Journal of Research in Crime and Delinquency*, January 1966, pp. 27-46.

Part II

CULTURE AND SOCIALIZATION

Different strokes for different folks.

Sly and the Family Stone

... he reads the news of the day, imprinted in characters invented by the ancient Semites by a process invented in Germany upon a material invented in China. As he scans the latest editorial pointing out the dire results to our institutions of accepting foreign ideas, he will not fail to thank a Hebrew God in an Indo-European language that he is a one-hundred percent (decimal system invented by the Greeks) American (from Amerigo Vespucci, Italian geographer).

Ralph Linton

Introduction to Part II:
(Culture & Socialization)

An old proverb states that "children grow up and develop their own personalities in spite of their parents." While we could accept the implied wisdom of this, we should also add that children do not grow up in spite of their culture.

The connecting variables between the individual and his culture are many: the family, peer groups, school, informal and formal associations. However, the structure of culture molds and modifies the individual character the same way that the ocean shapes its inhabitants.

Another analogy suggests that the last thing which fish are able to perceive is the water in which they live. A similar statement could be made about man and his consciousness of his culture. But to understand man, his past, his present state, and perhaps his future, is to understand the system of his myths, beliefs, ideas, artifacts, art, knowledge, or, in sum, his culture. The culture becomes a part of each man through the process of socialization. Some of us become so thoroughly socialized that we see the culture *for* man. Others of us resist socialization so that we see culture *against* man. All in all, perhaps that is the way it has always been and may always be. It would be rather unfortunate for us if we failed to understand this delicate interaction between the individual and culture.

Professor Miner's article, "Body Ritual Among the Nacirema," demonstrates the impact of culture patterns upon individuals while basically viewing the process from a culture-against-man frame of reference. In another article, "Magic, Sorcery, and Football Among the Urban Zulu. . .," Professor N. A. Scotch demonstrates how a sport from a different culture has become integrated in a totally different context, as a consequence of acculturation.

The importance of *socialization* as a process is a central tenet contained in Professor Becker's work, "Becoming a Marihuana User." Re-socialization, demonstrates more aptly the impact of internalization of a new set of norms which is a basic process in interaction between individual and his social environment. Finally, a lack of culture resulting in absence of "man as *human* being" is the central point of Professor Davis' contribution in "Final Note on a Case of Extreme Isolation."

4.   BODY RITUAL AMONG THE NACIREMA

HORACE MINER

The anthropologist has become so familiar with the diversity of ways in which different peoples behave in similar situations that he is not apt to be surprised by even the most exotic customs. In fact, if all of the logically possible combinations of behavior have not been found somewhere in the world, he is apt to suspect that they must be present in some yet undescribed tribe. This point has, in fact, been expressed with respect to clan organization by Murdock (1949:71). In this light, the magical beliefs and practices of the Nacirema present such unusual aspects that it seems desirable to describe them as an example of the extremes to which human behavior can go.

Reprinted from *The American Anthropologist*, Vol. 58, No. 3, (June 1956), pp. 503-507, by permission of the author and the publisher, American Anthropological Association.

Professor Linton first brought the ritual of the Nacirema to the attention of anthropologists twenty years ago (1936:326), but the culture of this people is still very poorly understood. They are a North American group living in the territory between the Canadian Cree, the Yaqui and Tarahumare of Mexico, and the Carib and Arawak of the Antilles. Little is known of their origin, although tradition states that they came from the east. According to Nacirema mythology, their nation was originated by a culture hero, Notgnihsaw, who is otherwise known for two great feats of strength—the throwing of a piece of wampum across the river Pa-To-Mac and the chopping down of a cherry tree in which the Spirit of Truth resided.

Nacirema culture is characterized by a highly developed market economy which has evolved in a rich natural habitat. While much of the people's time is devoted to economic pursuits, a large part of the fruits of these labors and a considerable portion of the day are spent in ritual activity. The focus of this activity is the human body, the appearance and health of which loom as a dominant concern in the ethos of the people. While such a concern is certainly not unusual, its ceremonial aspects and associated philosophy are unique.

The fundamental belief underlying the whole system appears to be that the human body is ugly and that its natural tendency is to debility and disease. Incarcerated in such a body, man's only hope is to avert these characteristics through the use of the powerful influences of ritual and ceremony. Every household has one or more shrines devoted to this purpose. The more powerful individuals in the society have several shrines in their houses and, in fact, the opulence of a house is often referred to in terms of the number of such ritual centers it possesses. Most houses are of wattle and daub construction, but the shrine rooms of the more wealthy are walled with stone. Poorer families imitate the rich by applying pottery plaques to their shrine walls.

While each family has at least one such shrine, the rituals associated with it are not family ceremonies but are private and secret. The rites are normally only discussed with children, and then only during the period when they are being initiated into these mysteries. I was able, however, to establish sufficient rapport with the natives to examine these shrines and to have the rituals described to me.

The focal point of the shrine is a box or chest which is built into the wall. In this chest are kept the many charms and magical

potions without which no native believes he could live. These preparations are secured from a variety of specialized practitioners. The
most powerful of these are the medicine men, whose assistance must
be rewarded with substantial gifts. However, the medicine men do
not provide the curative potions for their clients, but decide what
the ingredients should be and then write them down in an ancient
and secret language. This writing is understood only by the medicine
men and by the herbalists who, for another gift, provide the required
charm.

The charm is not disposed of after it has served its purpose, but
is placed in the charm-box of the household shrine. As these magical
materials are specific for certain ills, and the real or imagined
maladies of the people are many, the charm-box is usually full to
overflowing. The magical packets are so numerous that people forget
what their purposes were and fear to use them again. While the
natives are very vague on this point, we can only assume that the
idea in retaining all the old magical materials is that their presence
in the charm-box, before which the body rituals are conducted, will
in some way protect the worshipper.

Beneath the charm-box is a small font. Each day every member
of the family, in succession, enters the shrine room, bows his head
before the charm-box, mingles different sorts of holy water in the
font, and proceeds with a brief rite of ablution. The holy waters are
secured from the Water Temple of the community, where the priests
conduct elaborate ceremonies to make the liquid ritually pure.

In the hierarchy of magical practitioners, and below the
medicine men in prestige, are specialists whose designation is best
translated "holy-mouth-men." The Nacirema have an almost pathological horror of and fascination with the mouth, the condition of
which is believed to have a supernatural influence on all social relationships. Were it not for the rituals of the mouth, they believe that
their teeth would fall out, their gums bleed, their jaws shrink, their
friends desert them, and their lovers reject them. They also believe
that a strong relationship exists between oral and moral characteristics. For example, there is a ritual ablution of the mouth for children which is supposed to improve their moral fiber.

The daily body ritual performed by everyone includes a mouth-
rite. Despite the fact that these people are so punctilious about care
of the mouth, this rite involves a practice which strikes the
uninitiated stranger as revolting. It was reported to me that the ritual
consists of inserting a small bundle of hog hairs into the mouth, along

with certain magical powders, and then moving the bundle in a highly formalized series of gestures.

In addition to the private mouth-rite, the people seek out a holy-mouth-man once or twice a year. These practitioners have an impressive set of paraphernalia, consisting of a variety of augers, awls, probes, and prods. The use of these objects in the exorcism of the evils of the mouth involves almost unbelievable ritual torture of the client. The holy-mouth-man opens the client's mouth and, using the above mentioned tools, enlarges any holes which decay may have created in the teeth. Magical materials are put into these holes. If there are no naturally occurring holes in the teeth, large sections of one or more teeth are gouged out so that the supernatural substance can be applied. In the client's view, the purpose of these ministrations is to arrest decay and to draw friends. The extremely sacred and traditional character of the rite is evident in the fact that the natives return to the holy-mouth-men year after year, despite the fact that their teeth continue to decay.

It is to be hoped that, when a thorough study of the Nacirema is made, there will be careful inquiry into the personality structure of these people. One has but to watch the gleam in the eye of a holy-mouth-man, as he jabs an awl into an exposed nerve, to suspect that a certain amount of sadism is involved. If this can be established, a very interesting pattern emerges, for most of the population shows definite masochistic tendencies. It was to these that Professor Linton referred in discussing a distinctive part of the daily body ritual which is performed only by men. This part of the rite involves scraping and lacerating the surface of the face with a sharp instrument. Special women's rites are performed only four times during each month, but what they lack in frequency is made up in barbarity. As part of this ceremony, women bake their heads in small ovens for about an hour. The theoretically interesting point is that what seems to be a preponderantly masochistic people have developed sadistic specialists.

The medicine men have an imposing temple, or *latipso*, in every community of any size. The more elaborate ceremonies required to treat very sick patients can only be performed at this temple. These ceremonies involve not only the thaumaturge but a permanent group of vestal maidens who move sedately about the temple chambers in distinctive costume and headdress.

The *latipso* ceremonies are so harsh that it is phenomenal that a fair proportion of the really sick natives who enter the temple ever recover. Small children whose indoctrination is still incomplete have been known to resist attempts to take them to the temple because "that is where you go to die." Despite this fact, sick adults are not only willing but eager to undergo the protracted ritual purification, if they can afford to do so. No matter how ill the supplicant or how grave the emergency, the guardians of many temples will not admit a client if he cannot give a rich gift to the custodian. Even after one has gained admission and survived the cermonies, the guardians will not permit the neophyte to leave until he makes still another gift.

The supplicant entering the temple is first stripped of all his or her clothes. In every-day life the Nacirema avoids exposure of his body and its natural functions. Bathing and excretory acts are performed only in the secrecy of the household shrine, where they are ritualized as part of the body-rites. Psychological shock results from the fact that body secrecy is suddenly lost upon entry into the *latipso*. A man, whose own wife has never seen him in an excretory act, suddenly finds himself naked and assisted by a vestal maiden while he performs his natural functions into a sacred vessel. This sort of ceremonial treatment is necessitated by the fact that the excreta are used by a diviner to ascertain the course and nature of the client's sickness. Female clients, on the other hand, find their naked bodies are subjected to the scrutiny, manipulation and prodding of the medicine men.

Few supplicants in the temple are well enough to do anything but lie on their hard beds. The daily ceremonies, like the rites of the holy-mouth-men, involve discomfort and torture. With ritual precision, the vestals awaken their miserable charges each dawn and roll them about on their beds of pain while performing ablutions, in the formal movements of which the maidens are highly trained. At other times they insert magic wands in the supplicant's mouth or force him to eat substances which are supposed to be healing. From time to time the medicine men come to their clients and jab magically treated needles into their flesh. The fact that these temple ceremonies may not cure, and may even kill the neophyte, in no way decreases the people's faith in the medicine men.

There remains one other kind of practitioner, known as a "listener." This witch-doctor has the power to exorcise the devils that lodge in the heads of people who have been bewitched. The Nacirema believe that parents bewitch their own children. Mothers are particularly suspected of putting a curse on children while teaching them the secret body rituals. The counter-magic of the witch-doctor is unusual in its lack of ritual. The patient simply tells the "listener" all his troubles and fears, beginning with the earliest difficulties he can remember. The memory displayed by the Nacirema in these exorcism sessions is truly remarkable. It is not uncommon for the patient to bemoan the rejection he felt upon being weaned as a babe, and a few individuals even see their troubles going back to the traumatic effects of their own birth.

In conclusion, mention must be made of certain practices which have their base in native esthetics but which depend upon the pervasive aversion to the natural body and its functions. There are ritual fasts to make fat people thin and ceremonial feasts to make thin people fat. Still other rites are used to make women's breasts larger if they are small, and smaller if they are large. General dissatisfaction with breast shape is symbolized in the fact that the ideal form is virtually outside the range of human variation. A few women afflicted with almost inhuman hypermammary development are so idolized that they make a handsome living by simple going from village to village and permitting the natives to stare at them for a fee.

Reference has already been made to the fact that excretory functions are ritualized, routinized, and relegated to secrecy. Natural reproductive functions are similarly distorted. Intercourse is taboo as a topic and scheduled as an act. Efforts are made to avoid pregnancy by the use of magical materials or by limiting intercourse to certain phases of the moon. Conception is actually very infrequent. When pregnant, women dress so as to hide their condition. Parturition takes place in secret, without friends or relatives to assist, and the majority of women do not nurse their infants.

Our review of the ritual life of the Nacirema has certainly shown them to be a magic-ridden people. It is hard to understand how they have managed to exist so long under the burdens which they have imposed upon themselves. But even such exotic customs as these take on real meaning when they are viewed with the insight provided by Malinowski when he wrote (1948:70):

> Looking from far and above, from our high places of safety in the developed civilization, it is easy to see all the crudity and irrelevance of magic. But without its power and guidance early man could not have mastered his practical difficulties as he has done, nor could man have advanced to the higher stages of civilization.

REFERENCES

Linton, Ralph. *The Study of Man*. New York: D. Appleton-Century Co., 1936.
Malinowski, Bronislaw. *Magic, Science, and Religion*. Glencoe: The Free Press, 1948.
Murdock, George P. *Social Structure*. New York: The Macmillan Co., 1949.

5. MAGIC, SORCERY, AND FOOTBALL AMONG URBAN ZULU: A CASE OF REINTERPRETATION UNDER ACCULTURATION[1]

N. A. SCOTCH

In discussing beliefs in witchcraft in Africa, Gluckman[2] points out that native beliefs in witchcraft not only persist in the face of continuing acculturation but often expand and change to meet the exigencies of new life situations. In fact, the impact of science, and particularly the impact of modern medicine, on previously nonliterate Africans actually inhibits their traditional beliefs and practices much less than might be expected; and although it would be incorrect to assert that Africans have rejected modern medicine—rejected, say modern germ theories of disease—the fact remains that they sustain the basic structure of their traditional beliefs in spite of elemental contradictions between those beliefs and scientific explanations.

But how can opposing explanations of cause and effect be held simultaneously? According to Gluckman, concepts of science and witchcraft fulfill different functions: science explains *how* a given process occurs, as in the course of a disease, for example, whereas witchcraft explains *why* the process occurs at all, or why one man and not another contracts the disease. From the African point of view, modern medicine is extremely limited in explaining total situations. It may contribute dependable probabilities, as when it predicts that ten per cent of a tribal population will die of tuberculosis, or when it prognosticates a specific disease in the individual; but it fails to explain, from the African perspective, why one particular child among ten sharing the same conditions contracts tuberculosis whereas the remaining nine do not, and it is this last explanation that witchcraft continues to provide with assurance for modern Africans. As Gluckman (2, p. 101) observes: "The difficulty of destroying beliefs in witchcraft is that they form a system which can absorb and explain many failures and apparently contradictory evidence."

This functional aspect of witchcraft may explain, to a very great extent, its persistence in the belief system of Africans, its expansion and peculiar adaptability to industrialized Euroamerican modes of life. As Gluckman points out:

> African life nowadays is changing rapidly, and witchcraft accusations now involve circumstances arising from Africa's absorption in Western economy and polity. Conflicts between old and new social principles

Reprinted from the *Journal of Conflict Resolutions*, Vol. V (1961), pp. 70-74, by permission of the author and the publisher, Center of Research on Conflict Resolution.

produce new animosities, which are not controlled by custom, and these open the way to new forms of accusation. Charges, previously excluded, as by a Zulu against his father, are now made. The system of witchcraft beliefs, originally tied to certain social relations, can be adapted to new situations of conflict—to competition for jobs in towns, to the rising standard of living, made possible by new goods, which breaches the previous egalitarianism, and so forth [2, p. 101].

One example of such innovation in the application of magic and sorcery—terms which I prefer to witchcraft—to cultural change and urban living came to my attention during my recent research among the Zulu in South Africa. It illustrates not only how the changing pattern of magic is related to the changing way of life, but it does the reverse as well, and shows how innovations can only be built on previous cultural patterns. In Durban the Africans show a great enthusiasm for soccer, or, to use the local term, football. Much of the limited leisure of the native male population is devoted to watching, discussing, and participating in this game, and organized football leagues resembling, in their hierarchies of skill, our own major and minor leagues in baseball, engage in complex rivalries no less extreme, bitter, and unremitting than in Chicago or Cleveland. This exemplifies the "new situations of conflict" to which Gluckman refers. Interpersonal and intergroup hostility and aggression are much greater in an urban setting than in the more traditional rural Zulu community. Unnaturally crowded conditions and competition for scarce employment opportunities lead to more frequent accusations of sorcery in the city. Football, it may be hypothesized, serves a dual function in this context: first, it is one of the few opportunities open to the Zulu for release from the anxiety and tensions of anomic urban life; and more specifically, it allows the expression of the increased aggression and hostility that arises in the city between Africans, within the framework of a modern, acceptable form.

It is common knowledge, and not surprising, that in an effort to produce winning teams each of these football teams employs an *inyanga*, or Zulu doctor, who serves the dual purpose of strengthening his own team by magic and ritual, and of forestalling the sorcery directed at his team by rival *inyangas*. Although no *inyanga* with whom I talked would admit that he employed sorcery against opposing teams, each was convinced that this was the practice of rival *inyangas*. Actually magic in Durban football is so widespread that although in searching for players there exists at least a minimal recognition of individual talent, few players known to be the object of *umtagathi*, or sorcerers, would be considered by a team regardless of their ability; moreover, success or failure of a team is invariably attributed to the skills of the *inyangas*, as well as to the natural talent of the players. However, when a team consistently loses it is the *inyanga* who is replaced, not the players. When, on the other hand, an individual player is suspected of being the object of sorcery he may be dropped from the team for fear that the spell might generalize to include the teammates of the unfortunate victim.

That football holds a place of extreme importance to the African community is demonstrated in several ways. Players of considerable talent are much sought after and part of the work of the trainer is to scout other teams and to attempt to entice skilled players of opposing teams into joining his own. In fact, although ostensibly this is an amateur sport, players of promise are frequently paid a salary from the treasury of the team as a means of keeping them. If a skilled player has had difficulty in finding employment, it is incumbent on all members of the team to find suitable and well-paying employment for the star. So involved are the efforts of teammates to keep them happy that star players are known to pass from club to club for the "best deal."

Because of this, and for other reasons as well, strict discipline is maintained on the team. The trainer—or what we would call coach—is in a position of supreme authority. All the normal rules of status and interpersonal relationships which have long traditions and history may be discarded in the interests of winning games. Thus, it is even possible for a trainer to strike a man older than himself—perhaps considerably older—if the trainer feels he is not doing his share. This, of course, is a gross transgression against important Zulu norms regarding seniority and status.

The supernatural is enlisted in every possible way to aid in the production of a successful football team. Thus, ritual and ceremony are used on a number of occasions, connected with football, and serve the functions of sanctioning and supporting the efforts of a team. Before the season even opens, the team slaughters a goat "to open the doors to luck" and the season's end is marked by another slaughter.

Much of the ritual is propitiative as in the example of the slaughter cited above, but most ceremonies combine propitiation with positive attempts to combat sorcery. The following is an account, related by an educated Zulu health educator of the ritual conducted by *inyangas* on the night preceding a match:

> All the football teams have their own *inyanga* who doctors them all for each match. The night before a match they must "camp" together around a fire. They all sleep there together, they must stay naked and they are given *umuthi* and other medicines by the *inyanga*. Incisions

are made on their knees, elbows, and joints. In the morning they are made to vomit. They must all go together on the same bus to the match, and they must enter the playing grounds together. Almost every team I know has an *inyanga* and does this—it is necessary to win. Even though players are Christians and have lived in towns for a long time, they do it, and believe in it.

Another informant gave as the reasons for this practice of camping-out the following account:

The purpose is to avoid liquor, sexual intercourse, mixing with enemy players who might bewitch them, and mixing with other persons who might affect them with ill-luck.

The camping group is composed of the starting team and reserves, plus administrative members of the club, loyal and enthusiastic supporters, and the *inyanga*. The morning after the camping the whole group moves to the playing grounds together. A certain procedure is followed: the group keeps a very tight formation with every man touching the man in front of, behind and beside him, the pace is very slow and stylized and the group may be likened to a millipede—one organism with a million legs. Even when the group has to take a bus from one part of town to another where the football field is, they still make every effort to maintain their formation. The players themselves are placed right in the center of the group in order that they might be protected. Moving out onto the actual playing field with their stylized trotting step, the group acts very hostile to outsiders for fear that intruders will attempt to bewitch the players or in some way to weaken the "umuthi" or the medicine of the *inyanga*.

Now, when we compare the description of the ritual magic involved in "camping-out" with accounts by Bryant[1] (p. 501) and Krige[3] (p. 272) of doctoring of Zulu warriors in the time of Shaka during the early 1800's, we perceive many elements of unmistakable similarity: the circle around the fire; the medicines to endow strength and courage; the medicine on the weapons (currently, on football jerseys and shoes) to increase their potency (currently, to make them slippery); and the purificatory emetic which, in Shaka's time, was taken on the morning of the battle, and nowadays on the morning before the football match.

Further, the formation followed in reaching the playing field derives, without doubt, from historical military formations. The avoidance of sex on the eve of battles can also be traced back to earlier customs connected with warfare. These are but a few examples of the basic similarities of the ritual and ceremony used currently by football teams and formerly by army regiments.

There is an interesting parallel to be found to the above example of cultural syncretism. Sundkler [4], in describing Zulu leadership patterns in separatist churches, has shown that the traditional roles of chief and medical specialist are carried over into the modern Christian church in much the same way as these roles are found in modern football teams.

Returning to the point made earlier—why does a belief in magic in football exist at all? As Gluckman says, because such a belief explains the inexplicable. Why does one football team win consistently and another lose? Certainly the winning team will have players who are more talented—but why, in the first place, do these teams manage to gather more talented players, and, in the second place, why are these players more talented, where does their skill come from? Why is it that the talented players avoid sorcery? These are the questions with which magic deals.

That beliefs in magic help to explain the inexplicable is illustrated by the following account:

> We health educators started a team and did very well. We made a point of not using an *inyanga*. We advertised the fact that we did not use one. We even invited a few outsiders on to our team so that they would see that we used no witchcraft, and we hoped that they would tell others about this. Well, we won a lot of games—and do you know what the people said? They said that because we work with European doctors we were given injections to make us strong so that we could win. We could not convince them otherwise.

By this account a number of things are made clear. Modern medicine is viewed as essentially similar to the magic of the Zulu doctor, except in this case it is the magic of the European. Formerly, Zulu avoided European doctors (except in the case of trauma) in the belief that they could only help or cure Europeans. Today, they accept the fact that an African can be helped in many cases by modern Western medicine. Nonetheless, it is still believed that there are some diseases—which they refer to as Bantu diseases—which cannot be helped by the European. Such diseases as *umfufuyana, chayiza* and *spoiliyana*, which are essentially psychosomatic, hysterical-type personality disorders, are rarely taken to the European doctor.

On the other hand, the injections used by European doctors are viewed as being entirely magical, and Zulu who come to the European doctor for help of any kind always insist on a *jovo*—an injection—as part of any treatment. No distinction is drawn between the *jovo* of the white jacketed European doctor or the roots or herbs of the *inyanga* clad in skins. Thus, when we view the football team we clearly see how the winning of matches is almost always explained by references to magic. In usual cases it is magic of the *inyanga,* while in unusual cases, like that of the health educator team, the magic of the European doctors.

Retention by urban Zulu of magical beliefs and practices also throws some light on the persistence of conflict patterns in a changing culture. The use of sorcery practices and warfare rituals within the framework of the game of soccer introduced by Europeans illustrates the adaptation of old methods of expressing hostility to the new and highly frustrating urban situation.

REFERENCES

1. Bryant, A. T. *The Zulu People.* Pietermaritzburg: Shuter and Schooter, 1949.
2. Gluckman, M. *Custom and Conflict in Africa.* London: Oxford University Press, 1955.
3. Krige, E. J. *The Social System of the Zulus.* London: Longmans, 1936.
4. Sundkler, B. *Bantu Prophets in South Africa.* London: Lutterworth, 1948.

[1] I wish to thank M. J. Herskovits, A. Vilakazi, R. LeVine, and W. Elmendorf for having read and made valuable suggestions regarding this paper. The responsibility for this final version is, of course, completely my own. I also wish to thank the National Institutes of Health, the Program of African Studies at Northwestern University, Washington State University, and the Russell Sage Foundation for the financial support that made possible the field work and analysis of data on which this paper is based. This is a revised version of a paper read at the 1959 meetings of the American Anthropological Association.

6. BECOMING A MARIHUANA USER*

Howard S. Becker

The use of marihuana is and has been the focus of a good deal of attention on the part of both scientists and laymen. One of the major problems students of the practice have addressed themselves to has been the identification of those individual psychological traits which differentiate marihuana users from nonusers and which are assumed to account for the use of the drug. That approach, common in the study of behavior categorized as deviant, is based on the premise that the presence of a given kind of behavior in an individual can best be explained as the result of some trait which predisposes or motivates him to engage in the behavior.[1]

Reprinted from *The American Journal of Sociology,* Vol. LIX, November, 1953, pp. 235-242, by permission of the author and the publisher, The University of Chicago Press.

*Paper read at the meetings of the Midwest Sociological Society in Omaha, Nebraska, April 25, 1953. The research on which this paper is based was done while I was a member of the staff of the Chicago Narcotics Survey, a study done by the Chicago Area Project, Inc., under a grant from the National Mental Health Institute. My thanks to Solomon Kobrin, Harold Finestone, Henry McKay, and Anselm Strauss, who read and discussed with me earlier versions of this paper.

This study is likewise concerned with accounting for the presence or absence of marihuana use in an individual's behavior. It starts, however, from a different premise: that the presence of a given kind of behavior is the result of a sequence of social experiences during which the person acquires a conception of the meaning of the behavior, and perceptions and judgments of objects and situations, all of which make the activity possible and desirable. Thus, the motivation or disposition to engage in the activity is built up in the course of learning to engage in it and does not antedate this learning process. For such a view it is not necessary to identify those "traits" which "cause" the behavior. Instead, the problem becomes one of describing the set of changes in the person's conception of the activity and of the experience it provides for him.[2]

This paper seeks to describe the sequence of changes in attitude and experience which lead to *the use of marihuana for pleasure*. Marihuana does not produce addiction, as do alcohol and the opiate drugs; there is no withdrawal sickness and no ineradicable craving for the drug.[3] The most frequent pattern of use might be termed "recreational." The drug is used occasionally for the pleasure the user finds in it, a relatively casual kind of behavior in comparison with that connected with the use of addicting drugs. The term "use for pleasure" is meant to emphasize the noncompulsive and casual character of the behavior. It is also meant to eliminate from consideration here those few cases in which marihuana is used for its prestige value only, as a symbol that one is a certain kind of person, with no pleasure at all being derived from its use.

The analysis presented here is conceived of as demonstrating the greater explanatory usefulness of the kind of theory outlined above as opposed to the predispositional theories now current. This may be seen in two ways: (1) predispositional theories cannot account for that group of users (whose existence is admitted)[4] who do not exhibit the trait or traits considered to cause the behavior and (2) such theories cannot account for the great variability over time of a given individual's behavior with reference to the drug. The same person will at one stage be unable to use the drug for pleasure, at a later stage be able and willing to do so, and, still later, again be unable to use it in this way. These changes, difficult to explain from a predispositional or motivational theory, are readily understandable in terms of changes in the individual's conception of the drug as is the existence of "normal" users.

The study attempted to arrive at a general statement of the sequence of changes in individual attitude and experience which have always occurred when the individual has become willing and able to use marihuana for pleasure and which have not occurred or not been permanently maintained when this is not the case. This generalization is stated in universal terms in order that negative cases may be discovered and used to revise the explanatory hypothesis.[5]

Fifty interviews with marihuana users from a variety of social backgrounds and present positions in society constitute the data from which the generalization was constructed and against which it was tested.[6] The interviews focused on the history of the person's experience with the drug, seeking major changes in his attitude toward it and in his actual use of it and the reasons for these changes. The final generalization is a statement of that sequence of changes in attitude which occurred in every case known to me in which the person came to use marihuana for pleasure. Until a negative case is found, it may be considered as an explanation of all cases of marihuana use for pleasure. In addition, changes from use to nonuse are shown to be related to similar changes in conception, and in each case it is possible to explain variations in the individual's behavior in these terms.

This paper covers only a portion of the natural history of an individual's use of marihuana,[7] starting with the person having arrived at the point of willingness to try marihuana. He knows that others use it to "get high," but he does not know what this means in concrete terms. He is curious about the experience, ignorant of what it may turn out to be, and afraid that it may be more than he has bargained for. The steps outlined below, if he undergoes them all and maintains the attitudes developed in them, leave him willing and able to use the drug for pleasure when the opportunity presents itself.

I

The novice does not ordinarily get high the first time he smokes marihuana, and several attempts are usually necessary to induce this state. One explanation of this may be that the drug is not smoked "properly," that is, in a way that insures sufficient dosage to produce real symptoms of intoxication. Most users agree that it cannot be smoked like tobacco if one is to get high:

> Take in a lot of air, you know, and . . . I don't know how to describe it, you don't smoke it like a cigarette, you draw in a lot of air and get it deep down in your system and then keep it there. Keep it there as long as you can.

Without the use of some such technique[8] the drug will produce no effects, and the user will be unable to get high:

> The trouble with people like that [who are not able to get high] is that they're just not smoking it right, that's all there is to it. Either they're not holding it down long enough, or they're getting too much air and not enough smoke, or the other way around or something like that. A lot of people just don't smoke it right, so naturally nothing's gonna happen.

If nothing happens, it is manifestly impossible for the user to develop a conception of the drug as an object which can be used for pleasure, and use will therefore not continue. The first step in the sequence of events that must occur if the person is to become a user is that he must learn to use the proper smoking technique in order that his use of the drug will produce some effects in terms of which his conception of it can change.

Such a change is, as might be expected, a result of the individual's participation in groups in which marihuana is used. In them the individual learns the proper way to smoke the drug. This may occur through direct teaching:

> I was smoking like I did an ordinary cigarette. He said, "No, don't do it like that." He said, "Suck it, you know, draw in and hold it in your lungs till you . . . for a period of time."
> I said, "Is there any limit of time to hold it?"
> He said, "No, just till you feel that you want to let it out, let it out."
> So I did that three or four times.

Many new users are ashamed to admit ignorance and, pretending to know already, must learn through the more indirect means of observation and imitation:

> I came on like I had turned on [smoked marihuana] many times before, you know. I didn't want to seem like a punk to this cat. See, like I didn't know the first thing about it—how to smoke it, or what was going to happen, or what. I just watched him like a hawk—I didn't take my eyes off him for a second, because I wanted to do everything just as he did it. I watched how he held it, how he smoked it, and everything. Then when he gave it to me I just came on cool, as though I knew exactly what the score was. I held it like he did and took a poke just the way he did.

No person continued marihuana use for pleasure without learning a technique that supplied sufficient dosage for the effects of the drug to appear. Only when this was learned was it possible for a conception of the drug as an object which could be used for pleasure to emerge. Without such a conception marihuana use was considered meaningless and did not continue.

II

Even after he learns the proper smoking technique, the new user may not get high and thus not form a conception of the drug as something which can be used for pleasure. A remark made by a user suggested the reason for this difficulty in getting high and pointed to the next necessary step on the road to being a user:

> I was told during an interview, "As a matter of fact, I've seen a guy who was high out of his mind and didn't know it."
> I expressed disbelief: "How can that be, man?"
> The interviewee said, "Well, it's pretty strange, I'll grant you that, but I've seen it. This guy got on with me, claiming that he'd never got high, one of those guys, and he got completely stoned. And he kept insisting that he wasn't high. So I had to prove to him that he was."

What does this mean? It suggests that being high consists of two elements: the presence of symptoms caused by marihuana use and the recognition of these symptoms and their connection by the user with his use of the drug. It is not enough, that is, that the effects be present; they alone do not automatically provide the experience of being high. The user must be able to point them out to himself and consciously connect them with his having smoked marihuana before he can have this experience. Otherwise, regardless of the actual effects produced, he considers that the drug has had no effect on him: "I figure it either had no effect on me or other people were exaggerating its effect on them, you know. I thought it was probably psychological, see." Such persons believe that the whole thing is an illusion and that the wish to be high leads the user to deceive himself into believing that something is happening when, in fact, nothing is. They do not continue marihuana use, feeling that "it does nothing" for them.

Typically, however, the novice has faith (developed from his observation of users who do get high) that the drug actually will produce some new experience and continues to experiment with it until it does. His failure to get high worries him, and he is likely to ask more experienced users or provoke comments from them about it. In such conversations he is made aware of specific details of his experience which he may not have noticed or may have noticed but failed to identify as symptoms of being high:

> I didn't get high the first time. . . . I don't think I held it in long enough. I probably let it out, you know, you're a little afraid. The second time I wasn't sure, and he [smoking companion] told me, like I asked him for some of the symptoms or something, how would I know, you know. . . . So he told me to sit on a stool. I sat on—I think I sat

on a bar stool—and he said, "Let your feet hang," and then when I got down my feet were real cold, you know.

And I started feeling it, you know. That was the first time. And then about a week after that, sometime pretty close to it, I really got on. That was the first time I got on a big laughing kick, you know. Then I really knew I was on.

One symptom of being high is an intense hunger. In the next case the novice becomes aware of this and gets high for the first time:

They were just laughing the hell out of me because like I was eating so much. I just scoffed [ate] so much food, and they were just laughing at me, you know. Sometimes I'd be looking at them, you know, wondering why they're laughing, you know, not knowing what I was doing. [Well, did they tell you why they were laughing eventually?] Yeah, yeah, I come back, "Hey, man, what's happening?" Like, you know, like I'd ask, "What's happening?" and all of a sudden I feel weird, you know. "Man, you're on, you know. You're on pot [high on marihuana]." I said, "No, am I?" Like I don't know what's happening.

The learning may occur in more indirect ways:

I heard little remarks that were made by other people. Somebody said, "My legs are rubbery," and I can't remember all the remarks that were made because I was very attentively listening for all these cues for what I was supposed to feel like.

The novice, then, eager to have this feeling, picks up from other users some concrete referents of the term "high" and applies these notions to his own experience. The new concepts make it possible for him to locate these symptoms among his own sensations and to point out to himself a "something different" in his experience that he connects with drug use. It is only when he can do this that he is high. In the next case, the contrast between two successive experiences of a user makes clear the crucial importance of the awareness of the symptoms in being high and re-emphasizes the important role of interaction with other users in acquiring the concepts that make this awareness possible:

[Did you get high the first time you turned on?] Yeah, sure. Although, come to think of it, I guess I really didn't. I mean, like that first time it was more or less of a mild drunk. I was happy, I guess, you know what I mean. But I didn't really know I was high, you know what I mean. It was only after the second time I got high that I realized I was high the first time. Then I knew that something different was happening.

[How did you know that?] How did I know? If what happened to me that night would of happened to you, you would've known, believe me. We played the first tune for almost two hours—one tune! Imagine, man! We got on the stand and played this one tune, we started at nine o'clock. When we got finished I looked at my watch, it's a quarter to eleven. Almost two hours on one tune. And it didn't seem like anything.

I mean, you know, it does that to you. It's like you have much more time or something. Anyway, when I saw that, man, it was too much. I knew I must really be high or something if anything like that could happen. See, and then they explained to me that that's what it did to you, you had a different sense of time and everything. So I realized that that's what it was. I knew then. Like the first time, I probably felt that way, you know, but I didn't know what's happening.

It is only when the novice becomes able to get high in this sense that he will continue to use marihuana for pleasure. In every case in which use continued, the user had acquired the necessary concepts with which to express to himself the fact that he was experiencing new sensations caused by the drug. That is, for use to continue, it is necessary not only to use the drug so as to produce effects but also to learn to perceive these effects when they occur. In this way marihuana acquires meaning for the user as an object which can be used for pleasure.

With increasing experience the user develops a greater appreciation of the drug's effects; he continues to learn to get high. He examines succeeding experiences closely, looking for new effects, making sure the old ones are still there. Out of this there grows a stable set of categories for experiencing the drug's effects whose presence enables the user to get high with ease.

The ability to perceive the drug's effects must be maintained if use is to continue; if it is lost, marihuana use ceases. Two kinds of evidence support this statement. First, people who become heavy users of alcohol, barbiturates, or opiates do not continue to smoke marihuana, largely because they lose the ability to distinguish between its effects and those of the other drugs.[9] They no longer know whether the marihuana gets them high. Second, in those few cases in which an individual uses marihuana in such quantities that he is always high, he is apt to get this same feeling that the drug has no effect on him, since the essential element of a noticeable difference between feeling high and feeling normal is missing. In such a situation, use is likely to be given up completely, but temporarily, in order that the user may once again be able to perceive the difference.

III

One more step is necessary if the user who has now learned to get high is to continue use. He must learn to enjoy the effects he has just learned to experience. Marihuana-produced sensations are not automatically or necessarily pleasurable. The taste for such experience is a socially acquired one, not different in kind from acquired tastes for oysters or dry martinis. The user feels dizzy, thirsty; his scalp tingles; he misjudges time and distances; and so on. Are these things pleasurable? He isn't sure. If he is to continue marihuana use, he must decide that they are. Otherwise, getting high, while a real enough experience, will be an unpleasant one he would rather avoid.

The effects of the drug, when first perceived, may be physically unpleasant or at least ambiguous:

> It started taking effect, and I didn't know what was happening, you know, what it was, and I was very sick. I walked around the room, walking around the room trying to get off, you know; it just scared me at first, you know. I wasn't used to that kind of feeling.

In addition, the novice's naïve interpretation of what is happening to him may further confuse and frighten him, particularly if he decides, as many do, that he is going insane:

> I felt I was insane, you know. Everything people done to me just wigged me. I couldn't hold a conversation, and my mind would be wandering, and I was always thinking, oh, I don't know, weird things, like hearing music different. . . . I get the feeling that I can't talk to anyone. I'll goof completely.

Given these typically frightening and unpleasant first experiences, the beginner will not continue use unless he learns to redefine the sensations as pleasurable:

> It was offered to me, and I tried it. I'll tell you one thing. I never did enjoy it at all. I mean it was just nothing that I could enjoy. [Well, did you get high when you turned on?] Oh, yeah, I got definite feelings from it. But I didn't enjoy them. I mean I got plenty of reactions, but the were mostly reactions of fear. [You were frightened?] Yes. I didn't enjoy it. I couldn't seem to relax with it, you know. If you can't relax with a thing, you can't enjoy it, I don't think.

In other cases the first experiences were also definitely unpleasant, but the person did become a marihuana user. This occurred, however, only after a later experience enabled him to redefine the sensations as pleasurable:

> [This man's first experience was extremely unpleasant, involving distortion of spatial relationships and sounds, violent thirst, and panic produced by these symptoms.] After the first time I didn't turn on for about, I'd say, ten months to a year. . . . It wasn't a moral thing; it was because I'd gotten so frightened, bein' so high. An' I didn't want to go through that again, I mean, my reaction was, "Well, if this is what they call being' high, I don't dig [like] it." . . . So I didn't turn on for a year almost, accounta that. . . .

Well, my friends started, an' consequently I started again. But I didn't have any more, I didn't have that same initial reaction, after I started turning on again.

[In interaction with his friends he became able to find pleasure in the effects of the drug and eventually became a regular user.]

In no case will use continue without such a redefinition of the effects as enjoyable.

This redefinition occurs, typically, in interaction with more experienced users who, in a number of ways, teach the novice to find pleasure in this experience which is at first so frightening.[10] They may reassure him as to the temporary character of the unpleasant sensations and minimize their seriousness, at the same time calling attention to the more enjoyable aspects. An experienced user describes how he handles newcomers to marihuana use:

Well, they get pretty high sometimes. The average person isn't ready for that, and it is a little frightening to them sometimes. I mean, they've been high on lush [alcohol], and they get higher that way than they've ever been before, and they don't know what's happening to them. Because they think they're going to keep going up, up, up till they lose their minds or begin doing weird things or something. You have to like reassure them, explain to them that they're not really flipping or anything, that they're gonna be all right. You have to just talk them out of being afraid. Keep talking to them, reassuring, telling them it's all right. And come on with your own story, you know: "The same thing happened to me. You'll get to like that after awhile." Keep coming on like that; pretty soon you talk them out of being scared. And besides they see you doing it and nothing horrible is happening to you, so that gives them more confidence.

The more experienced user may also teach the novice to regulate the amount he smokes more carefully, so as to avoid any severely uncomfortable symptoms while retaining the pleasant ones. Finally, he teaches the new user that he can "get to like it after awhile." He teaches him to regard those ambiguous experiences formerly defined as unpleasant as enjoyable. The older user in the following incident is a person whose tastes have shifted in this way, and his remarks have the effect of helping others to make a similar redefinition:

A new user had her first experience of the effects of marihuana and became frightened and hysterical. She "felt like she was half in and half out of the room" and experienced a number of alarming physical symptoms. One of the more experienced users present said, "She's dragged because she's high like that. I'd give anything to get that high myself. I haven't been that high in years."

In short, what was once frightening and distasteful becomes, after a taste for it is built up, pleasant, desired, and sought after. Enjoyment is introduced by the favorable definition of the experience that one acquires from others. Without this, use will not continue, for marihuana will not be for the user an object he can use for pleasure.

In addition to being a necessary step in becoming a user, this represents an important condition for continued use. It is quite common for experienced users suddenly to have an unpleasant or frightening experience, which they cannot define as pleasurable, either because they have used a larger amount of marihuana than usual or because it turns out to be a higher-quality marihuana than they expected. The user has sensations which go beyond any conception he has of what being high is and is in much the same situation as the novice, uncomfortable and frightened. He may blame it on an overdose and simply be more careful in the future. But he may make this the occasion for a rethinking of his attitude toward the drug and decide that it no longer can give him pleasure. When this occurs and is not followed by a redefinition of the drug as capable of producing pleasure, use will cease.

The likelihood of such a redefinition occurring depends on the degree of the individual's participation with other users. Where this participation is intensive, the individual is quickly talked out of his feeling against marihuana use. In the next case, on the other hand, the experience was very disturbing, and the aftermath of the incident cut the person's participation with other users to almost zero. Use stopped for three years and began again only when a combination of circumstances, important among which was a resumption of ties with users, made possible a redefinition of the nature of the drug:

> It was too much, like I only made about four pokes, and I couldn't even get it out of my mouth, I was so high, and I got real flipped. In the basement, you know, I just couldn't stay in there anymore. My heart was pounding real hard, you know, and I was going out of my mind; I thought I was losing my mind completely. So I cut out of this basement, and this other guy, he's out of his mind, told me, "Don't, don't leave me, man. Stay here." And I couldn't.
>
> I walked outside, and it was five below zero, and I thought I was dying, and I had my coat open; I was sweating, I was perspiring. My whole insides were all . . . , and I walked about two blocks away, and I fainted behind a bush. I don't know how long I laid there. I woke up, and I was feeling the worst, I can't describe it at all, so I made it to a bowling alley, man, and I was trying to act normal, I was trying to shoot pool, you know, trying to act real normal, and I couldn't lay and I couldn't stand up and I couldn't sit down, and I went up and laid down where some guys that spot pins lay down, and that didn't

help me, and I went down to a doctor's office. I was going to go in there and tell the doctor to put me out of my misery . . . because my heart was pounding so hard, you know. . . . So then all week end I started flipping, seeing things there and going through hell, you know, all kinds of abnormal things. . . . I just quit for a long time then.

[He went to a doctor who defined the symptoms for him as those of a nervous breakdown caused by "nerves" and "worries." Although he was no longer using marihuana, he had some recurrences of the symptoms which led him to suspect that "it was all his nerves."] So I just stopped worrying, you know; so it was about thirty-six months later I started making it again. I'd just take a few pokes, you know. [He first resumed use in the company of the same user-friend with whom he had been involved in the original incident.]

A person, then, cannot begin to use marihuana for pleasure, or continue its use for pleasure, unless he learns to define its effects as enjoyable, unless it becomes and remains an object which he conceives of as capable of producing pleasure.

IV

In summary, an individual will be able to use marihuana for pleasure only when he goes through a process of learning to conceive of it as an object which can be used in this way. No one becomes a user without (1) learning to smoke the drug in a way which will produce real effects; (2) learning to recognize the effects and connect them with drug use (learning, in other words, to get high); and (3) learning to enjoy the sensations he perceives. In the course of this process he develops a disposition or motivation to use marihuana which was not and could not have been present when he began use, for it involves and depends on conceptions of the drug which could only grow out of the kind of actual experience detailed above. On completion of this process he is willing and able to use marihuana for pleasure.

He has learned, in short, to answer "Yes" to the question: "Is it fun?" The direction his further use of the drug takes depends on his being able to continue to answer "Yes" to this question and, in addition, on his being able to answer "Yes" to other questions which arise as he becomes aware of the implications of the fact that the society as a whole disapproves of the practice: "Is it expedient?" "Is it moral?"[11] Once he has acquired the ability to get enjoyment out of the drug, use will continue to be possible for him. Considerations of morality and expediency, occasioned by the reactions of society, may interfere and inhibit use, but use continues to be a possibility in terms of his conception of the drug. The act becomes impossible only when the ability to enjoy the experience of being high is lost, through a change in the user's conception of the drug occasioned by certain kinds of experience with it.

In comparing this theory with those which ascribe marihuana use to motives or predispositions rooted deep in individual behavior, the evidence makes it clear that marihuana use for pleasure can occur only when the process described above is undergone and cannot occur without it. This is apparently so without reference to the nature of the individual's personal makeup or psychic problems. Such theories assume that people have stable modes of response which predetermine the way they will act in relation to any particular situation or object and that, when they come in contact with the given object or situation, they act in the way in which their makeup predisposes them.

This analysis of the genesis of marihuana use shows that the individuals who come in contact with a given object may respond to it at first in a great variety of ways. If a stable form of new behavior toward the object is to emerge, a transformation of meanings must occur, in which the person develops a new conception of the nature of the object.[12] This happens in a series of communicative acts in which others point out new aspects of his experience to him, present him with new interpretations of events, and help him achieve a new conceptual organization of his world, without which the new behavior is not possible. Persons who do not achieve the proper kind of conceptualization are unable to engage in the given behavior and turn off in the direction of some other relationship to the object or activity.

This suggests that behavior of any kind might fruitfully be studied developmentally, in terms of changes in meanings and concepts, their organization and reorganization, and the way they channel behavior, making some acts possible while excluding others.

[1]See, as examples of this approach, the following: Eli Marcovitz and Henry J. Meyers, "The Marihuana Addict in the Army," *War Medicine*, VI (December, 1944), 382-91; Herbert S. Gaskill, "Marihuana, an Intoxicant," *American Journal of Psychiatry*, CII (September, 1945), 202-4; Sol Charen and Luis Perelman, "Personality Studies of Marihuana Addicts," *American Journal of Psychiatry*, CII (March, 1946), 674-82.

[2]This approach stems from George Herbert Mead's discussion of objects in *Mind, Self, and Society* (Chicago: University of Chicago Press, 1934), pp. 277-80.

[3]Cf. Roger Adams, "Marihuana," *Bulletin of the New York Academy of Medicine*, XVIII (November, 1942), 705-30.

[4]Cf. Lawrence Kolb, "Marihuana," *Federal Probation*, II (July, 1938), 22-25; and Walter Bromberg, "Marihuana: A Psychiatric Study," *Journal of the American Medical Association*, CXIII (July 1, 1939), 11.

[5]The method used is that described by Alfred R. Lindesmith in his *Opiate Addiction* (Bloomington: Principia Press, 1947), chap. i. I would like also to acknowledge the important role Lindesmith's work played in shaping my thinking about the genesis of marihuana use.

[6]Most of the interviews were done by the author. I am grateful to Solomon Kobrin and Harold Finestone for allowing me to make use of interviews done by them.

[7]I hope to discuss elsewhere other stages in this natural history.

[8]A pharmacologist notes that this ritual is in fact an extremely efficient way of getting the drug into the blood stream (R. P. Walton, *Marihuana: America's New Drug Problem* [Philadelphia: J. B. Lippincott, 1938], p. 48).

[9]"Smokers have repeatedly stated that the consumption of whiskey while smoking negates the potency of the drug. They feel it very difficult to get 'high' while drinking whiskey and because of that smokers will not drink while using the 'weed' " (cf. New York City Mayor's Committee on Marihuana, *The Marihuana Problem in the City of New York* [Lancaster, Pa.: Jacques Cattell Press, 1944], p. 13).

[10]Charen and Perelman, *op. cit.*, p. 679.

[11]Another paper will discuss the series of developments in attitude that occurs as the individual begins to take account of these matters and adjust his use to them.

[12]Cf. Anselm Strauss, "The Development and Transformation of Monetary Meanings in the Child," *American Sociological Review*, XVII (June, 1952), 275-86.

7. FINAL NOTE ON A CASE OF EXTREME ISOLATION

Kingsley Davis

Early in 1940 there appeared in this *Journal* an account of a girl called Anna.[1] She had been deprived of normal contact and had received a minimum of human care for almost the whole of her first six years of life. At that time observations were not complete and the report had a tentative character. Now, however, the girl is dead, and, with more information available, [2] it is possible to give a fuller and more definitive description of the case from a sociological point of view.

Anna's death, caused by hemorrhagic jaundice, occurred on August 6, 1942. Having been born on March 1 or 6,[3] 1932, she was approximately ten and a half years of age when she died. The previous report covered her development up to the age of almost eight years; the present one recapitulates the earlier period on the basis of new evidence and then covers the last two and a half years of her life.

Reprinted from *The American Journal of Sociology*, Vol. LII, No. 5 (March 1947), pp. 432-437, by permission of the author and the publisher, The University of Chicago Press.

EARLY HISTORY

The first few days and weeks of Anna's life were complicated by frequent changes of domicile. It will be recalled that she was an illegitimate child, the second such child born to her mother, and that her grandfather, a widowed farmer in whose house her mother lived, strongly disapproved of this new evidence of the mother's indiscretion. This fact led to the baby's being shifted about.

Two weeks after being born in a nurse's private home, Anna was brought to the family farm, but the grandfather's antagonism was so great that she was shortly taken to the house of one of her mother's friends. At this time a local minister became interested in her and took her to his house with an idea of possible adoption. He decided against adoption, however, when he discovered that she had vaginitis. The infant was then taken to a children's home in the nearest large city. This agency found that at the age of only three weeks she was already in a miserable condition, being "terribly galled and otherwise in very bad shape." It did not regard her as a likely subject for adoption but took her in for a while anyway, hoping to benefit her. After Anna had spent nearly eight weeks in this place, the agency notified her mother to come to get her. The mother responded by sending a man and his wife to the children's home with a view to their adopting Anna, but they made such a poor impression on the agency that permission was refused. Later the mother came herself and took the child out of the home and then gave her to this couple. It was in the home of this pair that a social worker found the girl a short time thereafter. The social worker went to the mother's home and pleaded with Anna's grandfather to allow the mother to bring the child home. In spite of threats, he refused. The child, by then more than four months old, was next taken to another children's home in a near-by town. A medical examination at this time revealed that she had impetigo, vaginitis, umbilical hernia, and a skin rash.

Anna remained in this second children's home for nearly three weeks, at the end of which time she was transferred to a private foster-home. Since, however, the grandfather would not, and the mother could not, pay for the child's care, she was finally taken back as a last resort to the grandfather's house (at the age of five and a half months). There she remained, kept on the second floor in an attic-like room because her mother hesitated to incur the grandfather's wrath by bringing her downstairs.

The mother, a sturdy woman weighing about 180 pounds, did

a man's work on the farm. She engaged in heavy work such as milking cows and tending hogs and had little time for her children. Sometimes she went out at night, in which case Anna was left entirely without attention. Ordinarily, it seems, Anna received only enough care to keep her barely alive. She appears to have been seldom moved from one position to another. Her clothing and bedding were filthy. She apparently had no instruction, no friendly attention.

It is little wonder that, when finally found and removed from the room in the grandfather's house at the age of nearly six years, the child could not talk, walk, or do anything that showed intelligence. She was in an extremely emaciated and undernourished condition, with skeleton-like legs and a bloated abdomen. She had been fed on virtually nothing except cow's milk during the years under her mother's care.

Anna's condition when found, and her subsequent inprovement, have been described in the previous report. It now remains to say what happened to her after that.

LATER HISTORY

In 1939, nearly two years after being discovered, Anna had progressed, as previously reported, to the point where she could walk, understand simple commands, feed herself, achieve some neatness, remember people, etc. But she still did not speak, and, though she was much more like a normal infant of something over one year of age in mentality, she was far from normal for her age.

On August 30, 1939, she was taken to a private home for retarded children, leaving the county home where she had been for more than a year and a half. In her new setting she made some further progress, but not a great deal. In a report of an examination made November 6 of the same year, the head of the institution pictured the child as follows:

> Anna walks about aimlessly, makes periodic rhythmic motions of her hands, and, at intervals, makes gutteral and sucking noises. She regards her hands as if she had seen them for the first time. It was impossible to hold her attention for more than a few seconds at a time—not because of distraction due to external stimuli but because of her inability to concentrate. She ignored the task in hand to gaze vacantly about the room. Speech is entirely lacking. Numerous unsuccessful attempts have been made with her in the hope of developing initial sounds. I do not believe that this failure is due to negativism or deafness but that she is not

sufficiently developed to accept speech at this time. . . . The prognosis is not favorable. . . .

More than five months later, on April 25, 1940, a clinical psychologist, the late Professor Francis N. Maxfield, examined Anna and reported the following: large for her age; hearing "entirely normal"; vision apparently normal; able to climb stairs; speech in the "babbling stage" and "promise for developing intelligible speech later seems to be good." He said further that "on the Merrill-Palmer scale she made a mental score of 19 months. On the Vineland social maturity scale she made a score of 23 months."[4]

Professor Maxfield very sensibly pointed out that prognosis is difficult in such cases of isolation. "It is very difficult to take scores on tests standardized under average conditions of environment and experience," he wrote, "and interpret them in a case where environment and experience have been so unusual." With this warning he gave it as his opinion at that time that Anna would eventually "attain an adult mental level of six or seven years."[5]

The school for retarded children, on July 1, 1941, reported that Anna had reached 46 inches in height and weighed 60 pounds. She could bounce and catch a ball and was said to conform to group socialization, though as a follower rather than a leader. Toilet habits were firmly established. Food habits were normal, except that she still used a spoon as her sole implement. She could dress herself except for fastening her clothes. Most remarkable of all, she had finally begun to develop speech. She was characterized as being at about the two-year level in this regard. She could call attendants by name and bring in one when she was asked to. She had a few complete sentences to express her wants. The report concluded that there was nothing peculiar about her, except that she was feebleminded—"probably congenital in type."[6]

A final report from the school, made on June 22, 1942, and evidently the last report before the girl's death, pictured only a slight advance over that given above. It said that Anna could follow directions, string beads, identify a few colors, build with blocks, and differentiate between attractive and unattractive pictures. She had a good sense of rhythm and loved a doll. She talked mainly in phrases but would repeat words and try to carry on a conversation. She was clean about clothing. She habitually washed her hands and brushed her teeth. She would try to help other children. She walked well and could run fairly well, though clumsily. Although easily excited, she had a pleasant disposition.

INTERPRETATION

Such was Anna's condition just before her death. It may seem as if she had not made much progress, but one must remember the condition in which she had been found. One must recall that she had no glimmering of speech, absolutely no ability to walk, no sense of gesture, not the least capacity to feed herself even when the food was put in front of her, and no comprehension of cleanliness. She was so apathetic that it was hard to tell whether or not she could hear. And all this at the age of nearly six years. Compared with this condition, her capacities at the time of her death seem striking indeed, though they do not amount to much more than a two-and-a-half-year mental level. One conclusion therefore seems safe, namely, that her isolation prevented a considerable amount of mental development that was undoubtedly part of her capacity. Just what her original capacity was, of course, is hard to say; but her development after her period of confinement (including the ability to walk and run, to play, dress, fit into a social situation, and, above all, to speak) shows that she had at least this much capacity—capacity that never could have been realized in her original condition of isolation.

A further question is this: What would she have been like if she had received a normal upbringing from the moment of birth? A definitive answer would have been impossible in any case, but even an approximate answer is made difficult by her early death. If one assumes, as was tentatively surmised in the previous report, that it is "almost impossible for any child to learn to speak, think, and act like a normal person after a long period of early isolation," it seems likely that Anna might have had a normal or near-normal capacity, genetically speaking. On the other hand, it was pointed out that Anna represented "a marginal case, [because] she was discovered before she had reached six years of age," an age "young enough to allow for some plasticity."[7] While admitting, then, that Anna's isolation *may* have been the major cause (and was certainly a minor cause) of her lack of rapid mental progress during the four and a half years following her rescue from neglect, it is necessary to entertain the hypothesis that she was congenitally deficient.

In connection with this hypothesis, one suggestive though by no means conclusive circumstance needs consideration, namely, the mentality of Anna's forebears. Information on this subject is easier to obtain, as one might guess, on the mother's than on the father's side. Anna's maternal grandmother, for example, is said to have been college educated and wished to have her children receive a good education, but her husband, Anna's stern grandfather, apparently a shrewd, hard-driving, calculating farmowner, was so penurious that her ambitions in this direction were thwarted. Under the circumstances her daughter (Anna's mother) managed, despite having to do hard work on the farm, to complete the eighth grade in a country school. Even so, however, the daughter was evidently not very smart. "A schoolmate of [Anna's mother] stated that she was retarded in school work; was very gullible at this age; and that her morals even at this time were discussed by other students." Two tests administered to her on March 4, 1938, when she was thirty-two years of age, showed that she was mentally deficient. On the Stanford Revision of the Binet-Simon Scale her performance was equivalent to that of a child of eight years, giving her an I.Q. of 50 and indicating mental deficiency of "middle-grade moron type."[8]

As to the identity of Anna's father, the most persistent theory holds that he was an old man about seventy-four years of age at the time of the girl's birth. If he was the one, there is no indication of mental or other biological deficiency, whatever one may think of his morals. However, someone else may actually have been the father.

To sum up: Anna's heredity is the kind that *might* have given rise to innate mental deficiency, though not necessarily.

COMPARISON WITH ANOTHER CASE

Perhaps more to the point than speculations about Anna's ancestry would be a case for comparison. If a child could be discovered who had been isolated about the same length of time as Anna but had achieved a much quicker recovery and a greater mental development, it would be a stronger indication that Anna was deficient to start with.

Such a case does exist. It is the case of a girl found at about the same time as Anna and under strikingly similar circumstances. A full description of the details of this case has not been published, but, in addition to newspaper reports, an excellent preliminary account by a speech specialist, Dr. Marie K. Mason, who played an important role in the handling of the child, has appeared.[9] Also the late Dr. Francis N. Maxfield, clinical psychologist at Ohio State University, as was Dr. Mason, has written an as yet unpublished but penetrating analysis of the case.[10] Some of his observations have been included in Professor Zingg's book on feral man.[11] The following discussion is drawn mainly from these enlightening materials.

The writer, through the kindness of Professors Mason and Maxfield, did have a chance to observe the girl in April, 1940, and to discuss the features of her case with them.

Born apparently one month later than Anna, the girl in question, who has been given the pseudonym Isabelle, was discovered in November, 1938, nine months after the discovery of Anna. At the time she was found she was approximately six and a half years of age. Like Anna, she was an illegitimate child and had been kept in seclusion for that reason. Her mother was a deaf-mute, having become so at the age of two, and it appears that she and Isabelle had spent most of their time together in a dark room shut off from the rest of the mother's family. As a result Isabelle had no chance to develop speech; when she communicated with her mother, it was by means of gestures. Lack of sunshine and inadequacy of diet had caused Isabelle to become rachitic. Her legs in particular were affected; they "were so bowed that as she stood erect the soles of her shoes came nearly flat together, and she got about with a skittering gait."[12] Her behavior toward strangers, especially men, was almost that of a wild animal, manifesting much fear and hostility. In lieu of speech she made only a strange croaking sound. In many ways she acted like an infant. "She was apparently utterly unaware of relationships of any kind. When presented with a ball for the first time, she held it in the palm of her hand, then reached out and stroked my face with it. Such behavior is comparable to that of a child of six months."[13] At first it was even hard to tell whether or not she could hear, so unused were her senses. Many of her actions resembled those of deaf children.

It is small wonder that, once it was established that she could hear, specialists working with her believed her to be feeble-minded. Even on nonverbal tests her performance was so low as to promise little for the future. Her first score on the Stanford-Binet was 19 months, practically at the zero point of the scale. On the Vineland social maturity scale her first score was 39, representing an age level of two and a half years.[14] "The general impression was that she was wholly uneducable and that any attempt to teach her to speak, after so long a period of silence, would meet with failure."[15]

In spite of this interpretation, the individuals in charge of Isabelle launched a systematic and skillful program of training. It seemed hopeless at first. The approach had to be through pantomime and dramatization, suitable to an infant. It required one week of intensive effort before she even made her first attempt at vocalization. Gradually she began to respond, however, and, after the first hurdles had at last been overcome, a curious thing happened. She went through the usual stages of learning characteristic of the years from one to six not only in proper succession but far more rapidly than normal. In a little over two months after her first vocalization she was putting sentences together. Nine months after that she could identify words and sentences on the printed page, could write well, could add to ten, and could retell a story after hearing it. Seven months beyond this point she had a vocabulary of 1,500-2,000 words and was asking complicated questions. Starting from an educational level of between one and three years (depending on what aspect one considers), she had reached a normal level by the time she was eight and a half years old. In short, she covered in two years the stages of learning that ordinarily require six.[16] Or, to put it another way, her I.Q. trebled in a year and a half.[17] The speed with which she reached the normal level of mental development seems analogous to the recovery of body weight in a growing child after an illness, the recovery being achieved by an extra fast rate of growth for a period after the illness until normal weight for the given age is again attained.

When the writer saw Isabelle a year and a half after her discovery, she gave him the impression of being a very bright, cheerful, energetic little girl. She spoke well, walked and ran without trouble, and sang with gusto and accuracy. Today she is over fourteen years old and has passed the sixth grade in a public school. Her teachers say that she participates in all school activities as normally as other children. Though older than her classmates, she has fortunately not physically matured too far beyond their level.[18]

Clearly the history of Isabelle's development is different from that of Anna's. In both cases there was an exceedingly low, or rather blank, intellectual level to begin with. In both cases it seemed that the girl might be congenitally feeble minded. In both a considerably higher level was reached later on. But the Ohio girl achieved a normal mentality within two years, whereas Anna was still marked inadequate at the end of four and a half years. This difference in achievement may suggest that Anna had less initial capacity. But an alternative hypothesis is possible.

One should remember that Anna never received the prolonged and expert attention that Isabelle received. *The result of such attention, in the case of the Ohio girl, was to give her speech at an early stage, and her subsequent rapid development seems to have been a consequence of that.* "Until Isabelle's speech and language development, she had all the characteristics of a feeble-minded child." Had Anna, who, from the standpoint of psychometric tests and early history, closely resembled this girl at the start, been given a mastery of speech at an earlier point by intensive training, her subsequent development might have been much more rapid.[19]

The hypothesis that Anna began with a sharply inferior mental capacity is therefore not established. Even if she were deficient to start with, we have no way of knowing how much so. Under ordinary conditions she might have been a dull normal or, like her mother, a moron. Even after the blight of her isolation, if she had lived to maturity, she might have finally reached virtually the full level of her capacity, whatever it may have been. That her isolation did have a profound effect upon her mentality, there can be no doubt. This is proved by the substantial degree of change during the four and a half years following her rescue.

Consideration of Isabelle's case serves to show, as Anna's case does not clearly show, that isolation up to the age of six, with failure to acquire any form of speech and hence failure to grasp nearly the whole world of cultural meaning, does not preclude the subsequent acquisition of these. Indeed, there seems to be a process of accelerated recovery in which the child goes through the mental stages at a more rapid rate than would be the case in normal development. Just what would be the maximum age at which a person could remain isolated and still retain the capacity for full cultural acquisition is hard to say. Almost certainly it would not be as high as age fifteen; it might possibly be as low as age ten. Undoubtedly various individuals would differ considerably as to the exact age.

Anna's is not an ideal case for showing the effects of extreme isolation, partly because she was possibly deficient to begin with, partly because she did not receive the best training available, and partly because she did not live long enough. Nevertheless, her case is instructive when placed in the record with numerous other cases of extreme isolation. This and the previous article about her are meant to place her in the record. It is to be hoped that other cases will be described in the scientific literature as they are discovered (as unfortunately they will be), for only in these rare cases of extreme isolation is it possible "to observe *concretely separated* two factors in the development of human personality which are always otherwise only analytically separated, the biogenic and the sociogenic factors."[20]

[1]Kingsley Davis, "Extreme Social Isolation of a Child," *American Journal of Sociology*, XLV (January, 1940), pp. 554-65.

[2]Sincere appreciation is due to the officials in the Department of Welfare, Commonwealth of Pennsylvania, for their kind co-operation in making available the records concerning Anna and discussing the case frankly with the writer. Helen C. Hubbell, Florentine Hackbusch, and Eleanor Meckelnburg were particularly helpful, as was Fanny L. Matchette. Without their aid neither of the reports on Anna could have been written.

[3]The records are not clear as to which day.

[4]Letter to one of the state officials in charge of the case.

[5]Ibid.

[6]Progress report of the school.

[7]Davis, op. cit., p. 564.

[8]The facts set forth here as to Anna's ancestry are taken chiefly from a report of mental tests administered to Anna's mother by psychologists at a state hospital where she was taken for this purpose after the discovery of Anna's seclusion. This excellent report was not available to the writer when the previous paper on Anna was published.

[9]Marie K. Mason, "Learning To Speak after Six and One-Half Years of Silence," *Journal of Speech Disorders*, VII (1942), 295-304.

[10]Francis N. Maxfield, "What Happens When the Social Environment of a Child Approaches Zero." The writer is greatly indebted to Mrs. Maxfield and to Professor Horace B. English, a colleague of Professor Maxfield, for the privilege of seeing this manuscript and other materials collected on isolated and feral individuals.

[11]J. A. L. Singh and Robert M. Zingg, *Wolf-Children and Feral Man* (New York: Harper & Bros., 1941), pp. 248-51.

[12]Maxfield, unpublished manuscript cited above.

[13]Mason, op. cit., p. 299.

[14]Maxfield, unpublished manuscript.

[15]Mason, op. cit., p. 299.

[16]Ibid., pp. 300-304.

[17]Maxfield, unpublished manuscript.

[18]Based on a personal letter from Dr. Mason to the writer, May 13, 1946.

[19]This point is suggested in a personal letter from Dr. Mason to the writer, October 22, 1946.

[20]Singh and Zingg, *op. cit.*, pp. xxi-xxii, in a foreword by the writer.

Part III

INSTITUTIONS

It's getting hard to be someone,
But it all works out,
It doesn't matter much to me.

Lennon and McCartny

"You degrade us and then ask why we are degraded.
You shut our mouths and then ask why we don't
speak. You close your colleges and seminaries against
us, then ask why we don't know more."

Fredrick Douglass

College is a wonderful institution — for those who
want to grow up in an institution.

Arthur Hoppe

How do you marry and yet live like gentle lovers, or
at least like friendly roommates? Quite frankly, I do
not know the answer to that question.

Mervyn Cadwallader

Introduction to Part III:
(Institutions)

A concise statement about institutions was put forth early in this century by Sumner:

> Institutions and laws are produced out of mores. An institution consists
> of a concept (idea, notion, doctrine, interest) and a structure. The struc-
> ture is a framework, or apparatus, or perhaps only a number of func-
> tionaries set to cooperate in prescribed ways at a certain conjuncture.*

71

To put it simply, institutions are organized *ways* to take care of our most basic human needs.

Sociologists agree that the basic human institutions which are common to most cultures are: family, religion, polity, economy and most recently, education.

The selections which follow critically examine some aspects of the contemporary American scene in relation to the institutional structures. For example, Professor Charles Hobart examines the nature of value conflict within the family and relates such pattern to the changing patterns in this institution. The second selection in this part is devoted to an analysis of the institution of education. The Research Organizing Cooperatives demonstrate how education contributes to the maintenance of structured social inequality in American society. This thought-provoking article critically evaluates an increasingly important function which our educational institutions perform.

The role of religion in relation to the Black Americans is the topic of Professor Fichter's article. He demonstrates the impact of religion upon the individual and a subculture. Again, the structural significance of a social institution, religion, is demonstrated.

Professor Stuart Lynn, examining poverty in the United States, shows the impact of the economic organization upon the individual. In separating the myths from the facts, Lynn further illustrates the basic insensitivity of our economic institution to some basic human needs.

Finally, Professor S. P. Milgram, in discussing authority and acceptance of it, critically analyzes a significant aspect of the authority system as it is internalized by the individual.

8. COMMITMENT, VALUE CONFLICT AND THE FUTURE OF THE AMERICAN FAMILY

CHARLES W. HOBART

There are many attempts to characterize the nature of modern society: the affluent society, the other-directed society, the managerial

*from *Folkways*, 1906. by William Graham Sumner. Blaisdale Publishing Company.

Reprinted from the *Journal of Marriage and the Family*, Vol. 25 (November 1963), pp. 405-412, by permission of the author and the publisher, National Council of Family Relations.

society, the mass society, the expert society, the pluralistic society, the achieving society, the insane society. Most of these characterizations share at least one underlying assumption, that as a society we tread where man has never trod before, that there are qualitative differences between our society and earlier ones which make extrapolation on the basis of earlier societal experience unreliable at best, and often completely invalid.

One consequence is that the continued utility of many features fundamental to earlier societies becomes problematic. Examples include the segregation of sex roles, homogeneity of culture, widespread status ascription. It is both important and difficult to speculate about what further structural modifications may be in the offing. So long as an institution provides functions prerequisite to the survival of any human social system we must think in terms not of the disappearance of the institution but of the evolution of functional alternatives.

It is in this context that the following discussion of the future of the family is set. This paper deals first with the argument that the family as we know it is becoming obsolete, and with some recent changes in social structure which are contributing to this apparent obsolescence. Second there is a discussion of value conflicts and of future societal development given continued pre-eminence of materialistic values. Finally there is consideration of bases for anticipating a value revolution which would facilitate renewed commitment to family relationships.

There is no need to cite the varied evidence which seems to suggest the progressive obsolescence of the family as we know it. Some maintain that the family, no longer an economic necessity, is an inefficient, artificial, arbitrary, outmoded structuring of relationships. Barrington Moore, in his provocative "Thoughts of the Future of the Family" protests such "obsolete and barbaric features" as "the obligation to give affection as a duty to a particular set of persons on account of the accident of birth," "the exploitation of socially sanctioned demands for gratitude, when the existing social situation no longer generates any genuine feeling of warmth."[1] Moore concludes that "one fine day human society may realize that the part-time family, already a prominent part of our social landscape, has undergone a qualitative transformation into a system of mechanized and bureaucratized child rearing" since "an institutional environment can be . . . warmer than a family torn by obligations its members resent."[2]

In contradiction to this position, it is the thesis of this paper that though the family is from some value perspectives an outdated structural unit, defined in terms of responsibility and commitment it remains a necessary condition for the development and expression of humanity. Furthermore, if it in fact is such a necessary condition, concern for its effective survival should help to shape the course of the future development of society.

It must be admitted that the family is undergoing changes, both within itself and in relation to the rest of society which tend significantly to weaken its solidarity. At least four of these changes may be mentioned: 1) loss of functions; 2) increased personal mobility within society; 3) the decline of status ascription and the increase in status achievement; and 4) the ascendency of materialistic values.

1. In regard to loss of family functions, note that not only has the emergence of separate and distinct institutions accomplished the functional depletion of the once omnifunctional family, but active family membership has become optional in our day. Social status placement is primarily based on occupational achievement, rather than family ascription. There are now no imperious deterrents to a solitary family-alienated existence; all necessary services are available commercially. In fact, family responsibilities today distract and detract from single-minded pursuit of highly prized personal success in most occupations—scholarly, commercial, or professional.

Americans *are* getting married with greater frequency than ever before, a reflection, perhaps, of the increasing significance of companionship and emotional security within the family for people today. But if they marry for companionship and security, the high level of divorce rates[3] suggests that Americans seek divorce when they fail to attain these goals.

2. The rate of spatial mobility of Americans today is remarkable: in the last decade one half of all families in the States have moved every five years. Some consequences of this unprecedented movement have been 1) increase in the number and variety of readjustments which a family must make; 2) radical loss of support of the family by neighborhood, friendship, and kinship primary groups; and 3) weakened discouragement of separation and divorce by these groups. Thus increased mobility may be seen as 1) precipitating more crises and adjustment difficulties within the family, 2) stripping the family of external supports at the very time of heightened stress, and 3) weakening the opposition to traditionally disapproved means of resolving difficulties, such as divorce.

Since mobility involves physical removal from the informal controls exercised by primary groups, Howard S. Becker's conceptualization of commitment becomes relevant to this discussion. Becker conceives of commitment as an act, consciously or unconsciously accomplished, whereby a person involves additional interests of his ("side bets") directly in action he is engaged in, which were originally extraneous to this action. Becker emphasizes that the process is relative to the values or valuables of the person.[4] I am emphasizing its relativity to the importance of the reference groups in whose eyes he stands to gain or lose on his "side bets."

In Becker's terms, then, commitment in marriage was once strengthened by making side bets involving staking one's reputation on one's trustworthiness, loyalty, fidelity in marriage. These bets were secured by the scrutiny of unchanging reference groups: close neighbors, fellow parishioners, occupational associates. The increasing speed of physical mobility as well as the growth of value confusion and of heterogeneous sub-cultures have tended to sharply depreciate the coin with which side bets to marital commitment were once made. This devaluation further weakens the stability of marriage.

3. Another trend in American society which appears to have a powerful potential for further weakening the family is suggested by the phrase "proliferation of associations," "personality market," "individuation." These suggest a growing contrast with the recent past when most close relationships of people were traditionally defined ascribed relationships with mate and children, with other kin, with neighbors, with fellow parishioners. Today, more and more relationships are achieved. They are "cultivated" in school, at work, in voluntary associations; they are promoted through friends and professional or business contacts.

The significant point is that rather than being ascribed, and thus traditionally defined and delimited, relationships are now more often achieved and thus more idiosyncratic and potentially boundless. Herein lies their threat to the family, for they, like many other aspects of contemporary life, may readily infringe upon family claims, may alienate members from the family. Note that at one time only men, as sole bread winners of the family, were vulnerable to these possibilities, in work and voluntary association situations. Their colleagues in these situations were other men, thus posing no threat to devotion to the wife at home. But with the spectacular increase in the employment of married as well as unmarried women, both sexes are vulnerable, and increasingly their work and voluntary association relationships *may* endanger the marriage bond. With this bond under greater stress, the decline of the primary group discouragements to divorce becomes increasingly consequential.

The proliferation of achieved, and thus potentially unlimited relationships for both men and women is by no means exclusively dysfunctional. Restriction of "close" relationships to a small circle of sharply limited ascribed relationships tends to be delimiting as far as growth of the person is concerned. Mead and others have demonstrated that the personality is a social product, and personality growth can occur only in relationships. Hence a small circle of ascribed relationships tends to be stultifying in at least three ways. In the first place, since the limits of an ascribed relationship are traditionally defined in terms of convention and appropriateness, the personality potential in an ascribed relationship is far more limited than in the more open, uncircumscribed achieved relationship. Second, since the circle of ascribed relationships is more homogeneous than the range of possible achieved relationships, the latter may awaken a broader range of latent potentialities within the person. Third, the circle of ascribed relationships may soon be rather thoroughly explored and exhausted, especially given geographical immobility, early in life. By contrast, the opportunities for new achieved relationships may last until death and may be limited only by the activity and involvement of the person. Thus it seems that the increase in proportion of achieved relationships is a necessary condition for actualization of more human potential in society.

I noted above that any achieved relationship, particularly a cross sex one, may jeopardize the marriage bond and perhaps parental responsibilities. Yet, given extensive and rapid spatial and vertical mobility, almost all relationships tend to be shifting sand, lacking in dependability and security, providing no basis on which to build a life. The very impermanence of these manifold relationships heightens the need for *some* relationships which are dependable; which can be, invariably, counted on; which will not be weakened or destroyed by the incessant moving about of people. Such secure relationships can only be found, given the structural peculiarities for our society today, within the family. Actualization of this security within the family depends upon commitment, a commitment symbolized in the phrase "in sickness and in health, for better or for worse, for richer or for poorer, til death do you part."

4. A final source of instability within the family is the value confusion which appears to be one of the hallmarks of our age. The crucial significance of values depends upon the fact that man is a being

who must *live* his life since it is not lived for him by imperious drives or instincts, as Fromm says.[5] Man, thus emancipated from the security of nature's control, needs human community to humanize him and to structure his choice between the alternatives which confront him. The basis for choice is a set of values, generated in society, in terms of which choice priorities may be assigned.

One linkage between values and the family lies in the fact that the original unit of human community and the universal humanizing unit of all societies is the family. It is in the family that many of the most important values, bases for choice, are learned. The family not only transmits values; it is predicated on, and in fact symbolizes some of the distinctively "human" values: tenderness, love, concern, loyalty.

Man's capacity for consistent and responsible action depends on his being able to orient himself and to act on the basis of commitment to values; thus a certain level of value consistency is important. But a prominent feature of American society today is a pervasive value conflict. The family depends upon and symbolizes "inefficient values" of being, knowing, caring, loving, unconditionally committing oneself. These values are incompatible with the urban industrial values of production, achievement, exchange, quantification, efficiency, success. Simultaneous unlimited commitment to people—in love and concern—and to achievement, success, prosperity, is impossible. The resultant tension in a society which pays uncritical lip-service to both sets of values, is disruptive and potentially incapacitating. It tends toward resolution, in favor of the "inhuman" urban values. Fromm has noted that as a society we tend to *love things,* and *use people,* rather than the reverse. And Whyte has remarked that the "organization men" he interviewed seemed to prefer to sacrifice success in marriage to career success, if forced to choose between them.

This value confusion is, of course, a source of instability within the American family. A family presumes unlimited commitment between family members: "til death do you part" between husband and wife, "all we can do for the kids" on the part of parents toward children. But the priority of these love and concern values is directly challenged by success and achievement values which may imply that status symbols are more important than babies; that what a child *achieves* is more important that what he *is*; that what we *own* is more important than what we *are*. Thus the stage is set for conflict between a success oriented husband and a child-people welfare oriented wife, or for a rather inhuman family which values things over people, and which may raise children who have difficulty living down this experience of worthlessness.

The question may be raised whether what one does versus what one is are polar characteristics, or is not what one does a part of what one is? Purely logically the latter is of course true. But social psychologically speaking there are significant differences in the way these two value emphases influence the process and consequences of parent-child interaction. Briefly, parents who emphasize *doing* respond to their children in terms of conditional love, and the child comes to feel that he is unacceptable unless he conforms, and also unless he meets certain "production quotas." By contrast, parents who emphasize *being* respond to their children in terms of unconditional love, and their children come to feel that they are intrinsically acceptable and love worthy. Successful performance is thus a matter of much more anxious preoccupation for the former than for the latter ideal type of child.

This review of some changes in family and society—loss of functions, increased mobility, increased status achievement, and ascendancy of materialistic values—has pointed out that some of these changes have functional as well as dysfunctional consequences. What are the likely prospects for the future? Which way will the value conflict be resolved? What are the preconditions, the prospects, and the probable consequences of more explicit self-conscious commitment to the family?

Let us look first at some further consequences of the value predicament in our society today. Consider the emerging character type in America. Torn from family commitments by the demands of urban living—dedication to efficiency, success, etc., modern man is often alienated from himself and from others.[6] To escape the anxious awareness of his inability to express his humanity and to relate to others through his role as a functionary in a bureaucratic system, he is tempted to identify with the system, becoming, in Mills' terms, a "cheerful robot."[7] In Riesman's terms he is the "other-directed,"[8] forever adapting to the demands of the situation, of the people at hand; in Fromm's terms he is the "personality package," an exchangeable commodity to be sold for success.[9]

The ecology of the American city likewise reflects this value pattern and has important consequences for the family. Most cities can be characterized as central places for the merchandizing of goods and credits. They are the center of great webs of communication and transportation through which our economy of exchange functions. The natural areas of the city are determined by land values: the allocation of people and facilities is in accord with who can pay. Thus it is not for the family that the city functions, and it is not in accord with the values foundational to the family that people and facilities are located. Because the city is not a livable habitat for family units, families have fled to the suburbs. Here children can play, but here too, mothers are often stranded, driven to distraction by childish babbling from which there is no escape, and fathers are missing, early and late, commuting.

From an institutional perspective the family is weakening, and again our value confusion is involved. No longer a necessary economic unit, the family continues to provide for the socialization of children and for companionship. Yet even in these two remaining areas the family is losing significance. Children have more and more been turned over to schools, and, in some instances, nursery schools and Sunday schools, for a major portion of their socialization, as parents occupy themselves with other activities. More significant than the time turned over to such institutional socialization of children is the responsibility that parents more than willingly relinquish or do not recognize as theirs. There appears to be little concern in America today that the shaping of a human life, a human personality, a future of happiness or hell, which is best accomplished in a primary group, is turned over ever earlier and for longer periods to secondary, impersonal, social, agencies. In these agencies children can only be "handled" and manipulated in groups, rather than cared for as individuals.

Leisure time is used by some to cultivate companionship with wife and children. But for many it appears that what time is spent together is seldom spent primarily in *being* together, but rather in *doing* simultaneously: watching T.V., going someplace, being entertained. Leisure is thus often an escape from the tension of urban life which pulls people in different directions, a distraction from "the great emptiness."[10]

The family persists because people want and need the family. The problem is that, having often lost the family in its meaningful sense as a primary commitment, people want a fantasy; they compulsively seek security. They get disillusionment.[11] Pulled apart by the value conflict of our society they want both personal loving involvement and social efficient achievement, and often they can commit themselves to neither. Thus straddling both ways of life, they can only distract themselves from their predicament.

This admittedly pessimistic overview forces us to confront a further question. What kind of a *future* is in store for our society?

Will time tolerate the tension of values, will it tolerate the embarrassing persistence of the family? Some current trends suggest the resolution of the tension in favor of materialistic urban values which place a premium on man, the efficient doer.

To be more explicit, the character type of the future, according to some, will be the true functionary, the "cheerful robot." "Human engineering" seems determined to insuring that man is socialized into this mold, his human anxieties conditioned out. The power structure of the society will be even more centralized than the current structure. The city will rid itself of remaining small shops and other lingering evidences of human sentiment, so that where there is now variety and diversity, there will be functional monotony. With the rapid increase in urban population there is the prospect that the inefficiency of suburban living will be eliminated and people will be housed in compact apartments or even in some collective arrangement.

The family as we know it will be eliminated from this society, Moore has suggested,[12] and Skinner, in *Walden II*[13] agrees.[14] Children, housed separately, will not endanger the efficiency of adult activity. They will not be left to the haphazard care of their accidental parents but will be socialized by behavioral conditioning experts. Couples will have no use for life-long commitments and will often tend to go their separate ways. Each man for himself by himself will escape into the mass of interchangeable associates. Such is the vision of the future that some foresee.

But it seems undeniable that such a future would, in one sense, mean the end of human society. Human society is not an automatic process as are subhuman spheres of life. There is reason to believe that man, *as we know him*, has to care enough to carry on,[15] and to care enough he has to have a reason; life has to have some meaning. Without at least the illusion, the vision, of human ends that today's contradiction of values yet provides man, what would keep him going? Thus it seems impossible to conceive of the future of man in the above terms. Something more or less than man might emerge to carry on something more or less than human society, but such speculation is best left to science fiction writers.

But while the inhuman potential in current trends is not only sobering but frightening, the *human* possibilities are also unparalleled. An alternative future depends upon a value revolution in American society—not just the emergence of an unambiguous value hierarchy, but a displacement of the now pre-eminent success, efficiency, productivity, prosperity values by the more human oriented being, knowing, caring, loving values. This revolution is in fact overdue; it is prerequisite to our continued societal survival. It is heralded by Winston White's provocative discussion *Beyond Conformity* which maintains that we are even now undergoing "a shift from emphasis on the development of economic resources to the development of human resources—particularly the capacities of personalities."[16] A society of scarcity must encourage productivity and efficiency upon pain of greater scarcity, poverty and starvation. But in an affluent society, plagued not by *underproduction* but by *underconsumption*, production-increasing values *are in fact dysfunctional*, aggravating the chronic overproduction problem. In the affluent society, the implementation of "human" values is not only possible as it is not in a society of scarcity, it is also functional in the sense of diverting initiative and energy from the productive sphere, where they threaten to aggravate existing over-production, to other areas where they may serve to free people to be more themselves.

A key to this value change lies in renewed commitment to the family and in thus re-establishing the centrality of the commitment to inefficient, human values which the family relationship symbolizes. There are some who would try to solve the problems of our heterogeneous society in terms of restructuring (Fromm's work communities for example), of eliminating structurally some of the diversity and complexity of our society. But this is the kind of short-sightedness that tries to move forward by moving backward. To look wistfully at the beauty and relative simplicity of the rigidly structured life in a primitive society without at the same time realizing that our human potentialities are greater than would be realized in such a society is the kind of irresponsibility that evades the task at hand. This is the most significant point made in *Beyond Conformity*. White sees human personality as emancipated from ascriptive ties in contemporary society. Since man is no longer *determined* automatically by family, church, or occupation, greater individuality of personality is possible. In the absence of automatic structural determinants, man is "indeed, forced to be free," to become more individualistic.[17]

It follows from this that the family of the future must not be defined in terms of more structure, but in terms of less explicit structure. It must at once be flexible enough for increasingly individuated people, yet a stable basic unit for human life. The family as a commitment implies freedom in the definition of the marital relationship in order to meet the demands of the particular way of life of the two people involved. For its members, family relationships should be a part of a larger pattern of meaningful, involving relationships. Only thus, individually defined and not exclusive, can the family tie avoid being a trapping, arbitrarily binding, stultifying commitment for its members. Defined in this way, the family would be a sustaining, liberating, and humanizing influence since it would invest life in modern society with context, continuity, and direction. As a commitment, a limiting choice, an orienting value complex, it would permit a decisive stance in the urban sea of alternatives, not an artificial reduction of the alternatives.

Are there any alternative side bet possibilities in our day to shore up the marriage commitment, which have not suffered the erosion of effectiveness noted earlier in contemporary society? I think that the answer is yes. It is an answer which is not only compatible with, but dependent on the fact that since *doing* is inescapably becoming less important in contemporary society than *being*, husbands and wives are increasingly chosen because of the persons that they *are*, rather than what they can *do*. Increasingly mates may be known deeply and loved for what they are. To know and love the person in this way is to feel for and care for the person. Love in this sense, then, involves the inadvertent side bet of deeply feeling with and for and caring about this person. A risking of the marriage vows involves immediate apprehension of the pain this causes my mate, as my own pain. My empathy with and ego involvement with my mate guarantees a "side bet penalty" which is likely to be heavier than the attractiveness of what I stand to gain from my breach of commitment.

Here is a basis for a new, deeper commitment to the family, in so far as couple members dare to invest themselves to this extent, in each other. And in this deeper commitment, more of meaning in life would be discovered in the experience of human values, the intrinsic values of being, becoming, knowing and being known, caring and being cared for, in contrast to the values of doing and achieving. And out of this profound experiencing of human values might come the basis for the slow revolution in values which would further facilitate deeper commitment to the family, and in time the reorientation of contemporary society.

The implications of such a changed significance of the family and such a value revolution for future society are many. The character type which could emerge in this kind of family setting would be neither the chameleon-like, other-directed nor the rigid, artificially dogmatic inner-directed, to use Riesman's terms. Instead there could emerge the autonomous individual who is able to see and consciously choose between the alternatives; who knows himself and can express himself in decisive, directed action; who retains his sense of identity discovered *beyond* role, in the various roles he must play. Not merely functioning, having sold his soul "true believer" fashion, not living oblivious of alternatives, he could consciously exercise the greatest sense of freedom and responsibility that man has ever known; he could live Winston White's vision.[18]

With renewed emphasis on *being* rather than on *doing*, the family and the concern with human relationships which it symbolizes could once again be an organizing principle in society. With less emphasis on over-efficiency our society could significantly cut down the length of the working day. Such a work schedule would make possible an enriched home life. While older children were in school both men and women could work, if they chose, and thus perhaps develop specialized interests. The specialization of their work could be balanced by the vocations of homemaking and greater involvement in parenthood for both men and women, and by the opportunity to develop other interests in their leisure time. A shorter work day would mean that children could once again be socialized more within the family primary group. The school could accomplish its distinctive function of transmitting knowledge in half a day, leaving the humanization responsibility to the home. Here the inefficient process of growing up could take place in a context where there is time for each child, and where each child is valued and known as an individual. In the home children need not be collectively handled, regimented and manipulated as they must be at school, but might be better freed to become, to find themselves, to develop their unique potentials.

In addition to assuming the responsibility for socializing children, such a family could provide meaningful and sustaining relationships which are a prerequisite to open, undefended, loving relationships with others. As I noted above, it is inevitable that most relationships in an urban society will be time-bound, that the demands of complex and highly mobile living will pull people apart, but the family can offer the element of permanence which other relationships cannot. And thus safeguarded by their family-centered security against being left unbearably alone when the hour of separation came, people could dare to invest themselves in a number of invaluable but often short term relationships whose dissolution would otherwise be unbearable. Increased leisure time would enable individuals to develop these relationships both within and without the family.

The question arises, could people really bear to spend more time with their families than they now do? To this a number of things can be said. In the first place, people presumably would not have the same need that they do today to escape the emptiness of shallow, family-togetherness by constantly doing or being with different people. Time spent together could be on a more meaningful level than it can now be. Secondly, time would also be spent in other meaningful, involving relationships with non-family members which would mean that the family would not seem a trap and would not degenerate into a stagnating aggregate of individuals. The family would lose the compulsive exclusive security which makes it dull for those who spend most of their leisure time with their family and dare not do otherwise. Assuming a commitment of family members to each other more profound than any based merely on exclusion or external structure, family members could tolerate an element of genuine insecurity in their relationships which would not have to be evaded and would keep the relationship from being static and dull.

Finally young people, no longer stranded, disoriented, alienated from parents—as they often are now when neither adolescents nor parents know each other—would not have to escape compulsively, haphazardly into marriage. They could postpone marriage until they knew what they wanted, what they needed and what they were entering into.

There are a few shreds of evidence that the American family may in fact be evolving in the direction advocated in this paper. Hilsdale, in a rather sensitive interviewing study, sought to discover whether subjects entered marriage with an absolute commitment to marriage, or merely a commitment to trial of marriage. He found that 80% entered with an absolute commitment. This commitment was, significantly, associated with an "almost total absence of starry-eyed Hollywood-type 'romantic love.' "[19] Another finding of this study was the preoccupation of his subjects with communication: they felt that their marriage would last "because we can talk to each other, because we can discuss our problems together."[20] Hilsdale terms this faith "magical," but it can also be seen as a reaction to the fact that in an increasingly impersonal society, people cannot talk with each other. In this light it appears as both awareness by people of their need to really communicate with another, and a commitment to safeguard this highly valued and important aspect of the marriage relationship. Moreover, there is evidence that communication is related to marital adjustment.[21]

In this paper I have argued that if an affluent society is to survive, it must undergo a value revolution which will make what we have called human values pre-eminent over production values. Such a society-wide evaluation would eliminate a major source of the compromised commitment, of the value conflict between and within the family members, and of the inadequate and distorting socialization of children, which exist in the American family today. There seems to be reason for hoping that such a value revolution may come out of the changing pattern of husband-wife relationship. If this should continue such that the family were restructured along the lines suggested by these values, people could find the security and sustenance which they need, but often cannot find, in today's world. The nature of contemporary urban society makes this increasingly necessary for a number of reasons. Earlier alternative bases of family solidarity are disappearing, and thus commitment is an increasingly crucial bond. Increasingly, the family is the only security base available to man today. Where a commitment-based family security is dependably available to man, he will have a basis for relating fearlessly to the greater varieties of people available to him in a society organized in terms of achieved statuses, deepening and enriching himself and others in the process.

[1]Barrington Moore, "Thoughts on the Future of the Family," in Maurice R. Stein, Arthur J. Vidich and David M. White, *Identity and Anxiety*, Glencoe Eds., Ill.: The Free Press, 1960, pp. 393-94.

[2]*Ibid.*, p. 401.

[3]See, for example, U.S. Bureau of the Census, *Statistical Abstract of the United States*, Washington, D.C., 1961, p. 48.

[4]Howard S. Becker, "Notes on the Concept of Commitment." *American Journal of Sociology*, 66 (July, 1960), p. 35.

[5]Erich Fromm, *The Sane Society*, New York: Holt, Rinehart, and Winston, 1960, p. 24.

[6]A few recent titles in the growing literature on alienation in modern man include: *American Journal of Psychoanalysis*, A Symposium on Alienation and the Search for Identity, Vol. 21, no. 2, 1961; Eric and Mary Josephson, *Man Alone*, Alienation in Modern Society, New York: Dell Publishing Co., 1962; Robert Nisbet, *The Quest for Community*, New York: Oxford University Press, 1953; Fritz Pappenheim, *The Alienation of Modern Man*, New York: Monthly Review Press, 1959; Maurice Stein, *The Eclipse of Community*, Princeton: Princeton University Press, 1960; Maurice Stein, Arthur Vidich and David White, Eds., *Identity and Anxiety*; Survival of the Person in Mass Society, Glencoe, Ill.: Free Press, 1960; Allen Wheelis, *The Quest for Identity*, New York: W. W. Norton, 1958.

[7]C. Wright Mills, *The Sociological Imagination*, New York: Oxford University Press, 1959, p. 171.

[8]David Riesman, Nathan Glazer, Reuel Denny, *The Lonely Crowd*, New York: Doubleday Anchor Books, 1956.

[9]Erich Fromm, *The Art of Loving*, New York: Harper and Bros., 1956, p. 3.

[10]Robert MacIver, "The Great Emptiness," in Eric Larrabee and Rolf Meyersohn, Eds., *Mass Leisure*, Glencoe, Illinois: The Free Press, 1958, pp. 118-122.

[11]Charles W. Hobart, "Disillusionment in Marriage and Romanticism," *Marriage and Family Living*, Vol. 20 (May, 1958), pp. 156-162.

[12]Barrington Moore, op. cit.

[13]B. F. Skinner, Walden Two, New York: The Macmillan Co., 1948.

[14]But note that the evolution of child handling procedures in the Jewish communal Kibbutzim is in the direction of granting parents more access to their children and permitting children to spend more time in their parents' apartments. John Bowlby, Maternal Care and Mental Health, Geneva: World Health Organization, 1952, pp. 42-43.

[15]William H. R. Rivers, "The Psychological Factor," in W. H. R. Rivers, ed, Essays on the Depopulation of Melanesia, Cambridge, England: The University Press, 1922.

[16]Winston White, Beyond Conformity, New York: The Free Press of Glencoe, Ill., 1961, p. 162.

[17]Ibid., p. 164.

[18]Winston White, op. cit.

[19]Paul Hilsdale, "Marriage as a Personal Existential Commitment," Marriage and Family Living, 24 (May, 1962), p. 142.

[20]Ibid., p. 143.

[21]Charles W. Hobart and William J. Kausner, "Some Social Interactional Correlates of Marital Role Disagreement and Marital Adjustment," Marriage and Family Living, 21 (Aug., 1959), p. 263.

9.   EDUCATION AND THE MAINTENANCE OF SOCIAL CLASSES*

by The Research Organizing Cooperative

"To get a good job, get a good education."

America is the "land of opportunity" because everyone has a chance to get a good education. That's why we have free public schools from kindergarten to high school. And here in California, that's why we have "mass" higher education. Right?

Wrong.

Many people put up with the way their lives are run—hard work, low take-home pay, prices and rents going up all the time—because they believe that their children, at least, have a chance to make a decent life for themselves. If your kid studies hard and if he's got something on the ball, maybe he can make it.

This is a myth.

The reality? A factory worker's son has a smaller chance of getting a four-year college diploma today than he had ten years ago. For Third World children—those of African, Asian, Latin American and American Indian descent—the situation is even worse. At San

Francisco State College in 1960, for example, 12 percent of the students were black. By 1968 this had dropped to 3 percent.

How did this happen? For the answer, we have to go back to the late 1950s.

Thanks to the post-war "baby boom," the number of children in school was expected to double between 1960 and 1970. The bonus crop of babies who were born after World War II was growing up, and there had been a steady migration of families to California. Just to keep up with this increase—not to mention improving education—the state would have to build as many schools in one decade as it had built in the previous forty or fifty years.

Books, teachers, school buses—all would have to be doubled. And college facilities would have to be expanded too. Where was the money to come from?

As usual it would come from California's working people, the people the state squeezes most of its income from. These are the families who make less than $10,000 a year—and they pay the lion's share of the retail sales, cigarette, alcoholic beverage, motor vehicle and gasoline taxes. Together these taxes bring in 55 percent of the state's revenue. And these same people pay a generous share of the state's personal income tax, as well.

What about the corporations? Last year, bank and corporate taxes brought in less than 12 percent of California's tax revenues. Could they afford any more?

The huge war industries of California are bloated with dollars. Lockheed Aircraft made a profit of $54 million in 1967; North American Rockwell made $68 million; Standard Oil of California, $421 million—and this is only what these companies report.

Any one of these corporations could cough up another $10 million in taxes without straining. But they don't have to because they control the governor's office and the state legislature. (By making big contributions to both political parties, the corporation bosses come out on top no matter who wins the election.)

In short, there was no way to pay for mass higher education. The workers had already been taxed to the gills. And the corporations refused to pay. Obviously something had to go.

What "went" was the notion that higher education was for everybody. In 1959 the state legislature authorized the Regents to figure out ways to cut the costs of education and make the school system more "efficient." In February 1960 the Regents came out with their report, the "Master Plan for Higher Education" in California. Two months later the report was enacted into law, killing any hope for equal opportunity in education. And it all had the approval of Democratic Governor Edmund "Pat" Brown.

The Master Plan had two major effects. It established the tracking system throughout the state. And it cut down on the number of working-class students who attend college and reduced spending on those who do attend.

What is the "tracking system"? Since the Master Plan there have been two standard "tracks" in the elementary and high schools of California. One is for children who are considered "college material," the other for those who are "not academically inclined." If your child is placed on the "college" track, he will be in a classroom with other children who are headed for college. What he is taught will prepare him for college.

If your child is placed on the "vocational" track, he will be taught different materials, by teachers who know that he is not likely to go to college. And they are right. Once he is put on this track he hasn't much chance of getting off.

Why is there a tracking system? In America today, the number of good jobs is limited, and there are many jobs that are poorly paid. If everyone got a good education, it would be hard to find people to fill the poorer jobs. Also, the extra education would be "wasted"—there would be no way for the bosses to make money out of it.

Even more important, the people who have good jobs now are not satisfied just to have good jobs. They want to make sure their children have them too. But in a fair competition for the good jobs, many privileged kids of average ability would be edged out by brighter working-class kids.

The tracking system solves this "problem." It eliminates most working-class children from the competition for good jobs, by preventing them from getting the education they need to compete. Yet it seems normal to many working people. Why is this?

Very early in their school careers—usually by the third grade —children are placed on either the college track or the other track, on the basis of seemingly "objective" reading and "IQ" tests. But in fact these tests are far from objective.

They measure "intelligence" by comparing a child's test scores to those of an average group of white, privileged city children of the same age. But the "IQ" test is based in part on things that a child living in a higher-income city neighborhood is more likely to know about. So if you are a factory worker and you live in a neighborhood of other workers, or if you live on a farm, your child will be handicapped in the test. And the cultural bias of IQ tests makes it extra hard on black and brown children.

It is not a matter of the privileged children having a "better background" or being "better prepared." Some of the questions on the Stanford-Binet IQ test for young children, for example, involve the use of wooden building blocks. Nearly all middle-class parents buy blocks like these for their children. A great many poorer children, on the other hand, have never seen a set of building blocks before the day of the IQ test. Clearly, the children who have played with them for many hours at home will do a better job with them than the children who have never seen them before. Does this make the practiced, middle-class child brighter? According to the IQ test it does.

When it comes right down to it, IQ tests measure income, not intelligence. It may be news to some parents that the IQ tests discriminate in this way. But teachers, professors and testers have known it all along.

In theory it is possible for a child to get onto the college track even if he starts on the lower track. But it is very difficult. Often, racial or class discrimination is at work. Teachers and guidance counselors cannot believe that a child from "that kind of background" could be "college material."

Often it is simply that once a teacher learns a child's "IQ," she "knows" how much to expect of the child—and children quickly understand when they are not expected to do well.

An experiment that took place in the New York City schools proved this. Some teachers were told that an objective test had identified some "late bloomers" in their classes. They were told that certain children who had been doing only average work would soon show a dramatic improvement in their classroom performance.

Actually the children were just average children, selected at random. But once the teachers believed that these children were about to do better, the children DID do better. The teachers "knew" they were not ordinary children and treated them more patiently and respectfully—and the children responded.

For ethical reasons, the people who ran this experiment did not try telling the teachers that any of the children had "no potential." They did perform that experiment on rats. The people who put rats through mazes were told that some of the rats were more intelligent and that other rats were dumber. Sure enough, the "intelligent" rats (actually they were all the same) did better in the mazes!

In effect the school system is doing the same thing to your children that the experimenters did to the rats. They tell the teachers that some children are not as bright as other children. And then these children do not do as well because they are not expected to.

The lesson is clear. Once a so-called "objective" system of testing like this takes hold, it will actually hold back the children from Third World and white working-class backgrounds.

The tracking system isn't the only problem Third World and white working-class children have to face in the schools of San Francisco. Just as important are the problems of blatant inequality in faculty, staff, facilities, supplies and curriculum. The highest paid teachers (the best and most experienced) are concentrated in the predominantly white schools, teaching students from the higher-income neighborhoods. And the least experienced and poorest trained teach the poorest students—in schools that are overwhelmingly black and Spanish-speaking.

More money is spent on each pupil at the "whiter," richer schools. This is because the channeling of funds favors the college-trackers over the vocational-trackers. And the biased tests push the wealthier white students into the pre-college program.

The Third World communities suffer most. The greatest overcrowding in San Francisco schools occurs in the black ghettoes of the Fillmore and Bayview-Hunters Point. And many of these schools are in older, deteriorating buildings, with bad plumbing, bad lighting, no playground equipment, inadequate fire escapes, etc.

Children from Third World communities rarely have teachers from a background similar to their own. Six out of ten public school students in San Francisco are nonwhite, but only one teacher in ten is nonwhite. Programs in ethnic studies developed by teachers at Polytechnic High, Mission High and Wilson High have not been seriously considered by the Board of Education.

The school system has been callous toward Third World children speaking foreign languages. There is no bilingual instruction in San Francisco, even in the primary grades where children from non-English speaking homes need help in making a transition. Yet one-third of the students come from homes where a language other than English is spoken.

What is the effect of all this? Let's just give one example: the results of a third grade reading test given at two elementary schools. At the wealthier, 70-percent-white Alamo Elementary School, the children were found to be reading a year *ahead* of their grade level. At poverty-ridden, nearly-all-black Golden Gate School, the children were more than a year *behind* their grade level, and two years behind the Alamo children.

That test spells bright careers and high salaries for most of the Alamo School class. It dooms the Golden Gate third-graders to lives of poverty and under-employment.

By the time they get out of high school, more than three-quarters of all graduates from the working-class schools either look for a job right away, take vocational training, or go into the Army. But what about those working-class and Third World students who still want to go to college? To understand their fate it is necessary to go back to the Master Plan for Higher Education.

The Master Plan, which became law in 1960, outlined the official policy of class discrimination that determines who gets into college.

> The State College and University admission requirements "should be exacting," the Plan stated, "because the junior colleges relieve them of the burden of doing remedial work."

Translation: Those Third World and white working-class children who have been crippled by the "educational" system can be kept out of the better colleges by using so-called "objective" entrance tests. They won't complain because they can always go to junior college.

> "Special admissions" should not exceed 2 percent of the regular enrollment.

Translation: If protests force the admission of students outside of the regular, discriminatory standards, at least they will be only a token group. The great mass of Third World and white working-class youth will be kept out. (This remains true despite the recent concession, which may raise the "special admissions" quota to a maximum of 10 percent at S.F. State—if the Legislature approves.)

> "A study of the transfer procedures (from the junior colleges to the four-year schools)" should be undertaken "with the view of tightening them."

Translation: The main purpose of junior colleges is to turn out skilled workers, not four-year college graduates. Make it more difficult for junior college students to get into a four-year program, or else they will get more education than they need to do their jobs.

> "Retention standards" at the junior colleges should be "rigid enough to guarantee that taxpayers' money is not wasted on individuals who lack the capacity or the will to succeed in their studies."

Translation: Instead of helping those students who were badly prepared by their high schools, flunk out as many as possible to keep costs down. That way you can preserve the myth that higher education is available to everyone, when in reality higher education is only intended for some.

> "Vigorous use of probation and the threat of dismissal may help some 'late bloomers' to flower sooner."

Translation: Train the workers to know who's boss. Get them used to being afraid. That will be useful to them on the job or in the Army.

Finally, the Master Plan conceded: "The selection and retention devices . . . will not guarantee that all able young Californians will go to college."

It was the understatement of the year.

All of these measures have worked out precisely as expected. Before the Master Plan was adopted, anyone in the top 33 percent of his high school class was supposed to be able to get into the University of California. And anyone in the top 70 percent could get into State College.

Today, only students in the top 12½ percent are supposed to be able to get into the University, and only the top 33 percent can get into State College. But good grades are not enough to get you into college any more. Since the Master Plan, you also have to do well on the College Board examinations.

Like the IQ tests for tracking students in school, the College Boards have a racial and class bias. Again, membership in the privileged classes gives you a better score.[1]

Adding the discriminatory College Board examination to the requirements for admission wiped out any chance that most Third World and white working-class high school graduates had of going on to college.

San Francisco's Mission High School, the lowest income school in the city, is a good example. In June 1966, only 2 percent of the graduating class went to either the University of California or San Francisco State College. In all, 5 percent of Mission's seniors went to some four-year college, as against 50 percent for Lowell, one of the highest income schools in the city. This is how the San Francisco school system serves its working-class and Third World majority.

A recent interview (March 1969) with the Dean of Admissions of San Francisco State College, Charles Stone, tells a lot about who gets to go to our "local" four-year college. Dean Stone admitted that 60 percent of San Francisco State freshmen come from outside the city. He also admitted that "almost half of the San Francisco people we admit come from private schools"—despite the fact that three-quarters of the high school students in the city go to public schools. This means that a boy or girl in private school has a three times better chance of getting into our publicly financed State College than a boy or girl from public school. Last year only 4 percent of San Francisco public school graduates enrolled at San Francisco State.

But Dean Stone's preferential treatment does not apply to just any private school. Take the Sacred Heart High School in the Western Addition, for example. Half of the student body of this low-tuition school is nonwhite. But San Francisco State accepted only five boys from Sacred Heart last year.

No, the Dean is talking about high-tuition, mostly white private schools like Stuart Hall for Boys in Pacific Heights, or St. Ignatius High School in the Richmond district. Last year Dean Stone admitted more students from the distant (and expensive) Bellarmine Preparatory School in San Jose than he did from Mission and Wilson High Schools combined.

The Dean was asked why this was so, when so many youths here in San Francisco want a college education. "You understand," he replied, "the boys at Bellarmine are mostly San Jose boys, so naturally they want to get away from home." To Dean Stone it means more that these rich boys should be able to go to school away from home than that poor boys and girls from our own city should go to college at all. The result is that the family income of the average State College student is $10,000 a year. (At the University of California, the average is even higher: $12,000.)

The main excuse the educators give is that everyone can go to a junior college. But even the two-year junior colleges—supposedly "open to everybody with a high school diploma"—are more exclusive than they pretend to be. Once admitted, many students are promptly flunked out—and no wonder, since most of them come from impossibly bad high schools. Most of those who enter City College of San Francisco, for example, do not complete two years there, and only 15 percent go on to higher education.

Given the systematic exclusion of black and Spanish-speaking people from State College and U.C., you would think they would show an extra high enrollment at junior colleges. But this is not the case. Black and brown people make up 22 percent of San Francisco's population—but only 16 percent of the students at City College of San Francisco.

Two-thirds of the students at the junior colleges come from

families earning less than $10,000 a year. These are the families, Third World and white working people, who actually pay most of California's taxes. Yet the junior colleges their children go to get only 10 cents out of every dollar the state spends on education. While their own kids get a second class education, working people subsidize quality education for the rich.

For the junior colleges are really nothing but glorified vocational high schools. Their job is to make workers out of the children of workers, just as the University's job is to make managers and professionals out of the children of managers and professionals. The corporations, which benefit, have found that this "educational division of labor" is more efficient for them.

Junior college facilities, libraries, teacher salaries and working conditions are all below standard. Their massive counseling and testing programs combine to discourage most students from going ahead to a four-year college. Instead, students are encouraged to become hairdressers, technicians or secretaries.

It doesn't "just happen" that so few junior college students go ahead to a four-year education—that's the way it is meant to be. At the College of San Mateo, for example, only 5 percent of the students normally go ahead to a four-year institution. However, when a "College Readiness Program" for Third World students there encouraged them to continue their education—and 90 percent of the Third World students in the program did so!—the director of the program was told that not enough of his students were going into vocational training. "I didn't know I had a quota," he told the administrators. "You don't," they replied, "but you still should have put more students into vocational training." Precisely because the College Readiness Program was succeeding, it had to be crippled.

Whenever you run into a strange situation like this—educators discouraging students from getting more education, "economy" at the expense of those who can least afford it—the question you have to ask is: Who benefits?

In California and the rest of America, it is the corporations. When Governor Reagan and Superintendent Rafferty get together to talk about how to create a real educational system that meets people's needs—they talk about the "manpower requirements" of private industry and the state. (Even the San Francisco State catalogue talks about serving "the technical and professional manpower requirements of the state.")

The fact is that higher education in California is controlled by big business. The Regents who control the University of California, the Trustees of the State Colleges, and the trustees who supervise every other public and private college in the state, are almost always members of the white business class. They range from officials of the biggest corporations and banks, to the presidents of important local businesses. They are almost all white, Protestant, male and over 50.

And they have made sure that the school system in the state of California contributes its share to the production of their most important product: Profits.

Appendix—Class Education in a Nutshell: Who Goes to College and Who Pays For It

	Family Income Under $10,000	Family Income Over $10,000
Percent of California families	71.9%	28.1%
Percent of San Francisco families	75.8%	24.2%
Percent of California Third World families	Over 90%	Under 10%
Percent of state non-corporate taxes paid	62%	38%

Colleges Attended			Problems of U.S. Capitalism
(Full-time student enrollment in California, 1967)			*Relative Amount Spent per Student*
			Out of every $100 of tax-payers' money spent by the State of California to educate students in public colleges . . .
Junior Colleges (217,000)	2/3 of students	1/3 of students	—an average of $10 is spent for each Junior College student.*
State Colleges (122,000)	1/2 of students	1/2 of students	—an average of $30 is spent for each State College student.
University of California (91,000)	1/3 of students	2/3 of students	—an average of $60 is spent for each University of California student.
Private colleges and universities (78,000)	1/4 of students	3/4 of students	

*While Junior Colleges are mainly financed by local rather than state taxes, local taxes are mainly property taxes which hit poor and working people hardest. The brunt falls on tenants (due to a shift from landlord to tenant) and on small homeowners.

WHAT THIS MEANS . . .
1. Seven out of 10 of the 270,000 who graduate from California public and parochial high schools come from families *with total income under $10,000*—the income group that pays most of the state's taxes.
BUT . . .
2. Fewer than 10 percent of the under-$10,000 high school graduates enroll at the University of California or State Colleges upon graduation. (Two percent go to private colleges; 41 percent enter Junior Colleges; and 47 percent of them go to no college at all.)
AND . . .
3. Nearly 35 percent of the over-$10,000 high school graduates enroll at the University of California or State Colleges. (Almost all go to college somewhere.)
THEREFORE . . .
4. Four-year college is mainly for the minority of higher-income families. But the lower-income families, most of whose children can't get in, pay most of the bill.

---

[1] The Scholastic Aptitude Test, the main part of the College Board exams, is only a variation of a test invented by Edward Thorndike, the "father" of intelligence testing—who believed that nonwhite people were genetically of lower intelligence than whites. This man, who has had a tremendous influence in American education, not only wanted to exclude people of color from the colleges, he wanted to exclude them from the human race. He wrote in 1940: "One sure service, about the only one, which the inferior and vicious [his term for nonwhite people] can perform is to prevent their genes from survival." Although he was most hostile to people of color, Thorndike wanted to deny all working people the right to an equal education. He opposed "extending culture to the masses," favoring instead "giving special education to the gifted (privileged) child."

10. AMERICAN RELIGION AND THE NEGRO

JOSEPH H. FICHTER

The role of organized religion in the current Negro freedom movement is symbolized by the leadership of Martin Luther King, who is primarily concerned neither with an appointment to a "white pulpit" nor with the dissolution of Negro church denominations. In other words, neither the mixing of the races nor the mixing of the

Reprinted from *Daedalus*, Vol. 94 (1965), by permission of the author and the publisher, Daedalus, the Journal of the American Academy of Arts and Sciences.

religions is the main objective of any churchman's participation in the movement for Negro rights. What is important is "freedom now" for both races, and "equality now" for all citizens, regardless of racial and religious affiliation. A free society can be pluralistic by the choice and decision of its citizens, but a pluralistic society can be free only if its major institutions support freedom for all.

Better than any other institution, organized religion ought to understand the terms of the struggle for racial freedom and equality. Religious-minded people ought to grasp more readily than others such concepts as reparation for wrong-doing, reconciliation of the estranged, resolution for improvement, commitment to values, firm purpose of amendment, fellowship and brotherhood, love and justice. The slogan of the rights movement, "freedom now," had great significance to the ancient Jews in bondage, to the early Christians in pagan Rome, to the Catholics in the English persecutions, to the Huguenots in the French persecutions. If the historical analogy between religious liberty and racial liberty is so close, one wonders why the churches delayed so long before entering the civil rights movement. But now that the commitment has been made and the struggle has been joined, one may speculate about further and fuller religious influence and participation in the movement.

Organized religion has certainly contributed to the moral awakening of Americans to the race problem, and the young generation of people now in the pulpits and pews of American churches and synagogues gives assurance that this will continue. These people do not accept the old caricature of religion as merely a personal and private affair. They have repudiated the peculiar notion that the race question is a political and legal matter, not a religious and moral concern. The "proper scope" of religious activity has been widened by them; we now frequently hear about the relevance of religion to modern life, to the crowded city, to business practices, to political organizations, to educational systems, and to racial and other minority problems.

Changes in religious activities are uneven, as they are in all institutionalized areas of society. There are major trends and minor counter-trends, but the main direction of religious influence in this regard is clear and ineluctable. There is criticism of white clergymen who have few Negroes in their own congregations, but who go South to engage in sit-ins at restaurants and to picket voting registrars. There is criticism of church leaders who use their moral influence more often for the desegregation of non-church institutions than they do for the desegregation of their own organizations. It is said, on the one hand, that "the present movement to do away with segregation as an ultimate ideal has stemmed mainly from the churches,"[1] and, on the other hand, that "as long as churches remain segregated through subtle techniques, they give moral sanction to segregation in other areas of social life."[2]

It has often been said, and by religious people themselves, that Sunday morning at church is the most segregated time in America; and it probably offers little consolation to insist that Saturday night at the country club is an even more segregated time. We do not expect the country club to set standards of moral principle and practice, but we do await guidance from the church in both respects. The church cannot afford to wait for the Congress, the President, and the Supreme Court to provide its moral standards and values. Yet, as Liston Pope has remarked, the church has "lagged behind the Supreme Court as the conscience of the nation on questions of race."[3]

White religionists have found this disconcerting, and Negro religionists have considered it a demonstration of white insincerity. As Embree wrote more than thirty years ago, "Segregation in Christian churches is an embarrassment. In a religion whose central teaching is brotherly love and the golden rule, preachers have to do a great deal of rationalizing as they expound their own gospel."[4] We are not limiting the present discussion to the extent to which the churches have remained internally conservative and segregated or have become internally progressive and integrated. We are interested also in the moral impact which the church has had on the larger society, the extent to which church people have promoted external, non-denominational integration and reconciliation of the races. Whatever their previous conservative stance has been, the churches have now become "spearheads of reform."[5]

The ways in which churches approach the problem of desegregation vary according to region and are the result both of the voluntary nature of church membership and of local cultural patterns. Thus, in the Southern states, where local customes—and often legal intimidation—prevent the races from associating voluntarily even in the churches, those interested in racial justice become involved in non-church desegregation, as of public facilities, schools, buses, libraries, parks, and voting. In the North and West, however, where Negroes and whites can associate more freely than in the South, the churches tend to promote the desegregation of their own congregations as well as of public and civic institutions.

I

What have the churches in America done about their own internal pattern of racial segregation? It must be said in all fairness that in the second half of the last century segregated patterns in religion came as a *consequence* of community practice and legislation.[6] In this sense, the church bowed to the culture instead of resisting and reforming it. The seeds of separation had been sown even before the Civil War, when large Southern Protestant denominations declared their independence. In the ensuing decades the separation of the Negro Protestant bodies came about either by expulsion from the white denominations or by the Negroes' own withdrawal to independent churches.

Negro religion in America is by definition segregated religion, but it embraces a wide range of structures, patterns, and attitudes. At one end are the completely separatist religious cults, the best known of which is now the Black Muslim Movement, which repudiates Christian and Caucasian civilization and turns to Asiatic culture and the religion of Islam.[7] An earlier Negro nationalist cult, now declining in influence, is the Moorish Temple of Science in America, which also repudiates the white man, his religion, and his culture.[8] These groups extoll the black man as superior to the white and scoff at the notion of reconciliation or integration with white Christians. One of the most spectacular anti-white movements was Marcus Garvey's Universal Mutual Improvement Association, which was both political and religious. It did not turn to Asia and Islam, but glorified Negritude with its black Christ and black God. It disparaged white culture and wanted to return to Africa for the fulfillment of a pure religion and a higher civilization.[9] The memory of Garvey as the "lost savior" of the race lingers among Negroes, and some of his former adherents are seeking the new savior among the Black Muslims.

These black religious and nationalist movements, because they are antagonistic to whites and fight against cultural assimilation, are opposed by most Negro leaders and feared by some whites. They speak boldly of the need for Negro courage and physical resistance to white discrimination and injustice. They are the most vocal protest of despair and frustration over the white man's failure to practice the ideals of Christianity and the principles of democracy in relation to American Negroes. They serve to dramatize the Negro's plight in America, and, while proclaiming the advantages of withdrawal from white America, they are also serving the latent function of arousing white America to the need for interracial justice and integration.[10]

The black nationalist groups make a direct appeal to the racial pride of the most disadvantaged Negroes and are effective in reforming the moral behavior of their members. They are puritanical in their rules on sexual behavior, smoking, drinking, dancing, and work habits. While repudiating Christianity they are emulating the Christian, Puritan, bourgeois way of life. The numerous Holiness sects also have great influence on the behavior of the lower classes of urban Negroes. These people seek personal sanctification and a sinless way of life. Their preachers concentrate on other-worldly sermons and the futility of worldly and material comforts, possessions, and status. They are seldom concerned about social justice, integration, and the civil rights movement. Instead of demanding separatism, as the Black Muslims do, they seem to accept it apathetically as a worldly evil, and for this they are chided by American Negro leadership.[11]

The positive segregation of the black nationalists and the negative segregation of the Holiness sects both are functions of their differing religious ideologies, and they both make their appeal to the poorest class of Negroes. The great majority of American Negroes belong to the large Protestant denominations, but they are also in a segregated church system. This must be said of the Baptist denomination, to which six out of ten Negro church members belong.[12] It must also be said of the Methodist denomination, which has the second largest Negro membership and which was reorganized in 1939 into five white geographical jurisdictions and one Negro Central Jurisdiction, embracing all Negro congregations regardless of their location.[13]

From the point of view of ultimate socio-religious integration, the large separate Negro Protestant churches present a double rationalization. The first is that their white fellow Protestants, especially in the Southeast, are not "ready" for integration and that if congregational integration were now to take place the Negro members would again be relegated to the fringes of church participation. The second is that Negroes have freer expression within their own congregations, enjoy a common meeting place and center of communication; they can discuss and promote the elimination of Negro disabilities. "The Negro church remains one of the few areas in which the Negro can retain his identity as an individual and yet have a vehicle for self-expression and the exercise of his own abilities."[14]

It can be argued that the *felix culpa* of the Negro Protestant denominations is that they have been a training ground for the most successful integrationist leaders. We must remember that Nat Turner, leader of the slave revolt in 1831, was a preacher, and many Negro political leaders during Reconstruction were recruited from the pulpit.[15] It was only when the Negro preacher advised patience and forbearance among his congregation that he came to earn "considerable good will among the whites," and religion was "assumed to be a force for good in all respects and, particularly, in race relations."[16] As Charles Johnson wrote a quarter of a century ago, "the indifference of the Negro church to current social issues and its emphasis on the values of a future life lent indirect but vital support to the race patterns."[17]

The relatively recent emergence of Negro preachers as outspoken proponents of civil rights has been accompanied by a loss of this "white good will." The burnings and bombings of Negro churches in the South by white racists clearly demonstrate that religion is no longer "good" for conservation of racial segregation. The anomaly, therefore, is that the segregated Negro Protestant church has been the most effective instrument in breaking down non-church segregation. If these people had been absorbed into the white Protestant denominations they may well have lost their leadership to whites, and would probably have lost the sense of solidarity that now characterizes their program of desegregation.[18]

Whatever the ambiguous position of the Negro clergy may have been before the 1950's, whether they had been a hindrance or a help to integration, whether they had been leaders or followers in the upsurge of Negro protest, there can be no doubt that they have contributed both techniques and ideology to the current civil rights movement.[19] They evolved a moral philosophy of non-violence, which draws upon the teachings of Ghandi and also presents a powerful example of Christian virtue. This effective weapon of passive resistance, Christian patience and love, must not be confused with the escapist philosophy that is still found among the Negro Holiness sects and is condemned by all prominent Negro leaders in the country.[20]

To what extent have the white Protestant denominations "cleaned their own house" of racial discrimination? At the national level every major Protestant Church body has gone on record in favor of desegregating its own congregations. Although preserving the Negro Central Jurisdiction, seventy-four Methodist bishops joined in a 1960 declaration on race relations, saying: "To discriminate against a person solely on the basis of his race is both unfair and un-Christian. There must be no place in the Methodist Church for racial discrimination or enforced segregation."[21]

The Baptists probably have a wider separation than do any of the other large denominations. The National Baptist Convention, USA, and the National Baptist Convention of America are the two largest Negro religious bodies in the country. Among the whites, the Southern Baptists differ quite sharply from the American Baptist Convention, for they continue to maintain and defend a formalized policy against internal integration. There is a similar problem of disagreement between the United Presbyterian Church and the Presbyterian Church of the United States, the latter being made up of Southern adherents who are reluctant to change segregated patterns.[22] The Protestant Episcopal Church does not have a "Southern Branch," and most of its bishops and lay leaders have spoken out clearly for racial unity, but some of its Southern officials have taken exception to this stand.[23]

The religious denomination is not the only social organization in which national and regional policies clash with local customs. The urban church congregation includes people who live mainly in racially separated residential areas. There have been genuine efforts to achieve desegregation in local Protestant churches, but these still tend to be exceptions to the pattern.[24] Despite all efforts to the contrary, the membership of a congregation does change when the population of the neighborhood shifts. For example, one Methodist congregation in Los Angeles deliberately planned total integration, but "rather than racial inclusiveness, what the church really achieved was a relatively trouble-free transition from a Caucasian to a Negro membership."[25] The experience of this congregation is probably a paradigm for local urban churches elsewhere. "There were Negroes in the community long before there were Negroes in this church. Negroes did not come to worship until the Caucasians had largely left. The Caucasian exodus accelerated when Negroes did begin to come in significant numbers. The implication would seem to be clear: for the most part these Caucasian churchmen did not wish to live alongside or worship God together with Negro churchmen. A further implication is that for the most part Negro churchmen return this particular compliment of their white brethren."[26]

There are several reasons that white Protestantism, even with the best will of its ministers and leading lay people, has not succeeded widely in integrating its churches: (a) Protestant denominations lack the coercive influence of ecclesiastical authority at the higher levels and therefore allow each local congregation to determine its own course of action and its own moral rationalization for not acting to desegregate. (b) The different local congregations do not take a united position on the race issue.[27] (c) The Protestant principle of face-to-face primary groupings and close fellowship is difficult to institute in the religious context when it does not exist between the races in other community activities. (d) Protestant congregations are often willing to pay the high cost of moving their church to another location in order to remain segregated.[28]

Except for a few places in Maryland, Kentucky, and Louisiana, the Roman Catholic Church has been almost exclusively a white church in America. It has had relatively little influence in the Southeastern states, where the majority of Negroes lived, and even with its high rate of urban conversions it can probably still claim only about five per cent of the Negro population. Although the Catholic Church followed local patterns in providing separate facilities for Negroes, there have always been Negroes who attended Mass in white PARISHES AND WHITES who attended Mass in Negro parishes. Myrdal pointed out that, in the South, "the Roman Catholic Church is the only one where Negroes are allowed to attend white churches," and he says later that because the Church includes persons from all classes in the same congregation "there is a relatively greater feeling of equality among Catholic laymen."[29]

The Catholic Church in America is not subdivided into regional or racial denominations, and it is thus in a strategic position to implement internal integration. Even in those places where segregated parishes and schools are still maintained—as in some Southern dioceses—the Negroes, priests, and others involved in them are under the jurisdiction of the same bishop and chancery office as are their neighboring white Catholics. The continuation of separate Negro parishes remains the major obstacle to complete Catholic racial integration. On it depend separate parochial schools, parents' clubs, local organizations such as the Holy Name Society, the Sodality, Altar and Rosary societies, choirs, acolytes, youth clubs, study groups, and so forth.[30] Catholic colleges and universities, and in some instances high schools, which are under the authority of diocesan officials and religious orders, are generally desegregated. Practically all seminaries, as well as novitiates and houses of study for religious Sisters, have by this time opened their doors to Negro candidates. There are, however, still a few segregated Catholic hospitals in the Southeastern states.

Like the leaders of the Protestant churches, the bishops of the

Catholic Church, individually and collectively, have condemned racism. The Popes have spoken on the subject as early as the sixteenth century. Bishop Waters of Raleigh, North Carolina, was the first of the Southern prelates to integrate the Churches of his diocese; and Archbishop Rummel, through the Catholic Committee of the South, preached about the immorality of segregation. Perhaps the most effective churchman in this regard was the late Father LaFarge, who founded the Catholic interracial Councils in various cities.[31]

It is probably true that the hierarchal structure of the Catholic Church, with its emphasis on episcopal authority in the realm of faith and morals, has an advantage in imposing integration "from above."[32] The threat of excommunication, though seldom employed, is also an effective instrument.[33] Perhaps of more importance is the fact that the typical urban parish tends to be a large, secondary association in which most parishioners are not expected to have the close social bonds of fellowship that one finds in Protestant congregations. In spite of the recent liturgical drive for communal awareness, the typical Catholic still tends to focus his attention on the altar more than on his fellow parishioners.[34]

In spite of the common religious commitment to the moral value of interracial brotherhood, there is an important difference between the *gemeinschaftlich* and the *gesellschaftlich* structure of a church congregation. This is roughly similar to the associational type of industrial labor union, which has indeed had greater success in assimilating Negro workers than has the more close-knit, primary, exclusive type of craft union. The "higher law" principle of human relations should be operative in both types, but internal, local, structural integration can be better achieved where there is more stress on the worship of God and less on the fellowship of human beings.

II

The ability of a religious denomination or local congregation to integrate its own membership is not the same as its capacity to influence race relations in the surrounding community. In this instance it appears that success in creating cooperation across racial lines, as it has been across creedal lines, is greatest when the moral issues are clearest and when the personal contacts are informal. There is a lesson here in the ecumenical experiences of the last decade. Ancient concepts of better or worse, of inferior or superior, had to be put aside. Respect for the dignity and worth of individuals of another religious persuasion underlay the whole approach to ecumenism. Taking the larger picture of the American society, we may ask in what ways religious bodies have affected the structure of race relations outside their own organizations. First, it must be mentioned that some of the most virulent propagandists for the preservation of racial segregation are fundamentalist preachers, that some Southern ministers have been members of the Ku Klux Klan, and that clergymen sometimes lend respectability to White Citizens' Councils by offering a prayer at their meetings.[35] These are, of course, a small and diminishing minority when compared to the vast number of American clergymen who stand in opposition to racial discrimination.

Since the end of the Second World War there has been an enormous increase in religious preachment about better race relations. One of the most widely publicized examples of this was "An Appeal to the Conscience of the American People," adopted at the close of the National Conference on Religion and Race in Chicago in 1963, in which more than seventy organizations representing the major religious denominations participated.[36] This appeal sought a reign of justice, love, courage, and prayer in the area of American race relations; and the closing plenary session accepted sixty-two practical program suggestions dealing with almost every conceivable aspect of the racial situation.[37] Subsequently, local councils on religion and race have been established throughout the country, including the deep South.

The day is long past when the pulpit was used to expound theological and Biblical arguments in favor of racial segregation. Only the racist extremists are attempting to revive these discredited arguments.[38] In fact, a flood of arguments favoring racial integration has come from the main religious representatives of the National Council of Churches, the National Catholic Welfare Conference, and the Synagogue Council of America. Perhaps no group has been so energetic in promoting the religious basis for civil rights and racial integration as the Anti-Defamation League of B'nai B'rith. Since there are very few Negro Jews, the temples and synagogues are not faced with the problem of integrating their congregations, but Jewish leaders have been very active in promoting better race relations.[39]

The great practical impact of the moral pronouncements of religious leaders about racial integration stems in part from the fact that they are so completely in accord with the democratic values of the American culture. Religious and political motivations are mutually supportive—the politican can use scripture to confirm constitutional arguments, and the religious spokesman can use the principles of democracy to confirm the need for brotherhood under God.[40] From a sociological point of view, one may debate, and perhaps never settle, whether in American society religion simply reflects the culture or whether cultural patterns are largely the consequence of religious values. The case of the Southeastern region must be considered in this regard since in the matter of racial beliefs and practices the regional differences are greater than the differences among the major religious denominations.

Compared to other sections of the nation, the Southeast was least influenced by the rational and religious reforms of the last century and by the social gospel movement at the beginning of this century.[41] In his most recent book, James Dabbs charges white Southern Protestants with failure. "The South tried to live, on the one hand, by a highly social culture, on the other by a highly individualistic religion. The culture did not support the religion, the religion did not support the culture."[42] In spite of its high rate of church affiliation and attendance at religious services, the white Southeast is still generally reluctant to accept the modern American and religious interpretation of civil rights and race relations.

In spite of Will Herberg's protestation that an American "culture religion" is developing and President Johnson's assertions that race relations constitute a "national problem," the issue is joined in the Southeastern states, and Negro Protestant clergymen now provide the most effective influence there. It is somewhat surprising, then, to find that the Negro clergy is under attack for refusing to participate in the civil rights struggle,[43] or to read that "neither religious ideology nor religious leaders were in any important way responsible for the increased restiveness and mood of protest among Negroes during the mid-1950's."[44] Negro ministers, and especially Martin Luther King, must be given credit for their role in developing the non-violent techniques of protest.

The significant contribution of Negro preachers and Negro churches toward the elimination of racial discrimination has sometimes been misunderstood. In his small, posthumous book, E. Franklin Frazier wrote that the Negro church was "the most important cultural institution created by Negroes," but that it was also "the most important institutional barrier to integration and the assimilation of Negroes." He speaks also of the few Negro individuals who have been "able to escape from the stifling domination of the church."[45] In his review of this book, Horace Cayton remarks that "Frazier did not live to witness the fervor of the continuing Negro rebellion and the position of leadership which the church and churchmen are taking in it. Perhaps, if he had, his final judgment on the importance and resilience of the Negro church might have been tempered."[46]

If religious organizations were not segregated, probably no other form of American organization would be segregated, and there would be no need for a springboard like the Negro churches from which an attack could be mounted against other forms of institutional segregation and discrimination. It seems true to say that, on the American scene, racial integration is resisted most in groups where the membership is voluntary, where the organizational status is private (that is, non-governmental), and where the relationships are personal and primary. These characteristics are present, at least conceptually, in the typical religious congregation, which is deliberately exempted from anti-segregation legislation and from official public pressure.

They are present too in the Negro church, and it seems symptomatic of their interpretation of different types of institutions that Negroes are more interested in integrating schools (70 per cent) than in going to church with whites (52 per cent).[47] Furthermore, the segregated congregation is a concomitant—if not always a consequence —of other social phenomena. For example, the cultural taboo against interracial marriage and the hard facts of residential segregation work against the kind of association that is ideally expected among members of the same religious congregation. The existence of integrated religious organizations would be a demonstration that these factors had been minimized, and that non-church types of segregation had decreased.

The organized church, the "most important Negro cultural institution," has provided continued protest against all forms of racial injustice and discrimination. The most famous slave insurrections were led by Negro preachers, Gabriel Prosser in 1800, Denmark Vesey in 1822, Nat Turner in 1831. Speaking from a historical perspective, Liston Pope has said that "the mounting spirit of revolt among Negroes, often robed in biblical teachings on release from bondage, revealed most especially in insurrections and revolts in the period between 1800 and 1831, was also related to the creation of separate Negro demoninations."[48]

Anyone who has been observing developments on the racial front since the 1955 Montgomery bus boycott need not be reminded that "Negro ministers constitute the largest segment of the leadership class." Obviously, as Thompson points out, the clergy must spend most of his time on pastoral duties. This is their primary professional function. Nevertheless, "there are a few prominent Negro ministers who can always be found in the vanguard of the Negro's march toward full participation in community affairs. These ministers are generally well-trained, articulate and courageous. Their churches are made available for mass meetings, forums, and other types of programs designed to acquaint the Negro masses with major social issues facing them."[49]

It must be remembered, too, that white clergymen, Christian and Jewish, also have a primary obligation to pastoral duties and that one cannot expect the majority of them to be involved mainly in action programs for civil rights. Anyone who has participated in Southern demonstrations, marches, and other civil rights programs has heard the cry of white segregationists that preachers should stay in their pulpits and not "meddle" in these affairs. In fact, the three bishops of Alabama, Catholic, Episcopal, and Methodist, said as much about non-Southern clergymen (and Sisters) who participated in the Selma-Montgomery demonstrations of 1965. They felt that these "outsiders" should stay home and "clean up their own backyard."

It may be argued that neither churches nor churchmen should be "used" as an instrument to promote "extraneous" purposes. Major institutions, economic, political, and educational, are said to function well in the American culture because the means they employ are focused exclusively on definite objectives. This is only relatively true, however, because all cultural institutions intermesh in daily life and affect each other's means and ends—a fact which is becoming increasingly evident. Only those who argue for "complete" separation of the religious and political institutions, Church and State, continue to be blind to the fact that neither can divorce itself "completely" from the other.

The Negro clergyman typically does not "mind his own business" in the restricted sense of remaining apart from the large social problems of his people, while the white clergyman, priest, or rabbi, in his segregated church or synagogue, often stays aloof from the larger social problems of the day. This contrast is sharpened when we realize that racial segregation has been forced upon Negro churches, has been instituted and perpetuated by white churches.[50] It requires a special effort by white clergymen to look outside their own groups and to recognize the areas of discrimination and injustice in the larger community. The importance of the Protestant "witness" as a servant church to the society has been the theme of the writing of Gibson Winter and Peter Berger in recent years.[51]

If white clergymen maintain a personal, individual philosophy of religious behavior, they are likely to withdraw completely from the area of civic behavior or even, as some have done, oppose their colleagues who are socially concerned. If they are aware of the social problems of their communities, they may limit themselves to the level of preaching and prayer or may operate at the level of action and involvement. Since the end of the Second World War there has been a continuous increase in the number of ministers, priests, and rabbis who preach and pray about race relations, and an even more rapid growth in the number who have involved themselves in action programs.

Clergymen were instrumental in changing California's laws on miscegenation and in desegregating their own high schools, colleges, and seminaries; they participated in the Freedom Rides, in demonstrations and sit-ins all over the South, in the march on Washington, and in the march on Montgomery. The sympathy marches that occurred all over the country following the murder of Reverend James Reeb and of Mrs. Viola Liuzzo were often promoted and always participated in by clergymen. The reluctance and reticence noted by Thomas Pettigrew among the ministers of Little Rock have since been far outbalanced by the vocal and physical presence of clergymen in the struggle for racial justice.[52]

When discussing the march on Washington in 1963, James Reston felt that moral reaction would have to precede political reaction. "This whole movement for equality in American life will have to return to first principles before it will 'overcome' anything."[53] This is the familiar argument, used by moralists and clergymen and by some psychologists, that there must be a "change of heart" and reformed attitudes among the people before we can expect law and customs to improve. There is no doubt that genuine spiritual conversion has a marked effect on the external behavior of the convert; thus the more converts there are to love and brotherhood, the more quickly will America rid itself of racial discrimination.

The march on Washington in 1963 was indeed followed by continued interest and action by organized religious bodies, and was followed also by the Civil Rights Law of 1964. One cannot prove a causal sequence here—the political action perhaps would have occurred without the intervening religious action. A clearer sequence is seen in the active religious leadership of the march on Montgomery in 1965, which was followed immediately by President Johnson's proposal for a voting rights law.[54] In this instance there can be no doubt that the "call to conscience" made by the moral and religious leaders of America led to practical results.

The involvement of organized religion in the race problems of

America has sharpened the recognition of the logical connection between prayer, study, and personal virtue, on the other. These are mutually reinforcing elements in the whole complex approach to a better human relationship between the races. College students concerned with religion have shifted "from study-involvement to involvement-study," as Paul Zietlow has remarked.[55] They started the sit-ins in 1960, initiated demonstrations in Birmingham, Jackson, Greensboro, Nashville, and other places in 1963, and participated in marches wherever they have occurred. A National Student Leadership Conference on Religion and Race also had ecumenical overtones in the cooperation of the B'nai B'rith Hillel Foundations, National Club Foundation, National Federation of Catholic College Students, and the National Student Christian Federation.

While trying to ameliorate present conditions of discrimination, Negroes are probably more interested today in the removal of unjust external racial practices than they are in the growth of love and kindness in the hearts of prejudiced people. There is ample evidence that white attitudes toward racial integration have improved in accompaniment to the legal and actual removal of racial barriers.[56] This has occurred even though we cannot make a universal application of this principle. "It is certainly true," wrote Gordon Allport in 1964, "that prejudiced attitudes do not always lead to prejudiced behavior. It is equally true that a person with equalitarian attitudes may engage in unjust discrimination, especially if he lives in South Africa or in Mississippi."[57]

III

Cultural change has affected religious people and religious institutions, as it has other areas of American life, and it has been so rapid that any precise forecast of combined religious and racial trends would be senseless. Who could have foreseen the effective impact of religious people and organizations on Washington officialdom before the 1960's? To go back further, who could have foreseen that the conservative religious forces which influenced Southern state legislatures even to the extent of textbook censorship, which urged the Congress to pass the Volstead Act, which intervened so strongly in the 1928 presidential campaign, would now have lost most of their influence?

Organized religion has had, and should have, a conservative and preservative role in the larger society, but in too many instances this role seems to function in a negative and reactionary fashion. What has come to the fore in the civil rights movement is the prophetic, creative, and positive role of religion, which has long been recognized almost exclusively in the area of personal piety and family morality. That the church has also a positive social function in the larger society has not always been clearly understood, perhaps because the society is much more morally complex than the individual human being. To be against sin, personal and social, is only one aspect of genuine religiosity. To be for virtue, personal and social, is a morally inalienable imperative of the church and its members.

Change and development have not led to an abandonment of the "old time" religion, or of the eternal truths, as some rigid racists would claim. We have not diluted or repudiated genuine religious truths, principles, and values. We have reviewed them in light of new knowledge about psychological and sociological phenomena. This creative social revolution, which churchmen now sponsor so vigorously, implies an expansion and fulfillment of divine precepts of behavior which we have always struggled to understand in an imperfect and human way.

Why are churchmen so deeply involved in the civil rights movement, and why are they impelled to continue this mission to the larger society? The principal motivation must always be that this is the right and moral thing to do. Store owners and factory managers may say that improved race relations are good for the economy. Mayors and governors may say that the racial solution must be found for the sake of peace and order in the community. National leaders may worry about the "world image" of American democracy that must offset Communist rivalries and meet the expectations of emerging nations. The religionist can certainly approve all of these reasons, but his most impelling motive is that the virtues of love and justice demand the removal of racism and all of its discriminatory effects and practices.

Aside from interim strategies and long-range programs, which may require the technical knowledge of social scientists more than the theological knowledge of churchmen, the church has had its greatest effect in the current drive for Negro freedom precisely because Americans are willing to listen to the moral argument. Whatever one may think of Myrdal's analysis of the American race problem, it is significant that he recognized the moral dilemma of the white man's conscience. As James Weldon Johnson has said, the solution of the race problem involves the salvation of the white man's soul and of the black man's body.[58] If the ordinary American has an uneasy conscience about the American record on race relations, he ought to be able to turn to his religion, the "keeper" of his conscience, for the grace and strength to do the right thing.

The much-discussed "failure" of church members and clergymen, of organized Protestants, Catholics, and Jews, has been so widely publicized that it has evoked wide-spread contrition. The current movement toward rectification of this failure and toward positive implementation of moral principles is bascially a religious movement. It is probably true to say that the postwar American experience of race relations has been a major catalyst for both the organizational and doctrinal perspectives of American religion. The self-analysis that has been forced upon religious-minded individuals, and upon the religious bodies to which they belong, has certainly clarified the American moral dilemma of race. Quite aside from these speculative considerations, this test of America's religious ideology has resulted in pragmatic decisions to reconstitute congregational membership; it has resulted, perhaps more significantly, in the deliberate moral impact of religious leaders on the extra-church institutions of the American culture.

REFERENCES

1. Anson Phelps Stokes *et al.*, *Negro Status and Race Relations in the United States* (New York, 1948), p. 50.
2. David Moberg, *The Church as a Social Institution* (Englewood Cliffs, N.J., 1962), p. 453.
3. Liston Pope, *The Kingdom Beyond Caste* (New York, 1957), p. 105.
4. Edwin R. Embree, *Brown America* (New York, 1931), pp. 208-209.
5. It is Myrdal's theory that the Church changes with the community. "Few Christian Churches have ever been, whether in America or elsewhere, the spearheads of reform." Gunnar Myrdal, *An American Dilemma* (New York, 1944), p. 877.
6. C. Vann Woodward, *The Strange Career of Jim Crow* (New York, 1955), has demonstrated that formal segregation of the races is a much more recent phenomenon than many people realized, especially in the Southeast.
7. See C. Eric Lincoln, *The Black Muslims in America* (Boston, 1961); and E. U. Essien-Udom, *Black Nationalism* (Chicago, 1962).
8. C. Eric Lincoln, *op. cit.*, p. 53.
9. Edmund D. Cronon, *Black Moses: The Story of Marcus Garvey and the Universal Negro Improvement Association* (Madison, Wis., 1955).
10. For an analysis of various Negro religious cults, see Arthur H. Fauset, *Black Gods of the Metropolis* (Philadelphia, 1954).
11. See the views of Benton Johnson, "Do Holiness Sects Socialize in Dominant Values?" *Social Forces*, Vol. 39 (May 1961), pp. 309-316. James Baldwin came out of this kind of religious environment. He has repudiated this philosophy, but has not embraced the ideology of the Black Muslims.
12. See Frank S. Loescher, *The Protestant Church and the Negro: A Pattern of Segregation* (New York, 1948).
13. Dwight W. Culver, *Negro Segregation in the Methodist Church* (New Haven, Conn., 1953).
14. Lyle E. Schaller, *Planning for Protestantism in Urban America* (New York, 1965), p. 188.
15. Myrdal, *op. cit.*, p. 861.

16. *Ibid.*, p. 862.
17. Charles S. Johnson, *Growing Up in the Black Belt* (Washington, D.C., 1941), pp. 135-136. See also the more recent analysis of Joseph R. Washington, "Are American Negro Churches Christian?" *Theology Today* (April 1963), pp. 76-86.
18. See Martin Luther King, *Stride Toward Freedom* (New York, 1958). "The non-violent movement in America has come not from secular forces but from the heart of the Negro church. This movement has done a great deal to revitalize the Negro church and to give its message a relevant and authentic ring." King, p. 165, in Mathew Ahmann (ed.), *Race: Challenge to Religion* (Chicago, 1963).
19. Norval Glenn, "Negro Religion and Negro Status in the United States," in Louis Schneider (ed.), *Religion, Culture and Society* (New York, 1964), pp. 623-638, argues as though the Negro preachers were only reluctantly drawn into the civil rights struggle. "The middle-class ministers of the city could hardly have avoided involvement in the boycott: King and several of the others organized and led it" (p. 633). Yet, nearly half (47 per cent) of the Negroes told the *Newsweek* poll that their ministers are "helping a lot." See William Brink and Louis Harris, *The Negro Revolution in America* (New York, 1963), Ch. 6, "The Role of the Negro Church," and the tables on pp. 220-223.
20. See James W. Vander Zanden, "The Non-Violent Resistance Movement Against Segregation," *American Journal of Sociology*, Vol. 68 (March 1963), pp. 544-550.
21. Reported in *The New York Times*, April 28, 1960. For the attitudes of Southern Methodist laymen on segregation, see Stotts and Deats, *Methodism and Society: Guidelines for Strategy* (Nashville, Tenn., 1959), Vol. 4, Appendix A.
22. See David M. Reimers, "The Race Problem and Presbyterian Union," *Church History* (June 1962), pp. 203-215; and also John L. Bell, "The Presbyterian Church and the Negro in North Carolina," *North Carolina Historical Review* (January 1963), pp. 15-36.
23. See the summary on the Protestant Churches by W. Seward Salisbury, *Religion in American Culture* (Homewood, Ill., 1964), pp. 472-475. See also the penetrating analysis by Thomas F. Pettigrew, "Wherein the Church Has Failed in Race," *Religious Education*, Vol. 59, No. 1 (January-February 1964), pp. 64-73; and Walter B. Posey, "The Protestant Episcopal Church; An American Adaptation," *Journal of Southern History* (February 1959), pp. 3-30.
24. For examples at the local church level see Robert W. Root, *Progress Against Prejudice* (New York, 1957).
25. Reported by Grover C. Bagby in Galen R. Weaver (ed.), *Religion's Role in Racial Crisis* (New York, 1964), p. 16.
26. *Ibid.*, p. 16; see also the research report by Henry Clark, "Churchmen and Residential Desegregation," *Review of Religious Research*, Vol. 5, No. 3 (Spring 1964), pp. 157-164.
27. The difficulty of getting inter-denominational consensus on the race question seems to reflect the lack of moral and doctrinal consensus among the Protestant denominations. See Kyle Haselden, *The Racial Problem in Christian Perspective* (New York, 1964).
28. These reasons are discussed by Lyle E. Schaller, *op. cit.*, pp. 187-190. He considers residential segregation an "excuse," but not a reason for the perpetuation of racial segregation in churches. See also the earlier article by Samuel S. Hill, "Southern Protestantism and Racial Integration," *Religion in Life*, Vol. 33, No. 3 (Summer 1964), pp. 421-429, where he discusses similar "factors" as operative in the South.
29. Myrdal, *op. cit.*, pp. 870, 1411. In the *Newsweek* poll, more Negroes (58 per cent) think that "Catholic priests" are helpful to the cause than say this about "white churches" (24 per cent). Brink and Harris, *op. cit.*, pp. 133, 233.
30. Joseph H. Fichter, "The Catholic South and Race," *Religious Education*, Vol. 59, No. 1 (January-February 1964), pp. 30-33; also Joseph H. Fichter and George L. Maddox, "Religion in the South, Old and New," in John McKinney and Edgar Thompson (eds.), *The South in Continuity and Change* (Durham, N.C., 1965).
31. John LaFarge, "Caste in the Church: The Roman Catholic Experience," *Survey Graphic*, Vol. 36 (January 1947), pp. 61 ff., 104-106; also *The Catholic Viewpoint on Race Relations* (Garden City, N.Y., 1960).
32. Liston Pope, *op. cit.*, p. 140, feels that this is "in line with the findings of social scientists in the last few years as the most effective means of achieving desegregation and the diminution of prejudice."
33. The excommunication of three Louisiana Catholics by Archbishop Rummel did

not seem to diminish their racist activities in the White Citizens' Council, although it probably acted as a deterrent to others.

34. The difference between "objective and subjective worship" of Catholicism and Protestantism was analyzed by James B. Pratt, *The Religious Consciousness* (New York, 1920), pp. 290-309, reprinted in Schneider, *op. cit.*, pp. 143-156. The way in which this applies to race relations among Catholics is indicated by Elizabeth M. Eddy, "Student Perspectives on the Southern Church," *Phylon*, Vol. 25, No. 4 (Winter 1964), pp. 369-381.

35. There seems to be a "pattern" in clergymen's attitudes. "The small-sect minister is typically segregationist and vocal, whereas the denomination minister is typically integrationist and silent." Ernest Q. Campbell, "Moral Discomfort and Racial Segregation—An Examination of the Myrdal Hypothesis," *Social Forces* (March 1961), p. 229.

36. Matthew Ahmann (ed.), *Race, Challenge to Religion* (Chicago, 1963), pp. 171-173, contains the original essays of the prominent speakers at the Conference.

37. Galen R. Weaver (ed.), *Religion's Role in Racial Conflict* (New York, 1963), Ch. 7, "Programmatic Recommendations."

38. The propaganda of the White Citizens' Councils in several Southeastern States abounds with these "Biblical proofs" that God was the First Segregationist, and with charges that integrationists, especially white clergymen, are the dupes of atheistic Communism. What Negroes think of Communism is shown in the fact that about the same minority (6 per cent) approve of the Black Muslim movement as believe (5 per cent) the Communist claim of no discrimination under their system. Brink and Harris, *op. cit.*, pp. 201, 225.

39. See, for example, the speeches of Rabbi Morris Adler, Dr. Julius Mark, and Dr. Abraham J. Heschel, in Matthew Ahmann (ed.), *op. cit.*, at the National Conference on Race and Religion.

40. For a few examples of this trend see William S. Nelson (ed.), *The Christian Way in Race Relations* (New York, 1948); Will Campbell, *Race and Renewal of the Church* (Philadelphia, 1962); and Benjamin E. Mays, *Seeking to be a Christian in Race Relations* (New York, n.d.).

41. See Kenneth K. Bailey, *Southern White Protestantism in the Twentieth Century* (New York, 1964); also James Sellers, *The South and Christian Ethics* (New York, 1962); and Robert M. Miller, *American Protestantism and Social Issues* (Chapel Hill, N.C., 1958).

42. James McBride Dabbs, *Who Speaks for the South?* (New York, 1965). That the Southerner, even in his religion, is not just another American, was also held by W. J. Cash, *The Mind of the South* (1940), C. Vann Woodward, *The Burden of Southern History* (1960), and Francis B. Simkins, *The Everlasting South* (1963). Others have seen the Southerner as American, for example, Harry Ashmore, *An Epitaph for Dixie* (1957), Charles Sellers, *The Southerner as American* (1960), Thomas D. Clark, *The Emerging South* (1961), and Howard Zinn, *The Southern Mystique* (1964).

43. This is the contention of Simeon Booker, *Black Man's America* (Englewood Cliffs, N.J., 1964).

44. See Norval Glenn, *op. cit.*, p. 632; also James W. Vander Zanden, "The Non-Violent Resistance Movement against Segregation," *American Journal of Sociology*, Vol. 68 (March 1963), pp. 544-550.

45. E. Franklin Frazier, *The Negro Church in America* (New York, 1963), pp. 70, 86.

46. Horace Cayton, "E. Franklin Frazier: A Tribute and a Review," *Review of Religious Research*, Vol. 5, No. 3 (Spring 1964), pp. 137-142 (p. 141).

47. Brink and Harris, *op. cit.*, pp. 223, 236.

48. Liston Pope, "The Negro and Religion in America," *Review of Religious Research*, Vol. 5, No. 3 (Spring 1964), pp. 142-152 (p. 144). He adds that "the Negro ministry is on the ascendancy in the eyes of all Americans" (p. 147). In the same issue of the *Review*, Walter Muelder, "Recruitment of Negroes for Theological Studies," pp. 152-156, says that "the ministry, once the chief outlet for Negro ambition, is declining significantly in relative importance among professionals. It should be noted that Negro enrollments in medicine and law have also been dropping" (p. 155).

49. Daniel C. Thompson, *The Negro Leadership Class* (Englewood Cliffs, N.J., 1963), p. 36.

50. The oft-repeated expression of white Southerners that "Negroes prefer to be by

themselves" has validity only if it means that they prefer this to unjust and discriminatory treatment in churches, schools, parks, buses, restaurants, and elsewhere.

51. See Gibson Winter, *The Suburban Captivity of the Churches* (New York, 1962) and *The New Creation as Metropolis* (1963); and Peter Berger, *The Noise of Solemn Assemblies* (1961) and *The Precarious Vision* (1963).
52. Ernest Q. Campbell and Thomas Pettigrew, *Christians in Racial Crisis* (Washington, D.C., 1959), and their article, "Racial and Moral Crisis: The Role of Little Rock Ministers," *American Journal of Sociology*, Vol. 64 (March 1959), pp. 509-516.
53. James Reston, "The Churches, the Synagogues, and the March on Washington," *Religious Education*, Vol. 59, No. 1 (January-February 1964), pp. 5 ff., reprinted from *The New York Times*, August 30, 1963.
54. It may be argued that the shocking brutality, official and unofficial, of the diehard segregationists in Alabama was the main galvanizing force for reform.
55. Carl P. Zietlow, "Race, Students, and Non-Violence," *Religious Education*, Vol. 59, No. 1 (January-February 1964), pp. 116-120.
56. See the study done for *Newsweek* by William Brink and Louis Harris, *The Negro Revolution in America* (New York, 1964); also the changes noted by Herbert Hyman and Paul Sheatsley, "How Whites View Negroes, 1942-1963," *New York Herald Tribune*, November 19, 1963; and "Attitudes Toward Desegregation—Seven Years Later," *Scientific American*, Vol. 211, No. 1 (July 1964).
57. Gordon W. Allport, "Prejudice: Is it Societal or Personal?" *Religious Education*, Vol. 59, No. 1 (January-February 1964), pp. 20-29.
58. James Weldon Johnson, *Along This Way* (New York, 1933), p. 318, quoted by Myrdal, *op. cit.*, p. 43.

11.

MYTHOLOGY AND ECONOMICS: POVERTY IN AMERICA TODAY

STUART R. LYNN

Now that the Viet Nam war is over, and the United States is once again offering to help rebuild the economy of our former enemy, some are asking the question, "But what of our own people? What of America's poor?" And the President who received three of every five American votes in 1972 gives us the same answer: "Ask not what government can do for me. Ask instead what I can do for myself."

That this solution is by and large acceptable testifies to the beliefs that Americans hold regarding poverty in our own country. The theme of this essay is that those beliefs, regardless of how widely held, do not correspond to reality. They comprise, instead, a new mythology.

I.

Webster defines myth as "A traditional story of unknown authorship, ostensibly with a historical basis, but serving usually to explain some phenomenon of nature, the origin of man, or the customs, institutions, religious rites, etc. of a people . . . any fictitious story, or unscientific account, theory, belief, etc. . . ." Essentially, myth offers an explanation of something that is not understood, and enables people to deal with something mysterious in a semi-rational way. Ignorance is replaced by knowledge, and man's fear of the unknown is appeased. Socially, myth provides a basis for dealing with problems. Security replaces bewilderment and helplessness. Order is established from chaos, and stability provides a frame of reference for policy.

The United States of America has acquired an extensive mythology, encompassing the relationships between the individual and his land, the individual and capital, and the individual and other individuals from the settlements in Jamestown and Plymouth (16) to and beyond the present time. A large portion of this body of myth concerns the differences between rich and poor: how wealth and poverty developed, how they exist today, and how this division is to be handled in the future.

Our concern here is the mythology of American poverty: the place of poverty in present day "capitalist" America, and the future of poverty embodied in attempts to "eradicate" it. We want to know how Americans perceive poverty and the poor. We want to examine the more popular ideas of how poverty is being, and is to be, eliminated, and point out objections to those ideas. Finally, we make a brief introduction to some radical alternatives to the present approach to the problem of poverty in the U.S.

Our point of reference is the failure of the declared and undeclared wars on poverty to significantly dent the problem. More important is the attitude that insists that these policies *have* worked, or should have worked, or perhaps may yet work. What do Americans believe, and how well are these beliefs substantiated? These are the questions posed here.

It should be recognized at this early stage that much of the argument around America's poverty problem is directed at the assumption that since most Americans are not poor, what is needed is only a minor adjustment on the part of either the economic system or on the part of the poor themselves. Thus Capitalism as such should not be the subject of criticism. (20)

To this way of thinking will be opposed another. The justification of capitalism as essentially beneficial is seen as an answer to the wrong question. There will be no denial that our form of capitalism has done a great deal for the development of the U.S. economy.

In this, there is no departure from the basic premise of Marx. The proper question then is not "Hasn't capitalism done a good job?" but is instead "Why isn't capitalism doing a *better* job?" or even "*Can* capitalism do a better job?" We seek to answer this question by examining the answers that our society has found for those who are poor, and the unexplored alternatives.

II.

Every year, the President's Council of Economic Advisors (9) makes a report to the President on the state of the American economy. The report of January, 1972 contained 128 tables. Only one of those tables had any information on the distribution of income in this country . . . but not very much. And what there was showed that things had actually gotten worse for the poor from 1969 to 1970. In 1970, the number of families earning under $3000 and single individuals earning under $1500 had *increased* from the previous year, and the figure for families was even a higher percentage than the year before. (Dollar figures for both years are measured at 1970 prices.)

But, presumably, the President is not interested in the distribution of income in the United States. If asked, he would probably say offhand that constant progress is being made toward a more proportional (even) distribution, but that this could only go so far because the economy requires a large amount of saving which only rich people and corporations can provide. Most of us would probably guess the same thing; that the New Deal and subsequent economic growth are bringing the incomes of the poorest part of the nation closer, even if slowly, to the incomes of the richest part.

The data show that nothing of the kind is happening. Income distributions for representative years since 1929 (Table 1) show that with the exception of boom years, in which the upper fifth claims *one-half or more* of all before-tax income, there has been a fairly constant income distribution for the last 40 years. (1, 21) And these figures actually understate the inequality that continues to exist. They omit income from capital gains, which is heavily concentrated in the upper income classes. (39) They omit real income hidden under expense accounts and non-money income, both of which go disproportionately to the rich. (21) And finally, they fail to account for non-reporting and under-reporting of income which makes the actual distribution even less proportional. (31)

In spite of the fact that more than ten years have passed since a few national political leaders were shocked into some kind of

Table 1.   Income Distribution in the United States.

Percent of Reported Money Income (Excluding Capital Gains)
Going To Each Fifth of Income Earners.

Year	Upper (a) (b)		2nd (a)	(b)	3rd (a)	(b)	4th (a)	(b)	Lower (a) (b)	
1929	51.3		18.8		14.4		10.1		5.4	
1934	46.7		20.4		15.5		11.5		5.9	
1941	50.0		22.0		16.0		9.0		3.0	
1945	45.0		24.0		16.0		11.0		4.0	
1950	44.1	42.6	23.5	23.5	17.1	17.4	11.2	12.0	4.1	4.5
1956	45.9	41.2	22.8	23.7	16.6	17.8	10.6	12.4	4.1	5.0
1960		42.0		23.6		17.6		12.0		4.9
1964		41.1		24.0		17.7		12.0		5.2
1968		40.6		23.7		17.7		12.4		5.7
1969		41.0		23.4		17.6		12.3		5.6
		50.9		24.3		13.7		7.7		3.4

NOTES: Column (a) is from Kolko (21), and column (b) is from Ackerman (1). Figures for 1941 and 1945 are rounded. Column (a) considers all income receiving units. Column (b) refers only to families, except for 1969 where figures are given both for families (above) and for unrelated individuals.

awareness of the poverty problem by Socialist Michael Harrington's book *The Other America* (17), and in spite of study after study indicating the responsibility of the society as a whole for allowing much of this situation to persist, especially in the areas of old-age poverty (35), dependent children and hunger (7, 8), non-poor Americans still retain the image of the poor as lazy people who simply refuse to find jobs that are advertised in the newspaper every day. Those who fall below the unrealistically low government "poverty figure" of $3553 for a non-farm family of four (in 1968) are seen as suffering from their own personality defects, rather than as victims of a society that could be, but is not, providing for them.

Although we may be aware of the data showing that the poor are undereducated, underfed, underemployed, and apparently under-white, it is still possible to consider the problem as one of personal initiative if one is not familiar with the startling facts relating to employment among the poor. It is true that most poor people do not work. But then almost half of the poor (43.5% in 1966) are under eighteen years old (and in polite society would be expected to be in school until at least that age), while another large chunk of the poor (18%) is at least sixty-five years old, and again non-poor Americans might well expect not to have regular or any employment during these years of their lives. (33)

And what of the remaining poor—the 38.5% who are in the normal working years? Of those who were "head of household" in 1966, almost half (44%) had *full-time jobs* for most or all of the year. Another 29% either had part-time jobs (because full-time positions for which they were qualified were not available), or worked full-time less than 40 weeks due to illness, job scarcity and other reasons. Of those who were not working at all, almost one half were mothers of dependent children. Another one-third were ill or disabled for all or most of the year. Of the remaining few, 40% were in school and 15% reported that they were looking for work but could not find jobs for which they were qualified.

These figures leave us with an empty feeling. Of the 30 million "lazy" poor people in the United States in 1966, approximately 100,000—or 0.3%—belong in the category of head of household, between the ages of 18 and 65, who were not working at all for some unspecified reason. Even of those, it is quite likely that many are in circumstances which do not occur to non-poor society but which, like unrecognized mental illness for example, may exclude them from meaningful participation in the labor force.

In spite of the fact that black Americans are disproportionately represented among the poor, widespread beliefs insist that they faced no greater problems than did several prior waves of ethnic immigrants to the large cities of the North—thus their poverty brands them as inferior. The point-by-point refutation of this argument was one of the significant aspects of the report of the National Advisory Commission on Civil Disorders (27). Aside from the fact that many ethnic groups have remained largely unassimilated for long periods of time, and remain poor, the Negro experience contains some elements which work against the process that brought success to many of the children of the foreign-born.

The most obvious of the disadvantages for the blacks has been their color. Blacks, as a target of prejudice, remain visible long after the children of ethnic minorities have vanished into white America, changed their names and become part of the mainstream of economic life. The nature of the economy is another aspect. The upward mobility associated with a relatively new, developing economy is more restricted than before. The jobs which remain to the black proletariat are mostly at the bottom of the ladder, while qualifications for jobs that might have been available earlier are now more demanding as the diploma mentality has taken hold.

Political and cultural differences exist as well, with blacks migrating from a slave society to a community whose culture was different and whose political and social structure was already established. The white political machine had stabilized, and could not provide the favors and mobility that it had previously offered to ethnic minorities. In spite of these obstacles, it is astonishing that many blacks *have* escaped poverty, in a period of time equalling other ethnic group progress, although perhaps invisibly as a consequence of their continued segregation in ghettos.

Even those who admit to the existence of widespread poverty, and perhaps recognize that social structural constraints may share a large part of the blame, are at a loss to explain how poverty remains when this poverty works to the benefit of no one. Leaving aside, for now, the relationship between poverty and the economic system—capitalism—it is interesting to note that there are many groups which *do* benefit from the continued existence of poverty and which in some cases lead existences which are justified *only* by the continuation of the situation.

Gans (14) describes fifteen "positive functions of poverty" for a society—many of which tie in with the economic critique of capitalism. In non-economic terms, consider the following: The poor create many professional opportunities for criminologists, social workers and public health workers. They are cited as the deviants through which society defines its norms and obtains vicarious thrills. They provide an outlet for the pity and energy of the unemployed rich, the churches and so on. They guarantee the status and upward mobility of the non-poor. And in political life, they provide a rallying point for the left and right, and subsidize the political power of those non-poor whose rates of political participation is higher. What would our society do without them?

III.

Granted the continued existence of poverty in the United States, and the inability of large numbers of people to escape poverty through their own efforts, one confronts the question of what should be done about it. The rather common myth that the United States represents a "market" or "capitalist" economy is extended to the idea that it is the restrictions of the market, the deviations from capitalism which may prevent us from reaching the goal of a no-poverty society.

Significantly, not even the right wing of the economic profession believes this. As represented by Milton Friedman (11), the conservatives believe that capitalism as a system is most consistent with personal liberty, but that without government intervention, this personal freedom guarantees that inequality will continue to exist. In this they agree with the non-Socialist left (20) that the market has done a good job, but must be somewhat modified to take care of the remaining problems. The differences exist mainly in the solutions proposed.

To find an opposing view, one must turn to the present-day Marxists. Baran and Sweezy (4) take the view that capitalism guarantees poverty not because of its reliance on individual freedom, but because its very nature denies true freedom and forces an underclass to exist in poverty. The accumulation of an economic surplus requires that people work for less than the value of their output according to Marxist theory. And although government may play at creating full employment, the control of the government and economy by the capitalists assures that full employment in any meaningful sense—not to mention the elimination of poverty—will never occur. (3)

What then is the record of the government which the right sees as a necessary evil and the left sees as hopelessly under control of the capitalists? It is widely believed that, without any special programs, the promotion of the growth of the economy as a whole, coupled with the progressive income tax which has been with us for many years, will assure that poverty can soon be eradicated. Yet it took over twenty years to reduce the number of families earning $3000 a year or less (accounting for price changes) from 8.4 million (1947) to 4.4 million (1969). (9) One year later, 4.6 million *families*, a higher figure, existed on $3000 a year or less, after many years of economic expansion. Many more lived on only slightly more than that. In the same period of time, the number of "unrelated individuals" earning $1500 a year or less fell—if you can call it that—from 3.7 million (1947) to 3.6 million (1970). Although these figures of course indicate a smaller percentage of the population, they show that for a minimum of 25 million people—more than 10% of the country—extreme poverty remains a way of life. Millions more are still very close.

We have seen that there has been no change in the pre-tax distribution of income, but doesn't the progressive tax system in the United States redistribute income substantially? Unfortunately it is only the federal income tax which is, for the most part, progressive. When *all* taxes are considered, the percentage of income paid in taxes by various income classes looks quite a bit different (see Table 2).

The startling facts are, then, that the overall tax system in this country is merely proportional in the income ranges from $2000 to $15,000 while taxing the poor heavily. And this trend is likely to continue as more state and local governments impose and increase their regressive taxes.

Table 2.   Taxes Paid As a Percent of Income Received.

Income Class	Federal	State and Local	Total	Federal	State and Local	Total
		(1958)			*(1965)*	
Under $2,000	9.6	11.3	21.0	19	25	44
$2000-$4000	11.0	9.4	20.4	16	11	27
$4000-$6000	12.1	8.5	20.6	17	10	27
$6000-$8000	13.9	7.7	21.6	17	9	26
$8000-$10000	13.4	7.2	20.6	18	9	27
$10000-$15000	15.1	6.5	21.6	19	9	27
Over $15000	28.6	5.9	34.4	32	7	38

Data for 1958 are from Kolko(22); for 1965 are from Pechman(30). Totals may not add correctly due to rounding.

Since the growth of the American economy has left millions in poverty, and the tax structure makes things even worse for the lowest group of income earners, can something be done? At the present time, the closest America comes to systematic relief of poverty is the welfare system. For the working poor of America, however, the welfare setup in the United States means absolutely nothing. Those hard-working, yet poor citizens over whom we sometimes shower so much sympathy and romanticizing are just plain out of luck. Welfare does not apply to them.

One of the favorites of the welfare myths is that since one cannot work and get welfare, many of the poor—able-bodied men, of course—are content to quit their jobs and stay on welfare. Those who hold this myth are probably not those who have tried to support a family in a city on a couple of thousand dollars a year. As we have seen, almost all of the poor who can work *are* working. And those who are on welfare? According to the United States government (HEW in 5), after one accounts for children and their mothers, and old and disabled people, there remains a hard core of "able-bodied males" who could work, but are on welfare. Their number in 1968 was 80 thousand—*less than 1% of the total welfare rolls!*

No, it is not work that poor people quit to go on welfare. It is mainly their families that poor men leave, so that mothers and children can go on welfare, receiving more than those men are earning in the jobs they can find. A poor man who is working cannot get welfare for his family, but if he runs away, disappears into the "uncountables" that the census mentions and leaves a family alone, then they can get help. Those mothers, left alone but who would like to look after their children, are then subjected to the most demeaning interference with their private lives ever devised in this country. If they wish to work and can find work, they may be frustrated by the virtual impossibility of finding a decent place to leave their children.

But there is another form of welfare which we generally do not talk about. This comes under such names as subsidy, tax incentive, low-cost loan and superior public services. These names all refer to government assistance, and they have one more characteristic in common: they almost always go to the middle-income and rich people. Consider subsidies to large corporations and the government's questionable commitments to such firms as Penn Central and Lockheed Aircraft. Do the poor gain much from these actions? Consider again such tax incentives as accelerated depreciation and the investment tax credit. Do the extra profits and jobs go to the poor, or to the rich and middle-income classes? Or take the tax exemption of interest on local government bonds (29), and reduction of tax rates on capital gains. And consider various forms of housing assistance given by the government which in 1962 amounted to twice as much for the rich as for the poor (18). All these items put money in the pockets of the rich, but rather than call them "welfare" we give them more business-like names, occasionally justifying some in the name of economic growth, and trying to hide the rest. Where is the indignant cry of the opponents of welfare when it is for large farms and corporations rather than for our poor?

And what of programs specifically designed to help the poor? An example of the fate of such programs is the story of urban renewal. Through this program—renamed "Negro removal" by its victims—more dwelling units were destroyed than were rebuilt in the 1950's and early '60s. Those homes which were built were largely more expensive than those that were destroyed—housing middle- and high-income earners at the expense of poor people (2). Those people who were not provided new homes which they could afford presumably disappeared into the already-existing quarters which they could afford—along with the people already there. Attempts to remove some of the ghetto-character of new public housing units by dispersing them throughout other residential areas are met with stiff opposition by those who imagine they would not enjoy the proximity to minority groups—including poor whites (19).

Recently, economists and social critics on the "left" and right have been agreeing on a major program of welfare assistance as a replacement for or adjunct to some existing programs: this is the "guaranteed annual income." Throughout most discussions on the benefits and possible ills of this idea, one problem remains relatively ignored: Will the standard of living provided by the guaranteed annual income be high enough to end poverty, but low enough to be afforded in economic and social terms? It has been estimated that a program to bring all families up to a level of 25% over the official poverty line (that would have been about $4600 for a family of four at the time) would cost "only" 30 billion dollars in 1968 (about 3% of our Gross National Product). (20) Using other estimates of what an "adequate" (but nonetheless below average) budget should be (about $8000 for a family of four), and the features generally proposed for a program of this type, Glick (15) suggests that the United States could not afford to allow everyone this decent standard of living without almost equalizing income and seriously damaging the necessary link between income and work in a capitalist economy, with disastrous consequences for the system. Who would do all those low paying jobs?

But these difficulties do not even arise under presently considered income-guarantee plans. When President Nixon introduced his legislative proposals under the politically attractive heading of "workfare," his income floor was $1600 a year for a family of four, and included such proposals as eliminating food stamps and forcing mothers of dependent children to accept employment. These proposals have since been shelved, and it is doubtful that any meaningful steps toward any guaranteed annual income will be taken for some time.

But while government solutions either die, become distorted or reap disastrous consequences, an important element of myth remains: the ultimate ability of capitalism to modify itself, and to embrace all segments of the population into its workings for the benefit of all. The capitalist mystique is such that our problems dissolve into attempts to give some, then others, a "piece of the rock" until none but a few malcontents remain. To a great extent, capitalism has succeeded, bringing into its fold in a systematic manner the major representatives of "the people."

Consider government regulation of business. Prior to the twentieth century, government facilitated business growth through outright gifts and by ignoring the consequences of the concentration of economic power. Then came "reform." The establishment of the major regulatory commissions in the years of Theodore Roosevelt and Woodrow Wilson, and the major role in the promotion of economic progress assumed by the New Deal of Franklin Roosevelt were supposed to be the means by which business activity was restrained to function within the boundaries of the public interest. Unfortunately, the interests served by the regulatory commissions were primarily not those of the public, but of big business itself, (23 25) while the New Deal deflected the potential upheaval from the

Depression to ways of allowing the economic contestants to work out their problems within the system which had produced the catastrophe (40).

Thus organized labor, the voice of the workingman, became accepted into the upper levels of economic decision-making. This development was celebrated by the liberal John Kenneth Galbraith (12), and has since been deified to the point where many Americans seem to believe that labor unions, through their bargaining power, lead the large corporations around on a leash. But while labor has acquired a large measure of power, as an organized force it often strongly defends the status quo (for example its resistance to desegregation at the union level, its frequent opposition to environmental measures and some significant defections to George Wallace and Richard Nixon), and not everyone agrees that its power is very significant.

For one thing, labor unions account for less than one-fourth of the American labor force, and in many industries where they are strong, they exhibit a strong degree of cooperation with the general tendencies of the large corporations (28). In short, Big Labor does not negate the power of Big Business in favor of the consumer. In fact, many consider that union leadership is by and large not even responsive to the union rank and file (34). The lesson is, perhaps, not that large size should be offset by large size, but rather that bigness in itself may be inherently harmful due to its inevitable accretions of power.

But doesn't the power of large corporations depend on their stockholders? And aren't a greater number of people becoming stockholders? Isn't "People's Capitalism" a way of controlling industry for the benefit of the little man, the consumer? The number of stockholders is indeed growing rapidly in recent years. After falling from about 10 million in 1930 to 6.5 million in 1952, the number has surged to 30 million in 1970 (38). But this number—about 15% of the population—hardly means "People's Capitalism." By 1962, when the number was 17 million, some 9% of all spending units, control of corporate wealth and power was still heavily concentrated. Only 1.6% of all stockholders owned 80% of the *value* of corporate stock, as well as 88.5% of the value of corporate bonds (24). One would be hard pressed to consider this evidence of a widening distribution of corporate power.

And still one more attempt is being made to convince poor people that the system can be made to work for them, that "self-help" is the answer to poverty, and that the society can be absolved

of its responsibility. This is the attempt to appeal to a large portion
of those victimized by American society in its own creations, the city
slums, and this time the rallying cry is "Black Capitalism."

The very idea of "Black Capitalism" appears as a contradiction
in terms to those who see black poverty and black ghettos as the
result of a capitalist system which requires such a social segregation (4),
If this analysis is correct, and certainly there is much evidence in
its favor, then black capitalism means no more than elevating a few
blacks to management and ownership positions (almost exclusively
in the ghettos) while the black proletariat and "unemployables"
remain exploited as before (6).

Further, black capitalism has advantages to the capitalist system
as a whole. First, it allows the system and the society to wash its
hands of the problem. A few loans, a few training programs and the
responsibility of the system to those it has exploited is officially
ended; black people hence should be able to make it on their own
without any basic changes required of society. Second, black capitalism maintains the exploitative link between the corporate capitalism
of the economy as a whole and the black community. Individual
entrepreneurs in the black community are linked to the rest of the
corporate structure, and are too weak to do other than to transmit
the consequences of corporate capitalism to ghetto residents. The
black community, although large and growing, nevertheless represents a minority market which, divided among small businessmen,
prevents any significant economic power from accruing to the community. In the face of these objections, many blacks are calling for
a sort of black socialism—community control of the means of production—as the only way to prevent continued subservience to white
corporate capitalism (36).

IV.

With the myths cleared away, what then are we to make of a system
that admits to a propensity for inequality and thrives on poverty?
What to suggest to a system in which modifications fail to eliminate
the problem and government programs regularly make things worse
for some and little better for others? It has been our primary intent
here to focus on the problems as a basis from which to begin the
construction of solutions. No single solution is proposed here;
indeed to do so in any detail would require volumes. But it is proper
here to indicate alternative *approaches* which have been suggested
by others. Human problems are rarely solved by single solutions,
and no doubt no "ideal system" can be established. Yet there may
be ideas which can be fruitfully pursued.

One of these approaches promises not better things, but indicates a way of thinking which will require solutions to even greater problems. Employment is a core of our present industrial system, and we have never really come to grips with it except at the height of World War II. In the late sixties, the unemployment rate was down below 3.5% for a time—a modern miracle—but we have been hovering above 5% for some time and the Nixon Administration shows signs of considering this "normal." (These are official government figures. They understate the problem by not counting part-time unemployment, those who are no longer looking for jobs because they can't be found, and those uncounted by the census. They also hide such structural problems such as rates as high as 30-40% among ghetto teenagers.) This tendency to up the "normal" unemployment rate may increase as more structural problems appear in the economy, as automation advances slowly, as population increases, and as women continue to assume their rightful place of equality in the work force and society as a whole.

A proposed solution, although rarely labelled for what it is, contemplates the provision of jobs conventionally thought of as menial and downright dirty, but under conditions and titles which give them "dignity." (See 26 for a description of a specific program to accomplish this under the Great Society.) If we specifically reject this approach, recognizing that a dirty job is a dirty job no matter what you call it, and concentrate on *eliminating* these jobs, rather than filling them with poor people (13) we drastically increase the magnitude of the problem we are dealing with. Nevertheless, this might well be an objective of a decent society.

But why stop with eliminating dirty jobs? What might be the consequence of eliminating most jobs, or at least a large number which could be conceivably handled by machine? This idea has a curious connection with the problem of eliminating poverty. It is suggested (37) that the American economy has such a great productive potential, and such a potential for mechanizing and automating, that we can afford—even need—to revise our entire ethic relating to the work-income linkage. We can perhaps eliminate the boring jobs—the ones the sociologists often refer to in their studies of worker alienation—and yet produce enough to guarantee every individual a decent life.

The economic implications of such a situation are the least of the problems. What is necessary is an entire revision of our ideas of what determines the worth of an individual, what an individual's rights may be as a member of an affluent society. Our imaginations would be put to the test in constructing alternative uses for our time. Creative people would be free to create without worrying about having to maintain themselves "productively." Non-machine jobs could provide outlets for those whose interests remained in more conventional channels. And of course the need to socialize people toward non-destructive uses of their time could claim the energies of millions.

Finally, one of the most widely debated approaches to the restructuring of our society is that of Socialism. Here we confront a series of myths centering around the idea that Socialism (and very few can even differentiate it as a concept from Communism and totalitarianism) necessarily means that all property is owned by the state, and freedom cannot exist. To many, however, Socialism implies simply that people have control over the decisions which affect their lives. This means more than voting for political representatives every two or four years. It means that the social structures, the institutions, through which people learn, work and play, are subjected to democratic control—with limitations to deny the possible tyranny of majorities so that humane values are maintained and enforced.

Few would claim that such goals are easily obtained. Human nature has always been influenced to some extent by the uncontrolled evolution of even those aspects of society which are introduced with the most benevolent of intents, let alone those which are designed to hurt. It is no easy job to organize a society, and size frequently breeds unimaginable complexity. But certainly the intentional continuation of a system whose results—however good they have been for some—are clearly detrimental to many and which to some extent may stifle us all is unthinkable.

BIBLIOGRAPHY

1. ACKERMAN, Frank, Howard Birnbaum, James Wetzler, and Andrew Zimbalist, "Income Distribution in the United States," *The Review of Radical Political Economics*, Vol. 3, No. 3, Summer, 1971.
2. ANDERSON, Martin, "The Consequences of Urban Renewal," in David Mermelstein, ed., *Economics—Mainstream Readings and Radical Critiques*, Random House, New York, 1970.
3. BARAN, Paul, *The Political Economy of Growth*, Monthly Review Press, New York, 1957.
4. ———, and Paul Sweezy, *Monopoly Capital*, Monthly Review Press, New York, 1966.
5. BELL, Carolyn Shaw, *The Economics of the Ghetto*, Pegasus, New York, 1970.
6. BOGGS, James, "The Myth and Irrationality of Black Capitalism," in Helen Ginsburg, *Poverty, Economics and Society*, Little, Brown, Boston, 1972.
7. CITIZENS' Board of Inquiry into Hunger and Malnutrition in the United States, "Hunger, U.S.A.," in David Mermelstein, ed., *Economics—Mainstream Readings and Radical Critiques*, Random House, New York, 1970.
8. CLARK Subcommittee, United States Senate, "Hunger and Malnutrition in the United States," in Helen Ginsburg, ed., *Poverty, Economics and Society*, Little, Brown, Boston, 1972.

9. COUNCIL Of Economic Advisors, "Annual Report," in the *Economic Report of the President, 1972*, U.S. Government Printing Office, Washington, 1972.
10. ECKSTEIN, Otto, *Public Finance*, 2nd edition, Prentice-Hall, Englewood Cliffs, N.J., 1967.
11. FRIEDMAN, Milton, *Capitalism and Freedom*, University of Chicago Press, Chicago, 1962.
12. GALBRAITH, John Kenneth, *American Capitalism*, Revised edition, Houghton Mifflin, Boston, 1956.
13. GANS, Herbert J., "Income Grants and 'Dirty Work,'" in David Mermelstein, ed. *Economics—Mainstream Readings and Radical Critiques*, Random House, New York, 1970.
14. ———, "The Positive Functions of Poverty," in the *American Journal of Sociology*, Vol. 78, No. 2, September, 1972.
15. GLICK, Brian, "GAI: The Guaranteed Annual Game," in David Mermelstein, ed. *Economics—Mainstream Readings and Radical Critiques*, Random House, New York, 1970.
16. GREGORY, Richard C., *No More Lies*, Harper and Row, New York, 1971.
17. HARRINGTON, Michael, *The Other America*, Penguin Books, Baltimore, 1963.
18. ———, *Toward a Democratic Left*, Penguin Books, Baltimore, 1969.
19. HARTMAN, Chester W., "The Politics of Housing," in Jeremy Larner and Irving Howe, *Poverty—Views from the Left*, William Morrow, New York, 1968.
20. HEILBRONER, Robert L., *The Economic Problem*, 3rd edition, Prentice-Hall, Englewood Cliffs, N.J., 1972.
21. KOLKO, Gabriel, "Inequality Under Capitalism," in Tom Christoffel, et. al. eds., *Up Against the American Myth*, Holt, Rinehart and Winston, New York, 1970.
22. ———, "The Myth of Progressive Taxation," in Tom Christoffel, et. al., eds., *Up Against the American Myth*, Holt, Rinehart and Winston, New York, 1970.
23. ———, "The Progressive Era: The Triumph of Conservatism," in David Mermelstein, ed., *Economics—Mainstream Readings and Radical Critiques*, Random House, New York, 1970.
24. LUNDBERG, Ferdinand, *The Rich and The Super-Rich*, Bantam Books, New York, 1968.
25. McCONNELL, Grant, "Self-Regulation: The Politics of Business," in David Mermelstein, ed., *Economics—Mainstream Readings and Radical Critiques*, Random House, New York, 1970.
26. MINNIS, Jack, "How the Great Society Solves the Servant Problem," in Marvin Gettleman and David Mermelstein, eds., *The Great Society Reader—The Failure of American Liberalism*, Vintage Books, New York, 1967.
27. NATIONAL Advisory Commission on Civil Disorders, "Comparing the Immigrant and Negro Experience," in David Mermelstein, ed., *Economics—Mainstream Readings and Radical Critiques*, Random House, New York, 1970.
28. NOSSITER, Bernard D., "Corporate Dominance and the Myth of Pluralism," in Tom Christoffel, et. al., eds., *Up Against the American Myth*, Holt, Rinehart and Winston, New York, 1970.
29. OTT, David and Attiat, "The Tax Subsidy Through Exemption of State and Local Bond Interest," in *The Economics of Federal Subsidy Programs*, submitted to the Joint Economic Committee, Congress of the United States, U.S. Government Printing Office, Washington, 1972.
30. PECHMAN, Joseph A., "The Rich, the Poor, and the Taxes They Pay," in Lloyd Reynolds, et. al., eds., *Current Issues of Economic Policy*, Richard D. Irwin, Homewood, Illinois, 1973.
31. ———, and Benjamin A. Okner, "Individual Tax Erosion by Income Class," in *The Economics of Federal Subsidy Programs*, submitted to the Joint Economic Committee, Congress of the United States, U.S. Government Printing Office, Washington, 1972.
32. PERLO, Victor, "'People's Capitalism' and Stock-Ownership," in David Mermelstein, ed., *Economics—Mainstream Readings and Radical Critiques*, Random House, New York, 1970.
33. PRESIDENT'S Commission on Income Maintenance Programs, "The Meaning of Poverty," in Helen Ginsburg, ed., *Poverty, Economics and Society*, Little, Brown, Boston, 1972.

34. SAYLES, Leonard R., and George Strauss, *The Local Union*, Harcourt, Brace and World, New York, 1967.
35. SELIGMAN, Ben B., "The Poverty of Aging," in Jeremy Larner and Irving Howe, eds., *Poverty—Views from The Left*, William Morrow, New York, 1968.
36. TABB, William K., *The Political Economy of the Black Ghetto*, W.W. Norton, New York, 1970.
37. THEOBALD, Robert, *Free Men and Free Markets*, Anchor Books, Garden City, New York, 1965.
38. U.S. BUREAU of the Census, *Statistical Abstract of the United States: 1972* (93rd edition), Washington, D.C., 1972.
39. U.S. DEPARTMENT of the Treasury, Internal Revenue Service, Publication 198 (2-72), Preliminary 1970 *Statistics of Income, Individual Income Tax Returns (S of I)*, Washington, 1972.
40. WILEY, Brad, "The Myth of New Deal Reform," in Tom Christoffel, et. al., eds., *Up Against the American Myth*, Holt, Rinehart and Winston, New York, 1970.

12. SOME CONDITIONS OF OBEDIENCE AND DISOBEDIENCE TO AUTHORITY

STANLEY MILGRAM

The situation in which one agent commands another to hurt a third turns up time and again as a significant theme in human relations. It is powerfully expressed in the story of Abraham, who is commanded by God to kill his son. It is no accident that Kierkegaard (1843), seeking to orient his thought to the central themes of human experience, chose Abraham's conflict as the springboard to his philosophy.

War too moves forward on the triad of an authority which commands a person to destroy the enemy, and perhaps all organized hostility may be viewed as a theme and variation on the three elements of authority, executant, and victim. We describe an experimental program, recently concluded at Yale University, in which a particular expression of this conflict is studied by experimental means. . . .

One aim of the research was to study behavior in a strong situation of deep consequence to the participants, for the psychological forces operative in powerful and lifelike forms of the conflict may not be brought into play under diluted conditions.

This approach meant, first, that we had a special obligation to protect the welfare and dignity of the persons who took part in the study; subjects were, of necessity, placed in a difficult predicament, and steps had to be taken to ensure their wellbeing before they were discharged from the laboratory. Toward this end, a careful post-experimental treatment was devised and has been carried through for subjects in all conditions.[1]

Reprinted from *Human Relations*, Vol. 18, (1965), pp. 57-75, by permission of the author and the publisher, Fred B. Rothman & Co. c/o John Harvard-Watts.

TERMINOLOGY

If Y follows the command of X we shall say that he has obeyed X; if he fails to carry out the command of X, we shall say that he has disobeyed X. The terms *to obey* and *to disobey*, as used here, refer to the subject's overt action only, and carry no implication for the motive or experimental states accompanying the action. . . .

A subject who complies with the entire series of experimental commands will be termed an *obedient* subject; one who at any point in the command series defies the experimenter will be called a *disobedient* or *defiant* subject. As used in this report, the terms refer only to the subject's performance in the experiment, and do not necessarily imply a general personality disposition to submit to or reject authority.

SUBJECT POPULATION

The subjects used in all experimental conditions were male adults, residing in the greater New Haven and Bridgeport areas, aged 20 to 50 years, and engaged in a wide variety of occupations. Each experimental condition described in this report employed 40 fresh subjects and was carefully balanced for age and occupational types. The occupational composition for each experiment was: workers, skilled and unskilled: 40 per cent; white collar, sales, business: 40 per cent; professionals: 20 per cent. The occupations were intersected with three age categories (subjects in 20s, 30s, and 40s, assigned to each condition in the proportions of 20, 40, and 40 percent respectively).

THE GENERAL LABORATORY PROCEDURE

The focus of the study concerns the amount of electric shock a subject is willing to administer to another person when ordered by an experimenter to give the 'victim' increasingly more severe punishment. The act of administering shock is set in the context of a learning experiment, ostensibly designed to study the effect of punishment on memory. Aside from the experimenter, one naive subject and one accomplice perform in each session. On arrival each subject is paid $4.50. After a general talk by the experimenter, telling how little scientists know about the effect of punishment on memory, subjects are informed that one member of the pair will serve as teacher and one as learner. A rigged drawing is held so that the naive subject is always the teacher, and the accomplice becomes the learner. The learner is taken to an adjacent room and strapped into an "electric chair."

The naive subject is told that it is his task to teach the learner a list of paired associates, to test him on the list, and to administer punishment whenever the learner errs in the test. Punishment takes the form of electric shock, delivered to the learner by means of a shock generator controlled by the naive subject. The teacher is instructed to increase the intensity of electric shock one step on the generator on each error. The learner, according to plan, provides many wrong answers, so that before long the naive subject must give him the strongest shock on the generator. Increases in shock level are met by increasingly insistent demands from the learner that the experiment be stopped because of the growing discomfort to him. However, in clear terms the experimenter orders the teacher to continue with the procedure in disregard of the learner's protests. *Thus, the naive subject must resolve a conflict between two mutually incompatible demands from the social field. He may continue to follow the orders of the experimenter and shock the learner with increasing severity, or he may refuse to follow the orders of the experimenter and heed the learner's pleas. The experimenter's authority operates not in a free field, but against evermounting countervailing pressures from the person being punished.*

A few technical points need to be considered before the findings of the study are described. For the purpose of delivering shock, a simulated shock generator is used, with 30 clearly marked voltage levels that range from 15 to 450 volts (and each activated by one of 30 individual lever switches set in a horizontal line). The naive subject is given a sample shock of 45 volts to convince him of the authenticity of the instrument. The generator bears verbal designations that range from "Slight Shock" to "Danger: Severe Shock."

The responses of the victim are standardized on tape, and each protest is coordinated to a particular voltage level on the shock generator. Starting with 75 volts the learner begins to grunt and moan. At 150 volts he demands to be let out of the experiment. At 180 volts he cries out that he can no longer stand the pain. At 300 volts he refuses to provide any more answers to the memory test, insisting that he is no longer a participant in the experiment and must be freed. In response to this last tactic, the experimenter instructs the naive subject to treat the absence of an answer as equivalent to a wrong answer, and to follow the usual shock procedure. The experimenter reinforces his demand with the statement: "You have no other choice, you must go on!" (This imperative is used whenever the naive subject tries to break off the experiment.) If the subject refuses to give the next higher level of shock, the experiment is considered at an end. A quantitative value is assigned to the subject's performance based on the maximum intensity shock he administered before breaking off. Thus any subject's score may range from zero (for a subject unwilling to administer the first shock level) to 30 (for a subject who proceeds to the highest voltage level on the board). For any particular subject and for any particular experimental condition the degree to which participants have followed the experimenter's orders may be specified with a numerical value, corresponding to the metric on the shock generator. . . .

PILOT STUDIES

Pilot studies for the present research were completed in the winter of 1960; they differed from the regular experiments in a few details; for one, the victim was placed behind a silvered glass, with the light balance on the glass such that the victim could be dimly perceived by the subject (Milgram, 1961).

Though essentially qualitative in treatment, these studies pointed to several significant features of the experimental situation. At first no vocal feedback was used from the victim. It was thought that the verbal and voltage designations on the control panel would create sufficient pressure to curtail the subject's obedience. However, this was not the case. In the absence of protests from the learner, virtually all subjects, once commanded, went blithely to the end of the board, seemingly indifferent to the verbal designations ("Extreme Shock" and "Danger: Severe Shock"). This deprived us of an adequate basis for scaling obedient tendencies. A force had to be introduced that would strengthen the subject's resistance to the experimenter's commands, and reveal individual differences in terms of a distribution of breakoff points.

This force took the form of protests from the victim. Initially, mild protests were used, but proved inadequate. Subsequently, more vehement protests were inserted into the experimental procedure. To our consternation, even the strongest protests from the victim did not prevent all subjects from administering the harshest punishment ordered by the experimenter; but the protests did lower the mean maximum shock somewhat and created some spread in the subject's performance; therefore, the victim's cries were standardized on tape and incorporated into the regular experimental procedure.

The situation did more than highlight the technical difficulties of finding a workable experimental procedure: it indicated that subjects would obey authority to a greater extent than we had sup-

posed. It also pointed to the importance of feedback from the victim in controlling the subject's behavior.

One further aspect of the pilot study was that subjects frequently averted their eyes from the person they were shocking, often turning their heads in an awkward and conspicuous manner. One subject explained: "I didn't want to see the consequences of what I had done."

This suggested that the salience of the victim may have, in some degree, regulated the subject's performance. If, in obeying the experimenter, the subject found it necessary to avoid scrutiny of the victim, would the converse be true? If the victim were rendered increasingly more salient to the subject, would obedience diminish? The first set of regular experiments was designed to answer this question.

IMMEDIACY OF THE VICTIM

This series consisted of four experimental conditions. In each condition the victim was brought "psychologically" closer to the subject giving him shocks.

In the first condition (Remote Feedback) the victim was placed in another room and could not be heard or seen by the subject, except that, at 300 volts, he pounded on the wall in protest. After 315 volts he no longer answered or was heard from.

The second condition (Voice Feedback) was identical to the first except that voice protests were introduced. As in the first condition the victim was placed in an adjacent room, but his complaints could be heard clearly through a door left slightly ajar, and through the walls of the laboratory.[2]

The third experimental condition (Proximity) was similar to the second, except that the victim was now placed in the same room as the subject, and 1½ feet from him. Thus he was visible as well as audible, and voice cues were provided.

The fourth, and final, condition of the series (Touch-Proximity) was identical to the third, with this exception: the victim received a shock only when his hand rested on a shockplate. At the 150-volt level the victim again demanded to be let free and, in this condition, refused to place his hand on the shockplate. The experimenter ordered the naïve subject to force the victim's hand onto the plate. Thus obedience in this condition required that the subject have physical contact with the victim in order to give him punishment beyond the 150-volt level.

Forty adult subjects were studied in each condition. The data revealed that obedience was significantly reduced as the victim was rendered more immediate to the subject. . . .

Expressed in terms of the proportion of obedient to defiant subjects, the findings are that 34 per cent of the subjects defied the experimenter in the Remote condition, 37.5 percent in Voice Feedback, 60 per cent in Proximity, and 70 percent in Touch-Proximity.

How are we to account for this effect? A first conjecture might be that as the victim was brought closer the subject became more aware of the intensity of his suffering and regulated his behavior accordingly. This makes sense, but our evidence does not support the interpretation. There are no consistent differences in the attributed level of pain across the four conditions (i.e. the amount of pain experienced by the victim as estimated by the subject and expressed on a 14-point scale). But it is easy to speculate about alternative mechanisms.

EMPATHIC CUES

In the Remote and to a lesser extent the Voice Feedback condition, the victim's suffering possesses an abstract, remote quality for the subject. He is aware, but only in a conceptual sense, that his actions cause pain to another person; the fact is apprehended, but not felt. . . . It is possible that the visual cues associated with the victim's suffering trigger empathic responses in the subject and provide him with a more complete grasp of the victim's experience. Or it is possible that the empathic responses are themselves unpleasant, possessing drive properties which cause the subject to terminate the arousal situation. Diminishing obedience, then, would be explained by the enrichment of empathic cues in the successive experimental conditions.

Denial and Narrowing of the Cognitive Field

The Remote condition allows a narrowing of the cognitive field so that the victim is put out of mind. The subject no longer considers the act of depressing a lever relevant to moral judgement, for it is no longer associated with the victim's suffering. When the victim is close it is more difficult to exclude him phenomenologically. He necessarily intrudes on the subject's awareness since he is continuously visible. In the Remote conditions, his existence and reactions are made known only after the shock has been administered. The auditory feedback is sporadic and discontinuous. In the Proximity conditions his inclusion in the immediate visual field renders him a continuously salient element for the subject. The mechanism of denial can no longer be brought into play. One subject in the Remote condition said: "It's funny how you really begin to forget that there's a guy out there, even though you can hear him. For a long time I just concentrated on pressing the switches and reading the words."

Reciprocal Fields

If in the Proximity condition the subject is in an improved position to observe the victim, the reverse is also true. The actions of the subject now come under proximal scrutiny by the victim. Possibly, it is easier to harm a person when he is unable to observe our actions than when he can see what we are doing. His surveillance of the action directed against him may give rise to shame, or guilt, which may then serve to curtail the action. Many expressions of language refer to the discomfort or inhibitions that arise in face-to-face confrontation. It is often said that it is easier to criticize a man "behind his back" than to "attack him to his face". . . . In short, in the Proximity condition, the subject may sense that he has become more salient in the victim's field of awareness. Possibly he becomes more self-conscious, embarrassed, and inhibited in his punishment of the victim.

Phenomenal Unity of Act

In the Remote condition it is more difficult for the subject to gain a sense of *relatedness* between his own actions and the consequences of these actions for the victim. There is a physical and spatial separation of the act and its consequences. The subject depresses a lever in one room, and protests and cries are heard from another. The two events are in correlation, yet they lack a compelling phenomenological unity. The structure of a meaningful act—*I am hurting a man*—breaks down because of the spatial arrangements, in a manner somewhat analogous to the disappearance of phi phenomena when the blinking lights are spaced too far apart. The unity is more fully achieved in the Proximity condition as the victim is brought closer to the action that causes him pain. It is rendered complete in Touch-Proximity.

Incipient Group Formation

Placing the victim in another room not only takes him further from the subject, but the subject and the experimenter are drawn relatively closer. There is incipient group formation between the experimenter and the subject, from which the victim is excluded. The wall between the victim and the others deprives him of an intimacy which the experimenter and subject feel. In the Remote condition, the victim is truly an outsider, who stands alone, physically and psychologically.

When the victim is placed close to the subject, it becomes easier to form an alliance with him against the experimenter. Subjects no longer have to face the experimenter alone. They have an ally who is close at hand and eager to collaborate in a revolt against the experimenter. Thus the changing set of spatial relations leads to a potentially shifting set of alliances over the several experimental conditions.

Acquired Behavior Dispositions

It is commonly observed that laboratory mice will rarely fight with the litter mates. Scott (1958) explains this in terms of passive inhibition. He writes: "By doing nothing under . . . circumstances [the animal] learns to do nothing, and this may be spoken of as passive inhibition . . . this principle has great importance in teaching an individual to be peaceful, for it means that he can learn not to fight simply by not fighting." Similarly, we may learn not to harm others simply by not harming them in everyday life. Yet this learning occurs in a context of proximal relations with others, and may not be generalized to that situation in which the person is physically removed from us. Or possibly, in the past, aggressive actions against others who were physically close resulted in retaliatory punishment which extinguished the original form of response. In contrast, aggression against others at a distance may have only sporadically led to retaliation. Thus the organism learns that it is safer to be aggressive toward others at a distance, and precarious to be so when the parties are within arm's reach. Through a pattern of rewards and punishments, he acquires a disposition to avoid aggression at close quarters, a disposition which does not extend to harming others at a distance. And this may account for experimental findings in the remote and proximal experiments. . . .

CLOSENESS OF AUTHORITY

If the spatial relationship of the subject and victim is relevant to the degree of obedience, would not the relationship of subject to experimenter also play a part?

There are reasons to feel that, on arrival, the subject is oriented primarily to the experimenter rather than to the victim. He has come to the laboratory to fit into the structure that the experimenter—not the victim—would provide. He has come less to understand his behavior than to *reveal* that behavior to a competent scientist, and he is willing to display himself as the scientist's purposes require. Most subjects seem quite concerned about the appearance they are making before the experimenter, and one could argue that this preoccupation in a relatively new and strange setting makes the subject somewhat insensitive to the triadic nature of the social situation. In other words, the subject is so concerned about the show he is putting on for the experimenter that influences from other parts of the social field do not receive as much weight as they ordinarily would. This overdetermined orientation to the experimenter would account for the relative insensitivity of the subject to the victim, and would also lead us to believe that alterations in the relationship between subject and experimenter would have important consequences for obedience.

In a series of experiments we varied the physical closeness and degree of surveillance of the experimenter. In one condition the experimenter sat just a few feet away from the subject. In a second condition, after giving initial instructions, the experimenter left the laboratory and gave his orders by telephone; in still a third condition the experimenter was never seen, providing instructions by means of a tape recording activated when the subjects entered the laboratory.

Obedience dropped sharply as the experimenter was physically removed from the laboratory. The number of obedient subjects in the first condition (Experimenter Present) was almost three times as great as in the second, where the experimenter gave his orders by telephone. Twenty-six subjects were fully obedient in the first condition, and only 9 in the second (Chi square obedient *vs.* defiant in the two conditions, $1 \, df = 14.7; \, p < .001$). Subjects seemed able to take a far stronger stand against the experimenter when they did not have to encounter him face to face, and the experimenter's power over the subject was severely curtailed.

Moreover, when the experimenter was absent, subjects displayed an interesting form of behavior that had not occurred under his surveillance. Though continuing with the experiment, several subjects administered lower shocks than were required and never informed the experimenter of their deviation from the correct procedure. (Unknown to the subjects, shock levels were automatically recorded by an Esterline-Angus event recorder wired directly into the shock generator; the instrument provided us with an objective record of the subject's performance.) Indeed, in telephone conversations some subjects specifically assured the experimenter that they were raising the shock level according to instruction, whereas in fact they were repeatedly using the lowest shock on the board. This form of behavior is particularly interesting; although these subjects acted in a way that clearly undermined the avowed purposes of the experiment, they found it easier to handle the conflict in this manner than to precipitate an open break with authority.

Other conditions were completed in which the experimenter was absent during the first segment of the experiment, but reappeared at the point that the subject definitely refused to give higher shocks when commanded by telephone. Although he had exhausted his power via telephone, the experimenter could frequently force further obedience when he reappeared in the laboratory.

Experiments in this series show that the physical *presence* of an authority is an important force contributing to the subject's obedience or defiance. Taken together with the first experimental series on the proximity of the victim, it would appear that something akin to fields of force, diminishing in effectiveness with increasing psychological distance from their source, have a controlling effect on the subject's performance. As the victim is brought closer, the subject finds it harder to administer shocks to him. When the victim's position is held constant relative to the subject, and the authority is made more remote, the subject finds it easier to break off the experiment. This effect is substantial in both cases, the manipulation of the experimenter's position yielded the more powerful results. . . .

TENSIONS

The description of final scores does not fully convey the character of the subjects' performance, and it would be useful to interrupt our reporting of quantitative relationships to remark on the subjects' general reaction to the situation.

One might suppose that a subject would simply break off or continue as his conscience and temperament dictated. Yet this is very far from what happened. There were powerful reactions of tension and emotional strain in a substantial proportion of the participants. Persons were observed to sweat, tremble, stutter, bite their lips, and groan as they found themselves increasingly implicated in the experimental conflict. Some sense of the subjects' mood can be gotten from a transcript of their remarks at breakoff point. Here are the remarks of two defiant subjects:

> Is he banging? . . . Is he hurt out there? Well, I don't want to be responsible for anything that happens to him. No, I can't go on with it. I don't know whether he's all right or not. I mean he may have a heart condition or something; I wouldn't feel right doing it. He's banging for help. He's evidently in trouble or he wouldn't bang . . . I don't see any sense to this—to knocking him out or something. I just can't see it.
>
> *(Subject refuses to administer shocks) (Subject 0108)*

> The man is banging. He wants to get out . . . I'm sorry. If the man wants to get out I'd just as soon stop . . . I don't want to administer any more [extremely excited] . . . I will gladly refund the check, but I will not harm this man . . . I'm sorry, I will not give him any more if he obviously wartts to get out. There is no money in the world that will make me hurt another individual. *(Subject 010X)*

And here is a transcript from an obedient subject. He began the experiment calmly, but became increasingly tense as the experiment proceeded. After administering the 150-volt shock, he began to address the experimenter in agitated tones:

> *150 volts delivered.* You want me to keep going?
> *165 volts delivered.* That guy is hollering in there. There's a lot of them here. He's liable to have heart condition. You want me to go on?
> *180 volts delivered.* He can't stand it! I'm not going to kill that man in there! You hear him hollering? He's hollering. He can't stand it. What if something happens to him? . . . I'm not going to get that man sick in there. He's hollering in there. You know what I mean? I mean I refuse to take responsibility. He's getting hurt in there. He's in there hollering. Too many left here. Geez, if he gets them wrong. There's too many of them left. I mean who is going to take responsibility if anything happens to that gentleman?
> *(The experimenter accepts responsibility.)* All right.
> *195 volts delivered.* You see he's hollering. Hear that. Gee. I don't know. *(The experimenter says: "The experiment requires that you go on.")* —I know it does, sir, but I mean—hugh—he don't know what he's in for. He's up to 195 volts.
> *210 volts delivered*
> *225 volts delivered*
> *240 volts delivered.* Aw, no. You mean I've got to keep going up with the scale? No sir. I'm not going to kill that man! I'm not going to give him 450 volts! *(The experimenter says: "The experiment requires that you go on.")*—I know it does, but that man is hollering in there, sir . . .

Despite his numerous, agitated objections, which were constant accompaniments to his actions, the subject unfailingly obeyed the experimenter, proceeding to the highest shock level on the generator. He displayed a curious dissociation between word and action. Although at the verbal level he had resolved not to go on, his actions were fully in accord with the experimenter's commands. This subject did not want to shock the victim, and he found it an extremely disagreeable task, but he was unable to invent a response that would free him from the experimenter's authority. Many subjects cannot find the specific verbal formula that would enable them to reject the role assigned to them by the experimenter. Perhaps our culture does not provide adequate models for disobedience.

One puzzling sign of tension was the regular occurrence of nervous laughing fits. In the first four conditions 71 of the 160 subjects showed definite signs of nervous laughter and smiling. The laughter seemed entirely out of place, even bizarre. Full-blown, uncontrollable seizures were observed for 15 of these subjects. On one occasion we observed a seizure so violently convulsive that it was necessary to call a halt to the experiment. In the post-experimental interviews subjects took pains to point out that they were not sadistic types and that the laughter did not mean they enjoyed shocking the victim.

In the interview following the experiment subjects were asked to indicate on a 14-point scale just how nervous or tense they felt at the point of maximum tension. . . . [O]bedient subjects reported themselves as having been slightly more tense and nervous than the defiant subjects at the point of maximum tension. . . .

BACKGROUND AUTHORITY

In psychophysics, animal learning, and other branches of psychology, the fact that measures are obtained at one institution rather than another is irrelevant to the interpretation of the findings, so long as the technical facilities for measurement are adequate and the operations are carried out with competence.

But it cannot be assumed that this holds true for the present study. The effectiveness of the experimenter's commands may depend in an important way on the larger institutional context in which they are issued. The experiments described thus far were conducted at Yale University, an organization which most subjects regarded with respect and sometimes awe. In post-experimental interviews several participants remarked that the locale and sponsorship of the study gave them confidence in the integrity, competence, and benign purposes of the personnel; many indicated that they would not have shocked the learner if the experiments had been done elsewhere.

This issue of background authority seemed to us important for an interpretation of the results that had been obtained thus far; moreover it is highly relevant to any comprehensive theory of human obedience. Consider, for example, how closely our compliance with the imperatives of others is tied to particular institutions and locales in our day-to-day activities. On request, we expose our throats to a man with a razor blade in the barber shop, but would not do so in a shoe store; in the latter setting we willingly follow the clerk's request to stand in our stockinged feet, but resist the command in a bank. . . . *One must always question the relationship of obedience to a person's sense of the context in which he is operating.*

To explore the problem we moved our apparatus to an office building in industrial Bridgeport and replicated experimental conditions, without any visible tie to the university. . . . The experiments were conducted in a three-room office suite in a somewhat run-down commercial building located in the downtown shopping area. The laboratory was sparsely furnished, though clean, and marginally respectable in appearance. When subjects inquired about professional affiliations, they were informed only that we were a private firm conducting research for industry. . . .

As it turned out, the level of obedience in Bridgeport, although somewhat reduced, was not significantly lower than that obtained at Yale. A large proportion of the Bridgeport subjects were fully obedient to the experimenter's commands (48 percent of the Bridgeport subjects delivered the maximum shock *vs.* 65 percent in the corresponding condition at Yale). . . .

LEVELS OF OBEDIENCE AND DEFIANCE

. . . The proportion of obedient subjects greatly exceeded the expectations of the experimenter and his colleagues. At the outset, we had conjectured that subjects would not, in general, go above the level of "Strong Shock." In practice, many subjects were willing to administer the most extreme shocks available when commanded by the experimenter. For some subjects the experiment provides an occasion for aggressive release. And for others it demonstrates the extent to which obedient dispositions are deeply ingrained, and are engaged irrespective of their consequences for others. Yet this is not the whole story. Somehow, the subject becomes implicated in a situation from which he cannot disengage himself. . . .

In Figure 1, we compare the predictions of forty psychiatrists at a leading medical school with the actual performance of subjects in the experiment. The psychiatrists predicted that most subjects would not go beyond the tenth shock level (150 volts; at this point the victim makes his first explicit demand to be freed). They further predicted that by the twentieth shock level (300 volts; the victim refuses to answer) 3.73 percent of the subjects would still be obedient; and that only a little over one-tenth of one percent of the subjects would administer the highest shock on the board. But, as the graph indicates, the obtained behavior was very different. Sixty-two percent of the subjects obeyed the experimenter's commands fully. Between expectation and occurrence there is a whopping discrepancy.

Why did the psychiatrists underestimate the level of obedience? Possibly, because their predictions were based on an inadequate conception of the determinants of human action, a conception that focuses on motives *in vacuo*. This orientation may be entirely adequate for the repair of bruised impulses as revealed on the psychiatrist's couch, but as soon as our interest turns to action in larger settings, attention must be paid to the situations in which motives are expressed. A situation exerts an important press on the individual. It exercises constraints and may provide push. In certain circumstances it is not so much the kind of person a man is, as the kind of situation in which he is placed, that determines his actions.

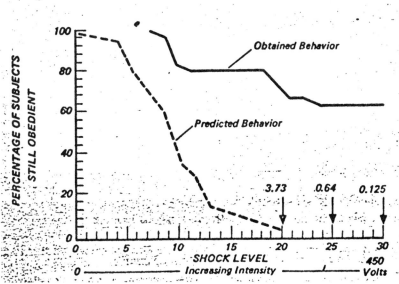

Figure 1. Predicted and Obtained Behavior in Voice Feedback

Many people, not knowing much about the experiment, claim that subjects who go to the end of the board are sadistic. Nothing could be more foolish as an overall characterization of these persons. It is like saying that a person thrown into a swift-flowing stream is necessarily a fast swimmer, or that he has great stamina because he moves so rapidly relative to the bank. The context of action must always be considered. The individual, upon entering the laboratory, becomes integrated into a situation that carries its own momentum. The subject's problem then is how to become disengaged from a situation which is moving in an altogether ugly direction.

The fact that disengagement is so difficult testifies to the potency of the forces that keep the subject at the control board. Are these forces to be conceptualized as individual motives and expressed in the language of personality dynamics, or are they to be seen as the effects of social structure and pressures arising from the situational field?

A full understanding of the subject's action will, I feel, require that both perspectives be adopted. The person brings to the laboratory enduring dispositions toward authority and aggression, and at the same time he becomes enmeshed in a social structure that is no less an objective fact of the case. . . .

But whatever the motives involved—and it is far from certain that they can ever be known—action may be studied as a direct function of the situation in which it occurs. This has been the approach of the present study, where we sought to plot behavioral regularities against manipulated properties of the social field. Ultimately, social psychology would like to have a compelling *theory of situations* which will, first, present a language in terms of which situations can be defined; proceed to a typology of situations; and then point to the manner in which definable properties of situations are transformed into psychological forces in the individual.

POSTSCRIPT

. . . With numbing regularity good people were seen to knuckle under the demands of authority and perform actions that were callous and severe. Men who are in everyday life responsible and decent were seduced by the trappings of authority, by the control of their perceptions, and by the uncritical acceptance of the experimenter's definition of the situation, into performing harsh acts. . . .

The results, as seen and felt in the laboratory, are to this author disturbing. They raise the possibility that human nature, or—more specifically—the kind of character produced in American democratic society, cannot be counted on to insulate its citizens from brutality and inhumane treatment at the direction of malevolent authority. . . .

In an article titled "The Dangers of Obedience," Harold J. Laski (1929) wrote:

> . . . civilization means, above all, an unwillingness to inflict unnecessary pain. Within the ambit of that definition, those of us who heedlessly accept the commands of authority cannot yet claim to be civilized men.
>
> . . . Our business, if we desire to live a life not utterly devoid of meaning and significance, is to accept nothing which contradicts our basic experience merely because it comes to us from tradition or convention or authority. It may well be that we shall be wrong; but our self-expression is thwarted at the root unless the certainties we are asked to accept coincide with the certainties we experience. That is why the condition of freedom in any state is always a widespread and consistent skepticism of the canons upon which power insists.

NOTES

1. It consisted of an extended discussion with the experimenter and, of equal importance, a friendly reconciliation with the victim. It is made clear that the victim did not receive painful electric shocks. After the completion of the experimental series, subjects were sent a detailed report of the results and full purposes of the experimental program. A formal assessment of this procedure points to its overall effectiveness. Of the subjects, 83.7 percent indicated that they were glad to have taken part in the study; 15.1 percent reported neutral feelings; and 1.3 percent stated that they were sorry to have participated. A large number of subjects spontaneously requested that they be used in further experimentation. Four fifths of the subjects felt that more experiments of this sort should be carried out, and 74 percent indicated that they had learned something of personal importance as a result of being in the study. Furthermore, a university psychiatrist, experienced in outpatient treatment, interviewed a sample of experimental subjects with the aim of uncovering possible injurious effects resulting from participation. No such effects were in evidence. Indeed, subjects typically felt that their participation was instructive and enriching.

2. It is difficult to convey on the printed page the full tenor of the victim's responses, for we have no adequate notation for vocal intensity, timing, and general qualities of delivery. Yet these features are crucial to producing the effect of an increasingly severe reaction to mounting voltage levels. (They can be communicated fully only by sending interested parties the recorded tapes.) In general terms, however, the victim indicates no discomfort until the 75-volt shock is administered, at which time there is a light grunt in response to the punishment. Similar reactions follow the 90- and 105-volt shocks, and at 120 volts the victim shouts to the experimenter that the shocks are becoming painful. Painful groans are heard on administration of the 135-volt shock, and at 150 volts the victim cries out, "Experimenter, get me out of here! I won't be in the experiment any more! I refuse to go on!" Cries of this type continue with generally rising intensity, so that at 180 volts the victim cries out, "I can't stand the pain," and by 270 volts his response to the shock is definitely an agonized scream. Throughout, he insists that he be let out of the experiment. At 300 volts the victim shouts in desperation that he will no longer

provide answers to the memory test; and at 315 volts, after a violent scream, he reaffirms with vehemence that he is no longer a participant. From this point on, he provides no answers, but shrieks in agony whenever a shock is administered; this continues through 450 volts. Of course, many subjects will have broken off before this point.

Part IV

STRATIFICATION

The rich man eats when he wishes, the poor man
when he can.

Peter, Paul and Mary

If you are not careful, the newspapers will have you
hating the people who are being oppressed and loving the people who are doing the oppressing.

Malcolm X

Introduction to Part IV
(Stratification)

Every known human group, particularly the modern industrial society, stratifies its members according to certain criteria which are
structurally defined. For the student of society, an understanding of
the social classes is of fundamental importance. To understand social
classes, and their consequences for the individual, means appreciation of the importance of social structure.

One's social class determines one's life chances. The aforemen-
tioned statement seems to contradict the American dream of class-
lessness. There is sufficient evidence, however, to justify this contradiction and state as a fact that the American dream, so far, has
been at best only a dream.

Professor Antonovsky's article, "Social Class, Life Expectancy,
and Overall Mortality," presents statistical data of some thirty studies
from Western countries. The data suggest the importance of social
class as a factor determining one's life expectancy and life chances.

The second selection in this section, "Caste in India and the
United States," by Professor Berreman, illustrates the existence of a
"caste" system in the Southern portion of the United States. This
rather closed system, Berreman points out, is a function of race, as
well as economic inequality.

The last article in this section, "The Positive Functions of Poverty," by Professor Herbert Gans, demonstrates another dimension of the stratification system: the functionalist perspective and its implications from a structural point of view.

13. SOCIAL CLASS, LIFE EXPECTANCY AND OVERALL MORTALITY*

Aaron Antonovsky

. . . recalling what happened when an "unsinkable" trans-Atlantic luxury liner, the *Titanic*, rammed an iceberg on her maiden voyage in 1912 . . . The official casualty lists showed that only 4 first class female passengers (3 voluntarily chose to stay on the ship) of a total of 143 were lost. Among the second class passengers, 15 of 93 females drowned; and among the third class, 81 of 179 female passengers went down with the ship.[1]

Death is the final lot of all living beings. But, as the tragic experience of the *Titanic* passengers dramatically illustrates, the time at which one dies is related to one's class. The intent of this paper is to examine the evidence which bears upon the closeness of this relationship, ranging as far back as the data will allow. It will first focus on the question of life expectancy at birth, and subsequently turn to that of overall mortality.

STUDIES OF LIFE EXPECTANCY

The average infant born today in the Western world can look forward, barring unforeseen events and radical changes in present trends, to a life span of about 70 years. That this has not always been the case for the human infant—and still is not for by far most infants born today—is well known. Whatever the situation prior to the era of recorded history, for the greater part of this era, that is, until the nineteenth century, most men lived out less than half their Biblical span of years.

In what is probably the first study of a total population, Halley, using data for the city of Breslau, Germany, for 1687 to 1691, calculated an average life expectancy at birth of 33.5 years.[2] Henry's estimate for the expectation of life of Parisian children born at the beginning of the eighteenth century was 23.5 years.[3] Half a century later, in the Vienna of 1752 to 1755, of every 1,000 infants born alive,

Reprinted from the *Milbank Memorial Fund Quarterly*, Vol. XLV, No. 2, April, 1967, by permission of the publisher, Milbank Memorial Fund Quarterly.

only 590 survived their first year, 413 their fifth year, and 359 their fifteenth year.[4] . . .

Ansell found a life expectation at birth for the total British population in 1874 of about 43 years.[5] At about the same time, the reported figures for Italy were somewhat lower: 35 years (1871 to 1880); 36.2 years for males, 35.65 years for females (1881-1882).[6]

Whatever the discrepancies and unreliabilities of these various sets of data, they consistently paint a picture of the Western world up to recent centuries which is quite similar to that of the world of presently "developing" societies until the last decade or two. Moreover, in the period of recorded history prior to the eighteenth century, no sizable increment had been added to the average life span. But if, from Greco-Roman times through the eighteenth or perhaps even the nineteenth century, the mythical "average" infant could anticipate living some 20 to 30 years, does any evidence indicate that dramatic class differences existed? Though the evidence is perforce limited, the answer would seem to be no.[7]

In other words, given a society which, though it manages to survive, does so at or near what might be called a rock-bottom level of life expectancy, one is not likely to find great differences among the strata of that society.

The data suggest the possibility that the trend in the nineteenth century, and perhaps even earlier, was toward a substantial widening of class differences. No report is available comparing the life expectancies of social strata of the population prior to the nineteenth century.

Can any conclusion be drawn from these data,[8] most of which are admittedly tenuous and not overly reliable? A crude picture . . . could be inferred which indicates the following. The bulk of recorded history was one of high birth and high death rates, which offset each other and led to at most a very small increase in population. During the first 16 centuries of the Christian era, world population increased from about one-quarter to one-half billion people, an annual growth rate of about .005 per cent. Conceivably, throughout this period, no substantial differentials in life expectancy could be found among different social strata of the population. From 1650 to 1850 world population again doubled, most of the increase being in the Western world, representing an average annual increase of .05 per cent. These two centuries would seem to mark the emergence of an increasing class gap in life expectancy, starting slowly but gathering increasing momentum and reaching its peak about the time Malthus made his observations. On the one hand, the life expectancy of the middle and upper strata of the population increased at a rapid rate. On the other, the lowest strata's life expectancy may have increased much more slowly or, conceivably, even declined as an industrial proletariat emerged. At some time during the nineteenth century, probably in the latter half, this trend was reversed, and the class gap began to diminish. This is reflected in the doubling of the world's population, again mostly in the West, this time in the 80 years from 1850 to 1930. In recent decades, the class gap has narrowed to what may be the smallest differential in history, but evidence of a linear gradient remains, with a considerable differential, given man's life span.

This supposition—not claimed to be more than that—seems to be of more than historical interest. It is, for two important reasons, most germane to the concern of this paper. In the first place, the scientist, no less than the lay person, often seems, in considering the question of the relationship between class and health, to be beset by a nineteenth century notion of perpetual progress. Ideologically committed, in this area, to the desirability of the disappearance of the class gap, he tends to assume, with or without data, that the historical picture is unilinear; the history of mankind, in his view, shows steady progress in this respect. The realization that this may well be an inaccurate image, that the relationship is more complex, suggests a more cautious orientation. Such an orientation would suggest various possibilities: a narrowing gap being transformed into one which is widening; differing positions, on any given index of health, of different strata of the population at various times.

The second reason for stressing the possibility of a curvilinear relationship between class and life expectancy over time is that such a relationship may help in forming an adequate idea of the relationship between class and health, and, more broadly, an adequate theory of disease. Once the search begins for explanations of why, in a given period, one stratum seems to be making more health progress than another, and less so in another period, factors are uncovered which must be integrated into a theory of disease.

Thus, for example, McKeown and Brown, arguing that the increase in the population of England in the eighteenth century was overwhelmingly due to the decline in mortality, attribute that decline to improvements in the environment (housing, water supply, refuse disposal, nutrition) rather than to any advances in medical care.[9] Supposedly, such improvements first appeared in the upper strata of society, and only slowly percolated downward. This would explain the increasing class differences in life expectancy. Once the environmental sanitation gap began to narrow, some reversal in the trend could be expected which, however, might soon be offset by other factors; e.g., the malnutrition of poverty. The point is that a very careful collection of data over time and the search for ups and downs may serve to pinpoint the various factors, and their modes of interaction, which influence overall mortality or the course of any specific disease.

CLASS DIFFERENCES IN MORTALITY
BEFORE WORLD WAR II

Twentieth century investigators have by and large focused on class differences in mortality rates. Chapin's study of Providence, Rhode Island, probably provides the earliest relevant information. Using census and tax records of 1865, he located all but about 200 of the 2,000 taxpayers, covering a total of 10,515 individuals. Every deceased person in that year was assigned to either the taxpayer or non-taxpayer group. Chapin then calculated the death rates per thousand in each group. The crude annual death rate of the latter (24.8 per 1,000 living) was more than double that of the taxpayers (10.8). This disparity is found in all but the five- to nine-years age cohort, and is greatest in the productive years (30 to 49) and in the 70 and over cohort. Since the non-taxpayer group includes more than 80 per cent of the population, had Chapin been able to make a finer class breakdown he presumably would have found even greater differences between the top and bottom strata. . . .

The earliest data presented by Collins refer to Danish mortality rates from 1865 to 1874, the 1870 census having been used to obtain denominator information.[10] Individuals were assigned to high, middle or poor classes on the basis of the head of household's occupation. . . . The age-adjusted mean annual death rates, by sex, of the population aged 20 and over in Copenhagen and in other towns . . . the data show that class differences are greater in Copenhagen than in provincial towns, and greater among males than among females. More significantly, although the rates show primarily an inverse class gradient, the differences between the high and middle classes are relatively small compared to the gap between them and the poor class. . . .

The first of many ecological studies was Rowntree's well-known survey of York, England, in 1899.[11] Rowntree divided the wage-earner areas of the city of York into three levels. The overall death rates per thousand persons (not age-standardized) he reports for 1899 are: highest, 13.5; middle, 20.7; poorest, 27.8 (ratios of 100:153:206). In this case, unlike the earlier Danish data, the inverse gradient is quite regular.

In a paper focusing on later data, Britten calculates overall death rates for 1900 in the nine states and the District of Columbia, which then comprised the death registration area.[12] He compared white-collar rates to those for the "laboring and servant" class in three age groups. Taking the white-collar death rate as 100, the ratios for the lower class group were: for ages 15-24, 151; for ages 25-44, 165; and for ages 45-64, 159.

As a prologue to her analysis of 1950 death rates, Guralnick presents, without analysis, the full set of data upon which Britten evidently based his calculations, as well as similar date for 1890.[13] . . . The most striking fact about these data is the very sizable difference, at all ages, between the "laboring and servant" class and all other groups. In both 1890 and 1900, the ratio of this class is highest in ages 25-44 and 45-64, somewhat lower at ages 15-24, and lowest .—though still relatively high—in the 65 and over category. An interesting pattern is shown by the clerical and official group: in the youngest age category its ratio is quite high, in 1900 approaching that of the lowest class; in each successive age category its ratio goes down, so that in the 65 and over category it has by far the lowest mortality rate. . . .

Huber[14] examined occupational mortality in France for 1907-1908, calculating death rates on the basis of the 1906 census. His figures are primarily for individual occupations, but he does give age-specific death rates for four broad groups. . . . Managers and officials consistently show the lowest rates. Clerical workers have, at ages 25-34, the highest rates, but thereafter craftsmen and kindred workers have higher rates. The rates of these two groups are, throughout, closer to each other than to those of the managerial group. Class differentials are greatest at ages 45-54. Private household workers, presumably a low status group, have relatively low rates. Since the data refer only to males, who presumably served primarily in well-to-do households, such rates need not be inexplicable. . . .

In a relatively early review of morbidity and mortality data, Sydenstricker, one of the pioneers in the field, cites Bruno's study of 22,600 deaths among 1.3 million wage-earners in 1915-1916, with life insurance in 12 American companies, showing a clear inverse occupational gradient.[15] The death rates per 1,000 policyholders were: professional and semiprofessionals, 3.3; skilled workmen, 3.7; semiskilled workmen, 4.5; unskilled workmen, 4.8. Using the rate of the professional class as 100, the ratios of the other three were 112, 136 and 145.

Whitney's study using 1930 data was the first large-scale American study following the pattern which had been set by the British Registrar General.[16] Death certificate data were obtained from ten states: Alabama, Connecticut, Illinois, Kansas, Massachusetts, Minnesota, New Jersey, New York, Ohio and Wisconsin. These states contained 39 per cent of the gainfully employed. The census was used to obtain denominator information. Analysis was limited to males aged 15 to 64, in an attempt to limit the unreliability introduced by retirement. Age-standardized data are presented within the social-economic classification developed by Edwards and used standardly by the United States Census.

As can be seen in Table 1, mortality rates vary inversely with class in the total age group of 15-64. Only the proprietor group is out of line. If retail dealers, whose rate is 8.4, are excluded from this category, the rate would be 7.0, making a linear relationship. The curve, however, is not smooth, as can be seen clearly from the ratios presented in the table. The largest difference is found between unskilled and semiskilled workers, with a sizable difference between the latter and skilled workers. Beyond this level the differences, although existent, are relatively small.

Table 1. Annual Death Rates per 1,000 Gainfully Occupied Males, Aged 15 to 64 Years (Age-Standardized) by Age Groups According to Socioeconomic Class, 1930[17]

Socioeconomic Class	Age Groups*							
	15-64		15-24		25-44		45-64	
	Rate	Ratio**	Rate	Ratio	Rate	Ratio	Rate	Ratio
All gainfully employed males	9.1	100	3.2	100	5.5	100	17.9	100
Professional men	6.7	74	2.3	72	3.5	64	16.2	90
Proprietors, Managers and officials	7.9	87	3.1	97	4.2	76	15.8	88
Clerks and kindred workers	7.8	86	2.3	72	4.1	74	16.5	92
Skilled workers and foremen	8.3	91	3.0	94	4.9	89	17.1	96
Semiskilled workers	10.1	111	3.2	100	6.1	111	20.8	116
Unskilled workers	14.5	159	4.7	147	9.6	174	24.8	138

*The age-standardized figures for the age group 15-64 are based on the 53 occupational groups with 500 or more deaths (Whitney, Table 8, p. 32). These cover 79 per cent of the gainfully employed. This set of data was selected as more reliable than the figures for all deaths, given by Whitney in Table 1, p. 17. The trends in the two sets of data are very similar. The age-specific data are only available in Whitney's Table 1, and cover the entire surveyed population.

**Rate for all gainfully employed males = 100.

The same general pattern appears in each of the three age-specific sets of data. The spread, however, is greatest in the 25-44 age group and least in the oldest group. In the latter, differences among the four occupational categories from skilled workers and up are almost nonexistent. This study indicates, then, that class is most intimately related to mortality rates among the unskilled and, secondarily among the semiskilled workers, and during middle age.[17]

Sheps and Watkins[18] sought to overcome the weakness of ecological studies by utilizing information obtained in careful sociological study which grouped areas in New Haven, Connecticut, into "natural areas." The boundary lines of these areas were such that information about census tracts could be used for purposes of setting denominators and standardizing for age. . . . The seven areas were ranked from best to worst, based on a composite of factors including rental, delinquency rates, social standing and financial dependency. All data were age-adjusted.

Taking the average annual death rate over the five-year period of the best area (8.0 per 1,000 persons) as 100, the ratios of the other six areas, going down the socioeconomic scale, were: 111, 110, 128, 136, 145, 148. Other than the fact that the rates for the second and third highest areas are almost identical, a clear inverse linear relationship is found. When the authors combined the seven areas into three, the range was substantially narrowed (100:114:134). The strongest relationship between mortality rates and economic level were found at ages 0-5 and 25-64.

WORLD WAR II TO THE PRESENT

Mortality rates in the Netherlands are among the lowest in the world. In this context, determination of social class differences becomes of particular interest. DeWolff and Meerdink[19] studied the mortality rates of gainfully employed males, aged 15-64 in Amsterdam in 1947-1952, using the 1947 census to provide denominator information. . . . The difference between the most favored group and the workers (117:100) barely reaches statistical significance. In contrast to the findings of all other studies, unskilled workers do not differ from skilled workers. Only the clerical group is relatively high (though a death rate of 5.1 is, as such, quite low). The authors suggest two reasons for this rate. First, the clerical workers do not reach the standards of physical fitness required to obtain civil service employment, which would have placed them in the top level. Second, many are probably children of manual workers and are not sufficiently fit to work.

By the 1950s, the number of studies of socioeconomic mortality differentials had increased considerably. . . . Tayback[20] divided Baltimore's 168 census tracts on the basis of the 1950 median tract rentals, grouping them into equal-sized population quintiles. . . . In overall terms, a clear inverse class gradient is seen, the male slope being somewhat steeper than the female slope, with very few figures being out of line. The gap tends to be quite large in the younger age groups, where the death rate is low. Class differences in middle age (35-54) are very sizable. At this age, the major differences seem to be at the top and bottom, between the highest and next-highest and between the lowest and second-lowest economic levels. Differences remain considerable at ages 55-64, but tend to become much smaller thereafter.

Ellis conducted a very similar study in Houston.[21] The index used to rank census tracts was a modification of the index of social rank developed by Shevky and Williams, which utilizes measures of education, occupation and median family income. Tracts were grouped into quintiles, each of which contained 12 or 13 tracts. . . . Although class differentials do appear, they differ from those in other studies. The range of differences is smaller, though still substantial. The two top groups of tracts, for males, and the three top, for females, are quite similar in their death rates. Most puzzling, perhaps, is the fact that males in the lowest tract level have a lower rate than do those in the adjacent level. Ellis suggests as a possible explanation the availability of free medical treatment for the lowest group. Group 4, not having such an advantage but having a limited income, may utilize funds for the females, who do have a lower rate than the females in group 5, whereas the males go on working and refrain from using such funds for themselves. . . .

Stockwell, whose concern was methodological as well as substantive, presents data exactly parallel to the above. . . . He also used a modified form of the Shevky-Williams index, studied deaths in 1949-1951, and included about one-fifth of the number of tracts in each socioeconomic level. Stockwell's data pertain to Providence and Hartford. The class differentials in these two cities are quite similar to those in Houston. In Providence, little difference is found among the top three levels of males or the top two levels of females. Hartford females do not differ among all five strata; levels 2 and 3 and levels 4 and 5 have almost identical rates.

Stockwell proceeded to compute rank order correlation coefficients between the census tracts in each city ranked by age-sex-standardized death rates and each of eight socioeconomic variables (occupation, two education variables, two income variables, two rent variables, crowding). In all cases, the correlation coefficients were significant.[22]

Since the British Registrar General system of social classification is the richest source of data on mortality differences over time among different socioeconomic levels, a number of attempts have been made to construct a comparable ranking in the United States. Breslow and Buell,[23] using the 1950 census for denominator data, classified all deaths of California males, aged 20-64, from 1949 to 1951, in one of five occupational classes. . . .

For the entire age group, a rough inverse gradient is seen between class and mortality. . . .

A more ambitious attempt along the same lines was conducted by Guralnick, who analyzed all male deaths in age group 20 to 64 in the United States in 1950.[24] In view of the fact that one primary purpose was to compare the United States data with the British, Guralnick collapsed classes II to IV to make this intermediate group comparable in the two countries. . . . For the entire age group, the picture is quite similar to that presented in the California study: a linear inverse gradient, with the intermediate occupational level being closer to class I, and the major gap occurring between class V and the intermediate group. Another publication by Guralnick,[25] in which standard mortality ratios are given separately for the five classes, presents figures almost identical with the California figures. The standardized mortality ratios for all United States males aged 20-64, in 1950, from class I to class V, are: 83, 84, 96, 97, 120. These ratios are for whites only, except for class I, which contains a few nonwhites. Once again classes I and II do not differ, nor do classes III and IV.

Examination of the age-specific rates . . . shows the largest class gap to lie in the 25 to 44 age group, with classes II to IV being closer to class I than to class V. A considerable gap remains at ages 45-54, but it is substantially narrowed by ages 55-64.

Guralnick also analyzed the same 1950 data along more traditional American lines, using the occupational classification developed by Edwards for the United States Census.[26] This scheme seeks to rank occupations by socioeconomic levels. The standardized mortality ratios presented in Table 2, for white males aged 25-59, shows an inverse gradient, but one which does not distinguish among all of the eight occupational groups. The lowest ratios are found among the top three groups; they are followed closely by sales, skilled and semiskilled workers, whose ratios are identical. Service workers fare

Table 2. Annual Death Rates per 1,000, and Ratios, White Males, by Age and Major Occupation Group, United States, 1950[26]

MAJOR OCCUPATION GROUP	25-29 SMR**	Age Group												
		20-24		25-29		30-34		35-44		45-54		55-59		60-64	
		X	Y*	X	Y	X	Y	X	Y	X	Y	X	Y	X	Y
All occupations	93	1.7	100	1.6	100	2.0	100	3.9	100	10.1	100	19.4	100	28.8	100
Professional, technical, kindred	82	1.2	73	1.2	70	1.5	76	3.2	81	9.4	93	18.9	98	29.2	101
Managers, officials, proprietors, nonfarm	85	1.5	86	1.3	79	1.5	76	3.3	85	9.5	94	18.9	98	28.9	100
Clerical, kindred	83	0.9	54	1.3	78	1.5	76	3.3	86	9.6	95	18.2	94	26.9	93
Sales	94	1.1	62	1.1	66	1.7	82	3.6	94	11.0	109	21.7	112	31.8	110
Craftsmen, foremen, kindred	94	1.8	103	1.6	97	2.0	99	4.0	102	10.1	100	20.8	107	32.1	111
Operatives, kindred	94	1.8	106	1.8	108	2.2	107	4.1	106	10.3	102	19.4	100	28.6	99
Service, except private household	116	1.2	72	1.6	98	2.4	117	5.1	133	13.8	136	22.4	116	29.2	101
Laborers, except farm and mine	131	2.6	149	2.8	171	3.6	178	6.5	167	14.5	144	23.8	123	34.9	121

*X = death rate per 1,000. Y = ratio, computed on the basis of rate for all occupations in each age category = 100.
**Standardized mortality ratios are computed on the basis of the entire population. Since nonwhite are excluded in this table, SMRs can fall below 100.
[26]Guralnick, Lillian, Mortality by Occupation and Industry Among Men 20 to 64 Years of Age, U.S., 1950, Vital Statistics, Special Reports, 53, 59, 61, 84-86, September, 1962.

substantially poorer, and, finally, laborers have a considerably higher mortality ratio.

This pattern does not hold in all age groups. Prior to age 30, only the roughest gradient appears, though laborers fare markedly worst. A clear gradient appears in the 30-34 groups, which is maintained in the next ten year cohort. In both cases, the ratios of the top three occupational groups are nearly identical. This pattern holds in ages 45-54 and 55-59 in part. Three mortality levels can be distinguished in these groups, which do not conform to the socioeconomic ranking: non-manual workers except sales workers; sales, skilled and semiskilled workers; and service and unskilled workers. In the oldest age category only laborers continue to differ from all other groups.

Hansluwka's review of Austrian mortality data[27] begins with reference to a number of early studies which were based upon workers covered by social insurance, reflecting only a very small part of the population. He does, however, present data for the entire employed population for 1951-1953. . . . For the very gross categories of "middle and upper class" and "working class" occupations, few sizable differences emerge, though the latter's rates are higher. At ages 14-17, the former's rate is appreciably higher. At ages 60-64, however, the working class has a much higher death rate. Hansluwka also presents a bar chart showing mortality in Vienna in 1951-1953. The city's 23 districts were classified on the percentage of workers of the labor force in each district and grouped into four categories. The data, he concludes, show "a clearcut pattern of social grading of mortality."

A problem which has consistently bedeviled those who seek to study socioeconomic differentials on mortality by use of death certificates and census records is the frequent noncomparability of data in the two sources, which leads to overestimation of the denominator in some occupations and underestimation in others, or difficulty in making any calculations. The nature of the problem has been explored, theoretically and empirically, by several writers.[28] Among these Kitagawa and Hauser have sought to overcome the difficulties by individual matching of 340,000 death certificates from deaths occurring in the United States from May through August, 1969, with census information recorded for these individuals in the 1960 census. In addition, personal interviews were conducted with individuals knowledgeable about 94 per cent of a sample of 9,500 of the decedents.

A preliminary analysis of the data using education and family income for white persons has been reported, though not yet published.[29] Consideration of the education variable, which is broken down into four levels of completed education by persons 25 and older, shows an inverse gradient of mortality rates by amount of education for both sexes in ages 25 to 64. Interestingly enough, this gradient disappears for males 65 and over, but remains quite strong for females of this age.

The latest mortality study available is Tsuchiya's presentation of standardized mortality ratios for an occupational industrial categorization of Japanese males, age 15 and over, in 1962.[30] No clear occupational gradient emerges from the data. The ratios, ranked from low to high, are: "management," 58; "clerks," 67; "mechanics and simple," 88; "sales," 89; "professional and technical," 92; "transporting and communicating," 135.

CLASS MORTALITY DIFFERENTIALS IN ENGLAND AND WALES

Since William Farr initiated the systematic study of occupational mortality statistics in 1851, the decennial reports of the British Registrar General for England and Wales have served as the outstanding source of information on the relationship of social class and mortality. For many years, the focus was on differential mortality risks of specific occupations. In the analysis of the 1910-1912 data, the various occupations were, for the first time, grouped together into five social classes. . . .

In 1930-1932 a further step was taken in moving from a concern with occupational hazards toward one with comparison of mortality risks of people sharing a given social environment: the mortality of married women classified according to husband's occupation was introduced as a systematic part of the data analysis. Since this time, despite reclassification of various occupations, the five-class scheme of the Registrar General has been maintained.[31]

The five social classes are described as follows (the proportion of occupied and retired men aged 15 and over in 1951 is given in brackets):

Class I. Higher administrative and professional occupations and business directorships (3.3 per cent).

Class II. Other administrative, professional and managerial, and shopkeepers: persons responsible for initiating policy and others without this responsibility, but with some responsibility over others (15 per cent).

Class III. Clerical workers, shop assistants, personal service, foremen, skilled workers: skilled workers with a special name, special responsibility and adaptability (52.7 per cent).

Class IV. Semiskilled workers: persons who are doing manual work which needs no great skill or training but who are doing it habitually and in association with a particular industry (16.2 per cent).

Class V. Unskilled workers: laborers, cleaners and other lowly occupations (12.8 per cent). . . .

Farmers and farm managers are included in class II and agricultural workers in class IV. Also, class III, which includes more than half the population, is composed of both manual and non-manual workers.

From the great amount and variety of data available in the reports of the Registrar General and papers based on these reports, those that seem to be the most important have been selected for present purposes. These are presented in Table 3. Collins' analysis of the 1910-1912 data for occupied and retired males aged 15 and over, which refers to classes I, III and V and excludes textile workers, miners and agricultural laborers, shows a regular inverse gradient, with the largest gap being between class III and class V.[32] Stevenson's figures for the same period,[33] which also exclude the same three occupational categories, but refer to males aged 25-64 in the five social classes, show a similar gradient. The ratios for classes II, III and IV, however, are nearly identical, and not very much higher than for class I. Stevenson argued that about ten per cent of the laborers on the census are misclassified as class IV rather than class V, which tends to lower the rates for the former and increase those for the latter. Changing the denominators to this extent would, he notes, produce a smoother gradient, as shown in Table 3. Collins also took the 1900-1902 and 1890-1892 data for 100 specific occupations and classified them as they had been classified in 1910, adjusting the death rates for age. . . . Collins proceeded to analyze the age-specific rates, which show that class differentials were largest in the 25-54 age groups. This is supported by Stevenson's analysis.

A similar picture emerges from the data for 1921-1923, despite the significant changes in classification. The gap between classes I and II is somewhat greater than in the previous decade. Classes II and III have near-identical ratios and class IV a somewhat higher ratio, while class V is still widely distinct from the others. Britten's analysis[34] of the age-specific rates compares class I to class III and class III to class V. For the former comparison, the greatest gap is at ages 16-19, and declines with regularity at each succeeding age.

The pattern of the class V: III ratio, however, is different. Here the greatest gap is at ages 35-44 and, though a bit less so, at 45-54.

Table 3.   Standardized Death Rates per 1,000 and Standardized Mortality Ratios, England and Wales, for Selected Age-Sex Groups and Time Periods, by Social Class

Time Period	I	II	III	IV	V	Population Group
1910-12						
Death rate per 1,000	12.0	—	13.6	—	18.7	Occupied and retired
Ratio (I = 100)	100	—	114	—	156	males, age 15+, excludes textile workers, miners, agricultural laborers
Standardized mortality ratio	88	94	96	93	142	Males, age 25-64, excludes textile, miners, agricultural laborers
Standardized mortality ratio	88	94	96	107	128	As immediately above, modified by Stevenson
1921-23						
Death rate per 1,000	7.4	8.6	8.7	9.2	11.5	Males
Ratio (I = 100)	100	116	117	124	155	
Standardized mortality ratio	82	94	95	101	125	Males, 20-64
1930-32						
Standardized	90	94	97	102	111	Males, 20-64
mortality ratio	81	89	99	103	113	Married women, 20-64
1949-53						
Standardized	98	86	101	94	118	Males, 20-64
mortality ratio	96	88	101	104	110	Married women, 20-64
	100	90	101	104	118	Occupied males, 20-64, adjusted to control for occupational changes since 1930-32
Death rate per 1,000	6.6		6.4		9.5	Males, 20-64, excludes
Ratio (I = 100)	100		97		144	agricultural workers

By 1930, class differentials, though now presenting a regular inverse gradient, had narrowed, with standardized mortality ratios of 90 for class I and 111 for class V, for males, aged 20-64. The innovation introduced in the data analysis for these years shows that general socioeconomic differences rather than specific occupational hazards were crucial in the relationship between class and mortality. This is seen in the data for married women classified by husband's occupation, in which the gradient is somewhat more steep than for the males.

The latest available data, for 1949-1953, show a rather different picture than that of previous decades. Class V still has a substantially higher ratio than the other classes; for the males, it is even higher than in 1930. Class II, however, now has the lowest ratio, followed by classes IV, I and III, in that order. For married women, the inverse gradient persists, except that here too, as among the males, class II has a lower ratio than class I. The relatively low ratio of class IV may well be an artifact of classificational changes from one social class to another. Adjustment of the data for occupied males to take account of these changes "has had the important effect of raising the SMR of Social Class IV from 94, where it was second lowest, to 104, where it occupies the second highest position, as it did in 1921-1923 and 1930-1932."[35] Guralnick's analysis of the British data,[36] excluding all gainfully employed in agriculture, and collapsing classes II-IV, shows that this latter group had a very slightly lower death rate than class I, while class V remains very much higher.

Moriyama and Guralnick,[37] in their attempt to compare data for males from the United States and England and Wales, present age-specific ratios for the latter combining the three middle classes and excluding all engaged in agriculture, for 1950 only. For most age groups, little difference is seen between class I and classes II-IV; this is particularly true from age 45 upwards. Class V has consistently higher rates; but whereas this is the case to a moderate degree at ages 20-24, the differential increases thereafter, reading a peak at ages 35-44, after which it declines again and nearly disappears at ages 60-64. (The respective ratios of the three class groups I, II-IV and V, taking the rate of all occupations as 100, are: at ages 20-24, 102, 94, 122; at ages 25-34, 90, 95, 138; at ages 35-44, 83, 96, 143; at ages 45-54, 98, 97, 129; at ages 55-59, 99, 99, 115; and at ages 60-64, 100, 101, 106.)

Viewing the data for England and Wales in overall terms, class differentials in mortality in the twentieth century both have and have not declined. On the one hand, the differentials between the middle levels (among whom mortality rates differed little even in the earlier years) and class I have more or less disappeared. On the other hand, class V is still strikingly worse off than the rest of the population. Though indications are that its relative position improved in the earlier decades of the century, this does not seem to be the case between 1930 and 1950.

CONCLUSIONS

This statistical examination clearly provides no basis to reject the inference drawn from the figures of the *Titanic* disaster. Despite the multiplicity of methods and indices used in the 30-odd studies cited, and despite the variegated populations surveyed, the inescapable conclusion is that class influences one's chance of staying alive. Almost without exception, the evidence shows that classes differ in mortality rates. Only three such exceptions were found, indicating no or almost no class difference. Altenderfer, comparing 1939-1940 mortality rates of 92 United States cities classified into three mean income groups, shows a relatively small difference among them. Szabady, comparing nonagricultural manual and non-manual workers in Hungary in 1959-1960, shows the same. In both cases, the classification is so gross as to minimize differences which a finer analysis might reveal. Only DeWolff and Meerdink's study in Amsterdam in 1947-1952 can legitimately be regarded as strongly contradictory of the link between class and mortality. Their data, however, must be seen in the context of a population which has just about the lowest death rate ever recorded. This is not to dismiss the importance of their findings. On the contrary, it suggests the extremely important hypothesis that as the overall death rate of a population is lowered, class differentials may similarly decline.

This hypothesis finds support in an overall trend reflected in the studies reported. In the earlier studies, the differential between the mortality rates of extreme class groups is about a 2:1 ratio, but later studies show a narrowing of this differential, so that by the 1940s, a 1.4:1 or 1.3:1 ratio is much more typical. As can be seen from studying the death rates, three years witnessed a progressive decline in the overall death rate. At the same time, a cautionary note must be exercised. Despite an undoubted overall decline in mortality in the past three decades, the trend in the earlier decades of the century toward the closing of the class gap has been checked, if not halted.

This indication focuses on the differences between mortality rates of the lowest class and other classes. A more accurate picture of the overall pattern would be to suggest that what has happened is a blurring, if not a disappearance, of a clear class gradient, while class differences remain. On the basis of the existent data—using, for the sake of convenience, a five-fold class distinction, this being the most popular—it is difficult to conclude whether classes I to IV now no longer differ in their mortality rates, or whether classes I and II have the lowest rates, and III and IV have higher rates, though not necessarily substantially so. What seems to be beyond question is that, whatever the index used and whatever the number of classes considered, almost always a lowest class appears with substantially higher mortality rates. Moreover, the differential between it and other classes evidently has not diminished over recent decades.

At this point discussion of the complex question of explanations for such patterns would not be appropriate. A possibility could be suggested, however. The truly magnificent triumphs over infectious diseases have been crucial in both narrowing the overall class differentials and in nearly eliminating differentials among all but the lowest class. In recent decades, however, access to good medical care, preventive medical action, health knowledge, and limitation of delay in seeking treatment have become increasingly important in combating mortality, as chronic diseases have become the chief health enemy in the developed world. In these areas, lower class people may well be at a disadvantage. As such factors become more and more important, as the historical supposition presented in the first pages of this paper suggests, increasing class differentiation may occur. This approach does not necessarily preclude consideration of genetic selection and what has commonly come to be called "the drift hypothesis."

The data reviewed lead to a further conclusion. With amazing consistency, the class differentials are largest in the middle years of life. This is no less true in the latest than in the earliest studies. Over and over again, the greatest gap is found in young and middle adulthood. The predominant pattern characterizing class differentials by age is that in which class differences are moderately high in the younger ages, rise to a peak at ages 30 to 44, begin to decline at that point and tend to disappear beyond age 65. Where a given set of data varies from this pattern, it is in one of two directions: in the former cases, class differentials are lowest in the younger and older groups; in the latter, the decline in class differentials only begins in late middle age.

This pattern of greatest class differences in middle adulthood may be linked to the two historical suppositions which have heretofore been presented. To hypothesize in more general terms, when mortality rates are extremely high or extremely low, class differences will tend to be small. In other words, when men are quite helpless before the threat of death, or when men have made great achievements in dealing with this threat, life chances will tend to be equitably distributed. On the other hand, when moderate progress is being made in dealing with this threat, differential consequences are to be expected. The crucial idea that may be involved here is that of preventable deaths, at any given level of knowledge, technique and social organization. Where and/or when such deaths are concentrated, class differentials will be greatest, unless appropriate social action is taken. This differential is not inevitable.

Much more, of course, could be said in summary, with reference to both substantive and methodological issues. Needless to say, consideration of patterns of class differences by cause of death is essential for a full understanding of this relationship. But this would have extended the paper into a book.

[1]Hollingshead, August B. and Redlich, Frederick C., *Social Class and Mental Illness*, New York, John Wiley & Sons, Inc., 1958, p. 6, citing Lord, Walter, *A Night to Remember*, New York, Henry Holt, 1955, p. 107.

[2]Cited in Dublin, Louis I., Lotka, Alfred J. and Spiegelman, Mortimer, *Length of Life*, revised edition, New York, Ronald Press, 1949, pp. 34, 30-43. The book as a whole is one of the most detailed treatments of the subject of life expectancy.

[3]Henry, Louis, The Population of France in the 18th Century, *in* Glass, David V. and Eversley, D.E.C. (Editors), *Population in History*, London, Edward Arnold, 1965, p. 444.

[4]Peller, Sigismund, Births and Deaths Among Europe's Ruling Families Since 1500, *in* Glass and Eversley, *op. cit.*, p. 94.

[5]Ansell, C., Vital Statistics of Families in the Upper and Professional Classes, *Journal of the Royal Statistical Society*, 37, 464, 1874, cited in Titmuss, Richard, *Birth, Poverty and Wealth*, London, Hamish Hamilton Medical Books, 1943, p. 19.

[6]Cipolla, Carlo M., Four Centuries of Italian Demographic Development, *in* Glass and Eversley, *op. cit.*, pp. 578, 582.

[7]Dublin, Lotka and Spiegelman, *op. cit.*, pp. 31-32; Peller, *op. cit.*, p. 95.

[8]Pages reviewing the data are omitted. The studies containing the data are listed here (C.S.H.). Villerme, Louis R., *Tableau de L'état Physique et Moral des Ouvriers*, Vol. 2, Paris, Jules Renouard et Cie., 1840, pp. 251, 376-385; Farren, *Observations on the Mortality Among the Members of the British Peerage*, cited *in* Titmuss, *op. cit.*, p. 17; Morris, Jeremy N., *Uses of Epidemiology*, second edition, Edinburgh and London, E. and S. Livingstone, 1964, pp. 161-162; Titmuss, *op. cit.*, p. 18; Bailey, A.H. and Day, A., On the Rate of Mortality Prevailing Amongst the Families of the Peerage During the 19th Century, *Journal of the Institute of Actuaries*, 9, 305, cited in Collins, Selwyn D., *Economic Status and Health*, Washington, United States Government Printing Office, 1927, p. 14; Farr, William, *Vital Statistics. A Memorial Volume of Selections from the Reports and Writings of William Farr*, Humphreys, N.A. (Editor), London, The Sanitary Institute, 1885, pp. 393-394, also cited *in* Titmuss, *op. cit.*, pp. 17-18; Ansell, C., cited *in* Titmuss, *op. cit.*, p. 19; Mayer, Albert J. and Hauser, Phillip, Class Differentiations in Expectation of Life at Birth, *in* Bendix, Reinhard and Lipset, Seymour M. (Editors), *Class, Status and Power*, Glencoe, Illinois, Free Press, 1953, pp. 281-284; Tietze, Christopher, Life Tables for Social Classes in England, Milbank Memorial Fund *Quarterly*, 21, 182-187, April, 1943; Yeracaris, Constantine A., Differential Mortality, General and Cause-Specific, in Buffalo, 1939-41, *Journal of the American Statistical Association*, 50, 1235-1247, December, 1955; Tayback, Matthew, The Relationship of Socioeconomic Status and Expectation of Life, *Baltimore Health News*, 34, 139-144, April, 1957.

[9]McKeown, Thomas and Brown, R.G., Medical Evidence Related to English Population Changes in the Eighteenth Century, *Population Studies*, 9, 119-241, 1955 (reprinted in Glass and Eversley, *op. cit.*, pp. 285-307).

[10]Collins, *op. cit.*, p. 13.

[11]Rowntree, Seebohm B., *Poverty and Progress: A Second Social Survey of York*, London, Longmans, Green & Co., 1941, p. 296.

[12]Britten, Rollo H., Mortality Rates by Occupational Class in the U.S., *Public Health Reports*, 49, 1102, September, 1934.

[13]Guralnick, Lillian, Mortality by Occupation and Industry Among Men 20 to 64 Years of Age, U.S., 1950, *Vital Statistics, Special Reports*, 53, 56, September, 1962.

[14]Huber, Michel, *Bulletin Statistique General de la France*, fasc IV, 1912, quoted in Daric, Jean, Mortality, Occupation, and Socio-Economic Status, *Vital Statistics, Special Reports*, 33, 175-187, September, 1951.

[15]Bruno, Frank J., Illness and Dependency, *Miscellaneous Contributions*, No. 9, The Committee on the Costs of Medical Care, Washington, 1931, cited in Sydenstricker, Edgar, *Health and Environment*, New York, McGraw-Hill Book Company, 1933, p. 94.

[16]Whitney, Jessamine S., *Death Rates by Occupation, Based on Data of the U.S. Census Bureau*, 1930, New York, National Tuberculosis Association, 1934, pp. 17, 32.

[17]Whitney's data are quoted and discussed by Britten, *op. cit.*, and Guralnick, *op. cit.*

[18]Sheps, Cecil and Watkins, J.H., Mortality in the Socio-Economic Districts of New Haven, *Yale Journal of Biology and Medicine*, 20, 51-80, October, 1947.

[19]DeWolff, P. and Meerdink, J., Mortality Rates in Amsterdam According to Profession, *Proceedings of the World Population Conference*, 1954, Vol. I, New York, United Nations (E/Conf. 13/413), pp. 53-55.

[20]Tayback, *op. cit.*, p. 142.

[21]Ellis, John M., Socio-Economic Differentials in Mortality from Chronic Diseases, *Social Problems*, 5, 30-36, July, 1957. Reprinted in expanded form in Jaco, E. Gartly (Editor), *Patients, Physicians and Illness*, Glencoe, Illinois, Free Press, 1958, p. 32.

[22]Stockwell, Edward G., *Socio-Economic Mortality Differentials in Hartford, Conn. and Providence, R.I.: A Methodological Critique*, unpublished doctoral dissertation, Brown University, 1960. Relevant papers published by Stockwell based on his dissertation include: ———, A Critical Examination of the Relationship Between Socioeconomic Status and Mortality, *American Journal of Public Health*, 53, 956-964, June, 1963; ———, Socioeconomic Status and Mortality, *Connecticut Health Bulletin*, 77, 10-13, December, 1963.
Stockwell investigated the difference made in the analysis of socioeconomic mortality data when different indices of class are used. He notes that the precise conclusions one draws will "vary considerably with the methodological conditions characterizing a particular study," however the overall patterns are sufficiently similar so that, for present purposes, it is adequate to refer to only one or two of his measures. Since many studies reported in the present paper used median rental, however, it is important to note that Stockwell's data indicate that, of all eight variables, this is the poorest predictor of mortality rates.

[23] Breslow, Lester and Buell, Philip, Mortality from Coronary Heart Disease and Physical Activity of Work in California, *Journal of Chronic Diseases*, 11, 421-44, April, 1960.

[24]Guralnick, Lillian, Socioeconomic Differences in Mortality by Cause of Death: United States, 1950 and England Wales, 1949-1953, in *International Population Conference*, Ottawa, 1963, *op. cit.*, p. 298.

[25]———, Mortality by Occupation Level and Cause of Death Among Men 20 to 64 Years of Age, U.S., 1950, *Vital Statistics, Special Reports*, 53, 452-481, September, 1963. For an earlier paper reporting provisional death rates in the same population by the five classes and seven age categories, see Moriyama, Iwao M. and Guralnick, Lillian, Occupational and Social Class Differences in Mortality, in *Trends and Differentials in Mortality*, New York, Milbank Memorial Fund, 1956, p. 66.

[27]Hansluwka, Harold, Social and Economic Factors in Mortality in Austria, in *International Population Conference, Ottawa, 1963, op. cit.*, pp. 315-344.

[28]Buechley, Robert, Dunn, John E. Jr., Linden, George and Breslow, Lester, Death Certificate Statement of Occupation: Its Usefulness in Comparing Mortalities, *Public Health Reports*, 71, 1105-1111, November, 1956; Kitagawa, Evelyn M. and Hauser, Philip M., Methods Used in a Current Study of Social and Economic Differentials in Mortality, in *Emerging Techniques of Population Research*, New York, Milbank Memorial Fund, pp. 250-266; and ———, Social and Economic Differentials in Mortality in the U.S., 1960: A Report on Methods, in *International Population Conference, Ottawa, 1963, op. cit.*, pp. 355-367.

[29]Kitagawa, Evelyn M. and Hauser, Philip M., Social and Economic Differentials in Mortality, United States, 1960. Paper presented at the 1966 annual meeting of the Population Association of America.

[30]Tsuchiya, Kenzaburo, The Relation of Occupation to Cancer, Especially Cancer of the Lung, *Cancer*, 18, 136-144, February, 1965.

[31]. . . Registrar General's *Decennial Supplement, England and Wales, 1951, Occupational Mortality*, Part II, Vol. 1, *Commentary*, London, Her Majesty's Stationery Office, 1958, pp. 12-13. This system of classification is also described *in* Logan, W.P.D., Social Class Variations in Mortality, in *Proceedings of the World Population Conference, op. cit.*, pp. 185-188; and Brockington, Fraser C., *The Health of the Community*, third edition, London, J. & A. Churchill Ltd., 1965, pp. 325-334. The percentage distribution of the social classes is taken from Logan, p. 201. For further discussions of the antecedents and development of the Registrar General system of classification, *see* Greenwood, Major, *Medical Statistics from Graunt to Farr*, Cambridge, University Press, 1948; and ——, Occupational and Economic Factors of Mortality, *British Medical Journal*, 1, 862-866, April, 1939.

[32]Collins, *op. cit.*, p. 15.

[33]Stevenson, T.H.C., The Social Distribution of Mortality from Different Causes in England and Wales, 1910-1912, *Biometrika*, 15, 384-388, 1923; Logan, *op. cit.*, p. 204. Logan's paper was also published, with variations, under the same title, in *British Journal of Preventive and Social Medicine*, 8, 128-137, July, 1954, and in *Public Health Reports*, 69, 1217-1223, December, 1954.

[34]Britten, Rollo H., Occupational Mortality Among Males in England Wales, 1921-1923, *Public Health Reports*, 43, 1570, June, 1928.

[35]Registrar General, *op. cit.*, p. 20.

[36]Guralnick, *op. cit.* (International Population Conference), p. 298.

[37]Moriyama and Guralnick, *op. cit.*, p. 69.

4. CASTE IN INDIA AND THE UNITED STATES[1]

GERALD D. BERREMAN

Many writers who have contributed to the vast literature on the caste system in India have emphasized its unique aspects and ignored or denied the qualities it shares with rigid systems of social stratification found in other societies. Others have claimed to find caste systems or caste groups in such widely scattered areas as Arabia, Polynesia, Africa, Guatemala, and Japan.[2] Some observers refer to Negro-white relations in the United States, and particularly in the South, as being those of caste,[3] a usage which others, including C. S. Johnson, Oliver C. Cox, and, more recently, G. E. Simpson and J. M. Yinger, have criticized. This paper will compare the relationship between "touchable," especially twice-born, and "untouchable" castes in India with that between Negroes and whites in the southern United States.

Caste can be defined so that it is applicable only to India, just as it is possible to define narrowly almost any sociocultural phenomenon. Indianists have traditionally held to specific, usually enumerative, definitions. Indeed, the caste system in India has

Reprinted from *The American Journal of Sociology*, Vol. 66, September 1970, by permission of the author and the publisher, The University of Chicago Press.

several unique features, among which are its religious aspects, its complexity, and the degree to which the caste is a cohesive group that regulates the behavior of its members. Within India there is considerable variation in the characteristics of, and the relations among, the groups to which the term "caste" is applied.

However, caste can be accurately defined in broader terms. For many purposes similar social facts may be usefully categorized together, despite differences which, while not denied, are not crucial to the purposes at hand. For purposes of cross-cultural comparison this is necessary: for the study of social process, and with the aim of deriving generalizations, caste is a concept which might well be applied cross-culturally. For these purposes a caste system may be defined as a *hierarchy of endogamous divisions in which membership is hereditary and permanent*. Here hierarchy includes inequality both in status and in access to goods and services. Interdependence of the subdivisions, restricted contacts among them, occupational specialization, and/or a degree of cultural distinctiveness might be added as criteria, although they appear to be correlates rather than defining characteristics.

This definition is perhaps best viewed as describing an ideal type at one end of a continuum along which systems of social stratification might be ranged. There can be little doubt that the systems in India and the southern United States would fall far toward the caste extreme of the continuum.[4] It now becomes necessary to look at the differences cited as crucial by those who object to use of the term "caste" in both societies. The objections raised by those interested in structure, relationships, and interaction will be discussed here; the objections of those interested in specific content will be ignored—not because the latter objections are less cogent, but because they are less relevant to the comparison of social systems.[5]

Johnson sees many similarities in the two systems but objects to identifying both as caste, since "a caste system is not only a separated system, it is a stable system in which changes are socially impossible; the fact that change cannot occur is accepted by all, or practically all, participants. . . . No expenditure of psychological or physical energy is necessary to maintain a caste system."[6] Simpson and Yinger agree with Johnson and further object that, in the United States, "we lack a set of religious principles justifying a rigid system of social stratification and causing it to be willingly accepted by those at all levels."[7] Cox lists a number of features of a caste system (i.e., caste in India) which distinguish it from an interracial situation (i.e., Negro-white relations in America), important among which are its "nonconflictive," "nonpathological," and "static" nature, coupled with absence of "aspiration and progressiveness."[8]

Central to these distinctions is that caste in India is passively accepted and indorsed by all on the basis of religio-philosophical explanations which are universally subscribed to, while Negro-white relations in America are characterized by dissent, resentment, guilt, and conflict. But this contrast is invalid, resulting, as it does, from an idealized and unrealistic view of Indian caste, contrasted with a more realistic, pragmatic view of American race relations; Indian caste is viewed as it is supposed to work rather than as it does work; American race relations are seen as they do work rather than as they are supposed, by the privileged, to work. The traditional white southerner, asked to describe relations between the races, will describe the Negro as happy in his place, which he may quote science and Scripture to justify. This is similar to the explanations offered for the Indian system by the advantaged.

The point here is that ideal intercaste behavior and attitudes in India are much like those in America, while the actual interaction and attitudes are also similar. Commonly, ideal behavior and attitudes in India have been contrasted with real behavior and attitudes in America—a fact which has led to a false impression of difference. Similarly, comparisons of race relations in the rapidly changing urban or industrial South with caste relations in slowly changing rural or agrarian India lead to erroneous conclusions. Valid comparison can be made at either level, but must be with comparable data. The impact on intergroup relations of the social and economic changes which accompany urban life seems to be similar in both societies. Recent literature on village India and on the changing caste functions and caste relations in cities and industrial areas presents a realistic picture which goes far toward counteracting traditional stereotypes of Indian caste.[9]

In a study of caste functioning in Sirkanda, a hill village of northern Uttar Pradesh, India, I was struck by the similarity of relations between the twice-born and untouchable castes to race relations in the southern United States.[10] In both situations there is a genuine caste division, according to the definition above. In the two systems there are rigid rules of avoidance between castes, and certain types of contacts are defined as contaminating, while others are non-contaminating. The ideological justification for the rules differs in the two cultures, as do the definitions of the acts themselves; but these are cultural details. The tabooed contacts are symbolically rather than literally injurious as evidenced by the many inconsistencies in application of the rules.[11] Enforced deference, for example, is a prominent feature of both systems. Lack of deference from low castes is not contaminating, but it is promptly punished, for it implies equality. The essential similarity lies in the fact that the function of the rules in both cases is to maintain the caste system with institutionalized inequality as its fundamental feature. In the United States, color is a conspicuous mark of caste, while in India there are complex religious features which do not appear in America, but in both cases dwelling area, occupation, place of worship, and cultural behavior, and so on, are important symbols associated with caste status. The crucial fact is that caste status is determined, and therefore the systems are perpetuated, by birth: membership in them is ascribed and unalterable. Individuals in low castes are considered inherently inferior and are relegated to a disadvantaged position, regardless of their behavior. From the point of view of the social psychology of intergroup relations, this is probably the most important common and distinct feature of caste systems.

In both the United States and India, high castes maintain their superior position by exercising powerful sanctions, and they rationalize their status with elaborate philosophical, religious, psychological, or genetic explanations. The latter are not sufficient in themselves to maintain the systems, largely because they are incompletely accepted among those whose depressed position they are thought to justify. In both places castes are economically interdependent. In both there are great differences in power and privilege among, as well as class differences within, castes and elaborate barriers to free social intercourse among them.

Similarities in the two caste systems extend throughout the range of behavior and attitudes expressed in relations among groups. An important and conspicuous area of similarity is associated with competition for certain benefits or "gains" which are personally gratifying and/or socially valued and which by their nature or under the circumstances cannot be enjoyed by all equally. Competitive striving is, of course, not unique to caste organization; it is probably found to some extent in all societies. It is subject to a variety of social controls resulting in a variety of forms of social stratification, one of which is a caste system as defined here. However, the genesis of caste systems is not here at issue.[12]

The caste system in India and in the United States has secured gains for the groups established at the top of the hierarchy. Their desire to retain their position for themselves and their children accounts for their efforts to perpetuate the system. John Dollard, in his discussion of "Southern-town," identifies their gains as economic, sexual, and in prestige.

In the economic field, low-caste dependence is maintained in India as in America by economic and physical sanctions. This assures not only greater high-caste income but a ready supply of free service and cheap labor from the low castes. It also guarantees the continuing availability of the other gains. In India it is the most explicitly recognized high-caste advantage.

The sexual gain for the southern white caste is defined by Dollard, quoting whom I will substitute "high caste" and "low caste" for "white" and "Negro," respectively. In this form his definition fits the Indian caste system equally well.

In simplest terms, we mean by a "sexual gain" the fact that [high-caste] men, by virtue of their caste position, have access to two classes of women, those of the [high] and [low] castes. The same condition is somewhat true of the [low-caste] women, except that they are rather the objects of the gain than the choosers, though it is a fact that they have some degree of access to [high-caste] men as well as men of their own caste. [Low-caste] men and [high-caste] women, on the other hand, are limited to their own castes in sexual choices.[13]

This arrangement is maintained in the Indian caste system, as it is in America, by severe sanctions imposed upon any low-caste man who might venture to defy the code, by the toleration accorded high-caste men who have relations with low-caste women, and by the precautions which high-caste men take to protect their women from the low castes.

High-caste people gain, by virtue of their caste status alone, deference from others, constant reinforcement of a feeling of superiority, and a permanent scapegoat in the lower castes. Dollard has stated the implications of this gain in prestige, and, again substituting a caste designation for a racial one, his statement describes the Indian system perfectly:

> The gain here . . . consists in the fact that a member of the [high] caste has an automatic right to demand forms of behavior from [low-caste people] which serve to increase his own self-esteem.
> It must always be remembered that in the end this deference is demanded and not merely independently given.[14]

Ideally the high-caste person is paternalistic and authoritarian, while the low-caste person responds with deferential, submissive, subservient behavior. Gallagher might have been describing India rather than America when he noted: "By the attitudes of mingled fear, hostility, deprecation, discrimination, amused patronage, friendly domination, and rigid authoritarianism, the white caste generates opposite and complementary attitudes in the Negro caste."[15]

An additional high-caste gain in India is the religious tradition which gives people of high caste promise of greater rewards in the next life than those of low caste. People can increase their rewards in the next life by fulfilling their traditional caste duty. For high castes, this generally results in increasing the economic advantages and prestige acquired in this life, while it requires that the low castes subordinate their own economic gains and prestige in this life to the service and honor of high castes. Thus, for high-caste people, behavior leading to immediate rewards is consistent with ultimate rewards, while, for low-caste people, behavior required for the two rewards is contradictory.

These advantages are significant and recognized reasons for maintenance of the system by the privileged groups.[16] They are expressed in folklore, proverbs, and jokes; for instance, a story tells that, as the funeral procession of an old landlord passed two untouchable women going for water, one hand of the corpse fell from under the shroud and flopped about. One of the women turned to the other and remarked, "You see, Takur Singh is dead, but he still beckons to us." Other stories recount the avariciousness of Brahmins in their priestly role, the hard-heartedness of landlords and the like.

The compensatory gains for low-caste people are cited more often by high-caste advocates of the system than by those alleged to enjoy them. They are gains common to authoritarian systems everywhere and are usually subject to the will of the dominant groups.

As noted above, India is frequently cited as an example of a society in which people of deprived and subject status are content with their lot, primarily justifying it by religion and philosophy. This is the characteristic of caste in India most often cited to distinguish it from hereditary systems elsewhere, notably in the southern United States. On the basis of my research and the literature, I maintain that this is not accurate and therefore not a valid distinction. Its prevalence is attributable in part, at least, to the vested interests of the advantaged and more articulate castes in the perpetuation of the caste system and the maintenance of a favorable view of it to outsiders. The same arguments and the same biases are frequently presented by apologists for the caste system of the southern United States.

In both systems there is a tendency to look to the past as a period of halcyon amity and to view conflict and resentment as resulting from outside disturbances of the earlier normal equilibrium. Alien ideas, or large-scale economic disturbances, or both, are often blamed for reform movements and rebellion. Such explanations may account for the national and regional reform movements which find their advocates and followers primarily among the educated and social elites; they do not account for the recurrent grass-roots attempts, long endemic in India, to raise caste status; for the state of mind which has often led to low-caste defections from Hinduism when the opportunity to do so without fear of major reprisals has presented itself; nor for the chronic resentment and tension which characterizes intercaste relations in even so remote a village as Sirkanda, the one in which I worked.

Among the low or untouchable castes in Sirkanda, there was a great deal of readily expressed resentment regarding their caste position. Specific complaints revolved around economic, prestige, and sexual impositions by the high castes. Although resentment was suppressed in the presence of people of the dominant high castes, it was readily expressed where there was no fear of detection or reprisal.[17] Low-caste people felt compelled to express village loyalties in public, but in private acts and attitudes caste loyalties were consistently and intensely dominant when the two conflicted.

Caste, as such, was not often seriously questioned in the village. Objections were characteristically directed not at "caste" but at "my position in the caste hierarchy."

In the multicaste system of India, abolition of the system evidently seems impossible from the point of view of any particular caste, and a change in its rank within the system is viewed by its members as the only plausible means of improving the situation. Moreover, abolition would destroy the caste as a group which is superior to at least some other groups, and, while it would give caste members an opportunity to mingle as equals with their superiors, it would also force them to mingle as equals with their inferiors. Abolition, even if it could be accomplished, would thus create an ambivalent situation for any particular caste in contrast to the clear-cut advantages of an improvement in rank.

In the dual system of the southern United States where the high caste is clearly dominant, abolition of the caste division may be seen by the subordinate group as the only plausible remedy for their deprived position. Furthermore, they have nothing to lose but their inferior status, since there are no lower castes. There are, of course, Negroes and organized groups of Negroes, such as the black suprem-

acist "Muslims" recently in the news in the United States, who want
to invert the caste hierarchy; conversely, there are low-caste people
in India who want to abolish the entire system. But these seem to
be atypical viewpoints. The anticaste religions and reform movements which have from time to time appealed with some success
to the lower castes in India, for example, Buddhism, Islam, Christianity, Skhism, have been unable, in practice, to remain casteless.
This seems to be a point of real difference between Indian and
American low-caste attitudes, for in America objection is more
characteristically directed toward the system as such.[18]

In Sirkanda those low-caste people who spoke most piously
against high-caste abuses were likely to be equally abusive to their
caste inferiors. However, no low caste was encountered whose members did not seriously question its place in the hierarchy. A sizable
literature is accumulating concerning castes which have sought to
alter their status.[19] Such attempts were made in Sirkanda. A more
common reaction to deprived status on the part of low-caste people
was what Dollard calls "passive accommodation" coupled with occasional ingroup aggression.[20]

In both America and India there is a tendency for the person
of low caste to "laugh it off" or to become resigned. In Sirkanda
low-caste people could not avoid frequent contacts with their
superiors, because of their proximity and relative numbers. Contacts
were frequently informal, but status differences and the dangers of
ritual pollution were not forgotten. An untouchable in this village
who covered up his bitter resentment by playing the buffoon
received favors denied to his more sullen caste fellows. The irre-
sponsible, simple-minded untouchable is a widespread stereotype
and one which he, like the Negro, has found useful. Similarly, sullen
resignation, with the attendant stereotype of lazy shiftlessness, is a
common response, typified in the southern Negro axiom, "Do what
the man says." This, too, helps him avoid trouble, although it does
little for the individual's self-respect. Aggression against the economically and numerically dominant high castes in Sirkanda was too dangerous to be a reasonable alternative. It was discussed by low-caste
people in private but was rarely carried out. Even legitimate complaints to outside authority were avoided in view of the general
belief that the high-caste's wealth would insure an outcome unfavorable to the low castes—a belief well grounded in experience.

Since they harbored indignation and resentment, a number of
rationalizations of their status were employed by low-caste people,
apparently as mechanisms to lessen the sting of reality. Thus, they

often attributed their caste status to relative wealth and numbers: "If we were wealthy and in the majority, we would make the high castes untouchable."

Three more explanations of their caste status were consistently offered by low-caste people. These had the effect of denying the legitimacy of their low-caste position:

1. Members of the entire caste (or subcaste) group would deny that they deserved the low status to which they had been assigned. One example:

> Englishmen and Muslims are untouchables because they have an alien religion and they eat beef. This is as it should be. We are Hindus and we do not eat beef, yet we, too are treated as untouchables. This is not proper. We should be accorded higher status.

No group would admit to being lowest in the caste hierarchy.

2. People might grant that the caste of their clan, lineage, or family was of low status but deny that their particular group really belonged to it. I have not encountered a low-caste group which did not claim high-caste ancestry or origin. Thus a typical comment is:

> Yes, we are drummers by occupation, but our ancestor was a Brahmin who married a drummer woman. By rights, therefore, we should be Brahmins, but in such cases the high castes here go against the usual custom and assign the child the caste of his low-caste parent rather than of his father, from whom a person inherits everything else.

3. A person might grant that his own caste and even his lineage or family were of low status, but his explanation would excuse him from responsibility for it. Such explanations were supplied by Brahmins who, as the most privileged caste and the recipients of religiously motivated charity from all castes, have a vested interest in maintenance of the system and its acceptance by those at all levels. An individual's horoscope would describe him as having been of high caste and exemplary behavior in a previous life and therefore destined for even greater things in the present life. However, in performing some religiously meritorious act in his previous existence, he inadvertently sinned (e.g., he was a raja, tricked by dishonest servants who did not give to the Brahmin the charity he intended for them). As a result he had to be punished in this life with a low rebirth.

Thus, no one said, in effect, "I am of low status and so are my family members and my caste-fellows, and justly so, because of our misdeeds in previous lives." To do so would lead to a psychologically untenable position, though one advocated by high-caste people and by orthodox Hinduism. Rationalizations or beliefs such as these form a consistent pattern—they are not isolated instances. Neither are they unique to the village or culture reported here: the literature reveals similar beliefs elsewhere in North India.[21] They evidently indicate something less than enthusiastic acceptance of caste position and, meanwhile, they perhaps alleviate or divert resentment.

That people remain in an inferior position, therefore, does not mean that they do so willingly, or that they believe it is justified, or that they would do anything in their power to change it, given the opportunity. Rationalizations of caste status which are consistent and convincing to those who are unaffected or who benefit from them seem much less so to those whose deprivation they are expected to justify or explain. Adherence to a religious principle may not significantly affect the attitudes and behavior to which logic would seem, or to which dogma attempts, to tie it. A comparison of the realities of caste attitudes and interaction in India and the United States suggests that no group of people is content to be low in a caste hierarchy—to live a life of inherited deprivation and subjection—regardless of the rationalizations offered them by their superiors or constructed by themselves. This is one of many points on which further cross-cultural comparison, and only cross-cultural comparison of caste behavior might be conclusive.

It should be evident that the range of similarities between caste in India and race relations in America, when viewed as relations among people, is wide and that the details are remarkably similar in view of the differences in cultural context. Without denying or belittling the differences, I would hold that the term "caste system" is applicable at the present time in the southern United States, if it is applicable anywhere outside of Hindu India, and that it can be usefully applied to societies with systems of hierarchical, endogamous subdivisions whose membership is hereditary and permanent, wherever they occur. By comparing caste situations, so defined, it should be possible to derive further insight, not only into caste in India, but into a widespread type of relations between groups—insight which is obscured if we insist upon treating Indian caste as entirely unique.

[1]Delivered in abbreviated form before the Fifty-eighth Annual Meeting of the American Anthropological Association in Mexico City, December, 1959, and based partly on research carried out in India under a Ford Foundation Foreign Area Training Fellowship during fifteen months of 1957-58 (reported in full in my "Kin, Caste, and Community in a Himalayan Hill Village" [unpublished Ph.D. dissertation, Cornell University, 1959]). I am indebted to Joel V. Berreman and Lloyd A. Fallers for their helpful comments.

[2]E. D. Chapple and C. S. Coon, *Principles of Anthropology* (New York: Henry Holt & Co., 1942), p. 437; S. F. Nadel, "Caste and Government in Primitive Society," *Journal of the Anthropological Society of Bombay*, New Series VIII (September, 1954), 9-22; M. M. Tumin, *Caste in a Peasant Society* (Princeton, N.J.: Princeton University Press, 1952); J. D. Donoghue, "An Eta Community in Japan: The Social Persistence of Outcaste Groups," *American Anthropologist*, LIX (December, 1957), 1000-1017.

[3]E.G., Allison Davis, Kingsley Davis, John Dollard, Buell Gallagher, Gunnar Myrdal, Kenneth Stampp, Lloyd Warner.

[4]The Tira of Africa, for example, would not fall so far toward this extreme (cf. Nadel, *op. cit.*, pp. 18 ff.).

[5]As a matter of fact, ignorance of the details of content in the patterns of relations between whites and Negroes in the United States has prevented many Indianists from seeing very striking similarities. Two contrasting views of the cross-cultural applicability of the concept of caste have appeared since this paper was written: F. C. Bailey, "For a Sociology of India?" *Contributions to Indian Sociology*, No. 3 (July, 1959), 88-101, esp. 97-98; and E. R. Leach, "Introduction: What Should We Mean by Caste?" in *Aspects of Caste in South India, Ceylon and North-west Pakistan* ("Cambridge Papers in Social Anthropology," No. 2 [Cambridge: Cambridge University Press, 1959]), pp. 1-10.

[6]C. S. Johnson, *Growing Up in the Black Belt* (Washington, D.C.: American Council on Education, 1941), p. 326.

[7]G. E. Simpson and J. M. Yinger, *Racial and Cultural Minorities* (New York: Harper & Bros., 1953), p. 328.

[8]O. C. Cox, "Race and Caste: A Distinction," *American Journal of Sociology*, L (March, 1945), 360 (see also his *Caste, Class and Race* [Garden City, N.Y.: Doubleday & Co., 1948]).

[9]See, for example, the following community studies: F. G. Bailey, *Caste and the Economic Frontier* (Manchester: University of Manchester Press, 1957); Berreman, *op. cit.*; S. C. Dube, *Indian Village* (Ithaca, N.Y.: Cornell University Press, 1955); Oscar Lewis, *Village Life in Northern India* (Urbana: University of Illinois Press, 1958); McKim Marriott (ed.), *Village India* (American Anthropological Association Memoir No. 83 [Chicago: University of Chicago Press, 1955]); M. E. Opler and R. D. Singh, "The Division of Labor in an Indian Village," in *A Reader in General Anthropology*, ed. C. S. Coon (New York: Henry Holt & Co., 1948), pp. 464-96; M. N. Srinivas *et al.*, *India's Villages* (Development Department, West Bengal: West Bengal Government Press, 1955). See also, for example, the following studies of caste in the contemporary setting: Bailey, *op. cit.*; N. K. Bose, "Some Aspects of Caste in Bengal," *American Journal of Folklore*, LXXI (July-September, 1958), 397-412; Leach, *op. cit.*; Arthur Niehoff, *Factory Workers in India* ("Milwaukee Public Museum Publications in Anthropology," No. 5 [1959]); M. N. Srinivas, "Caste in Modern India," *Journal of Asian Studies*, XVI (August, 1957), 529-48; and the several articles comprising the symposium on "Caste in India" contained in *Man in India*, XXXIX (April-June, 1959), 92-162.

[10]The following discussion is based not exclusively on the Sirkanda materials but on observations and literature in non-hill areas as well. The hill area presents some distinct regional variations in caste structure, important among which is the absence of intermediate castes—all are either twice-born or untouchable. This leads to a dichotomous situation, as in the United States, but one which differs in that there are important caste divisions on either side of the "pollution barrier" (cf. Bailey, *op. cit.*, p. 8; Berreman, *op. cit.*, pp. 389 ff.). Relations across this barrier do not differ greatly from similar relations among plains castes, although somewhat more informal contact is allowed—pollution comes about less easily—in the hills.

[11]The symbolic acts—the "etiquette" of caste relations—in India and in America are often remarkably similar. The symbolism in America is, of course, not primarily religious as much as it is in India, although the sacred aspects in India are often far from the minds of those engaging in the acts and are not infrequently unknown to them.

[12]Cf. Nadel, *op. cit.*

[13]John Dollard, *Caste and Class in a Southern Town* ("Anchor Books" [Garden City, N.Y.: Doubleday & Co., 1957]), p. 135 (cf. Berreman, *op. cit.*, pp. 470 ff.).

[14]Dollard, op. cit., p. 174. Nadel speaking of caste in general, has noted that "the lower caste are despised, not only unhappily under-privileged; they bear a stigma apart from being unfortunate. Conversely, the higher castes are not merely entitled to the possession of coveted privileges, but are also in some way exalted and endowed with a higher dignity" (Nadel, op. cit., p. 16).

[15]B.G. Gallagher, American Caste and the Negro College (New York: Columbia University Press, 1038), p. 109.

[16]Cf. Pauline M. Mahar, "Changing Caste Ideology in a North Indian Village," Journal of Social Issues, XIV (1958), 51-65, esp. pp. 55-56; Kailash K. Singh, "Inter-caste Tensions in Two Villages in North India" (unpublished Ph.D. dissertation, Cornell University, 1957), pp. 184-85; and M. N. Srinivas, "The Dominant Caste in Rampura," American Anthropologist, LXI (1959), 1-16, esp. p. 4.

[17]Elaborate precautions were often taken by informants to insure against any possibility that their expressions of feeling might become known to their caste superiors, which is very similar to behavior I have observed among Negroes of Montgomery, Alabama.

[18]Whether this difference in attitude is widely correlated with multiple, as compared to dual, caste systems, or is attributable to other differences in the Indian and American situations, can be established only by further comparative work.

[19]E.G., Opler and Singh, op. cit., p. 476; B. S. Cohn, "The Changing Status of a Depressed Caste," in Marriott (ed.), op. cit., pp. 53-77; and Bailey, op. cit., pp. 220-26.

[20]Dollard, op. cit., p. 253.

[21]Cf. E. T. Atkinson, The Himalayan Districts of the North-Western Provinces of India (Allahabad: North-Western Provinces and Oudh Press, 1886), III, 446; B. S. Cohn, "The Camars of Senapur: A Study of the Changing Status of a Depressed Caste" (unpublished Ph.D. dissertation, Cornell University, 1954), pp. 112 ff.; and D. N. Majumdar, The Fortunes of Primitive Tribes (Lucknow: Universal Publishers Ltd., 1944), p. 193.

15.   THE POSITIVE FUNCTIONS OF POVERTY[1]

HERBERT J. GANS

Mertonian functional analysis is applied to explain the persistence of poverty, and fifteen functions which poverty and the poor perform for the rest of American society, particularly the affluent, are identified and described. Functional alternatives which would substitute for these functions and make poverty unnecessary are suggested, but the most important alternatives are themselves dysfunctional for the affluent, since they require some redistribution of income and power. A functional analysis of poverty thus comes to many of the same conclusions as radical sociological analysis, demonstrating anew Merton's assertion that functionalism need not be conservative in ideological outlook or implication.

I

Over 20 years ago, Merton (1949, p. 71), analyzing the persistence of the urban political machine, wrote that because "we should ordinarily . . . expect persistent social patterns and social structures to perform positive functions which are at the time not adequately fulfilled by other existing patterns and structures . . . perhaps this publicly maligned organization is, under present conditions, satisfying basic latent functions." He pointed out how the machine provided central authority to get things done when a decentralized local government could not act, humanized the services of the impersonal bureaucracy for fearful citizens, offered concrete help (rather than law or justice) to the poor, and otherwise performed services needed or demanded by many people but considered unconventional or even illegal by formal public agencies.

This paper is not concerned with the political machine, however, but with poverty, a social phenomenon which is as maligned as and far more persistent than the machine. Consequently, there may be some merit in applying functional analysis to poverty, to ask whether it too has positive functions that explain its persistence. Since functional analysis has itself taken on a maligned status among some American sociologists, a secondary purpose of this paper is to ask whether it is still a useful approach.[2]

II

Merton (1949, p. 50) defined functions as "those observed consequences which make for the adaptation or adjustment of a given system; and dysfunctions, those observed consequences which lessen the adaptation or adjustment of the system." This definition does not specify the nature or scope of the system, but elsewhere in his classic paper "Manifest and Latent Functions," Merton indicated that social system was not a synonym for society, and that systems vary in size, requiring a functional analysis "to consider a *range* of units for which the item (or social phenomenon H.G.) has designated consequences: individuals in diverse statuses, subgroups, the larger social system and cultural systems" (1949, p. 51).

In discussing the functions of poverty, I shall identify functions for *groups and aggregates;* specifically, *interest groups, socioeconomic classes,* and other population aggregates, for example, those with shared values or similar statuses. This definitional approach is based on the assumption that almost every social system—and of course every society—is composed of groups or aggregates with different interests and values, so that, as Merton put it (1949, p. 51), "items may be functional for some individuals and subgroups and dysfunctional for others." *Indeed, frequently one group's functions are another group's dysfunctions.*[3] For example, the political machine analyzed by Merton was functional for the working class and business interests of the city but dysfunctional for many middle class and reform interests. Consequently, functions are defined as those observed consequences which are positive *as judged by the values of the group under analysis*; dysfunctions, as those which are negative by these values.[4] Because functions benefit the group in question and dysfunctions hurt it, I shall also describe functions and dysfunctions in the language of economic planning and systems analysis as benefits and costs.[5]

Identifying functions and dysfunctions for groups and aggregates rather than systems reduces the possibility that what is functional for one group in a multigroup system will be seen as being functional for the whole system, making it more difficult, for example, to suggest that a given phenomenon is functional for a corporation or political regime when it may in fact only be functional for their officers or leaders. Also, this approach precludes reaching a priori conclusions about two other important empirical questions raised by Merton (1949, pp. 32-36), *whether any phenomenon is ever functional or dysfunctional for an entire society, and, if functional, whether it is therefore indispensable to that society.*

In a modern heterogeneous society, few phenomena are functional or dysfunctional for the society as a whole, and most result in benefits to some groups and costs to others. Given the level of differentiation in modern society, I am even skeptical whether one can empirically identify a social system called society. Society exists, of course, but it is closer to being a very large aggregate, and when sociologists talk about society as a system, they often really mean the nation, a system which, among other things, sets up boundaries and other distinguishing characteristics between societal aggregates.

I would also argue that no social phenomenon is indispensable; it may be too powerful or too highly valued to be eliminated, but in most instances, one can suggest what Merton calls "functional alternatives" or equivalents for a social phenomena, that is, other social patterns or policies which achieve the same functions but avoid the dysfunctions.

III

The conventional view of American poverty is so dedicated to identifying the dysfunctions of poverty, both for the poor and the nation, that at first glance it seems inconceivable to suggest that poverty could be functional for anyone. Of course, the slum lord and the loan shark are widely known to profit from the existence of poverty; but they are popularly viewed as evil men, and their activities are, at least in party, dysfunctional for the poor. However, what is less often recognized, at least in the conventional wisdom, is that *poverty also makes possible the existence or expansion of "respectable" professions and occupations, for example, penology, criminology, social work, and public health.* More recently, the poor have provided jobs for professional and paraprofessional "poverty warriors," as well as journalists and social scientists, this author included, who have supplied the information demanded when public curiosity about the poor developed in the 1960s.

Clearly, then, poverty and the poor may well serve a number of functions for many nonpoor groups in American society, and I shall describe 15 sets of such functions—economic, social, cultural, and political—that seem to me most significant.

First, the existence of poverty makes sure that "dirty work" is done. Every economy has such work: physically dirty or dangerous, temporary, dead-end and underpaid, undignified, and menial jobs. These jobs can be filled by paying higher wages than for "clean" work, or by requiring people who have no other choice to do the dirty work and at low wages. In America, poverty functions to provide a low-wage labor pool that is willing—or, rather, unable to be unwilling—to perform dirty work at low cost. *Indeed, this function is so important that in some Southern states, welfare payments have been cut off during the summer months when the poor are needed to work in the fields.* Moreover, the debate about welfare—and about proposed substitutes such as the negative income tax and the Family Assistance Plan—has emphasized the impact of income grants on work incentive, with opponents often arguing that such grants would reduce the incentive of—*actually, the pressure on*—the poor to carry out the needed dirty work if the wages therefore are no larger than the income grant. Furthermore, many economic activities which involve dirty work depend heavily on the poor; restaurants, hospitals, parts of the garment industry, and industrial agriculture, among others, could not persist in their present form without their dependence on the substandard wages which they pay to their employees.

Second, the poor subsidize, directly and indirectly, many

activities that benefit the affluent.[6] For one thing, they have long supported both the consumption and investment activities of the private economy by virtue of the low wages which they receive. This was openly recognized at the beginning of the Industrial Revolution, when a French writer quoted by T. H. Marshall (forthcoming, p. 7) pointed out that *"to assure and maintain the prosperities of our industries, it is necessary that the workers should never acquire wealth."* Examples of this kind of subsidization abound even today; for example, *domestics subsidize the upper middle and upper classes, making life easier for their employers and freeing affluent women for a variety of professional, cultural, civic, or social activities.* In addition, as Barry Schwartz pointed out (personal communication), *the low income of the poor enables the rich to divert a higher proportion of their income to savings and investment, and thus to fuel economic growth.* This, in turn, can produce higher incomes for everybody, including the poor, although it does not necessarily improve the position of the poor in the socioeconomic hierarchy, since the benefits of economic growth are also distributed unequally.

At the same time, the poor subsidize the governmental economy. Because local property and sales taxes and the ungraduated income taxes levied by many states are regressive, the poor pay a higher percentage of their income in taxes than the rest of the population, *thus subsidizing the many state and local governmental programs that serve more affluent taxpayers.*[7] In addition, the poor support medical innovation as patients in teaching and research hospitals, and *as guinea pigs in medical experiments, subsidizing the more affluent patients who alone can afford these innovations once they are incorporated into medical practice.*

Third, poverty creates jobs for a number of occupations and professions which serve the poor, or shield the rest of the population from them. As already noted, *penology would be miniscule without the poor, as would the police, since the poor provide the majority of their "clients."* Other activities which flourish because of the existence of poverty are the numbers game, the sale of heroin and cheap wines and liquors, pentecostal ministers, faith healers, prostitutes, pawn shops, and the peacetime army, which recruits its enlisted men mainly from among the poor.

Fourth, the poor buy goods which others do not want and thus prolong their economic usefulness, *such as day-old bread, fruit and vegetables* which would otherwise have to be thrown out, secondhand clothes, and deteriorating automobiles and buildings. *They also provide incomes for* doctors, lawyers, teachers, and others who are too old, poorly trained, or incompetent to attract more affluent clients.

In addition, the poor perform a number of social and cultural functions:

Fifth, the poor can be identified and punished as *alleged or real deviants* in order to uphold the legitimacy of dominant norms (Macarov 1970, pp. 31-33). The defenders of the desirability of hard work, thrift, honesty, and monogamy need people who can be accused of being lazy, spendthrift, dishonest, and promiscuous to justify these norms; and as Erikson (1964) and others following Durkheim have pointed out, the *norms themselves are best legitimated by discovering violations.*

Whether the poor actually violate these norms more than affluent people is still open to question. *The working poor work harder and longer than high-status jobholders, and poor housewives must do more housework to keep their slum apartments clean than their middle-class peers in standard housing.* The proportion of cheaters among welfare recipients is quite low and considerably lower than among income taxpayers.[8] Violent crime is higher among the poor, but the affluent commit a variety of white-collar crimes, and several studies of self-reported delinquency have concluded that middle-class youngsters are sometimes as delinquent as the poor. However, the poor are more likely to be caught when participating in deviant acts and, once caught, to be punished more often than middle-class transgressors. Moreover, they lack the political and cultural power to correct the stereotypes that affluent people hold of them, and thus continue to be thought of as lazy, spendthrift, etc., whatever the empirical evidence, by those who need living proof that deviance does not pay.[9] The actually or allegedly deviant poor have traditionally been described as undeserving and, in more recent terminology, culturally deprived or pathological.

Sixth, another group of poor, described as deserving because they are disabled or suffering from bad luck, provide the rest of the population with different emotional satisfactions; *they evoke compassion, pity, and charity, thus allowing those who help them to feel that they are altruistic, moral, and practicing the Judeo-Christian ethic.* The deserving poor also enable others to feel fortunate for being spared the deprivations that come with poverty.[10]

Seventh, as a converse of the fifth function described previously, the *poor offer affluent people vicarious participation in the uninhibited sexual, alcoholic, and narcotic behavior in which many poor people are alleged to indulge,* and which, being freed from the constraints of affluence and respectability, they are often thought to enjoy more than the middle classes. One of the popular beliefs about welfare recipients is that many are on a permanent sex-filled vacation. Although it may be true that the poor are more given to uninhibited behavior, studies by Rainwater (1970) and other observers of the lower class indicate that such behavior is as often motivated by despair as by lack of inhibition, and that it results less in pleasure than in *a compulsive escape from grim reality.* However, whether the poor actually have more sex and enjoy it more than affluent people is irrelevant; as long as the latter believe it to be so, they can share it vicariously and perhaps enviously when instances are reported in fictional, journalistic, or sociological and anthropological formats.

Eighth, poverty helps to guarantee the status of those who are not poor. In a stratified society, where social mobility is an especially important goal and class boundaries are fuzzy, people need to know quite urgently where they stand. As a result, the poor function as a reliable and relatively permanent measuring rod for status comparison, *particularly for the working class, which must find and maintain status distinctions between itself and the poor, much as the aristocracy must find ways of distinguishing itself from the nouveau riche.*

Ninth, the poor also assist in the upward mobility of the non-poor, for, as Goode has pointed out (1967, p. 5), "the privileged . . . try systematically to prevent the talent of the less privileged from being recognized or developed." By being denied educational opportunities or being stereotyped as stupid or unteachable, the poor thus enable others to obtain the better jobs. Also, an unknown number of people have moved themselves or their children up in the socioeconomic hierarchy through the incomes earned from the provision of goods and services in the slums: by becoming policemen and teachers, owning "Mom and Pop" stores, or working in the various rackets that flourish in the slums.

In fact, members of almost every immigrant group have financed their upward mobility by providing retail goods and services, housing, entertainment, gambling, narcotics, etc., to later arrivals in America (or in the city), most recently to blacks, Mexicans, and Puerto Ricans. Other Americans, of both European and native origin, have financed their entry into the upper middle and upper classes by owning or managing the illegal institutions that serve the poor, as well as the legal but not respectable ones, such as slum housing.

Tenth, just as the poor contribute to the economic viability of a number of businesses and professions (see function 3 above), they also add to the social viability of noneconomic groups. For one thing, they *help to keep the aristocracy busy*, thus justifying its continued existence. *"Society" uses the poor as clients of settlement houses and charity benefits;* indeed, *it must have the poor to practice its public-mindedness so as to demonstrate its superiority over the nouveaux riches who devote themselves to conspicuous consumption.* The poor play a similar function for philanthropic enterprises at the other levels of the socioeconomic hierarchy, including the mass of middle-class civic organizations and women's clubs engaged in volunteer work and fundraising in almost every American community. *Doing good among the poor has traditionally helped the church to find a method of expressing religious sentiments in action;* in recent years, militant church activity among and for the poor has enabled the church to hold on to its more liberal and radical members who might otherwise have dropped out of organized religion altogether.

Eleventh, the poor perform several cultural functions. They have played an unsung role in the creation of "civilization," having supplied the construction labor for many of the monuments which are often identified as the noblest expressions and examples of civilization, for example, the *Egyptian pyramids, Greek temples, and medieval churches.*[11] Moreover, they have helped to create a goodly share of the surplus capital that funds the artists and intellectuals who make culture, and particularly "high" culture, possible in the first place.

Twelfth, the "low" culture created for or by the poor is often adopted by the more affluent. *The rich collect artifacts from extinct folk cultures (although not only from poor ones),* and almost all Americans listen to *the jazz, blues, spirituals, and country music which originated among the Southern poor—as well as rock, which was derived from similar sources.* The protest of the poor sometimes becomes literature; in 1970, for example, *poetry written by ghetto children became popular in sophisticated literary circles.* The poor also serve as culture heroes and literary subjects, particularly, of course, for the Left, but the hobo, cowboy, hipster, and the mythical prostitute with a heart of gold have performed this function for a variety of groups.

Finally, the poor carry out a number of important political functions:

Thirteenth, the poor serve as symbolic constituencies and opponents for several political groups. *For example, parts of the revolutionary Left could not exist without the poor, particularly now that the working class can no longer be perceived as the vanguard of the revolution. Conversely, political groups of conservative bent need the "welfare chiselers" and others who "live off the tax-payer's hard-earned money" in order to justify their demands for reductions in welfare payments and tax relief.* Moreover, the role of the poor in upholding dominant norms (see function 5 above) also has a significant political function. An economy based on the ideology of laissez faire requires a deprived population which is allegedly unwilling to work; not only does the alleged moral inferiority of the poor reduce the moral pressure on the present political economy to eliminate poverty, *but redistributive alternatives can be made to look quite unattractive if those who will benefit from them most can be described as lazy, spendthrift, dishonest, and promiscuous.* Thus, conservatives and classical liberals would find it difficult to justify many of their political beliefs without the poor; but then so would modern liberals and socialists who seek to eliminate poverty.

Fourteenth, the poor, being powerless, can be made to absorb the economic and political costs of change and growth in American society. During the 19th century, *they did the backbreaking work that built the cities;* today, they are *pushed out of their neighborhoods to make room for "progress." Urban renewal projects to hold middle-class taxpayers and stores in the city and express-ways to enable suburbanites to commute downtown have typically been located in poor neighborhoods, since no other group will allow itself to be displaced.* For much the same reason, urban universities, hospitals, and civic centers also expand into land occupied by the poor. The major costs of the industrialization of agriculture in America have been borne by the poor, who are pushed off the land without recompense, just as in earlier centuries in Europe, they bore the brunt of the transformation of agrarian societies into industrial ones. The poor have also paid a large share of the human cost of the growth of American power overseas, for they have *provided many of the foot soldiers for Vietnam and other wars.*

Fifteenth, the poor have played an important role in shaping the American political process; *because they vote and participate less than other groups, the political system has often been free to ignore them.* This has not only made American politics more centrist than would otherwise be the case, but it has also added to the stability of the political process. *If the 15% of the population, below the federal "poverty line" participated fully in the political process, they would almost certainly demand better jobs and higher incomes, which would require income redistribution and would thus generate further political conflict between the haves and the have-nots.* Moreover, when the poor do participate, they often provide the Democrats with a captive constituency, for they can rarely support Republicans, lack parties of their own, and thus have no other place to go politically. This, in turn, has enabled the Democrats to count on the votes of the poor, allowing the party to be more responsive to voters who might otherwise switch to the Republicans, in recent years, for example, the white working class.

IV

I have described fifteen of the more important functions which the poor carry out in American society, enough to support the functionalist thesis that *poverty survives in part because it is useful to a number of groups in society.* This analysis is not intended to suggest that because it is functional, poverty *should* persist, or that it *must* persist. Whether it should persist is a normative question; whether it must, an analytic and empirical one, but the answer to both depends in part on whether the dysfunctions of poverty outweigh the functions. Obviously, poverty has many *dysfunctions, mainly for the poor themselves but also for the more affluent.* For example, their social order is upset by the pathology, crime, political protest, and disruption emanating from the poor, and the income of the affluent is affected by the taxes that must be levied to protect their social order. Whether the dysfunctions outweigh the functions is a question that clearly deserves study.

It is, however, possible to suggest alternatives for many of the functions of the poor. Thus, society's dirty work (function 1) could be done without poverty, some by automating it, the rest by paying the workers who do it decent wages, which would help considerably to cleanse that kind of work. Nor is it necessary for the poor to subsidize the activities they support through their low-wage jobs (function 2), for, like dirty work, many of these activities are essential enough to persist even if wages were raised. In both instances, however, costs would be driven up, resulting in higher prices to the customers and clients of dirty work and subsidized activity, with obvious dysfunctional consequences for more affluent people.

Alternative roles for the professionals who flourish because of the poor (function 3) are easy to suggest. Social workers could counsel the affluent, as most prefer to do anyway, and the *police could devote themselves to traffic and organized crime.* Fewer penologists would be employable, however, and *pentecostal religion would probably not survive without the poor.* Nor would parts of the second- and third-hand market (function 4), although even affluent people sometimes buy used goods. Other roles would have to be found for badly trained or incompetent professionals now relegated to serving the poor, and someone else would have to pay their salaries.

Alternatives for the deviance-connected social functions (functions 5-7) can be found more easily and cheaply than for the economic functions. Other groups are already available to serve as deviants to uphold traditional morality, for example, entertainers, hippies, and most recently, adolescents in general. These same groups are also available as alleged or real orgiasts to provide vicarious participation in sexual fantasies. The blind and disabled function as objects of pity and charity, and the poor may therefore not even be needed for functions 5-7.

The status and mobility functions of the poor (functions 8 and 9) are far more difficult to substitute, however. In a hierarchical society, some people must be defined as inferior to everyone else with respect to a variety of attributes, and the poor perform this function more adequately than others. They could, however, perform it without being as poverty-stricken as they are, and one can conceive of a stratification system in which the people below the federal "poverty line" *would receive 75% of the median income rather than 40% or less, as is now the case—even though they would still be last in the pecking order.*[12] Needless to say, such a reduction of economic inequality would also require income redistribution. *Given the opposition to income redistribution among more affluent people, however, it seems unlikely that the status functions of poverty can be replaced, and they—together with the economic functions of the poor, which are equally expensive to replace—may turn out to be the major obstacles to the elimination of poverty.*

The role of the poor in the upward mobility of other groups could be maintained without their being so low in income. However, if their incomes were raised above subsistence levels, they would begin to generate capital so that their own entrepreneurs could supply them with goods and services, thus competing with and perhaps rejecting "outside" suppliers. Indeed, this is already happening in a number of ghettos, where blacks are replacing white storeowners.

Similarly, if the poor were more affluent, they would make less willing clients for upper- and middle-class philanthropic and religious groups (function 10), although as long as they are economically and otherwise unequal, this function need not disappear altogether. Moreover, some would still use the settlement houses and other philanthropic institutions to pursue individual upward mobility, as they do now.

The cultural functions (11 and 12) may not need to be replaced. In America, the labor unions have rarely allowed the poor to help build cultural monuments anyway, and there is sufficient surplus capital from other sources to subsidize the unprofitable components of high culture. Similarly, other deviant groups are available to innovate in popular culture and supply new culture heroes, for example, the hippies and members of other counter-cultures.

Some of the political functions of the poor would, however, be as difficult to replace as their economic and status functions. Although the poor could probably continue to serve as symbolic constituencies and opponents (function 13) if their incomes were raised while they remained unequal in other respects, increases in income are generally accompanied by increases in power as well. Consequently, once they were no longer so poor, people would be likely to resist paying the costs of growth and change (function 14); and it is difficult to find alternative groups who can be displaced for urban renewal and technological "progress." Of course, it is possible to design city-rebuilding and highway projects which properly reimburse the displaced people, but such projects would then become considerably more expensive, thus raising the price for those now benefiting from urban renewal and expressways. Alternatively, many might never be built, thus reducing the comfort and convenience of those beneficiaries. Similarly, if the poor were subjected to less economic pressure, they would probably be less willing to serve in the army, except at considerably higher pay, in which case war would become yet more costly and thus less popular politically. Alternatively, more servicemen would have to be recruited from the middle and upper classes, but in that case war would also become less popular.

The political stabilizing and "centering" role of the poor (function 15) probably cannot be substituted for at all, since no other group is willing to be disenfranchised or likely enough to remain apathetic so as to reduce the fragility of the political system. Moreover, if the poor were given higher incomes, they would probably become more active politically, thus adding their demands for more to those of other groups already putting pressure on the political allocators of resources. The poor might continue to remain loyal to the Democratic party, but like other moderate-income voters, they could also be attracted to the Republicans or to third parties. While improving the economic status of the presently poor would not necessarily drive the political system far to the left, it would enlarge the constituencies now demanding higher wages and more public funds. It is of course possible to add new powerless groups who do not vote or otherwise participate to the political mix and can thus serve as "ballast" in the polity, for example, by encouraging the import of new poor immigrants from Europe and elsewhere, except that the labor unions are probably strong enough to veto such a policy.

In sum, then, several of the most important functions of the poor cannot be replaced with alternatives, while some could be replaced, but almost always only at higher costs to other people, particularly more affluent ones. Consequently, *a functional analysis must conclude that poverty persists not only because it satisfies a number of functions but also because many of the functional alternatives to poverty would be quite dysfunctional for the more affluent members of society.*[13]

V

I noted earlier that functional analysis had itself become a maligned phenomenon and that a secondary purpose of this paper was to demonstrate its continued usefulness. One reason for its presently low status is political; insofar as an analysis of functions, particularly latent functions, seems to justify what ought to be condemned, it appears to lend itself to the support of conservative ideological positions, although it can also have radical implications when it subverts the conventional wisdom. Still, as Merton has pointed out (1949, p. 43; 1961, pp. 736-37), functional analysis per se is ideologically neutral, and "like other forms of sociological analysis, it can be infused with any of a wide range of sociological values" (1949, p. 40). This infusion depends, of course, on the purposes—and even the functions—of the functional analysis, for as Wirth (1936, p. xvii) suggested long ago, "every assertion of a 'fact' about the social world touches the interests of some individual or group," and even if functional analyses are conceived and conducted in a neutral manner, they are rarely interpreted in an ideological vacuum.

In one sense, my analysis is, however, neutral; if one makes no judgment as to whether poverty ought to be eliminated—and if one can subsequently avoid being accused of acquiescing in poverty —then the analysis suggests only that *poverty exists because it is useful to many groups in society.*[14] If one favors the elimination of poverty, however, then the analysis can have a variety of political implications, *depending in part on how completely it is carried out.*

If functional analysis only identifies the functions of social phenomena without mentioning their dysfunctions, then it may, intentionally or otherwise, agree with or support holders of conservative values. Thus, to say that the poor perform many functions for the rich might be interpreted or used to justify poverty, just as Davis and Moore's argument (1945) that social stratification is functional because it provides society with highly trained professionals could be taken to justify inequality.

Actually, the Davis and Moore analysis was conservative because it was incomplete; it did not identify the dysfunctions of inequality and failed to suggest functional alternatives, as Tumin (1953) and Schwartz (1955) have pointed out.[15] Once a functional analysis is made more complete by *the addition of functional alternatives*, however, it can take on a liberal and reform cast, because the alternatives often provide ameliorative policies that do not require any drastic change in the existing social order.

Even so, to make functional analysis complete requires yet another step, an examination of the functional alternatives themselves. My analysis suggests that the alternatives for poverty are themselves dysfunctional for the affluent population, and it ultimately comes to a conclusion which is not very different from that of radical sociologists. To wit: *that social phenomena which are functional for affluent groups and dysfunctional for poor ones persist; that when the elimination of such phenomena through functional alternatives generates dysfunctions for the affluent, they will continue to persist; and that phenomena like poverty can be eliminated only when they either become sufficiently dysfunctional for the affluent or when the poor can obtain enough power to change the system of social stratification.*[16]

REFERENCES

Chernus, J. 1967. "Cities: A Study in Sadomasochism." *Medical Opinion and Review* (May), pp. 104-9.

Davis, K., and W. E. Moore. 1945. "Some Principles of Stratification." *American Sociological Review* 10 (April): 242-49.

Erikson, K. T. 1964. "Notes on the Sociology of Deviance." In *The Other Side*, edited by Howard S. Becker. New York: Free Press.

Gans, H. J. 1971. "Three Ways to Solve the Welfare Problem." *New York Times Magazine*, March 7, pp. 26-27, 94-100.

Goode, W. J. 1967. "The Protection of the Inept." *American Sociological Review* 32 (February): 5-19.

Gouldner, A. 1970. *The Coming Crisis of Western Sociology*. New York: Basic.

Herriot, A., and H. P. Miller. 1971. "Who Paid the Taxes in 1968." Paper prepared for the National Industrial Conference Board.

Macarov, D. 1970. *Incentives to Work*. San Francisco: Jossey-Bass.

Marshall, T. H. Forthcoming. "Poverty and Inequality." Paper prepared for the American Academy of Arts and Sciences volume on poverty and stratification.

Merton, R. K. 1949. "Manifest and Latent Functions." In *Social Theory and Social Structure*. Glencoe, Ill.: Free Press.

———. 1961. "Social Problems and Sociological Theory." In *Contemporary Social Problems*, edited by R. K. Merton and R. Nisbet. New York: Harcourt Brace.

Pechman, J. A. 1969. "The Rich, the Poor, and the Taxes They Pay." *Public Interest*, no. 17 (Fall), pp. 21-43.

Rainwater, L. 1970. *Behind Ghetto Walls*. Chicago: Aldine.

Schwartz, R. 1955. "Functional Alternatives to Inequality." *American Sociological Review* 20 (August): 424-30.

Stein, B. 1971 *On Relief*. New York: Basic.

Tumin, M. B. 1953. "Some Principles of Stratification: A Critical Analysis." *American Sociological Review* 18 (August): 387-93.

Wirth, L. 1936. "Preface." In *Ideology and Utopia*, by Karl Mannheim. New York: Harcourt Brace.

[1]Earlier versions of this paper were presented at a Vassar College conference on the war on poverty in 1964, at the 7th World Congress of Sociology in 1971, and in *Social Policy* 2 (July-August 1971): 20-24. The present paper will appear in a forthcoming book on poverty and stratification, edited by S. M. Lipset and S. M. Miller, for the American Academy of Arts and Sciences. I am indebted to Peter Marris, Robert K. Merton, and S. M. Miller for helpful comments on earlier drafts of this paper.

[2]The paper also has the latent function, as S. M. Miller has suggested, of contributing to the long debate over the functional analysis of social stratification presented by Davis and Moore (1945).

[3]Probably one of the few instances in which a phenomenon has the same function for two groups with different interests is when the survival of the system in which both participate is at stake. *Thus, a wage increase can be functional for labor and dysfunctional for management (and consumers), but, if the wage increase endangers the firm's survival, it is dysfunctional for labor as well.* This assumes, however, that the firm's survival is valued by the workers, which may not always be the case, for example, when jobs are available elsewhere.

[4]Merton (1949, p. 50) originally described functions and dysfunctions in terms of encouraging or hindering adaptation or adjustment to a system, although subsequently he has written that "dysfunction refers to the particular inadequacies of a particular part of the system for a designated requirement" (1961, p. 732). Since adaptation and adjustment to a system can have conservative ideological implications, Merton's later formulation and my own definitional approach make it easier to use functional analysis as an ideologically neutral or at least ideologically variable method, insofar as the researcher can decide for himself whether he supports the values of the group under analysis.

[5]It should be noted, however, that there are no absolute benefits and costs just as there are no absolute functions and dysfunctions; not only are one group's benefits often another group's costs, but every group defines benefits by its own manifest and

latent values, and a social scientist or planner who has determined that certain phenomena provide beneficial consequences for a group may find that the group thinks otherwise. For example, during the 1960s, advocates of racial integration discovered that a significant portion of the black community no longer considered it a benefit but saw it rather as a policy to assimilate blacks into white society and to decimate the political power of the black community.

[6]Of course, the poor do not actually subsidize the affluent. Rather, by being forced to work for low wages, they enable the affluent to use the money saved in this fashion for other purposes. The concept of subsidy used here thus assumes belief in a "just wage."

[7]Pechman (1969) and Herriott and Miller (1971) found that the poor pay a higher proportion of their income in taxes than any other part of the population: 50% among people earning $2,000 or less according to the latter study.

[8] Most official investigations of welfare cheating have concluded that less than 5% of recipients are on the rolls illegally, while it has been estimated that about a third of the population cheats in filing income tax returns.

[9] Although this paper deals with the functions of poverty for other groups, poverty has often been described as a motivating or character-building device for the poor themselves; and economic conservatives have argued that by generating the incentive to work, poverty encourages the poor to escape poverty. For an argument that work incentive is more enhanced by income than lack of it, see Gans (1971, p. 96).

[10] One psychiatrist (Chernus 1967) has even proposed the fantastic hypothesis that the rich and the poor are engaged in a sadomasochistic relationship, the latter being supported financially by the former so that they can gratify their sadistic needs.

[11]Although this is not a contemporary function of poverty in America, it should be noted that today these movements serve to attract and gratify American tourists.

[12]In 1971, the median family income in the United States was about $10,000, and the federal poverty line for a family of four was set at just about $4,000. Of course, most of the poor were earning less than 40% of the median, and about a third of them, less than 20% of the median.

[13]Or as Stein (1971, p. 171) puts it: *"If the non-poor make the rules . . . antipoverty efforts will only be made up to the point where the needs of the non-poor are satisfied, rather than the needs of the poor."*

[14]Of course, even in this case the analysis need not be purely neutral, but can be put to important policy uses, for example, by indicating more effectively than moral attacks on poverty the exact nature of the obstacles that must be overcome if poverty is to be eliminated. See also Merton (1961, pp. 709-12).

[15]Functional analysis can, of course, be conservative in value or have conservative implications for a number of other reasons, principally in its overt or covert comparison of the advantages of functions and disadvantages of dysfunctions, or in its attitudes toward the groups that are benefiting and paying the costs. Thus, a conservatively inclined policy researcher could conclude that the dysfunctions of poverty far outnumber the functions, but still decide that the needs of the poor are simply not as important or worthy as those of other groups, or of the country as a whole.

[16]On the possibility of radical functional analysis, see Merton (1949, pp. 40-43) and Gouldner (1970, p. 443). One difference between my analysis and the prevailing radical view is that most of the functions I have described are latent, whereas many radicals treat them as manifest: recognized and intended by an unjust economic system to oppress the poor. Practically speaking, however, this difference may be unimportant, for if unintended and unrecognized functions were recognized, many affluent people might then decide that they ought to be intended as well, so as to forestall a more expensive antipoverty effort that might be dysfunctional for the affluent.

Part V

WORK AND ORGANIZATIONS

I can't get no satisfaction.

Jagger and Richard

After God finished the rattlesnake, the toad and the vampire, He had some awful substance left with which He made a SCAB. A SCAB is a two-legged animal with a corkscrew soul, a water-logged brain and a combination backbone made of jelly and glue. Where others have hearts he carries a tumor of rotten principles. A strike-breaker is a traitor to his God, his Country, his family and his class!

Jack London

Introduction to Part V
(Work and Organizations)

Work behavior has been and continues to be an important area of sociological inquiry. Both men and women spend more of their cumulative lifetimes in work endeavors than in any other human activity.

In American society, as in most industrialized societies, work takes place in the context of a public or private complex organization or bureaucracy. It is the purpose of this section to reflect on a number of problems peculiar to work in an "organizational society." The work one does is of fundamental importance in determining the quality of life experiences which will be available to individuals in a capitalist society. The single most important source of status and prestige in our society derives from one's occupation. In addition to status, occupation will also determine one's income. Income, in turn, will drastically affect the quality of an individual's life. This is particularly the case in a society such as ours in which housing, food, medicine, education, even justice, are treated as commodities bought and sold in impersonal markets. In short, one's work is an important determinant of the kind of future that will be in store for ourselves, our children, and their children.

Professor Parlin's article raises some basic questions concerning the role of deception in our organizational society. It is argued that deception is a logical outgrowth of our cultural pre-occupation with mass consumption. The role of deception is analyzed in the context of the recruitment of new graduates into a large manufacturing organization.

Professor Miller's article points out the way in which the social class one is born into affects the probability that an individual will become a member of the business or political elite. Miller's data suggests that the Horatio Alger rags-to-riches legend is a myth of our culture.

The last article by Professors Lewis and Brisset points to our cultural pre-occupation with work. The authors suggest that even our most intimate leisure relationship (sex) cannot be enjoyed as leisurely fun. Their examination of institutional sex manuals points out that even sex must be perverted into a form of work performance. In sum, all three articles emphasize the impact of social structure on human beings.

16. AMERICAN HISTORIANS AND THE BUSINESS ELITE
WILLIAM MILLER
I

One might have supposed that historians, largely occupied as they have been with the activities of ruling classes, would have been among the first to study systematically the problem of the recruitment and tenure of elites. This problem is an especially interesting one in a country such as the United States which has had no official caste systems and no legally established hereditary hierarchies. Yet most American historians have shied away from it.[1] Few of them have even raised questions about the locus and transmission of power or status in modern times. Moreover, those who have discussed in particular the ascent of nineteenth- and early twentieth-century business leaders have tended to attribute their success simply to the possession of more shrewdness or trickiness or more pluck or luck or other private qualities than competitors who failed to rise; the very few historians who have considered social determinants

Reprinted from the *Journal of Economic History*, Vol. IX, (1949), pp. 184-208, by permission of the publisher, Economic History Association.

such as family background or work experience have, by stressing the alleged values of poverty or of starting business in boyhood, placed their emphasis, as we shall see, quite at the opposite pole from where it belongs.[2]

The present study of 190 business leaders of the first decade of the twentieth century and of 188 contemporary political leaders on whom data are presented for comparison aims to call historians' attention to the critical but neglected field of elite recruitment, to suggest a method by which data may be collected and analyzed,[3] and to present some of the results of applying this method to a particular area in which a few historians have speculated to strikingly misleading effect.

II

This essay is not wholly a pioneer effort to analyze the social characteristics of the American business elite, and a word should be said about the work already done in this field. I am not concerned with full-length biographies of business leaders, of which there are very few of value, nor with popular studies of groups of businessmen, such as Matthew Josephson's *The Robber Barons* or Frederick Lewis Allen's *The Lords of Creation*. Of somewhat greater interest, at least methodologically, are two books by Fritz Redlich—*History of American Business Leaders* and *The Molding of American Banking: Men and Ideas*.[4] These discuss certain "entrepreneurial" characteristics[5] of *sizable numbers* of business leaders; the first, leaders in the iron and steel industry in England, Germany, and the United States, largely in the nineteenth century; the second, American bankers and related politicos, 1781-1840. Unlike the more popular books, Redlich's are long on theory; but, like them, his are short on synthesis. Systematic summaries of his data can be made, but he has not made them.[6]

Most germane to the field of the present essay are the following *statistical* studies of American business leaders:[7] Pitirim Sorokin, "American Millionaires and Multi-Millionaires";[8] Chester M. Destler, "Entrepreneurial Leadership Among the 'Robber Barons': A Trial Balance";[9] C. Wright Mills, "The American Business Elite: A Collective Portrait";[10] and, the only full-length book, F.W. Taussig and C.S. Joslyn, *American Business Leaders: A Study in Social Origins and Social Stratification*.[11]

The first two, by Sorokin and Destler, are suggestive, but certain internal weaknesses reduce their scientific value. Sorokin lumps many kinds of millionaires and near millionaires; his 668 persons selected haphazardly (but not, statistically speaking, at random), over a period of some two hundred years, include actors, preachers, statesmen, and physicians as well as businessmen, and in his tables he seldom distinguishes the last group from the rest. The difficulty with Destler's work lies mainly in the vagueness of some of his categories, though the small number of businessmen studied by him (43) also diminishes confidence in his results.[12]

The essay by Mills and the book by Taussig and Joslyn, while satisfactory as starting points for additional studies, present their own problems, the first mainly because of the nature of its sample, the second partly because of the nature of its questionnaire. Mills selected his men only from the *Dictionary of American Biography.* The subjects for which were named on grounds that made some businessmen eligible for reasons that had little to do with their business achievements and others ineligible however eminent they may have been in the business community of their time.[13] Taussig and Joslyn, in turn, setting out to prove that heredity is more important than environment in business success, asked their respondents for so little information that, as William F. Ogburn said in a review of their book, they have "such a small fraction of the environment measured that they, in the nature of the case, cannot do much toward a solution of the problem."[14] Yet Taussig and Joslyn's initial data were carefully gathered and as presented in some of the tables in their book are available for more scholarly and scientific use.[15]

III

The present study is focused upon "career men"—bureaucrats, that is—who often must have been as occupied with getting and staying ahead in their companies as with keeping their companies ahead of the field. In studying the so-called "robber barons," Destler was impelled to consider also a few early "career men," an odd-sounding designation for "semi-piratical entrepreneurs who roamed the United States virtually unchecked before 1903."[16] I, in turn, have had to include some atavistic captains of industry. Nevertheless, except for a few partners in unincorporated investment-banking houses, the men discussed in these pages were all officeholders; many of them *never* organized a business of any kind.

Yet the dull titles by which these men are called and the bureaucratic maneuvering in which they must often have engaged should not suggest that these were petty men exercising small powers in petty domains. The mere fact that they were bureaucrats should suggest the contrary, for, while there are many examples of petty bureaucracies, generally speaking only large enterprises operating in large theaters need hierarchical structures. The fact is, the men discussed in this essay were at the apex of some of the mightiest organizations the world up to then had seen. In the vernacular of their times, their bureaucratic structures were among the first great industrial, commercial, and financial "trusts."

As late as 1896, except for some railroads, there were probably fewer than a dozen American corporations capitalized at more than $10 million. By 1903, again excepting railroads, there were more than three hundred corporations capitalized at $10 million or more, approximately fifty at $50 million or more, and seventeen at $100 million or more.[17] A similar change may be traced in the modern history of other capitalist nations in which, as in the United States, the startling upward curve in the productivity of workers, attributable in part to the new technology of electricity and alloys, helped bring about an unprecedented speeding up in the accumulation of money and power and in the combination of business firms.

In this period one after another of the key segments of the world's economy was engrossed by the world's business leaders, Americans not least among them. And in the United States as elsewhere it became possible in regard to scores of commodities and key services such as transportation, communication, and the granting of credit to name the corporations or clusters of corporations that dictated the quantities which could be produced or employed and the prices and places at which they could be sold. Such fateful decisions were in the domain of the early business bureaucrats studied here and were communicated to and carried out by the bureaucracies they controlled—organizations that would scarcely have been understood by early nineteenth-century entrepreneurs or by those Jacksonian politicians who had sought, in the name of equal entrepreneurial opportunity, to make the establishment of corporations so easy.

IV

At the start of this work I had decided that two hundred men were all that an individual could study in a reasonable time and that from that number (various contingencies reduced the final group to 190) statistically reliable results could be obtained.[18] If these men were selected from the largest companies regardless of field, the bulk of them would have come from the railroads; if, on the other hand, an equal number were taken from each major business field, representatives of small insurance companies and banks would have mingled with the elite while many from great railroads would have been excluded. This dilemma could be solved only arbitrarily.

The companies from which men were chosen were taken from the following major fields: (1) manufacturing and mining, (2) steam railroads, (3) public utilities, (4) finance (commercial banking, life insurance, investment banking).[19] Companies in the first three fields were ranked by capitalization, the commercial banks by deposits, and the life-insurance companies (no other types of insurance companies approach the life companies in size) by assets.[20] From the *Statistical Abstract of the United States* and other sources summarizing census information, I then took the capitalization of the entire manufacturing and mining, steam railroad, and public-utilities industries in the United States in or near 1910, the total deposits of the national banks, and the assets of the life-insurance companies. These I simply added together and distributed the leaders among the four fields more or less according to the proportion of the total represented by the figure used for each. This total of capital, deposits, and assets came to $57 billion. Table I shows how the leaders would have been distributed had the proportions been followed exactly, and how they actually are distributed in this study.

Table 1.   Distribution of Business Leaders by Type of Industry

Industry	Number of Men from Each Industry if Representation Were Proportionate to "Size" of Industry	Actual Number of Men from Each Industry
Manufacturing and Mining	65	64
Steam Railroads	58	58
Public Utilities	29	31
National Banking	16 ⎫	19 ⎫
Finance	29	28
Life Insurance	13 ⎭	9 ⎭
Total	181*	181*

*The nine investment bankers, selected on a different basis, are excluded from this table. See n. 20.

The next step was to choose the topmost positions from which these men should be selected. Should directors be included, or chairmen and members of key panels such as finance or executive committees? What of executive vice-presidents, general managers, or cashiers of banks? Investigation of the locus of different types of power in large corporations has only just begun;[21] for the period of this work it may fairly be said that there are no studies. The decision to limit this work to presidents and board chairmen of corporations and some partners of unincorporated investment-banking houses permitted me to choose men from a larger group of companies that would have been possible had men from more positions been selected; it may have caused some persons of great importance to be excluded, but all of those included, at any rate, were bound to be men of first rank.[22] These men and their companies are listed at the end of this section. No one who was president or board chairman in a listed company in the decade 1901-1910 has been excluded.[23]

One hundred and seventy-four of these men (information on this score is lacking for sixteen) held approximately 2,720 business directorships. A few held more than 100 each; the average was about 16.[24] Clearly, these men were leaders not only in their own companies but in the entire business community.

A List of the Men and Their Companies Used in This Study†

Size, in Millions, 1903	Company	Presidents and Chairmen (* denotes board chairman)
	A. Manufacturing and Mining Companies	
$1,370	United States Steel Corp.	Schwab, Charles M. Corey, William E. *Gary, Elbert H.
503	Consolidated Tobacco Co. } American Tobacco Co. }	Duke, James B.
201	American Smelting & Refining Co.	Nash, Edward W. Guggenheim, Daniel
175	Amalgamated Copper Co.	Rogers, Henry H. Ryan, John D.
170	International Mercantile Marketing Co.	Griscom, Clement A.
145	American Sugar Refining Co.	Havemeyer, Henry O. Thomas, Washington B.
130	United States Leather Co. Central Leather Co.	Horton, James Hoyt, Edward C. *Valentine, Patrick A.
120	International Harvester Co.	McCormick, Cyrus H. Deering, Charles
97	Standard Oil Co.	Rockefeller, John D.
84	Pittsburgh Coal Co.	Robbins, Francis L. Taylor, Matthew H. Field, William K.
82	American Can Co.	Norton, Edwin Assmann, Franz A. Graham, William T. *Reid, Daniel G.
74	Pullman Co.	Lincoln, Robert T.

Continued on p. 202

Size, in Millions, 1903	Company	Presidents and Chairman (* denotes board chairman)

A. Manufacturing and Mining Companies

Size, in Millions, 1903	Company	Presidents and Chairman
71	Corn Products Co. Corn Products Refining Co.	Matthiessen, Conrad H. Bedford, Edward T.
60	American Car & Foundry Co.	Bixby, William K. Eaton, Frederick H.
60	Crucible Steel Co. of America	Halcomb, Charles H. Smith, Frank B. Ramsey, Charles C. *Park, William G. *DuPuy, Herbert
58	United States Rubber Co.	Colt, Samuel P.
56	National Biscuit Co.	Crawford, Benjamin F. Green, Adolphus W.
56	Lackawanna Steel Co.	Scranton, Walter Clarke, Edmund A.S.
52	International Paper Co.	Chisholm, Hugh J. Burbank, Alonzo N.
50	United Copper Co.	Heinze, F. Augustus
50	American Locomotive Co.	Pitkin, Albert J. Marshall, Waldo H.
50	Distillers' Securities Corp.	Curley, Edmund J.
50	Cambria Steel Co.	Stackhouse, Powell Price, Charles S.
49	American Woolen Co.	Ayer, Frederick Wood, William M.
48	Colorado Fuel & Iron Co.	Osgood, John C. Kebler, Julian A. Hearne, Frank J. Welborn, Jesse F.
47	Republic Iron & Steel Co.	Thompson, Alexis W. Topping, John A. Guthrie, Tracy W. *French, G. Watson
46	General Electric Co.	Coffin, Charles A.
45	Associated Oil Co. of Calif.	Canfield, C.A. Chanslor, J.A. Herrin, William F.
44	Westinghouse Electric Corp.	Westinghouse, George Atkins, Edward F. *Ives, Brayton

B. Steam Railroads

Size, in Millions, 1903	Company	Presidents and Chairman
873	Pennsylvania Railroad Co.	Cassatt, Alexander McCrea, James
490	The Rock Island Co.	Leeds, William B. Mather, Robert Walker, Roberts *Yoakum, Benjamin F.
460	The Southern Pacific Co.	Hays, Charles M. *Tweed, Charles H.

Continued on p. 203

Size, in Millions, 1903	Company	Presidents and Chairman (* denotes board chairman)
	A. Manufacturing and Mining Companies	
458	Atchison, Topeka & Santa Fe Railway Co.	Ripley, Edward P.
451	Union Pacific Railroad Co.	Burt, Horace G. Harriman, Edward H. Lovett, Robert S.
394	The Reading Co.	Harris, Joseph S. Baer, George F.
392	Baltimore & Ohio Railroad Co.	Loree, Leonor F. Murray, Oscar G. Willard, Daniel
382	New York Central & Hudson River Railroad Co.	Callaway, Samuel R. Newman, William H. Brown, William C. *Depew, Chauncey M.
372	Erie Railroad Co.	Thomas, Eben B. Underwood, Frederick D.
365	Southern Railway Co.	Spencer, Samuel Finley, William W.
303	Chicago & Northwestern Railroad Co.	Hughitt, Marvin
297	Atlantic Coast Line Co.	Walters, Henry Elliott, Warren G. Jenkins, Michael
286	Northern Pacific Railway Co.	Mellen, Charles S. Elliott, Howard
233	Missouri Pacific Railroad Co.	Gould, George J.
230	Chicago, Milwaukee & St. Paul Railroad Co.	Earling, Albert J. *Miller, Roswell
226	Illinois Central Railroad Co.	Fish, Stuyvesant Harahan, James T.
205	Great Northern Railway	Hill, James J. Hill, Louis W.
152	Chicago, Burlington & Quincy Railroad Co.	Perkins, Charles E. Harris, George B. Miller, Darius
149	Missouri, Kansas & Texas Railway	Rouse, Henry C. Finney, Frederick N. Allen, Andrew A. *Joline, Adrian H. Hawley, Edwin
142	Norfolk & Western Railway Co.	Kimball, Frederick J. Fink, Henry Johnson, Lucius E.
138	Chesapeake & Ohio Railway	Stevens, George E. *Trumbull, Frank
127	Denver & Rio Grande Railroad Co.	Jeffery, Edward T.
119	Delaware, Lackawanna & Western Railroad	Truesdale, William H. *Sloan, Samuel

Continued on p. 204

Size, in   Presidents and Chairman
Millions, 1903   *Company*   (* denotes board chairman)

A. Manufacturing and Mining Companies

118	Western Maryland Railroad Co.	Hood, John M.

Pierce, Winslow S.
Ramsey, Joseph, Jr.
Bush, Benjamin F.

C. Public Utilities

| 392 | American Telephone & Telegraph Co. | Cochrane, Alexander |

Fish, Frederick P.
Vail, Theodore N.

| 224 | Metropolitan Securities Co. | Fowler, Thomas P. |

Vreeland, Herbert H.

| 176 | Public Service Co. of New Jersey | McCarter, Thomas N. |

| 170 | Brooklyn Rapid Transit Co. | Greatsinger, Jacob L. |

Winter, Edwin W.
*Brady, Anthony N.

| 150 | Consolidated Gas Co. of New York | Gawtry, Harrison E. |

Cortelyou, George B.

| 127 | Interborough Rapid Transit Co. } Interborough-Metropolitan Co. } | Belmont, August |

Bryan, Edward P.
Shonts, Theodore P.

| 121 | Western Union Telegraph Co. | Eckert, Thomas T. |

Clowry, Robert C.

| 117 | Philadelphia Rapid Transit Co. | Parsons, John B. |

Kruger, Charles O.

| 111 | Chicago Union Traction Co. } Chicago Railways Co. } | Roach, John M. |

*Foreman, Henry G.
*Blair, Henry A.

| 100 | United Gas Improvement Co. | Dolan, Thomas |

| 80 | North American Co. | Wetmore, Charles W. |

Campbell, James

| 76 | St. Louis Transit Co. | Carleton, Murray |

| 70 | United Railway & Electric Co. of Baltimore | Perin, Nelson |

House, William A.

| 69 | Massachusetts Electric Co. | Abbott, Gordon |

| 68 | Boston Elevated Railway Co. | Bancroft, William A. |

| 67 | People's Gas, Light & Coke Co. | Billings, Cornelius K.G. |

Knapp, George O.

D. Finance

1. National Banks

| 148 | National City Bank (New York) | Stillman, James |

Vanderlip, Frank A.

| 90 | National Bank of Commerce (New York) | Hendrix, Joseph C. |

Snyder, Valentine P.

| 84 | First National Bank (New York) | Baker, George F. |

Continued on p. 205

Size, in Millions, 1903	Company	Presidents and Chairman (* denotes board chairman)
	A. Manufacturing and Mining Companies	
75	National Park Bank (New York)	Delafield, Richard
74	Hanover National Bank (New York)	Woodward, James T.
59	United States Trust Co. (New York)	Stewart, John A. Gage, Lyman J. Sheldon, Edward W.
54	Mercantile Trust Co. (New York)	Deming, Henry C. Fitzgerald, Louis
92	First National Bank (Chicago)	Forgan, James B.
73	Illinois Trust and Savings Bank (Chicago)	Mitchell, John J.
46	Corn Exchange National Bank (Chicago)	Hamill, Ernest A.
46	National Bank of Commerce (St. Louis)	Thompson, William H. VanBlarcom, Jacob C.
47	National Shawmut Bank (Boston)	Stearns, James P. Gaston, William A.
	2. Life Insurance	
382	Mutual Life Insurance Co.	McCurdy, Richard A. Peabody, Charles A.
359	Equitable Life Assurance Co.	Alexander, James W. Morton, Paul
322	New York Life Insurance Co.	McCall, John A. Orr, Alexander E. Kingsley, Darwin P.
89	Metropolitan Life Insurance Co.	Hegeman, John R.
63	Aetna Life Insurance Co. (Hartford)	Bulkeley, Morgan G.
	3. Investment Bankers	Partners
	J.P. Morgan & Co.	Morgan, J. Pierpont Perkins, George W.
	Kuhn, Loeb & Co.	Schiff, Jacob H. Warburg, Paul M.
	Kidder, Peabody & Co.	Winsor, Robert Peabody, Frank E.
	Lee, Higginson & Co.	Higginson, Henry L. Lane, Gardner M.
	Speyer & Co.	Speyer, James

†Some of these men served in more than one listed company or in more than one eligible position in the same company. Each man is listed according to the first eligible position he held, and only there. Some of these companies changed names and otherwise were recognized during the decade studied; other expired during this decade. All companies are listed by their names in 1903; for some the new names are included in brackets.

V

As stated earlier in this essay, some general American historians have made enough casual remarks about the recruitment of modern business leaders to form a rough explanatory model. I want now to point out some of the facets of this model and then to introduce some of my own findings to show how obsolete it had become by the first decade of this century, if, indeed, it ever fitted the facts.

Virtually all the generalizations that go to make up this model are based upon a few remarkable life histories from the "robber baron" period; thus in most of the books that are at all concerned with the recruitment of business leaders one finds accounts of Andrew Carnegie, John D. Rockefeller, J. Pierpont Morgan, James J. Hill, and Edward H. Harriman. In *The Growth of the American People 1865-1940*, Arthur M. Schlesinger, Sr., cites in addition such older heroes as Cornelius Vanderbilt and Gustavus F. Swift but not later ones.[25] Charles A. and Mary R. Beard, in *The Rise of American Civilization*, add to the ubiquitous five Jay Gould, William H. Vanderbilt, Collis P. Huntington, Jay Cooke, William A. Clark, and Philip D. Armour.[26] Few general historians discuss a greater number of men than do the Beards; but much more significant, practically none discusses any *later* men.

The last extended discussion of the "typical" business leader by Samuel Eliot Morison and Henry Steele Commager in *The Growth of the American Republic*—a widely used textbook—follows (italics mine):

> The *most typical figure* of the industrial age was undoubtedly Andrew Carnegie. A *poor immigrant boy* from Scotland, he followed and helped to *perpetuate* the American tradition of rising *from poverty to riches*, and his success he ascribed entirely to the political and economic democracy which obtained in this country. By dint of unflagging industry and unrivalled business acumen and resourcefulness and especially through his extraordinary ability to choose as associates such men as Charles Schwab, Henry Frick, and Henry Phipps, and to command the devotion of his workmen, Carnegie built up the greatest steel business in the world, and retired in 1901 to chant the glories of "Triumphant Democracy" and to give away his enormous fortune of three and a half hundred millions.[27]

Arthur Schlesinger says vaguely of the latest group of business leaders he discusses that they arose "in most cases from obscure origins and unhindered by moral scruples, they were fired by a passionate will to succeed."[28] In the last discussion of business leaders in *The American Nation*, John D. Hicks says: "Typical of the railroad builders was James J. Hill," who, he points out, was an immigrant from Canada.[29] The Beards' analysis of the life histories of American business leaders ends with the eleven men named above, of whom they write:

> Of the group here brought under examination only two, Morgan and Vanderbilt, built their fortunes on the solid basis of family inheritances while only one had what may be called by courtesy a higher education: Morgan spent two years in the University of Göttingen. Carnegie began life as a stationary engineer; Jay Cooke as a clerk in a general store in Sandusky; Jay Gould as a surveyor and tanner; Huntington, Armour, and Clark as husky lads on their fathers' farms; Hill as a clerk for a St. Paul steamboat company; Harriman as an office boy in a New York broker's establishment; Rockefeller as a bookkeeper in Cleveland.[30]

The Beards' inference is that these men, starting from the lowliest jobs as exemplars of the tradition, rose from the most humble origins to the very top. This may actually have been so, not only of these few men but of the large majority of business leaders whom they are taken to represent. But, it may be asked, how many in modern times start much higher than these men did, even among the well-born, college-trained young men who, as *Fortune* put it, spend a few years in "the mummery of 'working in the plant' " before ascending to the highest executive levels?[31] Surely, of itself, an initial low-status job does not necessarily imply lowly origins.[32]

It is instructive to note that even the more perspicacious historians, when they err on the origins of business leaders, do so on the side of the tradition. Thus the Beards describe Rockefeller, the son of a "Barnumesque" itinerant entrepreneur, as "the son of a farmer";[33] and Henry B. Parkes writes of F. Augustus Heinze, the copper magnate who was born in Brooklyn, New York, into a comfortable business family, as a "young German immigrant."[34]

Though most historians say little about it, there has been in the United States for well over a century a sizable and growing working class, propertyless, segregated, often remarkably apathetic to the alleged opportunities of American business and political life. Into this class most immigrants, starting with the Irish in the 1840's, have been channeled. Historians generally imply by the individuals they select as examples that this class and (for so little is said in this connection of rich men's business-bred, college-educated sons) this class alone has supplied our business leaders, that their school, to quote Carnegie himself, was "the sternest of all schools—poverty," that they were graduated from it early in life into apprenticeships as "mechanics" or "poor clerks," and that "against the boy who swept the office, or who begins as a shipping clerk at fourteen," the college graduate "has little chance, starting at twenty."[35]

Yet to read the lives of business leaders, even of those who presumably are the pillars of this tradition, is to look almost in vain for working class or foreign origins, and even poor and unschooled farm boys are not conspicuous among such leaders. Of Rockefeller and Heinze I have already spoken. The historians themselves have accounted for J. Pierpont Morgan and William H. Vanderbilt. Jay Cooke's father, Eleutheros, was "a lawyer who was sent to Congress." Harriman's father, Orlando, was an Episcopal clergyman, "the one exception of his generation in a family of several brothers" who followed the family tradition of successful "trading and commercial pursuits." Harriman himself married the daughter of a banker and railroad president who started him on his railroad career. Even a farm boy such as Elbert H. Gary, who "experienced early in life the arduous regimen of work on a pioneer farm, an experience which endowed him with excellent health and a robust physique," was raised in a settlement named after his forebears and in a house that "was a large one for the time—the largest in the settlement . . . 'the big white house on the hill' it came to be called."[36]

Doubtless examples can be found in the period emphasized by the historians of men whose life histories more fully substantiate the tradition. What of the men in the later period to which the historians tacitly allow their explanations of origins and ascent to apply and which is the subject of this essay?

VI

Had the "typical" American business leader of the first decade of the twentieth century been an immigrant? Was he best represented in manufacturing, for example, by Franz A. Assmann, the German-born president of the American Can Company; or in railroading by Edward T. Jeffery, the English-born president of the Denver and Rio Grande; or in insurance by Alexander E. Orr, the Irish-born president of the New York Life; or in banking by Jacob H. Schiff, the German-born Jew who became senior partner of Kuhn, Loeb and Co.?

Simply to ask the question is to answer it. Of the 187 businessmen studied here whose birthplaces are known, only 18, or less than 10 per cent, were born abroad.[37] Surely these men were less "typical" of the topmost business leaders of their time than the 55 per cent who were born in the eastern part of the United States, in New England and the middle Atlantic states.[38]

Table II. American Business and Political Leaders by Region of Birthplace*

Birthplace	Business Leaders (per cent of)	Political Leaders (per cent of)
New England	18 ⎫ 55	22
Middle Atlantic	37 ⎭	27
East north central	22	27
South	9	11
West	4	7
United States	90	94
Foreign	10	6
Total cases(= 100 per cent)	187	188

* These are census regions. Combined in "South" are south Atlantic, south central, west south central; in "West" west north central, mountain, Pacific.

Of the eighteen business leaders who were foreign-born, moreover, scarcely two or three fit the historians' concept of the *poor* immigrant who made good, and even these men had been brought to the United States at such an early age that they may be said to have been bred if not born here. Two of the eighteen men were of rich, colonial American business families who happened to be residing temporarily in Canada when they were born. Four more, rich and highly placed abroad, either settled here as representatives of big foreign business firms or were brought over by fathers who represented such firms. At least two others had letters of introduction from their fathers or other relatives abroad to American bankers and merchants who helped to establish them here. Thus it appears to be unsafe in writing of elites to associate immigrant status, even where that fits, with the idea of poverty.

If not typically poor immigrants, were these business and political leaders the sons of foreigners? More of them were, surely, but the next table shows that the typical leader in each field was born into an American family.

Table III. American Business and Political Leaders by Region of Father's Birthplace

Father's Birthplace	Business Leaders (per cent of)	Political Leaders (per cent of)
New England	27	33
Middle Atlantic	31	28
East north central	4	5
South	12	17
United States, unspecified*	7	4
United States	81	87

Continued on p. 210

Father's Birthplace	Business Leaders (per cent of)	Political Leaders (per cent of)
Foreign	19	13
Total cases (= 100 per cent)	176	176

*Fathers of none of these men were known to have been born in the "West" as defined in Table II. All those known to have been born in the United States, the exact region being unknown, are counted here.

Moreover, these families themselves had, in most instances, been in America for many generations. Almost three fourths of the business and political leaders were at least of the fourth generation of their paternal lines to reside in America; many were of the seventh and even the eighth generations. Colonial families were represented by 73 per cent of the business leaders and 79 per cent of those in politics.[39] Fifty-six per cent of the former and 47 per cent of the latter were of families that had settled in America in the seventeenth century.

Even were they not of colonial ancestry, most of these leaders could point to British, and many to English, forebears.

Table IV. American Business and Political Leaders by Paternal Family's Origin*

Family Origin	Business Leaders (per cent of)	Political Leaders (per cent of)
England and Wales	53	56
Ireland..............................	14	13
Scotland	7	8
Canada..............................	3	1
British Empire, other, or unspecified ..	5	5
British Empire	82	83
Germany	12	8
Other countries	6	9
Total cases (= 100 per cent)	162	162

*Or country of leader's own origin if he was the first in the family to settle in America. In either case, *last country* before settlement in America.

They could claim Protestant, and often Episcopal or Presbyterian, backgrounds.

Table V. American Business and Political Leaders by Religious Background*

Denomination	Business Leaders (per cent of)	Political Leaders (per cent of)
Episcopal	25	12
Presbyterian.........................	21	17
Methodist	9	13
Baptist	5	7

Continued on p. 211

Denomination	Business Leaders (per cent of)	Political Leaders (per cent of)
Other Protestant......................	14	20
Protestant, unspecified................	16	25
Protestant	90	94
Catholic............................	7	4
Jewish	3	2
Total cases (= 100 per cent)	174	165

*In almost all instances this is the religion of the leader himself and most likely of his family as well. In a few instances where a shift in religion is known to have occurred, only the old religion is counted.

If not of recent foreign origin, was the typical American business leader of the early twentieth century a migrant from a farm?

Table VI shows that the political leaders far more frequently than those in business came from rural areas, that almost 60 per cent of the latter were recruited from the larger towns and cities. Indeed, more than 20 per cent of them were born in cities that around the middle of the nineteenth century had populations of 100,000 or more. Upon these men rural influences even in a predominantly rural society must have been at a minimum.

Table VI. American Business and Political Leaders by Size of Birthplace*

Size of Birthplace	Business Leaders (per cent of)	Political Leaders (per cent of)
Rural (under 2,500)....................	41 ⎫	75
Town (2,500-8,000)	19 ⎬59	9
City (over 8,000)	40 ⎭	16
Total cases (= 100 per cent)	164	180

*Population is from the census nearest each man's date of birth. In a few instances of men raised in places (that is, moved there before reaching the age of 7) sufficiently larger or smaller than their birthplaces to alter their classification in the scale used in the table, that place, not the birthplace, was used.

Yet more significant in answering the question are the occupations of the fathers of these business leaders. Here we find that even of those born in rural areas fewer than one third (and only 12 per cent of the whole group) had fathers who were mainly farmers. Fifty-six per cent of all the business leaders, on the other hand, had fathers who had been in business—often big business—before them; eight of ten, indeed, came from business or professional families.

Table VII. American Business and Political Leaders by Father's Occupation*

Occupation	Business Leaders (per cent of)	Political Leaders (per cent of)
Businessman	56 ⎫79	33
Professional	23 ⎭	18

Continued on p. 212

Occupation	Business Leaders (per cent of)	Political Leaders (per cent of)
Farmer...........................	12	38
Public official	7	9
Worker...........................	2	2
Total cases (= 100 per cent)	167	167

*Some fathers engaged in more than one occupation. The one used here was domi-
nant in the period in which each man was raised. In a few instances this was not
clear so a choice was made more or less arbitrarily (considering our lack of knowledge
of income and status factors in the early nineteenth century) by which business (including higher company positions as well as company ownership) took precedence
over farming and professional or public-official positions over both. This conforms
roughly to the ascending order of status used in classifying occupations today. In no
instance was there a problem of a father who was a worker (including wage as well
as salaried occupations). About one third of the professionals were lawyers or
engineers who might have been called businessmen, given the nature of their professional work; the others were clergymen, doctors, writers, etc. "Public official"
includes professional politicians (even if not officeholders) and lawyers who were
chiefly public men.

Darwin P. Kingsley, who was president of the New York Life
Insurance Company from 1907 to 1931 and chairman of the board
from 1931 to his death two years later, once said of his impoverished
early years:

> On the 40-acre farm, in Vermont, where I was born, everything we wore
> and everything we ate was grown on the farm, except a little sugar once
> in a while in place of maple sugar, which was indigenous, and a little
> tea. From a dozen sheep came wool which was first spun and then
> woven by hand into winter clothing. Our garden supplied flax which
> was made into summer garments. . . . I well remember the first time
> my father took his wool and swapped it for fulled cloth. We all regarded
> that as an epochal advance into a higher state of civilization.
> At Alburg, where I was born, there were not then (1857) enough houses
> to form even a hamlet. In the summer I attended the old "deestrict"
> school, a primitive affair innocent of any suggestion of higher education.
> In our home were very few books. Life there was clean through and
> through, self-respecting, and full of moral and religious discipline. But
> it was extremely narrow, uninspiring, and unimaginative. There was lit-
> tle or nothing to fire a boy with ambition or enthusiasm or to acquaint
> him with the world that lay beyond his "cabined, cribbed, and con-
> fined" sphere.[40]

Yet it was not this kind of poverty that Carnegie had in mind
when he recommended his "sternest of all schools"; this kind of
spiritual and intellectual poverty was probably most prevalent among
the poor, but this much at least they shared with large segments of
the population at all levels, including those born and raised among
the very rich. Call Kingsley's family poor in material things as well;

but compared with the sons of many urban and rural wage workers even in the 1850's he and other farmers' sons like him were not worse off.

Nevertheless, in the next table, showing the social status of the families of these business and political leaders, Kingsley and a few others with apparently similar or poorer backgrounds were classified as lower class. Men were classified as of the upper class when it was clear that their fathers, like those of August Belmont, Cornelius K. G. Billings, or Charles Deering, were themselves big business-men, or where their families, like those of Robert Todd Lincoln or Winslow Shelby Pierce, were politically eminent. Generally speak-ing, those in between—including some businessmen with no special claims to wealth or power or professionals like the average clergy-man, doctor, or lawyer—were ranked as of middle-class origins. This does not mean that their fathers were not of help to them. James B. Duke, for example, rose to wealth and power with a company founded by his father; George W. Perkins moved to a partnership in the House of Morgan—probably the acting head of the house at one stage—from a vice-presidency in the New York Life Insurance Company in which his father, a minor executive there, had given him his business start.

Not all the men ranked in the upper class, of course, had fathers as rich and powerful as those of Belmont or Billings, or families as well connected as those of Lincoln or Pierce. Many in the middle bracket, likewise, probably were not as fortunate in their upbringing as Elbert H. Gary, whose family is classified there; probably few so classified were as poor in material things as the Harrimans.

Table VIII. American Business and Political Leaders by Family Status

Status	Business Leaders (per cent of)	Political Leaders (per cent of)
Upper	50	36
Middle	45	50
Lower	5	14
Total cases (= 100 per cent)	179	180

Poor boys, as Carnegie rightly said, usually go to work early in life. Clearly few of these business and political leaders were poor boys. And, as the following table shows, few of them went to work at an early age.

Table IX. American Business and Political Leaders by age on Going to Work*

Age	Business Leaders (per cent of)	Political Leaders (per cent of)
15 or under	20	13
16-18	35	10
19 and over	45	77
Total cases (= 100 per cent)	179	182

*This is age on taking first regular business, professional, or other job (except work on father's or other relative's farm) after leaving school or, in a very few instances, after leaving the Union or Confederate armies.

Only one in five of these business leaders had a job before he was 16; slightly more than half of them had jobs before they were 19. Delaying the business debuts of most of the others—their late start, according to the tradition, being itself a handicap—was the pursuit of higher education, an undertaking that should so have altered their characters as to make them even poorer prospects for business success. The educational levels attained by all the leaders studied here are shown in the following table.[41]

Table X. American Business and Political Leaders by Highest Educational Level Attained*

Education	Business Leaders (per cent of)	Political Leaders (per cent of)
Grammar school	22	18
High school	37	27
Some college	12 }41	11 }55
College graduate	29	44
Total cases (= 100 per cent)	183	188

*I have reduced the many types of older schools to this modern terminology, including in "grammar school" institutions called by that name, as well as district, public, common, and similar schools; in "high school," academies and others of similar rank. Counted among grammar-school boys are those who had little or no formal education as well as graduates; among high-school boys, all those who attended whether graduates or not. A few who had private tutors well into their teens but did not attend college are counted with the high-school group.

Of the business leaders who did not go to work until they were 19 or older, 76 per cent had gone to college. Four out of five of these, in turn, were of the upper class. No group, if the traditional account of the origins and ascent pattern of the American business elite truly represented the facts, could have been worse off than this one in the competition for business eminence. Yet about 28 per cent of the business leaders are found in it.[42] These men shared *all* the alleged handicaps: upperclass upbringing, college education, a late business start; yet, if speed of ascent be taken as the measure of the *greatest* attainment, these men were actually the most successful of all. Not only did they spend less time after starting to work in getting to the top,[43] but, as the following table shows, they got there on the whole earlier in life than those allegedly most favored. This table shows the ages at which the two polar groups attained the high positions that made them eligible for this study.

Table XI. American Business Leaders by Age on Becoming President or Partner of Major Company*

Age	Late-Starting, Upper-Class, College Men (per cent of)	Early-Starting, Middle- and Lower-Class Noncollege Men (per cent of)
Under 45	43 } 66	26 48
45-49	23	22
50 and over	34	52
Total cases (= 100 per cent) ...	40	53

*Board chairmen are a special case in regard to age on attaining the position and were omitted from this table.

Still, one has to stretch a point to attribute to more than two or three general American historians *any* discussion of the speed of ascent of the business elite. More of them stress this elite's typically lower-class, foreign, or farm *origins* and speculate on the forces that impelled men upward from such insalubrious environs. Yet poor immigrant boys and poor farm boys together actually make up no more than 3 per cent of the business leaders who are the subject of this essay. If men with such backgrounds had been in fact representative of the great entrepreneurs of the later nineteenth century, they must have been supplanted with extraordinary rapidity by the higher status, more highly educated bureaucrats of the following generation. More likely, poor immigrant and poor farm boys who become business leaders have always been more conspicuous in American history books than in the American business elite.

----

[1] One reason for this may be that the traditional framework and the traditional assumptions of American history writing preclude serious questions about personal aspirations and the patterns of ascent. This framework is the "presidential synthesis," and one of the key assumptions is equality of opportunity. On this theme see Thomas C. Cochran, "The 'Presidential Synthesis' in American History," *American Historical Review*, LIII (1948), 748-59. See also N.W. Stephenson, "Roosevelt and the Stratification of Society," *Scripps College Papers*, No. 3 (1930), esp. pp. 71-72.

[2] The role of such social factors and of others to be considered here, such as education, nationality, and faith, in the selection of men even for training for high executive posts in modern corporations is brilliantly set forth by the former president of the New Jersey Bell Telephone Company, Chester I. Barnard, in his book, *The Functions of the Executive* (Cambridge: Harvard University Press, 1938). See also "The Thirty Thousand Managers," *Fortune*, February 1940.

[3] Sociologists (and a few others in special fields) were the first to adapt to the analysis of elite recruitment in social terms quantitative methods evolved by statisticians and used initially in elite studies by eugenists. For the early literature, see J. McKeen Cattell, *American Men of Science* (2d ed.; New York: The Science Press, 1910), p. 537.

[4] The first was published in 1940 by Edwards Brothers, Inc., Ann Arbor, Michigan; the second in 1947 by Hafner Publishing Co., New York.

[5] The problem of defining "entrepreneurial" functions in modern business and of locating the actual "entrepreneurs" in modern corporate bureaucracies, has been occupying economists and business historians for some years. Probably the best book on the subject, one rich in bibliography, is Robert A. Gordon's *Business Leadership in the Large Corporation* (Washington: The Brookings Institution, 1945). Also suggestive are the papers read at the 1946 meeting of the Economic History Association and collected in THE TASKS OF ECONOMIC HISTORY (Supplemental Issue of THE JOURNAL OF ECONOMIC HISTORY), Vol. VI (1946), and the papers and discussion at the 1948 meeting of the American Economic Association, published in the *American Economic Review* (1949), XXXIX, 322-55.

[6] For a provocative explanation of why Redlich himself has not synthesized his findings, see his preface to *The Molding of American Banking*.

[7] These are the major statistical studies. A few others discuss certain limited groups of business leaders or only one or two factors in the lives of national samples of the business elite. Of the first, one of the best, on New England railroad men in the later nineteenth century, is in Edward C. Kirkland, *Men, Cities and Transportation: A Study in New England History 1820-1900* (Cambridge: Harvard University Press, 1948), II, 452-79. Two examples of the second type are J.R. Shannon and Maxine Shaw, "Education of Business and Professional Leaders," *American Sociological Review*, V (1940), 381-83; Scott Nearing, "The Younger Generation of American Genius," *Scientific Monthly*, II (1916), 48-61. There are useful tables in Pitirim Sorokin, *Social Mobility* (New York: Harper & Brothers, 1927). A few tables appear in such inspirational books as B.C. Forbes, *Men Who Are Making America* (New York: B.C. Forbes Publishing Co., 1917), and B.C. Forbes, ed., *America's Fifty Foremost Business Leaders* (New York: B.C. Forbes & Sons Publishing Co., 1948). Popular but informative is "The Thirty Thousand Managers," *Fortune*, February 1940. Not designed as a study of business leaders but actually concerned with them in a social capacity is Hubert P. Beck, *Men Who Control Our Universities* (New York: King's Crown Press, 1947). An interesting study of English business leaders is Simon Haxey, *England's Money Lords, Tory M.P.* (New York: Harrison-Hilton Books, 1939). Useful statistical studies of leaders in other fields include Cortez A.M. Ewing, *The Judges of the Supreme Court 1789-1937* (Minneapolis: University of Minnesota Press, 1938); E. Pendleton Herring, *Federal Commissioners: a Study of Their Careers and Qualifications* (Cambridge: Harvard University Press, 1936); George H. Haynes, *The Senate of the United States, Its History and Practice* (Boston: Houghton Mifflin Co., 1938); C. Wright Mills, *The New Men of Power: America's Labor Leaders* (New York: Harcourt, Brace & Co., 1948); and Edwin L. Clarke, *American Men of Letters: Their Nature and Nurture* (New York: Columbia University Press, 1916).

[8] *The Journal of Social Forces*, III (1925), 627-40.

[9] THE TASKS OF ECONOMIC HISTORY (Supplemental Issue of THE JOURNAL OF ECONOMIC HISTORY), VI (1946), 28-49.

[10] THE TASKS OF ECONOMIC HISTORY (Supplemental Issue of THE JOURNAL OF ECONOMIC HISTORY), V (1945), 20-44.

[11] New York: The Macmillan Co., 1932.

[12] In extenuation it should be said that Destler's list makes his study more interesting than it would have been had he taken seriously the instructions to participants in the "program on entrepreneurial leadership" for which he wrote his paper. In a

note (p. 29) he says: "In a circular memorandum sent in advance . . . . to the con-
tributors to the program . . . . the suggestion was made that each select the 'typical
entrepreneur' of his epoch and then analyze his career in reference to his personal
life . . . ." No suggestion appears to have been made as to how such a "typical entrepreneur" could be selected without *first* making a study such as the one Destler
made. He continues: "A cursory examination of the personalities and careers of the
so-called 'robber barons' revealed that there was no one figure who might be regarded
as typical of the group. Instead of the study of an individual career, therefore, an
analysis of a relatively large group of 'robber barons' seemed called for if significant
results were to be attained."

[13] Mills was aware of this but concluded that the *DAB* nevertheless "forms a convenient point of departure for an over-all view of the social characteristics of eminent
American businessmen" (p. 20). On this no one yet really can gainsay him; by using
the *DAB* he naturally lost a number of the topmost business leaders, but any more
objectively composed list would also have lost some. In my list, for example (see
pp. 191-96), neither John D. Archbold nor Thomas F. Ryan appears; to have stretched
a point to include them would have meant to distort the objective criteria by which
the others were named or to alter those criteria in such ways that others would have
fallen out. Not until a good deal more is known about the whole universe of American
business leaders (for which a dictionary of such leaders would be an excellent starting
point) or about commensurable parts of that universe can anyone say with precision
how good or how bad the *DAB* is as a source of a representative sample of the business
elite; and not until we can make samples that we have confidence in—as market
researchers have confidence in national samples based on national censuses—will we
be able easily and scientifically to extend and deepen our knowledge of that universe.

[14] *The Journal of Political Economy*, XLII (1934), 404-6.

[15] Taussig and Joslyn used mail questionnaires to get information from about 7,000
businessmen, selected in a thoroughly objective fashion from Poor's 1928 national
Register of Directors, on the following points: age, age on first entering business,
most important position now held, age on assuming this position, size of company,
occupation of father and grandfather, education, assistance from relatives and friends.
Mills used the *DAB* for both his names and his information and sought the following
data for 1,464 business leaders born between 1570 and 1879: date of birth, region
of birth and of "success" (objectively defined by him), social class of family, education, father's occupation, political activity.

[16] Destler, "Entrepreneurial Leadership," THE TASKS OF ECONOMIC
HISTORY (Supplemental Issue of THE JOURNAL OF ECONOMIC HISTORY), VI
(1946), 28.

[17] See John Moody, *The Truth About the Trusts* (New York: Moody Publishing Co.,
1904), pp. 453-76.

[18] For a study of business bureaucrats it seemed reasonable to select the leaders
from among those who held the topmost *positions* in the largest business companies.
This was done without regard to the problem of getting biographical information on
the men who happened to hold these positions. As it turned out, most of the information sought (approximately thirty questions to be answered for each of these men were
put on a schedule, the answers then being coded and punched on Hollerith cards)
could be obtained for all but a few of these men. Only a part of this information
is analyzed in this essay; I hope in later studies to present more of it.

To describe in detail the sources used for information would use up far too much
of the space available here. Besides obvious sources such as individual biographies
(of which only eighteen of these business leaders have been subjects), the *DAB*
(which has essays on only fifty-six of these men), the *National Cyclopedia of American
Biography* (a much more useful source than the *DAB* and often more accurate), and
other encyclopedias, state and local histories, and diverse *Who's Who's*, I consulted
magazine articles, newspaper files, folders of clippings in morgues of newspapers and
magazines, and carried on an extensive correspondence with business companies, historical societies, and relatives of men discussed here.

[19] Of the seventy-four nonfinancial corporations represented by the men studied
here, fifty-eight (under original or other names) are among Berle and Means' two
hundred. Forty-five are among the two hundred (as of 1937) listed in Monograph 29,

"The Distribution of Ownership in the 200 Largest Nonfinancial Corporations," of the TNEC *Investigation of Concentration of Economic Power* (Government Printing Office, 1940). See pp. 346-47.

[20]Those in the first three fields were taken from Part VI of Moody's *The Truth About the Trusts*, published in 1904. Financial companies are not listed in Moody's book, hence they were taken from Moody's *Manual*, 1903. The leading investment-banking houses were named not on the basis of size but largely on that of testimony before the Pujo Committee, of which the following is a pertinent example: Louis Untermeyer questioning George F. Baker: "Will you be good enough to name a single transaction in the last 10 years of over $10,000,000 in amount which had been financed without the participation of Messrs. *Morgan & Co.*, or the City Bank, or *Kuhn, Loeb & Co.*, or *Speyer & Co.*, or *Lee, Higginson & Co.*, or *Kidder, Peabody & Co.*, of Boston, and the First National Bank and the Illinois Trust and Savings Bank, of Chicago?" Mr. Baker could not name one. See United States Congress, Committee on Banking and Currency, *Money Trust Investigation* (Government Printing Office, 1913), II, 1540. Men from all the banks named here are included in this study; those italicized are the five investment banking houses from which nine partners were selected.

[21]Among the leading studies in this field are those already cited, by Gordon, Barnard, and Berle and Means.

[22]I plan in another place to discuss in detail the selection of the 188 political leaders for this study. It is sufficient to state here that this number includes *all* the presidents, vice-presidents, cabinet members, and United States Supreme Court judges in the decade 1901-1910, these being 44 men plus 67 United States senators and 77 representatives. Twenty-three of the senators and 31 of the representatives held *all* the chairmanships in the 57th through the 61st Congresses of "major" committees in their respective houses, the list of committees being adapted from that in George H. Haynes, *The Senate of the United States*, II, 1059, and that in DeAlva Stanwood Alexander, *History and Procedure of the House of Representatives* (Boston: Houghton Mifflin Co., 1916), pp. 399-410. The remaining 44 senators and 46 representatives held all the chairmanships of certain other committees designated "minor" but sometimes of major importance in channeling legislation. Of the total of 144 senators and representatives, only 14 were not members of some "major" committee.

[23]The only exception is Bruce H. Ismay, an Englishman, who was president of the International Mercantile Marine Company beginning in 1904 and who served in this capacity abroad.

[24]This information is based on listings for 85 men in the *Directory of Directors*, City of New York, 1909-1910; for 58 men, in similar directories issued during the decade 1901-1910; for 31 men, on other sources. Two thousand seven hundred and twenty directorships is a conservative figure; were the maximum number ever held by each of these men available, the total would be appreciably higher.

[25]P. 129.

[26]II, 172-73.

[27]II, 134.

[28]*Growth of the American People*, p. 129.

[29]P. 168.

[30]*Rise of American Civilization*, II, 173.

[31]"The Thirty Thousand Managers," *Fortune*, February 1940, p. 61.

[32]In fairness to the Beards it should be pointed out that they were aware of changes in the recruitment of business leaders by the turn of the century. They write: "By the end of the century the government of American railways and staple industries, with exceptions of course, had been lost by the men who had grown up in the roundhouses and the mills through all the technical processes. On the whole, the high command in the empire of business was now in the hands of great banking corporations, and captains of industry were as a rule no longer evolved by natural selection; they were chosen by the dominant bankers who served as financial guardians."—*Rise of American Civilization*, II, 196-97. Two things must be said about this statement. (1) After making it, the Beards say nothing more about the leaders selected under the new conditions; they name no men and make no comparisons with the older group

discussed earlier in such detail. (2) Much more important, they fail to focus upon the lasting change that took place in the period of which they write. They say the new men no longer were selected from the plants. But whence, then, did they come? The Beards do not even raise this question. They do not, in fact, even establish that the older business leaders did rise from long years in "the roundhouses and the mills," and indeed it is more likely that, except for some in railroads, the older leaders started their own enterprises at early ages and rose *with* not *in* those enterprises. But whatever may be said of the older men, the majority of the *new* business leaders, along with hundreds of thousands of others who never rose out of the "ruck," did spend many years in the plant, or, in more instances, in the offices of their industries—for the problems of administration had already become complex enough to take an entire career to master. Bankers and other directors at the turn of the century did place "outsiders" at the head of the companies they financed—after all, many of these were newly organized or reorganized companies into which the introduction of outsiders early in their history probably was necessary and expedient. No one, to my knowledge, has studied the business backgrounds of these outsiders. I suggest that they were frequently experienced in the industries if not the companies into which they were placed. But the lasting change was not the importation of outsiders by the bankers; it was the tendency to select top bureaucrats from the hierarchy below. And the question of lasting social import is not whom did the bankers select from the outside but whom did the top bureaucrats select from the whole eager army of aspirants *within* the hierarchies to develop for, and finally install at, the top? Virtually all the candidates have been, in recent decades, so to speak, in business, often in *the* business. What then were the factors that differentiated the more from the less successful? If this was not the key question earlier in our history when business bureaucracies, in the main, were nonexistent, since the turn of the century it has been a question the answer to which has been of increasing social moment—a question, nevertheless, that most historians have not yet asked.

[33]*Rise of American Civilization,* II, 181. The adjective "Barnumesque" is Allan Nevins'; see his *John D. Rockefeller, the Heroic Age of American Enterprise* (New York: Charles Scribner's Sons, 1940), I, 15-16. See also I, 39-40, for Nevins' discussion of the role of the business background in Rockefeller's life. See, too, John D. Rockefeller, *Random Reminiscences of Men and Events* (New York: Doubleday, Page & Co., 1909) p. 33.

[34]Henry B. Parkes, *Recent America* (New York: Thomas Y. Crowell Co., 1945), p. 55. Heinze's father was a German immigrant.

[35]Andrew Carnegie, *The Empire of Business* (New York: Doubleday, Page & Co., 1902), pp. 107-11.

[36]The last quotation in this paragraph is from Ida M. Tarbell, *The Life of Elbert H. Gary* (New York: D. Appleton & Co., 1925), p. 20. The other quotations are from the *DAB.*

[37]The average age of the 190 business leaders in 1905 was 54 years; of the political leaders, 57 years.

[38]In his study of 1,464 businessmen born between 1570 and 1879, Mills found that 18.6 per cent had been foreign-born. He divided his men, by birth dates, into seven generations starting in the following years (in parentheses after each date is the proportion of foreign-born businessmen in the generation starting at that date): 1570 (78.4%), 1700 (28.3%), 1730 (28.1%), 1760 (22.3%), 1790 (10.2%), 1820 (17.5%), 1850 (10.9%). Thus, in each of these generations, except that born between 1790 and 1819, there was a greater percentage of foreign-born businessmen than in Mills' last generation, which is nearest to the period of the present study and in the group used in this study. (Mills, "The American Business Elite," THE TASKS OF ECONOMIC HISTORY (Supplemental Issue of THE JOURNAL OF ECONOMIC HISTORY), V, [1945], 22).

[39]Defining "colonial" families as those settled in America before 1776.

[40]Forbes, *Men Who Are Making America,* p. 232.

[41]Henry Lee Higginson, senior partner in Lee, Higginson & Co. early in this century, once said: "If there were just one thing I could tell the boys of this country it would be to tell them to be expert in whatever they set out to do. This country sorely needs experts. There is a scarcity of experts and a great opportunity for the

boy who wants to be of the greatest service."—Quoted from Samuel A. Eliot, *Biographical History of Massachusetts* (Boston: Massachusetts Biography Society, 1911-1918), Vol. IX (no pagination). Since Higginson spoke, this scarcity of experts in some lines has been so fully overcome that big corporations sometimes seem to be choked by them. The early business bureaucrats studied here, however, as a rule had no formal business or professional training. Those who went to college found few courses in business subjects when they were in attendance. About 9 per cent of the whole group attended secretarial, bookkeeping, or technical schools; 10 per cent had formal engineering training; 16 per cent had legal educations. Sixty-five per cent had no formal vocational, business, or professional education.

[42]Based on 180 business leaders about whom all three kinds of data are known.

[43]An estimate based on data about the presidents and partners studied here showing elapsed working time indicates that 61 per cent of the middle- and lower-class, non-college, early starters (before 19 years of age) spent *more* than thirty years at work before acquiring the position that made them eligible for this study while 66 per cent of the upper-class, college, late starters (19 years of age or older) spent *less* than thirty years.

17. DECEPTION AS AN AMERICAN NORM: THE CASE OF ORGANIZATIONAL RECRUITMENT

BRADLEY W. PARLIN

THE PROBLEM: AN OVERVIEW

A striking feature of modern industrialized countries is the extent to which the perpetuation of the cultures of these countries is dependent upon continual mass consumption of cultural objects for which there is often no apparent need. The consumption patterns of the citizens of the United States provide us with a plethora of examples. The seemingly mindless pursuit of fashion in the U.S. is one such example. On any given day, our shopping centers are filled with individuals of all ages and incomes rushing out to buy items of clothing that they didn't know they needed until they were cajoled or persuaded by the advertising establishment that they could no longer live comfortably without them. The list is long and never-ending: "hip huggers," "bell-bottoms," "halter tops," "platform shoes." "elephant baggies," etc. Of course, this consumption orientation does not stop with fashion. Popular music, automobiles, and patent medicines are routinely created for marketing, independent of any real or expressed need on the part of the consumer. In short, the hallmark of our contemporary capitalist society is the creation of need where none necessarily exists.

Jules Henry's cogent observation aptly summarizes the peculiar cultural configuration I am attempting to convey.

This formulation stands on its head the anthropological cliché that the function of culture is to satisfy a relatively fixed bundle of known needs, for in America, as elsewhere in industrialized cultures, it is only the deliberate creation of needs that permits the culture to continue.[1]

The creators of needs are the Madison Avenue advertising establishments who act as the handmaidens of consumer industry. Through slick advertising techniques, utilizing a variety of media, consumers are often misled, deceived, and manipulated into craving commodities which have little, if any, functional significance.

The American consumer is never allowed to be satisfied with his commodities because if he were satisfied he would no longer consume and the system would collapse. Thus, happiness becomes transient and the consumer drifts from purchase to purchase looking vainly for satisfaction or happiness. Old purchases or commodities become disliked, even hated. Clothing or automobiles which are not current or stylish become sources of embarrassment. Within the trappings of success are embodied the seeds of unhappiness, for the commodities we consume only temporarily satiate our desire for happiness and soon turn to ashes in our mouths as we continue our never-ending search for meaning with each new cultural object we purchase.

In sum, deception (with consumption) becomes normative, routine, commonplace: It is the epitome of modern corporate capitalism. This deception is apparent in a variety of contexts. Misleading, confusing, and worthless warranties on consumer commodities are commonplace. Patent medicines which claim to ease pain and suffering are found not only to be ineffective in providing relief but may even compound the malady the product is designed to alleviate. The cruelest and most poignant deception derives from the attempts of the advertising establishment to convince individuals that meaning and/or happiness can be found in the consumption of material goods.

Philip Slater, in his now-classic work entitled *Pursuit of Loneliness*, marvels at this cultural preoccupation with consumption.[2] Slater feels, however, that, ". . . men have achieved this miracle by making themselves into donkeys pursuing an inaccessible carrot."[3] Similarly, Cohen, discussing what he calls "The Anomia of Success," describes the loneliness which inevitably accompanies this consumption orientation. "He accumulates the money, the cars, the house in the suburbs, and realizes that he has wasted away his years always expecting the NEXT stage, the next promotion, the next raise in pay, the next purchase, to give him what he really wants. These never become ends in themselves; he strives after means and, once achieved, these are like water in his hands which drips away, non-solid, with little possibility of attachment. He starts to search for more again, dissatisfied, unfulfilled."[4] Loneliness is only one consequence of the consumption and deception described above. Mass consumption has also resulted in the proliferation of large scale organization in contemporary American society.

The Organizational Society

The emptiness and loneliness observed by Slater and Cohen are relatively personal consequences of the American preoccupation with consumption. The drivenness of American culture reflected in our consumption orientation is, in large part, responsible for what Max Weber has described as the increasing bureaucratization of western civilization.[5] Industrial bureaucracies or complex organizations have emerged to produce and distribute the items of consumption of American culture. In short, as Weber suggested, American culture has become and is becoming increasingly bureaucratized. Contemporary American society is thus, without question, an organizational society. Our babies enter the world in the delivery room of a complex organization and when we expire we will be prepared for burial or cremation in a complex organization. In the interim period, many of us will spend our work lives engaged in some aspect of the production of cultural objects or services for mass consumption. The day to day performance of our job-related tasks will take place within the context of a complex organization.

Recruitment Imperative

One of the imperatives of organizations is the constant need to find individuals to occupy the myriad of status roles which comprise the organization. This process is commonly referred to as the recruitment process. Each spring, on campuses throughout the United States, a curious ritual unfolds. Large numbers of representatives of American business and industry pour onto the nation's campuses in search of talented graduates to staff their manpower-hungry organizations. Like the legendary sirens who tempted the unwary sailor onto the rocky shores of the Aegean Sea, the modern corporate recruiter is equipped with the latest techniques and methods to entice the often reluctant students into the corporate monolith. Critics of the American business establishment have argued that the recruitment process is characterized by deceit and deception. The student is seen as an innocent victim of the organized efforts of the corporate bureaucracy to mislead him.[6] For the critics, the deception which allegedly permeates the organizational recruitment process is simply one small symptom of the more general malady affecting the American social structure. As we have seen, the consumption orientation of American society routinely necessitates advertisers to mislead or deceive the consumer in order to sell him a product which he neither wants nor needs. Thus, the consumer is often misled by the advertiser and manufacturer as he consumes, just as the student may be misled by a recruiter when he becomes a commodity on the labor market. In short, the deception which characterizes the interaction of actors in our economic system is alleged to be evident in the recruitment processes of complex organizations. Interestingly enough, there has been very little research on the recruitment process that would either confirm or deny the allegations of the critics cited above. Is deception an important part of the recruitment process in complex organizations as it is in our culture generally? It will be the purpose of this paper to provide an answer to this question through a systemic analysis of recruitment activity of new college graduates in a manufacturing organization.

II

ANALYSIS

The data for our analysis, of the role of deception in organizational recruitment, will have two sources. Data based on a case study of recruitment activity in a large midwestern manufacturing organization conducted by the author will be the primary source of information upon which this report is based. The data were gathered through participant observation while the author was employed as a technical recruiter in the firm which is the subject of the case study. Since it is always difficult to generalize from a case study, the researcher has also utilized the research reports of others to corroborate his findings. The recruitment activity to be described involved the hiring of new college graduates in engineering, science, business, social sciences and humanities for the period of one recruiting year. The recruiter behavior observed and analyzed included recruiters at both the corporate and plant levels of organization.

The basic argument to be developed is that elements of the formal structure of the organization under analysis constrained recruiters to use deception in their interactions with their clients. The particular element of the formal structure which was the source of constraint was the organizational reward system.

The Reward System

Managers in organizations spend considerable time and effort determining the most effective reward system for the motivation of employees. In this organization, it was decided that the best way to motivate the recruiting staff was to assign each a quantitative quota of new college hires to be met by the end of the recruiting season. The size of the quota would be based on the recruiter's aspirations and the number and size of the schools assigned to him. In addition, to maintain the pressure of the commitment to a quota, the corporate personnel staff would publish a bi-monthly information sheet entitled "The Recruiter" to reflect the progress of the individual recruiters toward their goals. This information would be sent to the general managers at division plant and corporate offices so that individual recruiter's relative progress would be known to his superiors. It was hoped that this would introduce a degree of competitiveness between recruiters through the exertion of peer and superior pressure.

In addition to the quota approach derived from the management by objective strategy, a predominant managerial philosophy affecting staff perspectives on recruiter productivity emerged from the manufacturing orientation of the executive management staff. A dominant philosophy of the executive management personnel was to interpret both line and staff function in terms of unit-output per unit-cost productivity norms. The recruiting staff was no exception with respect to this overriding philosophy.

In application to the recruiters' function, the productivity orientation was characterized by viewing individual recruiter's success or failure in terms of hiring costs which were computed by dividing the number of hires derived from each campus visit divided into the total costs of the campus visits. The higher the number of hires/per campus visit and cumulatively, the lower unit cost. Low unit cost through high output (hires) was thus an important index of recruiters' effectiveness and/or success. It was emphasized that part of the criteria for promotion, which all plant or division managers would be notified of, was success or failure in meeting their individual goals (quotas), and low unit costs. The formal goal or intention of the above reward system was to motivate recruiters to actively recruit the best possible qualified candidates for employment. As we shall see, the reward system had certain latent (unintended) consequences which served to frustrate the realization of the formal goal.

The Actors

Before describing the recruitment process, it is necessary to acquaint the reader with the actors in the organizational setting being described. The three basic parties involved include the recruiter, the operating department managers, and the students.

The recruiter was the individual assigned to travel to campuses to find likely candidates for employment.

The operating department managers were members of the organizational management for whom the student, if hired, would ultimately work. The recruiter would first screen candidates on campus and would invite likely prospects for further interviews with the operating department managers at the plant location. If the operating department managers were pleased with a recruiter's prospect, he would be made an offer of employment. Conversely, if the manager did not like the candidate, he would be rejected with the obvious implication for the recruiter's unit cost index.

The third party in the recruitment triad was the student candidate. The student, in both the campus and plant interview, would generally attempt to impress the potential employer with his attributes in hopes of receiving an offer for employment.

To structure subsequent analysis, we will restrict our discussion to two categories of relationships. These include the recruiter/manager relationship, and the recruiter/student relationship.

The Art of Deception: The Role of Recruiter

Playing any social role involves elements of deception which may be directed toward oneself or another actor in an interaction situation. Goffman, in his discussion of impression management, observes that elements of interaction are often characterized by direct attempts to convey misinformation through deceit and feigning.[7] As noted above, the position taken in this research is that one of the major unintended consequences of the formal structure of the recruiting function is to necessitate the skillful cultivation of the art of deception. Further, if one is to thoroughly understand the recruitment process, the nature of this deception must be analyzed.

The Recruiter/Manager Relationship

The extent of deception is most readily evident in the relationship of the recruiter to the operating department manager. As we have seen, the formal reward system which emphasizes quantitative quotas and productivity measured by unit output per unit cost makes the recruiter's success dependent upon the acceptability of his chosen candidates to the respective department manager. The formal reward system was reinforced by informal reports to the corporate recruiting manager on recruiter abilities by operating department managers. Whether these reports were good or bad depended on the degree to which candidates invited for plant visits met the expectations of operating department managers. The recruiter's success, then, was in large part dependent upon his emphatic abilities. The extent to which he was successful in ascertaining a manager's expectations and finding matching candidates determined his productivity. In most cases, however, satisfying an operating department manager (insuring success) required deceiving him. Seldom, however, was a manager ready to admit that he wanted a mediocre engineer who would be a non-threatening, conscientious plodder. More typically, the virtues of the "boy wonder of the Western business world" would characterize a manager's description of "his kind" of employee. Commonly, managers feared, and resisted attempts to place, bright, aggressive, and imaginative candidates. Many, if not most, managers preferred very average, non-threatening students who would not make waves. Often, managers were resistant to candidates with liberal political views, long hair, mod clothes or anything which might distinguish the candidate or make him stand out. Inasmuch as the operating department manager was not being honest in describing his "real" expectations of a potential employee, he was deceiving the recruiter.

The recruiter's deception of the operating manager began by conveying to him how "great" a candidate for a forthcoming plant visit was. The recruiter, prior to the candidate's actual visit, would often prepare the operating manager by praising the candidates for attributes they did not possess. Thus candidates who had been selected because of features like academic marginality, apparent lack of drive, low motivation, lack of imagination, conservative dress and/or political views were routinely passed off as hard driving, imaginative young men of promise. The recruiter knew (through experience or observation of previous departmental hires) that although the manager would never admit it, a marginal candidate was just what he wanted to hire. Typically, the recruiter would admit that the candidate had not been a "good" student, but would then push the candidate's inclination to ". . . roll up his shirt sleeves and take the bull by the horns attitude." That this kind of deception is not uncommon or unique in the recruitment process is evident in the following description of the same phenomenon in executive selection. Allan Cox, an executive recruiter, admits that, "In order to do my job well, . . . I have to create the impression that I am working wholeheartedly on behalf of people whose interests are, in fact, often inimical."[8] He goes on to demonstrate why the art of deception is so crucial to recruiter success. He gives the example of a company president who hired him to find ". . . only the best possible man,"[9] ". . . a sales manager who would turn the company around."[10] Cox notes, however, that "it soon became apparent that what the man really wanted was a weak sister who would put in long hours, get along with the rest of the boys and not really accomplish a thing."[11] The outcome of this situation is consistent with the outcome observed in the recruiting situation above.

Cox describes the outcome well. He assures his client that he believes his stated job description (above):

> . . .while behind the facade I realize that to satisfy him I shall have to deceive him and that to win the confidence of my candidate I shall have to praise him for weaknesses that will make him perfect for the job. I was able to find a man rather easily, incidently, but it was an unhappy business—priming the client to envision the candidate as a dynamo when I knew that he was no dynamo at all and that, in fact, a dynamo was the last thing in the world the client wanted.[12]

Put differently, Cox is suggesting that the formally stated descriptions of the ideal candidate are not nearly as important as the hidden job description, i.e.: the operating department manager's latent or undisclosed expectation. It is the necessity to respond to the manager's unstated expectations which leads to this kind of deception.

The Recruiter/Student Relationship

The deception does not stop in the recruiter/client relationship but extends to the recruiter/student relationship as well. One overriding criterion in the selection process is the student's possession of "maturity." Many recruiters' definitions of maturity are consistent with Jules Henry's. "Maturity," says Henry, "is the capacity not to care if you are misled."[13] Just as the recruiter deceives the operating manager, he also deceives the student. Recruiters routinely sell aspects of the company that, in fact, do not exist. Work situations characterized by boredom, underemployment and stifling managerial techniques were often described to student in terms such as challenge, excitement, and responsibility. If the student challenged the recruiter's descriptions, he was often rejected because of "lack of maturity" and/or for displaying arrogance. The recruiter who is interested in maximizing his productivity must not only sell the manager on the candidate but the candidate on the job. Many of the jobs the recruiters were trying to fill didn't appear to demand the level of expertise of even the marginal candidate. Consequently, recruiters were often inclined to oversell a candidate on the merits of his future job. This tendency to oversell, by imputing challenge, responsibility, mobility, etc., where none or little existed, created an additional informal dimension within the roles of personnel manager, recruiters, and operating department managers.

Cooling the Mark

The new role dimension created by the use of deception in the recruitment process corresponds to what Goffman has called "cooling the mark out."[14] "Cooling the mark" refers to the technique utilized by confidence men to discourage victims from calling the police once the victim discovers he has been taken. The intention is to get the victim to accept his disappointment. Similarly, the recruiter, personnel manager, or anyone in a position of responsibility is often faced with "cooling out" disappointed candidates whose expectations are not being met in his job. While the locus of disappointment is the job, the "cooling out" function actually has two sources. The first, discussed briefly above, derives from a sense of disappointment which occurs when the candidate has been "oversold." In this situation, the job does not measure up to the recruiter's descriptions. The second source of disappointment finds its origin in the occupational socialization which creeps into the students' courses and seminars. Students often leave the university socialized for a world that does not exist. Excitement, glamor, challenge, opportunity, and responsibility are among the features students are led to expect in a job. These images of the world of work are reinforced through slick advertising techniques and finally, the recruiter's "sell."

Jules Henry, for example, comments on the slick advertising

techniques utilized by employers which have little correspondence to the realities of the objective work situation.

> Through the advertisements, many of them a quarter of a page or more in size, run the themes of challenge, creativity, initiative, personnel growth, expansion, novelty, individuality, the taking of responsibility, stimulation through professional on-the-job contacts and achievement. The majority of American jobs, however, are remote from these. What is most striking is the realization that these things should be offered as inducements; the very form of the advertisements is an acknowledgement that in America most jobs are not challenges, that no creativity or initiative is desired.[15]

These images often turn to ashes in the new graduate's mouth when they give way to the realities of underemployment, boredom, lack of real responsibility and/or challenge, and to the realization that they have been misled and deceived. Many candidates, of course, know they are being misled (the "mature employee") and accept their disappointment or disillusionment quietly. They have been effectively socialized. Others are not willing to admit to themselves that success is dependent upon quietly accepting the fact that they are being deceived. These are the students who must be "cooled out" by whoever is the recipient of their anger and disillusionment.

Discussion of this problem with other recruiters and managers revealed a sort of informally institutionalized technique for "cooling the mark" in this company. Whenever a new employee would confront a staff member by suggesting to him that his job was not interesting or challenging, the staff member would attempt to displace the employee's anger by shifting the locus of responsibility. This was done through rap sessions whose essence focused on some variation of the following theme:

> Any job is not in itself any more or less challenging than any other job. A job is what you make it. Any job can be dull and uninteresting, or exciting and challenging. If you (the employee) are the kind of employee who will go places in this company you will demonstrate your imagination and inventiveness by approaching your job and making something out of it rather than demonstrating your incompetency and lack of imagination by bitching about it.

This theme effectively took the recruiter or another staff member off the hook and shifted the locus of responsibility onto the employee. This technique was not, of course, 100 percent effective, and considerable new graduate turnover could be attributed to disillusionment resulting from expectations and aspirations which were being frustrated. Terminating employees were required to have exit interviews with a member of the corporate recruiting staff. Frequently, particularly among recent new graduate hires, the reason for leaving was attributed to the inability of the company to meet the expectations of the new employee. The individual's expectations were generated through formal and informal occupational socialization, the recruiter's overzealous attempts to "sell" and deceptive advertising practices. Often the reason for "overselling" a candidate derived from the dull and uninteresting jobs the new graduates were being recruited to fill. If the recruiter was to succeed (meet his quotas and maintain low unit cost) he was forced to be dishonest and deceive the unsuspecting student. Unchallenging, boring jobs are not uncommon. A recent book by Ivar Berg suggests that most college graduates are underemployed.[16] The jobs they fill do not demand the level of expertise and training gained in college. This in turn results in high turnover rates among recent graduates. Berg observes that it is " . . readily acknowledged that the turnover of young executives varies only slightly; there is an average loss of half of all college graduates within the first five years of employment."[17] Jules Henry adds to this disappointing picture, observing that ". . . many recruitment ads fail to give a valid picture of the employer—a factor that tends to increase engineering turnover. The average engineer changes jobs about once every two and one half years. . ."[18] Noting that "most people do the job they have to do regardless of what they want to do, . . . "[19] Henry reflects on the disillusionment which often confronts the new graduate as he sells his labor to employers. "With a backward glance at the job dreams of his pre-'labor force' days the young worker enters the occupational system not where he would be but where he can; and his job-dream, so often an expression of his dearest self, is pushed down with all his other unmet needs to churn among them for the rest of his life."[20] Henry adds that, "What makes the renunciation particularly poignant is that it comes after an education that emphasizes exploitation of all the resources of the individual, and which has declared that the promise of democracy is freedom of choice."[21]

III

SUMMARY AND CONCLUSION

Our analysis of organizational hiring activities had demonstrated, above all else, that deception is the epitome of the recruitment process. Deception is the cornerstone of recruiter success. This deception was found to be primarily a latent function of the formal reward system of the organization being analyzed. This exemplifies the impact of social structure (in this case organizational structure) on human behavior. The reward system which emphasized quantitative quotas made recruiters responsive to the expectations of the operating department managers. Thus, a recruiter was not free to choose the candidate he may have felt was the most competent to do the job. If a recruiter was to be successful, he was forced to select the type of candidate which would be acceptable to the operating department manager. This enabled the recruiter to meet his quota and maintain low unit costs. Inviting a candidate for interviews in the plant who would not meet the operating department managers often latent expectations would result in a reject of the candidate as a suitable employee. This would not contribute to the recruiter's quota requirement and would raise his unit cost index. Thus, as we have seen, to be successful, the recruiter must be skilled in the art of deception. Among the consequences of the role of deception in organizational recruitments were frequently disappointed and disillusioned students who appeared ultimately as numbers in the companies' turnover statistics.

Early in this presentation it was suggested that American culture is permeated by deception deriving at least in part from our over emphasis of, and preoccupation with, mass consumption. Our examination of one small part of the organizational universe dramatically demonstrates the extent to which deception characterizes the interrelationship of individuals in their interaction within an organizational context. The deception which characterizes so much of the interaction in our culture is clearly evident in the recruitment process of large scale organizations.

BIBLIOGRAPHY

1. Jules Henry, *Culture Against Man*. (New York: Vintage Books, 1965) p. 19.
2. Philip Slater, *The Pursuit of Loneliness*. (Boston: Beacon Press, 1970).
3. ibid., p. 84.
4. Harry Cohen, "The Anomia of Success and the Anomia of Failure: A Study of Similarities In Opposites," *The British Journal of Sociology*, Volume XXIII, No. 3 (September 1972), p. 331.
5. Max Weber, *The Theory of Social and Economic Organization*, (New York: The Free Press).
6. Jules Henry, op. cit., See the section entitled "The Job and the Self," pp. 25-37.
7. Irving Goffman, *The Presentation of Self in Everyday Life*. (Garden City: Doubleday Anchor Books, 1959), p. 2.
8. Allan Cox, "Confessons of a Corporate Head-Hunter," *Playboy*, Volume XIX, No. 1, (January, 1972), p. 167.
9. ibid., p. 168.
10. ibid.
11. ibid.
12. ibid.

13. R. P. Cuzzort, *Humanity and Modern Sociological Thought*, (New York: Holt, Rinehart, and Winston, Inc., 1969), p. 263.
14. Irving Goffman, "On Cooling the Mark Out: Some Aspects of Adaptation to Failure," *Psychiatry*, Volume 15, (November, 1952), pp. 451-563.
15. Jules Henry, op. cit., pp. 34, 35.
16. Ivan Berg, *Education and Jobs*, (New York: Praeger Publishers, 1970) See Chapter III, "Job Requirements and Educational Achievement," pp. 38-61.
17. ibid. p. 75.
18. Jules Henry, op. cit., p. 36.
19. ibid. p. 35.
20. ibid. p. 25.
21. ibid.

18.

SEX AS WORK: A STUDY OF AVOCATIONAL COUNSELING*

LIONEL S. LEWIS AND DENNIS BRISSETT

This paper examines how sex play is represented in fifteen popular marriage manuals. The authors of these books are viewed as avocational counselors advising Americans about sexual activity in marriage. An analysis revealed that sex play is treated as work by these authors. Those engaged in sexual relations are urged to put forth a great deal of effort. The orgasm is portrayed as the product of marital sex. Other aspects of a job deemed necessary in sexual behavior are a work schedule and special techniques and equipment. Depicting sex as work is probably the consequence of the need of Americans to justify and dignify play and to resolve the contradictory values of work for work's sake and pleasure for pleasure's sake.

It is commonly accepted that America is a society of leisure. The society is said to have shifted from one of production to one of consumption.[1] The American of today spends little time working; he has a great deal of time to play.

With this surfeit of leisure, Americans have been called upon to engage in forms of consumption quite unknown to their inner-directed predecessors. There exist extensive opportunities for play, but little knowledge of how to conduct oneself in this play. As Riesman has remarked, "To bring the individual into unfrightening contact with the new range of opportunities in consumption often requires some guides and signposts."[2] Knowing how to play has become problematic; it is something the individual must learn. He must, in a word, be socialized into the art of play.

*This paper is in every respect a joint endeavor.
Reprinted from *Social Problems*, Vol. 15, No. 1, pp. 8-18, by permission of the authors and the publisher, Society for the Study of Social Problems.

Faced with this necessary socialization, the consuming American seeks out persons to teach him how to play. Very often this involves engaging the services of avocational counselors. The term avocational counseling ". . . describe[s] the activities undertaken by a number of relatively rapidly growing professions in the United States, including travel agents, hotel men, resort directors, sports teachers and coaches, teachers of the arts, including dancing teachers, and so on."[3] Each of the various counselors supplies the American public with advice on play and leisure. The advice of one such group of counselors is the subject matter of this paper.

Quite recently, Nelson Foote has observed that sex, since it is becoming increasingly dissociated from procreation, is becoming more and more a kind of play activity. He states that "the view that sex is fun can . . . hardly be called the invention of immoralists; it is every man's discovery."[4] The arena of consumption is extended to include the realm of man's sexual activity, and the avocational counselor finds himself a place advising people on the vicissitudes of sex as play.

Concomitant with this increasing amount of leisure time, and the attendant problem of learning how to play, it has been observed that the play of most Americans has become a laborious kind of play. "Fun, in its rather unique American form, is grim resolve. . . . We are as determined about the pursuit of fun as a desert-wandering traveler is about the search for water. . . ."[5] Consumption, to most Americans, has become a job. Like work, play has become a duty to be performed. This interpretation is supported by the emergence of what Wolfenstein has labeled a "fun morality." Here "play tends to be measured by standards of achievement previously applicable only to work . . . at play, no less than at work, one asks: 'Am I doing as well as I should?' "[6] Consumption very definitely has become production.

It is the purpose of this paper to examine the products of the avocational counselors of marital sex and to inquire as to their depiction of man's sexual behavior. If it is true that play is becoming work in the mass society, it might be necessary to amend Foote's notion of the character of sexual play. In focusing on how marital sex is handled by these avocational counselors, we will show how sex, an area of behavior usually not thought of as involving work, has been treated as such. We will emphasize how general work themes are presented as an essential part of sexual relations, and how the public is advised to prepare for sex just as they are advised to prepare for a job.

MARRIAGE MANUALS

The avocational counselors of sex with the widest audience are those who write what are frequently referred to as marriage manuals. These manuals are designed to explain all aspects of the sexual side of marriage. Their distribution is wide: many are in paperback and are readily available in drug stores; many can be found in multiple copies in public and university libraries; and some are distributed by facilities which offer service in sex, fertility, and contraception, such as Planned Parenthood clinics.

Fifteen manuals were selected from a listing of almost 50 for analysis in this study. They are listed in Appendix A. The first criterion for using a manual was wide circulation. This was determined by number of printings and number of copies sold. For example, one volume (15) in 1965 was in its forty-fifth printing and had sold more than one-half million copies in the United States; a second (13) was in its forty-eighth printing and had sold almost six hundred thousand; a third (3) was in its thirtieth printing[7] and has "been read by" two million eight hundred thousand[8]fl and a fourth (5) advertises on its cover "over a million and a half copies in print." Other criteria were that the book be still read and available. The fifteen volumes ranged from 14 page pamphlets to full-sized, indexed, hard-bound books.

Each manual was read by both authors, and principal themes were recorded. Notes were taken, compared, and classified. Only material about whose meaning both authors agreed was utilized in drawing conclusions about the themes in a book.

WORKING AT SEX

Marital sex, as depicted by the marriage manuals, is an activity permeated with qualities of work. One need not even read these books, but need only look at the titles or the chapter headings to draw this conclusion. Thus, we have books titled *The Sex Technique in Marriage* (10), *Modern Sex Techniques* (14), *Ideal Marriage: Its Physiology and Technique* (15). There are also chapters titled "How to Manage the Sex Act (3)," "Principles and Techniques of Intercourse (7)," "The Fourth Key to Soundly Satisfying Sex: A Controlled Sexual Crescendo (5)."

From the outset, as we begin to read the books, we are warned not to treat sex frivolously, indeed not to play at sex:

> An ardent spur-of-the-moment tumble sounds very romantic. . . .
> However, ineptly arranged intercourse leaves the clothes you had no
> chance to shed in a shambles, your plans for the evening shot, your

birth control program incomplete, and your future sex play under considerable better-be-careful-or-we'll-wind-up-in-bed-again restraint (5, pp. 34-35).

In other words, marital sex should not be an impromptu performance.

Moreover, sex should not be approached with a casual mien. Rather, we are counseled, sexual relations, at least good sexual relations, are a goal to be laboriously achieved. It is agreed that "satisfactory intercourse is the basis for happy marriage." However, it is added, "It does not occur automatically but must be striven for (12, p. 39)." In the plain talk of the avocational counselor, "Sexual relations are something to be worked at and developed (7, p. 6)."

This work and its development are portrayed as a taxing kind of endeavor; as behavior involving, indeed requiring, a good deal of effort. That sex involves effort is a pervasive theme in the 15 manuals. From the start one is advised to direct his effort to satisfying his or her mate so that mutual climax is achieved, sexual activity is continual, and one's partner is not ignored after climax. Thus, we are told:

> Remember, *couple* effort for *couple* satisfaction! That's the key to well-paced, harmonious sex play (5, p. 62).

Certain positions of intercourse are also seen as particularly taxing, in fact so taxing that certain categories of people are advised not to use them. One author, in discussing a particularly laborious position, remarks that "This is no position for a couple of grandparents, no matter how healthy and vigorous they are for their age, for it takes both effort and determination (4, p. 201)." Quite obviously, certain kinds of marital sex are reserved only for those persons who are "in condition."

The female is particularly cautioned to work at sex, for being naturally sexual seems a trait ascribed only to the male. The affinity of sex to her other work activities is here made clear: "Sex is too important for any wife to give it less call upon her energy than cooking, laundry, and a dozen other activities (5, p. 36)." To the housewife's burden is added yet another chore.

Even the one manual that takes great pains to depict sex as sport, injects the work theme. It is pointed out that

> You certainly can (strive and strain at having a climax)—just as you can . . . help yourself to focus on a complex musical symphony. . . . Just as you strive to enjoy a party, when you begin by having a dull time at it. Sex is often something to be worked and strained at—as an artist works and strains at his painting or sculpture (6, p. 122).

Sex, then, is considered a kind of work; moreover, a very essential form of labor. Regular sexual activity is said, for instance, to contribute to "physical and mental health (7, p. 27)," and to lead to "*spiritual unity* (14, frontpiece)." In the majestic functionalist tradition, "A happy, healthy sex life is vital to wholesome family life, which in turn is fundamental to the welfare of the community and of society (1, XIII)." Marital sex, most assuredly, is the cornerstone of humanity, but not any kind of marital sex—only that which leads to orgasm. "It is the orgasm that is so essential to the health and happiness of the couple . . . (10, p. 80)."

Indeed it is the orgasm which may be said to be the *product* of marital sexual relations. It is the *raison d'être* for sexual contact, and this orgasm is no mean achievement. In fact,

> Orgasm occasionally may be the movement of ecstasy when two people together soar along a Milky Way among stars all their own. This moment is the high mountaintop of love of which the poets sing, on which the two together become a full orchestra playing a fortissimo of a glorious symphony (4, pp. 182-183).

In masculine, and somewhat more antiseptic terms, "ejaculation is the aim, the summit and the end of the sexual act (15, 133)." Woe be to the couple who fail to produce this state as there are dire consequences for the unsuccessful, particularly for the woman.

> When the wife does not secure an orgasm, she is left at a high peak of sexual tension. If this failure to release tension becomes a regular thing, she may develop an aversion to starting any sex play that might lead to such frustrations. . . . Repeated disappointments may lead to headaches, nervousness, sleeplessness, and other unhappy symptoms of maladjustment (1, p. 65).

So important is it to reach orgasm, to have a product, that all the other sexual activities of marriage are seen as merely prosaic ingredients or decorative packaging of the product.

In fact, orgasm as a product is so essential that its occasion is not necessarily confined to the actual act of intercourse, at least for the women. Numerous counselors indicate that it may be necessary for the man to induce orgasm in the woman during afterplay. "A woman who has built up a head of passion which her husband was unable to requite deserves a further push to climax through intensive genital caress . . . (5, p. 111)." Particularly in the early years of marriage, before the husband has learned to pace his orgasm, he may have to rely on the knack of digital manipulation. In one author's imagery, "Sometimes it may be necessary for the husband to withdraw and continue the stimulation of his wife by a rhythmic fondling of clitoris and vulva until orgasm is attained (1, p. 66)."

The central importance of experiencing orgasm has led many of the authors to de-emphasize the traditional organs of intercourse. The male penis (member) is particularly belittled. It is considered "only one of the instruments creating sensation in the female, and its greatest value lies as a mental stimulant and organ of reproduction, not as a necessary medium of her sexual pleasure." The same author adds, ". . . the disillusioning fact remains that the forefinger is a most useful asset in man's contact with the opposite sex . . . (14, p. 71)." Futhermore, this useful phallic symbol should be directed primarily to the woman's seat of sensation, the clitoris. Only a man who is ignorant of his job directs his digital attention to the vulva, the female organ that permits conventional union.

One must often deny himself immediate pleasure when manufacturing the orgasm. One author, in referring to an efficient technique to attain orgasm, states that: "Unfortunately, some men do not care for this position. This, however, should be of little importance to an adequate lover, since his emotions are the less important of the two (14, p. 122)." Likewise, the woman may have to force herself in order to reach orgasm, even though she may not desire the activity which precedes it. It is specified that "If you conscientiously work at being available, you may ultimately find the feminine role quite satisfying even in the absence of ardor or desire (5, p. 38)." The work ethic of the sexual side of marriage, then, is one resting quite elaborately on what has been referred to as the "cult of the orgasm."

Still, one cannot easily perform one's job; its intricacies must first be mastered. After all, ". . . there is considerably more in the sexual relationship than . . . at first thought (8, p. 136)." "Remember that complete development of couple skills and adaptations takes literally years (5, p. 206)." There is a great deal to be learned. One author talks of eight steps "in order to facilitate sexual arousal and lead, finally, to satisfactory orgasm" and of seven "techniques which she and her mate may employ to help her attain full climax (6, pp. 124-126)."

All of this requires a good deal of mastery, a mastery that is necessary if the sex relationship is not to undergo "job turnover." Firstly, in the face of incompetence, the marriage partner may, at times, turn to auto-eroticism. One author stipulates that "There cannot be a shadow of a doubt that faulty technique, or a total lack of it on the man's part, drives thousands of wives to masturbation as their sole means of gratification (3, p. 140)." Moreover, if sexual skills are not acquired, the husband or wife may seek out new partners for sexual activity. The woman is admonished that adequate sexual relations will keep a man from "The Other Woman . . . (4, pp. 264-265)." The male also must be proficient in sexual encounters for "it is the male's habit of treating . . . [sexual relationships] as such [mechanically] which causes much dissatisfaction and may ultimately drive the wife to someone who takes it more seriously (14, p. 77)."

LEARNING SEX: PASSIVE AND ACTIVE

Marital sex is said to necessitate a good deal of preparation if it is to be efficiently performed. In one author's words: "This [complete satisfaction] cannot be achieved without study, practice, frank and open discussion . . . (12, p. 45)." This overall preparation seems to involve both a passive and an active phase. The passive phase seems most related to an acquisition of information previous to engaging in sexual, at least marital sexual, relations. The active phase best refers to the training, one might say on-the-job training, that the married couple receive in the sexual conduct of wedlock.

The matter of passive preparation receives a great deal of attention from the avocational counselors. Thirteen of the fifteen books call attention to the necessity of reading, studying and discussing the various facets of sexual relationships. After listing a number of these activities, one author advises that "If the two of them have through reading acquired a decent vocabulary and a general understanding of the fundamental facts listed above, they will in all likelihood be able to find their way to happiness (1, p. 20)." Another counselor cites the extreme importance of reciprocal communication by noting that " . . . the vital problem . . . must be solved through intelligent, practical, codified, and instructive discussion . . . (14, p. 7)." The general purpose of all this learning is, of course, to dispel ignorance, as ignorance is said to lead to "mistakes at work," and such cannot be tolerated. The learning of the other partner's physiology is particularly emphasized, most counselors devoting at least one chapter and a profusion of illustrations to relieve the ignorance of the marriage partners. One author, however, quite obviously feels that words and pictures are insufficient. Presenting a sketch of the woman's genitals, he asserts that "It should be studied; on the bridal night . . . the husband should compare the diagram with his wife's genital region . . . (14, p. 18)."

Together with learning physiology, the various manuals also stress the critical importance of learning the methodology of marital sex. Sexual compatibility seems not a matter of following one's natural proclivities, but rather "The technique of the sexual relation has to be learned in order to develop a satisfactory sex life (13, p. 172)." One must know one's job if one is to be successful at it. Not surprisingly, to like one's job also requires a learning experience, particularly for the woman. As one book scientifically asserts:

> There is a striking consensus of opinion among serious specialists (both men and women) that the average woman of our time and clime must *learn* to develop specific sexual enjoyment, and only gradually attains to the orgasm in coitus . . . they [women] have to *learn how* to feel both voluptuous pleasure and actual orgasm (15, p. 262).

In summary, then, passive learning involves the mastering of physiology and techniques. By the desexualized female of the marriage manuals, the fine art of emotional experience and expression is also acquired. And the naturally inept male must learn, for

> If the husband understands in even a general way the sexual nature and equipment of his wife, he need not give the slightest offense to her through ignorant blundering (1, p. 20).

This learning process, according to most of the manuals, eventually becomes subject to the actual experience of matrimonial sex. The marriage bed here becomes a "training" and "proving" ground. Again, wives seem particularly disadvantaged: "Their husbands have to be their guides (3, p. 108)." However, generally the training experience is a mutual activity. As one author suggests in his discussion of the various positions for coitus,

> In brief, the position to be used is not dictated by a code of behavior but should be selected as the one most acceptable to you and your mate. To find this you will examine your own tastes and physical conformations. By deliberate application of the trial and error method you will discover for yourselves which is most desirable for you both (11, p. 11).

In training, rigorous testing and practice is a must. In the words of one manual "experimentation will be required to learn the various responses within one's own body as well as those to be expected from one's beloved . . . (9, p. 7)," and also, "After a variable time of practice, husband and wife may both reach climax, and may do so at the same time (11, p. 10)."

Both the husband and wife must engage in a kind of "muscular control" training if the sex act is to be efficiently performed. The woman's plight during intercourse is picturesquely portrayed with the following advice. "You can generally contract these muscles by trying to squeeze with the vagina itself . . . perhaps by pretending that you are trying to pick up marbles with it (5, p. 97)." Fortunately, the man is able to practice muscular control at times other than during intercourse. Indeed, the man, unlike the woman, is permitted to engage in activities not normally related to sexual behavior while he is training. It is advised that "You can snap the muscles [at the base of the penile shaft] a few times while you are driving your car or sitting in an office or any place you happen to think of it . . . (5, p. 96)." The practice field, at least for the male, is enlarged.

In general, then, a careful learning and a studied training program are necessary conditions for the proper performance of marital sex. As seems abundantly true of all sectors of work, " 'Nature' is not enough . . . Man must pay for a higher and more complex nervous system by study, training, and conscious effort . . . (7, p. 34)."

THE JOB SCHEDULE

As in most work activities, the activity of marital sex is a highly scheduled kind of performance. There is first of all a specification of phases or stages in the actual conduct of the sex act. Although there is disagreement here, some authors indicating four or five distinct phases (15, p. 1), the consensus of the counselors seems to be that "Sexual intercourse, when satisfactorily performed, consists of three stages, only one of which is the sex act proper (11, p. 7)."

The sexual act therefore is a scheduled act and the participants are instructed to follow this schedule. "All three stages have to be fitted into this time. None of them must be missed and none prolonged to the exclusion of others (8, p. 155)." Practice and study is said to insure the proper passage from one phase to another (12, p. 42). Moreover, to guarantee that none of the phases will be excluded, it is necessary to engage in relations only when the sexual partners have a sizable amount of time during which they will not be distracted: ". . . husbands and wives should rarely presume to begin love-play that may lead to coitus unless they can have an hour free from interruptions (1, p. 51)." Even then, however, the couple must be careful, for there is an optimal time to spend on each particular phase. For instance, "Foreplay should never last less than fifteen minutes even though a woman may be sufficiently aroused in five (14, p. 43)." Likewise, the epilogue to orgasm should be of sufficient duration to permit the proper recession of passion.

Given this schedule of activity, the marriage manuals take great pains to describe the various activities required at each particular phase. It is cautioned, for instance, that "all contact with the female genital region . . . should be kept at an absolute minimum (14, pp. 42-43)" during foreplay. The man is warned furthermore to "refrain from any excessive activity involving the penis (14, p. 77)" if he wishes to sustain foreplay. Regarding afterplay, the advice is the same; the partners must not permit themselves "any further genital stimulation (15, p. 25)."

The "job specification" is most explicit, however, when describing the actual act of intercourse. It is particularly during this stage that the sexual partners must strain to maintain control over their emotions. Innumerable lists of "necessary activities" are found in the various manuals. The adequate lovers should not permit themselves to deviate from these activities. Sometimes, in fact, the male is instructed to pause in midaction, in order to ascertain his relative progress:

> After the penis has been inserted to its full length into the vagina, it is usually best for the husband to rest a bit before allowing himself to make the instinctive in-and-out movements which usually follow. He needs first to make sure that his wife is comfortable, that the penis is not pushing too hard against the rear wall of the vagina, and that she is as ready as he to proceed with these movements (1, p. 61).

TECHNIQUES

The "labor of love" espoused by the avocational counselors is one whose culmination is importantly based on the proper use of sexual technique. In fact, ". . . *miserable failure results from ignorance of technique* (3, p. 49)." Indeed "no sex relationship will have permanent value unless technique is mastered . . . (8, p. 177)." Thirteen of the fifteen books devote considerable space to familiarizing the reader with the techniques of sexual activity. These discussions for the most part involve enumerating the various positions of intercourse, but also include techniques to induce, to prolong, to elevate, and to minimize passion. Many times the depiction of particular coital positions takes on a bizarre, almost geometric, aura. In one such position, "The woman lies on her back, lifts her legs at right angles to her body from the hips, and rests them on the man's shoulders; thus she is, so to speak, doubly cleft by the man who lies upon her and inserts his phallus; she enfolds both his genital member and his neck and head. At the same time the woman's spine in the lumbar region is flexed at a sharp angle . . . (15, p. 218)." Often, however, the mastery of sexual technique seems to involve little more than being able to keep one's legs untangled, ". . . when the woman straightens her right leg the man, leaving his right leg between both of hers, puts his left one outside her right, and rolls over onto his left side facing her (1, 58)."

At times, in order to make love adequately, it is required of the participants that they supplement their technique with special equipment. Some of this equipment, such as lubricating jellies, pillows, and birth control paraphernalia, is simple and commonplace. Others are as simple but not as common, such as chairs, foot-high stools, and beds with footboards or footrails. Some, like aphrodisiacs, hot cushions, medicated (carbonic acid) baths, and sitz baths, border on the exotic. Still others actually seem to detract from the pleasure of intercourse. In this vein would be the rings of sponge rubber which are slipped over the penis to control depth of penetration and the various devices which make the male less sensitive, such as condoms and a local anesthetic applied to the glans.

This equipment that minimizes stimulation, while not particularly inviting, might be said to give greater pleasure than still other techniques that are suggested to add variety to the sex life. The latter, in fact, seem cruelly painful. For instance,

> . . . both partners tend to use their teeth, and in so doing there is naught abnormal, morbid or perverse. Can the same be said of the real love-bite that breaks the skin and draws blood? Up to a certain degree—yes (15, p. 157).

Indeed, a certain amount of aggression should be commonplace.

> . . . both of them can and do exult in a certain degree of male aggression and dominance. . . . Hence, the sharp gripping and pinching of the woman's arms and nates (15, p. 159).

At times, the authors seem to go so far as to indicate that the proper performance of the sex act almost requires the use of techniques that create discomfort. The element of irksomeness becomes an almost necessary ingredient of the conduct of marital sex.

CONCLUDING REMARKS

The kinds of impressions assembled here seem to support the notion that play, at least sexual play in marriage, has indeed been permeated with dimensions of a work ethic. The play of marital sex is presented by the counselors quite definitely as work.

This paradox, play as work, may be said to be an almost logical outcome of the peculiar condition of American society. First of all, it seems that in America, most individuals are faced with the problems of justifying and dignifying their play. In times past, leisure was something earned, a prize that was achieved through work. In the present era, it might be said that leisure is something ascribed or assumed. Indeed, as Riesman and Bloomberg have noted, "leisure, which was once a residual compensation for the tribulations of work, may become what workers recover from at work."[9]

The American must justify his play. It is our thesis that he has done this by transforming his play into work. This is not to say that he has disguised his play as work; it is instead to propose that his play has become work.[10] To consume is, in most cases, to produce. Through this transformation of play, the dignity of consumption is seemingly established; it is now work, and work is felt to carry with it a certain inherent dignity. The individual now is morally free to consume, and moreover free to seek out persons to teach him how to consume, for learning how to play is simply learning how to do one's job in society.

This transformation of play into work has been attended by another phenomenon that is also quite unique to contemporary American society. Given the fact that work has always been valued in American society, a cult of efficiency has developed. As a consequence, the productive forces in America have become very efficient, and an abundance of consumer goods have been created. So that such goods will be consumed, Americans have been socialized into being extremely consumption oriented. As Jules Henry[11] has noted, the impulse controls of most Americans have been destroyed. The achievement of a state of general satisfaction has become a societal goal. To experience pleasure is almost a societal dictum.

Thus there seem to be two antagonistic forces operating in American society. On the one hand, there is an emphasis on work and, on the other hand, there is an emphasis on attaining maximum pleasure. These two themes were recurrent in the fifteen manuals which we read, and as one writer put it:

> . . . it may well be that the whole level of sexual enjoyment for both partners can be stepped up and greatly enriched if the man is able to exercise a greater degree of deliberation and management (1, p. 33).

It was as if the avocational counselors were trying to solve a dilemma for their audience by reminding them to both "let themselves go" while cautioning them that they should "work at this." If sex be play it most assuredly is a peculiar kind of play.

APPENDIX A

1. Oliver M. Butterfield, Ph.D., *Sexual Harmony in Marriage*, New York: Emerson Books, 1964 (sixth printing).
2. Mary Steichen Calderone, M.D., M.S.P.H., and Phyllis and Robert P. Goldman, *Release from Sexual Tensions*, New York: Random House, 1960.
3. Eustace Chesser, M.D., *Love Without Fear*, New York: The New American Library, 1947 (twenty-ninth printing).
4. Maxine Davis, *Sexual Responsibility in Marriage*, New York: Dial Press, 1963.
5. John E. Eichenlaub, M.D., *The Marriage Art*, New York: Dell Publishing Co., 1961 (fourteenth printing).
6. Albert Ellis, Ph.D., and Robert A. Harper, Ph.D., *The Marriage Bed*, New York: Tower Publications, 1961.
7. Bernard R. Greenblat, B.S., M.D., *A Doctor's Marital Guide for Patients*, Chicago: Budlong Press, 1964.
8. Edward F. Griffith, *A Sex Guide to Happy Marriage*, New York: Emerson Books, 1956.
9. Robert E. Hall, M.D., *Sex and Marriage*, New York: Planned Parenthood-World Population, 1965.
10. Isabel Emslie Hutton, M.D., *The Sex Technique in Marriage*, New York: Emerson Books, 1961 (revised, enlarged, and reset edition following thirty-fifth printing in 1959).
11. Lena Levine, M.D., *The Doctor Talks with the Bride and Groom*, New York: Planned Parenthood Federation, 1950 (reprinted, February 1964).
12. S. A. Lewin, M.D., and John Gilmore, Ph.D., *Sex Without Fear*, New York: Medical Research Press, 1957 (fifteenth printing).
13. Hannah M. Stone, M.D., and Abraham Stone, M.D., *A Marriage Manual*, New York: Simon and Schuster, 1953.
14. Robert Street, *Modern Sex Techniques*, New York: Lancer Books, 1959.
15. Th. H. Van de Velde, M.D., *Ideal Marriage: Its Physiology and Technique*, New York: Random House, 1961.

[1]Leo Lowenthal, "The Triumph of Mass Idols," in *Literature, Popular Culture, and Society*, Englewood Cliffs, New Jersey: Prentice-Hall, 1961, pp. 109-140.

[2]David Riesman (with Nathan Glazer and Reuel Denney), *The Lonely Crowd*, Garden City, New York: Doubleday Anchor Books, 1953, p. 341.

[3]Riesman, *loc. cit.*

[4]Nelson Foote, "Sex as Play," in Eric Larrabee and Rolf Meyersohn, editors, *Mass Leisure*, Glencoe, Illinois: Free Press, 1958, p. 335.

[5]Jules Henry, *Culture Against Man*, New York: Random House, 1963, p. 43.

[6]Martha Wolfenstein, "The Emergence of Fun Morality," in Eric Larrabee and Rolf Meyersohn, *op. cit.*, p. 93.

[7]We were unable to obtain this most recent printing, and our copy was the twenty-ninth printing.

[8]These figures were published in *Newsweek*, October 18, 1965, p. 100.

[9]David Riesman and Warner Bloomberg, Jr., "Work and Leisure: Tension or Polarity," in Sigmund Nosow and William H. Form, editors, *Man, Work, and Society*, New York: Basic Books, Inc., 1962, p. 39.

[10]Many investigators have observed the intertwining of work and play. We are here only interested in one aspect of admixture, the labor of play.

[11]Henry, *op. cit.*, pp. 20-21.

Part VI

DEVIANCE

Sometimes I ain't so sho who's got ere a right to say
when a man is crazy and when he ain't. Sometimes
I think it ain't none of us pure crazy and ain't none
of us pure sane until the balance of us talks him that-
a-way. It's like it ain't so much what a fellow does,
but it's the way the majority of folks is looking at him
when he does it.

William Faulkner, AS I LAY DYING

Introduction to Part VI
(Deviance)

Deviance is deeply rooted in the structural features of communities
and societies. As poverty and inequality increase, so do the crime
rates. Gross economic inequalities in a society oriented toward consumption of commodities bought with the rewards of the stratification system unquestionably explain considerable deviance in American society. Deprivation, both absolute and relative, is an important
force pushing more and more individuals to the frustrations, disillu-
sionments, and hopelessness which drive individuals into careers in
deviance.

Professor Goffman's article exemplifies the way in which the
behavioral patterns of confidence men in their interactions with
their "marks" can be useful in facilitating an understanding of social
interaction in a wide variety of more "legitimate" social situations.

Professor Svalastoga's article illustrates the way in which structural variables such as status and class are involved with the crime
of rape. Most important, crime of any variety cannot be understood
independent of considerations of the influence of structural variables
such as social class.

19.

ON COOLING THE MARK OUT†

Some Aspects of Adaptation to Failure

ERVING GOFFMAN*

In cases of criminal fraud, victims find they must suddenly adapt themselves to the loss of sources of security and status which they had taken for granted. A consideration of this adaptation to loss can lead us to an understanding of some relations in our society between involvements and the selves that are involved.

In the argot of the criminal world, the term "mark" refers to any individual who is a victim or prospective victim of certain forms of planned illegal exploitation. The mark is the sucker—the person who is taken in. An instance of the operation of any particular racket, taken through the full cycle of its steps or phases, is sometimes called a play. The persons who operate the racket and "take" the mark are occasionally called operators.

The confidence game—the con, as its practitioners call it—is a way of obtaining money under false pretenses by the exercise of fraud and deceit. The con differs from politer forms of financial deceit in important ways. The con is practiced on private persons by talented actors who methodically and regularly build up informal social relationships just for the purpose of abusing them; white-collar crime is practiced on organizations by persons who learn to abuse positions of trust which they once filled faithfully. The one exploits poise; the other, position. Further, a con man is someone who accepts a social role in the underworld community; he is part of a brotherhood whose members make no pretense to one another of being "legit." A white-collar criminal, on the other hand, has no colleagues, although he may have an associate with whom he plans his crime and a wife to whom he confesses it.

*A.B. Univ. of Toronto 45; M.A., Sociology, Univ. of Chicago 49; Instr., Dept. of Social Anthropology, Univ. of Edinburgh, and field research in the Shetland Islands 49-51; admitted to candidacy for Ph.D. in Sociology, Univ. of Chicago; Rsc. Asst., Division of Social Sciences, Univ. of Chicago 52.

†Terminology regarding criminal activity is taken primarily from D. W. Maurer, *The Big Con* (New York, Bobbs-Merrill, 1940), and also from E. Sutherland, *The Professional Thief* (Chicago, Univ. of Chicago Press, 1937). The approach that this paper attempts to utilize is taken from Everett C. Hughes of the University of Chicago, who is not responsible for any misapplications of it which may occur here. The sociological problem of failure was first suggested to me by James Littlejohn of the University of Edinburgh. I am grateful to Professor E. A. Shils for criticism and to my wife, Angelica S. Goffman, for assistance.

Reprinted from *Psychiatry*, Vol. 15, Nov. 1952, pp. 451-563, by special permission of the author and the publisher, The William Alanson White Psychiatric Foundation, Inc.. Copyright is held by the Foundation.

The con is said to be a good racket in the United States only because most Americans are willing, nay eager, to make easy money, and will engage in action that is less than legal in order to do so. The typical play has typical phases. The potential sucker is first spotted, and one member of the working team (called the outside man, steerer, or roper) arranges to make social contact with him. The confidence of the mark is won, and he is given an opportunity to invest his money in a gambling venture which he understands to have been fixed in his favor. The venture, of course, is fixed, but not in his favor. The mark is permitted to win some money and then persuaded to invest more. There is an "accident" or "mistake," and the mark loses his total investment. The operators then depart in a ceremony that is called the blowoff or sting. They leave the mark but take his money. The mark is expected to go on his way, a little wiser and a lot poorer.

Sometimes, however, a mark is not quite prepared to accept his loss as a gain in experience and to say and do nothing about his venture. He may feel moved to complain to the police or to chase after the operators. In the terminology of the trade, the mark may squawk, beef, or come through. From the operators' point of view, this kind of behavior is bad for business. It gives the members of the mob a bad reputation with such police as have not yet been fixed and with marks who have not yet been taken. In order to avoid this adverse publicity, an additional phase is sometimes added at the end of the play. It is called cooling the mark out. After the blowoff has occurred, one of the operators stays with the mark and makes an effort to keep the anger of the mark within manageable and sensible proportions. The operator stays behind his team-mates in the capacity of what might be called a cooler and exercises upon the mark the art of consolation. An attempt is made to define the situation for the mark in a way that makes it easy for him to accept the inevitable and quietly go home. The mark is given instruction in the philosophy of taking a loss.

When we call to mind the image of a mark who has just been separated from his money, we sometimes attempt to account for the greatness of his anger by the greatness of his financial loss. This is a narrow view. In many cases, especially in America, the mark's image of himself is built up on the belief that he is a pretty shrewd person when it comes to making deals and that he is not the sort of person who is taken in by anything. The mark's readiness to participate in a sure thing is based on more than avarice; it is based on a feeling that he will now be able to prove to himself that he is the sort of person who can "turn a fast buck." For many, this capacity for high finance comes near to being a sign of masculinity and a test of fulfilling the male role.

It is well known that persons protect themselves with all kinds of rationalizations when they have a buried image of themselves which the facts of their status do not support. A person may tell himself many things: that he has not been given a fair chance; that he is not really interested in becoming something else; that the time for showing his mettle has not yet come; that the usual means of realizing his desires are personally or morally distasteful, or require too much dull effort. By means of such defenses, a person saves himself from committing a cardinal social sin—the sin of defining oneself in terms of a status while lacking the qualifications which an incumbent of that status is supposed to possess.

A mark's participation in a play, and his investment in it, clearly commit him in his own eyes to the proposition that he is a smart man. The process by which he comes to believe that he cannot lose is also the process by which he drops the defenses and compensations that previously protected him from defeats. When the blowoff comes, the mark finds that he has no defense for not being a shrewd man. He has defined himself as a shrewd man and must face the fact that he is only another easy mark. He has defined himself as possessing a certain set of qualities and then proven to himself that he is miserably lacking in them. This is a process of self-destruction of the self. It is no wonder that the mark needs to be cooled out and that it is good business policy for one of the operators to stay with the mark in order to talk him into a point of view from which it is possible to accept a loss.

In essence, then, the cooler has the job of handling persons who have been caught out on a limb—persons whose expectations and self-conceptions have been built up and then shattered. The mark is a person who has compromised himself, in his own eyes if not in the eyes of others.

Although the term, mark, is commonly applied to a person who is given short-lived expectations by operators who have intentionally misrepresented the facts, a less restricted definition is desirable in analyzing the larger social scene. An expectation may finally prove false, even though it has been possible to sustain it for a long time and even though the operators acted in good faith. So, too, the disappointment of reasonable expectations, as well as misguided ones, creates a need for consolation. Persons who participate in what is recognized as a confidence game are found in only a few social settings, but persons who have to be cooled out are found in many. Cooling the mark out is one theme in a very basic social story.

For purposes of analysis, one may think of an individual in reference to the values or attributes of a socially recognized character which he possesses. Psychologists speak of a value as a personal involvement. Sociologists speak of a value as a status, role, or relationship. In either case, the character of the value that is possessed is taken in a certain way as the character of the person who possesses it. An alteration in the kinds of attributes possessed brings an alteration to the self-conception of the person who possesses them.

The process by which someone acquires a value is the process by which he surrenders the claim he had to what he was and commits himself to the conception of self which the new value requires or allows him to have. It is the process that persons who fall in love or take dope call getting hooked. After a person is hooked, he must go through another process by which his new involvement finds its proper place, in space and time, relative to the other calls, demands, and commitments that he has upon himself. At this point certain other persons suddenly begin to play an important part in the individual's story; they impinge upon him by virtue of the relationship they happen to have to the value in which he has become involved. This is not the place to consider the general kinds of impingement that are institutionalized in our society and the general social relationships that arise: the personal relationship, the professional relationship, and the business relationship. Here we are concerned only with the end of the story, the way in which a person becomes disengaged from one of his involvements.

In our society, the story of a person's involvement can end in one of three general ways. According to one type of ending, he may withdraw from one of his involvements or roles in order to acquire a sequentially related one that is considered better. This is the case when a youth becomes a man, when a student becomes a practitioner, or when a man from the ranks is given a commission.

Of course, the person who must change his self at any one of these points of promotion may have profound misgivings. He may feel disloyal to the way of life that must be left behind and to the persons who do not leave it with him. His new role may require action that seems insincere, dishonest, or unfriendly. This he may experience as a loss in moral cleanliness. His new role may require him to forgo the kinds of risk-taking and exertion that he previously enjoyed, and yet his new role may not provide the kind of heroic and exalted action that he expected to find in it.[1] This he may experience as a loss in moral strength.

There is no doubt that certain kinds of role success require certain kinds of moral failure. It may therefore be necessary, in a sense, to cool the dubious neophyte in rather than out. He may have to be convinced that his doubts are a matter of sentimentality. The adult social view will be impressed upon him. He will be required to understand that a promotional change in status is voluntary, desirable, and natural, and that loss of one's role in these circumstances is the ultimate test of having fulfilled it properly.

It has been suggested that a person may leave a role under circumstances that reflect favorably upon the way in which he performed it. In theory, at least, a related possibility must be considered. A person may leave a role and at the same time leave behind him the standards by which such roles are judged. The new thing that he becomes may be so different from the thing he was that criteria such as success or failure cannot be easily applied to the change which has occurred. He becomes lost to others that he may find himself; he is of the twice-born. In our society, perhaps the most obvious example of this kind of termination occurs when a woman voluntarily gives up a prestigeful profession in order to become a wife and a mother. It is to be noted that this illustrates an institutionalized movement; those who make it do not make news. In America most other examples of this kind of termination are more a matter of talk than of occurrence. For example, one of the culture heroes of our dinner-table mythology is the man who walks out on an established calling in order to write or paint or live in the country. In other societies, the kind of abdication being considered here seems to have played a more important role. In medieval China, for instance, anchoretic withdrawal apparently gave to persons of quite different station a way of retreating from the occupational struggle while managing the retreat in an orderly, face-saving fashion.[2]

Two basic ways in which a person can lose a role have been considered; he can be promoted out of it or abdicate from it. There is, of course, a third basic ending to the status story. A person may be involuntarily deprived of his position or involvement and made in return something that is considered a lesser thing to be. It is mainly in this third ending to a person's role that occasions arise for cooling him out. It is here that one deals in the full sense with the problem of persons' losing their roles.

Involuntary loss seems itself to be of two kinds. First, a person may lose a status in such a way that the loss is not taken as a reflection upon the loser. The loss of a loved one, either because of an accident that could not have been prevented or because of a disease that could not have been halted, is a case in point. Occupational retirement because of old age is another. Of course, the loss will inevitably alter the conception the loser has of himself and the conception others have of him, but the alteration itself will not be treated as a symbol of the fate he deserves to receive. No insult is added to injury. It may be necessary, none the less, to pacify the loser and resign him to his loss. The loser who is not held responsible for his loss may even find himself taking the mystical view that all involvements are part of a wider con game, for the more one takes pleasure in a particular role the more one must suffer when it is time to leave it. He may find little comfort in the fact that the play has provided him with an illusion that has lasted a lifetime. He may find little comfort in the fact that the operators had not meant to deceive him.

Secondly, a person may be involuntarily deprived of a role under circumstances which reflect unfavorably on his capacity for it. The lost role may be one that he had already acquired or one that he had openly committed himself to preparing for. In either case the loss is more than a matter of ceasing to act in a given capacity; it is ultimate proof of an incapacity. And in many cases it is even more than this. The moment of failure often catches a person acting as one who feels that he is an appropriate sort of person for the role in question. Assumption becomes presumption, and failure becomes fraud. To loss of substance is thereby added loss of face. Of the many themes that can occur in the natural history of an involvement, this seems to be the most melancholy. Here it will be quite essential and quite difficult to cool the mark out. I shall be particularly concerned with this second kind of loss—the kind that involves humiliation.

It should be noted, parenthetically, that one circle of persons may define a particular loss as the kind that casts no reflection on the loser, and that a different circle of persons may treat the same loss as a symbol of what the loser deserves. One must also note that there is a tendency today to shift certain losses of status from the category of those that reflect upon the loser to the category of those that do not. When persons lose their jobs, their courage, or their minds, we tend more and more to take a clinical or naturalistic view of the loss and a nonmoral view of their failure. We want to define a person as something that is not destroyed by the destruction of one of his selves. This benevolent attitude is in line with the effort today to publicize the view that occupational retirement is not the end of all active capacities but the beginning of new and different ones.

A consideration of consolation as a social process leads to four general problems having to do with the self in society. First, where in modern life does one find persons conducting themselves as though they were entitled to the rights of a particular status and then having to face up to the fact that they do not possess the qualification for the status? In other words, at what points in the structures of our social life are persons likely to compromise themselves or find themselves compromised? When is it likely that a person will have to disengage himself or become disengaged from one of his involvements? Secondly, what are the typical ways in which persons who find themselves in this difficult position can be cooled out; how can they be made to accept the great injury that has been done to their image of themselves, regroup their defenses, and carry on without raising a squawk? Thirdly, what, in general, can happen when a person refuses to be cooled out, that is, when he refuses to be pacified by the cooler? Fourthly, what arrangements are made by operators and marks to avoid entirely the process of consolation?

In all personal-service organizations customers or clients sometimes make complaints. A customer may feel that he has been given service in a way that is unacceptable to him—a way that he interprets as an offense to the conception he has of who and what he is. The management therefore has the problem of cooling the mark out. Frequently this function is allotted to specialists within the organization. In restaurants of some size, for example, one of the crucial functions of the hostess is to pacify customers whose self-conceptions have been injured by waitresses or by the food. In large stores the complaint department and the floorwalker perform a similar function.

One may note that a service organization does not operate in an anonymous world, as does a con mob, and is therefore strongly obliged to make some effort to cool the mark out. An institution, after all, cannot take it on the lam; it must pacify its marks.

One may also note that coolers in service organizations tend to view their own activity in a light that softens the harsher details of the situation. The cooler protects himself from feelings of guilt by arguing that the customer is not really in need of the service he expected to receive, that bad service is not really deprivational, and that beefs and complaints are a sign of bile, not a sign of injury. In a similar way, the con man protects himself from remorseful images of bankrupt marks by arguing that the mark is a fool and not a full-fledged person, possessing an inclination towards illegal gain but not the decency to admit it or the capacity to succeed at it.

In organizations patterned after a bureaucratic model, it is customary for personnel to expect rewards of a specified kind upon fulfilling requirements of a specified nature. Personnel come to define their career line in terms of a sequence of legitimate expectations and to base their self-conceptions on the assumption that in due course they will be what the institution allows persons to become. Sometimes, however, a member of an organization may fulfill some of the requirements for a particular status, especially the requirements concerning technical proficiency and seniority, but not other requirements, especially the less codified ones having to do with the proper handling of social relationships at work. It must fall to someone to break the bad news to the victim; someone must tell him that he has been fired, or that he has failed his examinations, or that he has been by-passed in promotion. And after the blowoff, someone has to cool the mark out. The necessity of disappointing the expectations that a person has taken for granted may be infrequent in some organizations, but in others, such as training institutions, it occurs all the time. The process of personnel selection requires that many trainees be called but that few be chosen.

When one turns from places of work to other scenes in our social life, one finds that each has its own occasions for cooling the mark out. During informal social intercourse it is well understood that an effort on the part of one person (ego) to decrease his social distance from another person (alter) must be graciously accepted by alter or, if rejected, rejected tactfully so that the initiator of the move can save his social face. This rule is codified in books on etiquette and is followed in actual behavior. A friendly movement in the direction of alter is a movement outward on a limb; ego communicates his belief that he has defined himself as worthy of alter's society, while at the same time he places alter in the strategic position of being able to discredit this conception.

The problem of cooling persons out in informal social intercourse is seen most clearly, perhaps, in courting situations and in what might be called de-courting situations. A proposal of marriage in our society tends to be a way in which a man sums up his social attributes and suggests to a woman that hers are not so much better as to preclude a merger or partnership in these matters. Refusal on the part of the woman, or refusal on the part of the man to propose when he is clearly in a position to do so, is a serious reflection on the rejected suitor. Courtship is a way not only of presenting oneself to alter for approval but also of saying that the opinion of alter in this matter is the opinion one is most concerned with. Refusing a proposal, or refusing to propose, is therefore a difficult operation. The mark must be carefully cooled out. The act of breaking a date or of refusing one, and the task of discouraging a "steady" can also be seen in this light, although in these cases great delicacy and tact may not be required, since the mark may not be deeply involved or openly committed. Just as it is harder to refuse a proposal than to refuse a date, so it is more difficult to reject a spouse than to reject a suitor. The process of de-courting in which one person in a marriage maneuvers the other into accepting a divorce without fuss or undue rancor requires extreme finesse in the art of cooling the mark out.

In all of these cases where a person constructs a conception of himself which cannot be sustained, there is a possibility that he has not invested that which is most important to him in the soon-to-be-denied status. In the current idiom, there is a possibility that when he is hit, he will not be hit where he really lives. There is a set of cases, however, where the blowoff cannot help but strike a vital spot; these cases arise, of course, when a person must be dissuaded from life itself. The man with a fatal sickness or fatal injury, the criminal with a death sentence, the soldier with a hopeless objective—these persons must be persuaded to accept quietly the loss of life itself, the loss of all one's earthly involvements. Here, certainly, it will be difficult to cool the mark out. It is a reflection on the conceptions men have—as cooler and mark—that it is possible to do so.

I have mentioned a few of the areas of social life where it becomes necessary, upon occasion, to cool a mark out. Attention may now be directed to some of the common ways in which individuals are cooled out in all of these areas of life.

For the mark, cooling represents a process of adjustment to an impossible situation—a situation arising from having defined himself in a way which the social facts come to contradict. The mark must therefore be supplied with a new set of apologies for himself, a new framework in which to see himself and judge himself. A process of redefining the self along defensible lines must be instigated and carried along; since the mark himself is frequently in too weakened a condition to do this, the cooler must initially do it for him.

One general way of handling the problem of cooling the mark out is to give the task to someone whose status relative to the mark will serve to ease the situation in some way. In formal organizations, frequently, someone who is two or three levels above the mark in line of command will do the hatchet work, on the assumption that words of consolation and redirection will have a greater power to convince if they come from high places. There also seems to be a feeling that persons of high status are better able to withstand the moral danger of having hate directed at them. Incidentally, persons protected by high office do not like to face this issue, and frequently attempt to define themselves as merely the agents of the deed and not the source of it. In some cases, on the other hand, the task of cooling the mark out is given to a friend and peer of the mark, on the assumption that such a person will know best how to hit upon a suitable rationalization for the mark and will know best how to control the mark should the need for this arise. In some cases, as in those pertaining to death, the role of cooler is given to doctors or priests. Doctors must frequently help a family, and the member who is leaving it, to manage the leave-taking with tact and a minimum of emotional fuss.[3] A priest must not so much save a soul as create one that is consistent with what is about to become of it.

A second general solution to the problem of cooling the mark out consists of offering him a status which differs from the one he has lost or failed to gain but which provides at least a something or a somebody for him to become. Usually the alternative presented to the mark is a compromise of some kind, providing him with some of the trappings of his lost status as well as with some of its spirit. A lover may be asked to become a friend; a student of medicine may be asked to switch to the study of dentistry;[4] a boxer may become a trainer; a dying person may be asked to broaden and empty his worldly loves so as to embrace the All-Father that is about to receive him. Sometimes the mark is allowed to retain his status but is required to fulfill it in a different environment: the honest policeman is transferred to a lonely beat; the too zealous priest is encouraged to enter a monastery; an unsatisfactory plant manager is shipped off to another branch. Sometimes the mark is "kicked upstairs" and given a courtesy status such as "Vice President." In the game for social roles, transfer up, down, or away may all be consolation prizes.

A related way of handling the mark is to offer him another chance to qualify for the role at which he has failed. After his fall from grace, he is allowed to retrace his steps and try again. Officer selection programs in the army, for example, often provide for possibilities of this kind. In general, it seems that third and fourth chances are seldom given to marks, and that second chances, while often given, are seldom taken. Failure at a role removes a person from the company of those who have succeeded, but it does not bring him back—in spirit, anyway—to the society of those who have not tried or are in the process of trying. The person who has failed in a role is a constant source of embarrassment, for none of the standard patterns of treatment is quite applicable to him. Instead of taking a second chance, he usually goes away to another place where his past does not bring confusion to his present.

Another standard method of cooling the mark out—one which is frequently employed in conjunction with other methods—is to allow the mark to explode, to break down, to cause a scene, to give full vent to his reactions and feelings, to "blow his top." If this release of emotions does not find a target, then it at least serves a cathartic function. If it does find a target, as in "telling off the boss," it gives the mark a last-minute chance to re-erect his defenses and prove to himself and others that he had not really cared about the status all along. When a blow-up of this kind occurs, friends of the mark or psychotherapists are frequently brought in. Friends are willing to take responsibility for the mark because their relationship to him is not limited to the role he has failed in. This, incidentally, provides one of the less obvious reasons why the cooler in a con mob must cultivate the friendship of the mark; friendship provides the cooler with an acceptable reason for staying around while the mark is cooled out. Psychotherapists, on the other hand, are willing to take responsibility for the mark because it is their business to offer a relationship to those who have failed in a relationship to others.

It has been suggested that a mark may be cooled out by allowing him, under suitable guidance, to give full vent to his intial shock. Thus the manager of a commercial organization may listen with patience and understanding to the complaints of a customer, knowing that the full expression of a complaint is likely to weaken it. This possibility lies behind the role of a whole series of buffers in our society—janitors, restaurant hostesses, grievance committees, floor-walkers, and so on—who listen in silence, with apparent sympathy, until the mark has simmered down. Similarly, in the case of criminal trials, the defending lawyer may find it profitable to allow the public to simmer down before he brings his client to court.

A related procedure for cooling the mark out is found in what is called stalling. The feelings of the mark are not brought to a head because he is given no target at which to direct them. The operator may manage to avoid the presence of the mark or may convince the mark that there is still a slight chance that the loss has not really occurred. When the mark is stalled, he is given a chance to become familiar with the new conception of self he will have to accept before he is absolutely sure that he will have to accept it.

As another cooling procedure, there is the possibility that the operator and the mark may enter into a tacit understanding according to which the mark agrees to act as if he were leaving of his own accord, and the operator agrees to preserve the illusion that this was the case. It is a form of bribery. In this way the mark may fail in his own eyes but prevent others from discovering the failure. The mark gives up his role but saves his face. This, after all, is one of the reasons why persons who are fleeced by con men are often willing to remain silent about their adventure. The same strategy is at work in the romantic custom of allowing a guilty officer to take his own life in a private way before it is taken from him publicly, and in the less romantic custom of allowing a person to resign for delicate reasons instead of firing him for indelicate ones.

Bribery is, of course, a form of exchange. In this case, the mark guarantees to leave quickly and quietly, and in exchange is allowed to leave under a cloud of his own choosing. A more important variation on the same theme is found in the practice of financial compensation. A man can say to himself and others that he is happy to retire from his job and say this with more conviction if he is able to point to a comfortable pension. In this sense, pensions are automatic devices for providing consolation. So, too, a person who has been injured because of another's criminal or marital neglect can compensate for the loss by means of a court settlement.

I have suggested some general ways in which the mark is cooled out. The question now arises: what happens if the mark refuses to be cooled out? What are the possible lines of action he can take if he refuses to be cooled? Attempts to answer these questions will show more clearly why, in general, the operator is so anxious to pacify the mark.

It has been suggested that a mark may be cooled by allowing him to blow his top. If the blow-up is too drastic or prolonged, however, difficulties may arise. We say that the mark becomes "disturbed mentally" or "personally disorganized." Instead of merely telling his boss off, the mark may go so far as to commit criminal violence against him. Instead of merely blaming himself for failure, the mark may inflict great punishment upon himself by attempting suicide, or by acting so as to make it necessary for him to be cooled out in other areas of his social life.

Sustained personal disorganization is one way in which a mark can refuse to cool out. Another standard way is for the individual to raise a squawk, that is, to make a formal complaint to higher authorities obliged to take notice of such matters. The con mob worries lest the mark appeal to the police. The plant manager must make sure that the disgruntled department head does not carry a formal complaint to the general manager or, worse still, to the Board of Directors. The teacher worries lest the child's parent complain to the principal. Similarly, a woman who communicates her evaluation of self by accepting a proposal of marriage can sometimes protect her exposed position—should the necessity of doing so arise—by threatening her disaffected fiancé with a breach-of-promise suit. So, also, a woman who is de-courting her husband must fear lest he contest the divorce or sue her lover for alienation of affection. In much the same way, a customer who is angered by a salesperson can refuse to be mollified by the floorwalker and demand to see the manager. It is interesting to note that associations dedicated to the rights and the honor of minority groups may sometimes encourage a mark to register a formal squawk; politically it may be more advantageous to provide a test case than to allow the mark to be cooled out.

Another line of action which a mark who refuses to be cooled can pursue is that of turning "sour." The term derives from the argot of industry but the behavior it refers to occurs everywhere. The mark outwardly accepts his loss but withdraws all enthusiasm, good will, and vitality from whatever role he is allowed to maintain. He complies with the formal requirements of the role that is left him, but he withdraws his spirit and identification from it. When an employee turns sour, the interests of the organization suffer; every executive, therefore, has the problem of "sweetening" his workers. They must not come to feel that they are slowly being cooled out. This is one of the functions of granting periodic advancements in salary and status, of schemes such as profit-sharing, or of giving the "employee" at home an anniversary present. A similar view can be taken of the problem that a government faces in times of crisis when it must maintain the enthusiastic support of the nation's disadvantaged minorities, for whole groupings of the population can feel they are being cooled out and react by turning sour.

Finally, there is the possibility that the mark may, in a manner of speaking, go into business for himself. He can try to gather about him the persons and facilities required to establish a status similar to the one he has lost, albeit in relation to a different set of persons. This way of refusing to be cooled is often rehearsed in phantasies of the "I'll show them" kind, but sometimes it is actually realized in practice. The rejected marriage partner may make a better remarriage. A social stratum that has lost its status may decide to create its own social system. A leader who fails in a political party may establish his own splinter group.

All these ways in which a mark can refuse to be cooled out have consequences for other persons. There is, of course, a kind of refusal that has little consequence for others. Marks of all kinds may develop explanations and excuses to account in a creditable way for their loss. It is, perhaps, in this region of phantasy that the defeated self makes its last stand.

The process of cooling is a difficult one, both for the operator who cools the mark out and for the person who receives this treatment. Safeguards and strategies are therefore employed to ensure that the process itself need not and does not occur. One deals here with strategies of prevention, not strategies of cure.

From the point of view of the operator, there are two chief ways of avoiding the difficulties of cooling the mark out. First, devices are commonly employed to weed out those applicants for a role, office, or relationship who might later prove to be unsuitable and require removal. The applicant is not given a chance to invest him self unwisely. A variation of this technique, that provides, in a way, a built-in mechanism for cooling the mark out, is found in the institution of probationary period and "temporary" staff. These definitions of the situation make it clear to the person that he must maintain his ego in readiness for the loss of his job, or, better still, that he ought not to think of himself as really having the job. If these safety measures fail, however, a second strategy is often employed. Operators of all kinds seem to be ready, to a surprising degree, to put up with or "carry" persons who have failed but who have not yet been treated as failures. This is especially true where the involvement of the mark is deep and where his conception of self had been publicly committed. Business offices, government agencies, spouses, and other kinds of operators are often careful to make a place for the mark, so that dissolution of the bond will not be necessary. Here, perhaps, is the most important source of private charity in our society.

A consideration of these preventive strategies brings to attention an interesting functional relationship among age-grading, recruitment, and the structure of the self. In our society, as in most others, the young in years are defined as not-yet-persons. To a certain degree, they are not subject to success and failure. A child can throw himself completely into a task, and fail at it, and by and large he will not be destroyed by his failure; it is only necessary to play at cooling him out. An adolescent can be bitterly disappointed in love, and yet he will not thereby become, at least for others, a broken person. A youth can spend a certain amount of time shopping around for a congenial job or a congenial training course, because he is still thought to be able to change his mind without changing his self. And, should he fail at something to which he has tried to commit himself, no permanent damage may be done to his self. If many are to be called and few chosen, then it is more convenient for everyone concerned to call individuals who are not fully persons and cannot be destroyed by failing to be chosen. As the individual grows older, he becomes defined as someone who must not be engaged in a role for which he is unsuited. He becomes defined as something that must not fail, while at the same time arrangements are made to decrease the chances of his failing. Of course, when the mark reaches old age, he must remove himself or be removed from each of his roles, one by one, and participate in the problem of later maturity.

The strategies that are employed by operators to avoid the necessity of cooling the mark out have a counterpart in the strategies that are employed by the mark himself for the same purpose.

There is the strategy of hedging, by which a person makes sure that he is not completely committed. There is the strategy of secrecy, by which a person conceals from others and even from himself the facts of his commitment; there is also the practice of keeping two irons in the fire and the more delicate practice of maintaining a joking or unserious relationship to one's involvement. All of these strategies give the mark an out, in case of failure he can act as if the self that has failed is not one that is important to him. Here we must also consider the function of being quick to take offense and of taking hints quickly, for in these ways the mark can actively cooperate in the task of saving his face. There is also the strategy of playing it safe, as in cases where a calling is chosen because tenure is assured in it, or where a plain woman is married for much the same reason.

It has been suggested that preventive strategies are employed by operator and mark in order to reduce the chance of failing or to minimize the consequences of failure. The less importance one finds it necessary to give to the problem of cooling, the more importance one may have given to the application of preventive strategies.

I have considered some of the situations in our society in which the necessity for cooling the mark out is likely to arise. I have also considered the standard ways in which a mark can be cooled out, the lines of action he can pursue if he refuses to be cooled, and the ways in which the whole problem can be avoided. Attention can now be turned to some very general questions concerning the self in society.

First, an attempt must be made to draw together what has been implied about the structure of persons. From the point of view of this paper, a person is an individual who becomes involved in a value of some kind—a role, a status, a relationship, an ideology—and then makes a public claim that he is to be defined and treated as someone who possesses the value or property in question. The limits to his claims, and hence the limits to his self, are primarily determined by the objective facts of his social life and secondarily determined by the degree to which a sympathetic interpretation of these facts can bend them in his favor. Any event which demonstrates that someone has made a false claim, defining himself as something which he is not, tends to destroy him. If others realize that the person's conception of self has been contradicted and discredited, then the person tends to be destroyed in the eyes of others. If the person can keep the contradiction a secret, he may succeed in keeping everyone but himself from treating him as a failure.

Secondly, one must take note of what is implied by the fact that it is possible for a person to be cooled out. Difficult as this may be, persons regularly define themselves in terms of a set of attributes and then have to accept the fact that they do not possess them—and do this about-face with relatively little fuss or trouble for the operators. This implies that there is a norm in our society persuading persons to keep their chins up and make the best of it—a sort of social sanitation enjoining torn and tattered persons to keep themselves packaged up. More important still, the capacity of a person to sustain these profound embarrassments implies a certain looseness and lack of interpenetration in the organization of his several life activities. A man may fail in his job, yet go on succeeding with his wife. His wife may ask him for a divorce, or refuse to grant him one, and yet he may push his way onto the same streetcar at the usual time on the way to the same job. He may know that he is shortly going to have to leave the status of the living, but still march with the other prisoners, or eat breakfast with his family at their usual time and from behind his usual paper. He may be conned of his life's savings on an eastbound train but return to his home town and succeed in acting as if nothing of interest had happened.

Lack of rigid integration of a person's social roles allows for compensation; he can seek comfort in one role for injuries incurred in others. There are always cases, of course, in which the mark cannot sustain the injury to his ego and cannot act like a "good scout." On these occasions the shattering experience in one area of social life may spread out to all the sectors of his activity. He may define away the barriers between his several social roles and become a source of difficulty in all of them. In such cases the play is the mark's entire social life, and the operators, really, are the society. In an increasing number of these cases, the mark is given psychological guidance by professionals of some kind. The psychotherapist is, in this sense, the society's cooler. His job is to pacify and reorient the disorganized person; his job is to send the patient back to an old world or a new one, and to send him back in a condition in which he can no longer cause trouble to others or can no longer make a fuss. In short, if one takes the society, and not the person as the unit, the psychotherapist has the basic task of cooling the mark out.

A third point of interest arises if one views all of social life from the perspective of this paper. It has been argued that a person must not openly or even privately commit himself to a conception of himself which the flow of events is likely to discredit. He must not put himself in a position of having to be cooled out. Conversely, however, he must make sure that none of the persons with whom he has dealings are of the sort who may prove unsuitable and need to be cooled out. He must make doubly sure that should it become necessary to cool his associates out, they will be the sort who allow themselves to be gotten rid of. The con man who wants the mark to go home quietly and absorb a loss, the restaurant hostess who wants a customer to eat quietly and go away without causing trouble, and, if this is not possible, quietly to take his patronage elsewhere—these are the persons and these are the relationships which set the tone of some of our social life. Underlying this tone there is the assumption that persons are institutionally related to each other in such a way that if a mark allows himself to be cooled out, then the cooler need have no further concern with him; but if the mark refuses to be cooled out, he can put institutional machinery into action against the cooler. Underlying this tone there is also the assumption that persons are sentimentally related to each other in such a way that if a person allows himself to be cooled out, however great the loss he has sustained, then the cooler withdraws all emotional identification from him; but if the mark cannot absorb the injury to his self and if he becomes personally disorganized in some way, then the cooler cannot help but feel guilt and concern over the predicament. It is this feeling of guilt—this small measure of involvement in the feelings of others—which helps to make the job of cooling the mark out distasteful, wherever it appears. It is this incapacity to be insensitive to the suffering of another person when he brings his suffering right to your door which tends to make the job of cooling a species of dirty work.

One must not, of course, make too much of the margin of sympathy connecting operator and mark. For one thing, the operator may rid himself of the mark by application or threat of pure force or open insult.[5] In Chicago in the 1920's small businessmen who suffered a loss in profits and in independence because of the "protection" services that racketeers gave to them were cooled out in this way. No doubt it is frivolous to suggest that Freud's notion of castration threat has something to do with the efforts of fathers to cool their sons out of oedipal involvements. Furthermore, there are many occasions when operators of different kinds must act as middlemen, with two marks on their hands; the calculated use of one mark as a sacrifice or fall guy may be the only way of cooling the other mark out. Finally, there are barbarous ceremonies in our society, such as criminal trials and the drumming-out ritual employed in court-martial procedures, that are expressly designed to prevent the mark from saving his face. And even in those cases where the cooler makes an effort to make things easier for the person he is getting rid of, we often find that there are bystanders who have no such scruples.[6] Onlookers who are close enough to observe the blowoff but who are not obliged to assist in the dirty work often enjoy the scene, taking pleasure in the discomfiture of the cooler and in the destruction of the mark. What is trouble for some is Schadenfreude for others.

This paper has dealt chiefly with adaptations to loss; with defenses, strategies, consolations, mitigations, compensations, and the like. The kinds of sugar-coating have been examined, and not the pill. I would like to close this paper by referring briefly to the sort of thing that would be studied if one were interested in loss as such, and not in adaptations to it.

A mark who requires cooling out is a person who can no longer sustain one of his social roles and is about to be removed from it; he is a person who is losing one of his social lives and is about to die one of the deaths that are possible for him. This leads one to consider the ways in which we can go or be sent to our death in each of our social capacities, the ways, in other words, of handling the passage from the role that we had to a state of having it no longer. One might consider the social processes of firing and laying off; of resigning and being asked to resign; of farewell and departure; of deportation, excommunication, and going to jail; of defeat at games, contests, and wars; of being dropped from a circle of friends or an intimate social relationship; of corporate dissolution; of retirement in old age; and, lastly, of the deaths that heirs are interested in.

And, finally, attention must be directed to the things we become after we have died in one of the many social senses and capacities in which death can come to us. As one might expect, a process of sifting and sorting occurs by which the socially dead come to be effectively hidden from us. This movement of ex-persons throughout the social structure proceeds in more than one direction.

There is, first of all, the dramatic process by which persons who have died in important ways come gradually to be brought together into a common graveyard that is separated ecologically from the living community.[7] For the dead, this is at once a punishment and a defense. Jails and mental institutions are, perhaps, the most familiar examples, but other important ones exist. In America today, there is the interesting tendency to set aside certain regions and towns in California as asylums for those who have died in their capacity as workers and as parents but who are still alive financially.[8] For the old in America who have also died financially, there are old-folks homes and rooming-house areas. And, of course, large cities have their Skid Rows which are, as Park put it, ". . . full of junk, much of it human, i.e., men and women who, for some reason or other, have fallen out of line in the march of industrial progress and have been scrapped by the industrial organization of which they were once a part."[9] Hobo jungles, located near freight yards on the outskirts of towns, provide another case in point.

Just as a residential area may become a graveyard, so also certain institutions and occupational roles may take on a similar function. The ministry in Britain, for example, has sometimes served as a limbo for the occupational stillborn of better families, as have British universities. Mayhew, writing of London in the mid-nineteenth-century, provides another example: artisans of different kinds, who had failed to maintain a position in the practice of their trade, could be found working as dustmen.[10] In the United States, the jobs of waitress, cab driver, and night watchman, and the profession of prostitution, tend to be ending places where persons of certain kinds, starting from different places, can come to rest.

But perhaps the most important movement of those who fail is one we never see. Where roles are ranked and somewhat related, persons who have been rejected from the one above may be difficult to distinguish from persons who have risen from the one below. For example, in America, upper-class women who fail to make a marriage in their own circle may follow the recognized route of marrying an upper-middle class professional. Successful lower-middle class women may arrive at the same station in life, coming from the other direction. Similarly, among those who mingle with one another as colleagues in the profession of dentistry, it is possible to find some who have failed to become physicians and others who have succeeded at not becoming pharmacists or optometrists. No doubt there are few positions in life that do not throw together some persons who are there by virtue of failure and other persons who are there by virtue of success. In this sense, the dead are sorted but not segregated, and continue to walk among the living.

[1]Mr. Hughes has lectured on this kind of disappointment, and one of his students has undertaken a special study of it. See Miriam Wagenschein, " 'Reality Shock': A Study of Beginning School Teachers," M.A. thesis, Dept. of Sociology, Univ. of Chicago, 1950.

[2]See, for example, Max Weber, The Religion of China (H. H. Gerth, tr.); Glencoe, Ill., Free Press, 1951; p. 178.

[3]This role of the doctor has been stressed by W. L. Warner in his lectures at the University of Chicago on symbolic roles in "Yankee City."

[4]In his seminars, Mr. Hughes has used the term "second-choice" professions to refer to cases of this kind.

[5]Suggested by Saul Mendlovitz in conversation.

[6]Suggested by Howard S. Becker in conversation.

[7]Suggested by lectures of and a personal conversation with Mr. Hughes.

[8]Some early writers on caste report a like situation in India at the turn of the nineteenth century. Hindus who were taken to the Ganges to die, and who then recovered, were apparently denied all legal rights and all social relations with the living. Apparently these excluded persons found it necessary to congregate in a few villages of their own. In California, of course, settlements of the old have a voluntary character, and members maintain ceremonial contact with younger kin by the exchange of periodic visits and letters.

[9]R. E. Park, Human Communities; Glencoe, Ill.; Free Pess, 1952; p. 60.

[10]Henry Mayhew, London Labour and the London Poor; London, Griffin, Bohn, 1861; Vol. II, pp. 177-178.

20. RAPE AND SOCIAL STRUCTURE*

KAARE SVALASTOGA

THE PROBLEM

Rape, as shown by J. S. Brown, is a behavior pattern that is nearly universally met by very strong social sanctions.[1] Only incest, among

Reprinted from the Pacific Sociological Review, Vol. V, (1962), pp. 48-53, by permission of the author and the publisher, John MacGregor, Oregon State University.

*Revised version of paper presented at the American Sociological Association meetings, St. Louis, 1961. The author is strongly indebted to Professor Clarence Schrag of the University of Washington who read the first version of the paper and gave numerous valuable suggestions concerning form and content. For defects still present, the author is of course solely responsible.

sex offenses occurring in modern societies, encounters equally severe and universal social opposition.

Rape is commonly defined as enforced coitus.[2] But this very definition suggests that there is more to the offense than the use of force alone. This must be so, since no society has equipped itself with the means for measuring the amount of force applied in an act of coitus.

Hence, rape, like any other kind of crime, carries a heavy social component. The act itself is not a sufficient criterion. The act must be interpreted as rape by the female actee, and her interpretation must be similarly evaluated by a number of officials and agencies before the official designation of "rape" can be legitimately applied. Furthermore, rape is somewhat unique in that its negative evaluation in public opinion is very frequently extended to the victim as well as the offender.[3] This aspect of the crime is clearly instrumental in reducing the number of such offenses that are brought to the attention of the police.

This paper is not primarily concerned with force or the degree of its use in rape offenses. Rather, it investigates the role of *anonymity* and of *status differentials* between offenders and their victims as important components of the social situation that ordinarily accompanies this type of offense. In addition, variations in the *sex ratio* will be utilized in order to account for the unequal regional distribution of crimes of rape.

In formulating hypotheses concerning the variables mentioned, we have used an axiomatic-deductive procedure, assuming that this method will facilitate our search for invariances in the behavior under investigation.[4]

REVIEW OF PERTINENT RESEARCH

The author has been able to locate only one previous sociological treatment of rape, although several discussions of sex crimes in general are on record. For example, Hoegel found that Austrian sex offenders in 1900-1901 were chiefly from the class of manual workers and had a maximum incidence in the age group 16-20 years. Again, Wulffen found the highest incidence of rape and similar offenses in the warmer seasons of the year, the maximum occurring in July and the minimum in January, according to German data for the years 1883-1892. He also cites French data for the years 1827-1869 which reveal a maximum of sex crimes in June and a minimum in November. A study from Vienna, also reported by Wulffen, shows a maximum number of sex crimes and violent offenses on Sundays and a minimum number on Thursdays. Somewhat similar results have been reported in a number of other studies.[5]

Herz, an Austrian criminologist, stressed the sex ratio as a factor in the explanation of sex crimes, maintaining that these offenses increase according to the amount of deviation in either direction from an equilibrium ratio of 100. Herz's own data, however, show that the sex ratio is a rather poor predictor of sex crimes. Much better is the percentage of bachelors among males 24 years of age and older. This suggests that overall imbalance is not as crucial as sex ratio imbalance among unmarried adults in the peak marital propensity period. Hoegel's data for Austria in 1902-1903 point in the same direction.[6]

The most comparable previous study is that of LeMaire whose study of Danish offenders includes 104 rapists for the period 1929-1939. LeMaire demonstrates striking variations among ecological factors that are related to sex offenses. Thus, rape, incest among siblings, coitus with minors, and indecent behavior toward females all show a maximum concentration in rural areas, whereas other sex offenses are either concentrated in urban areas or are relatively evenly distributed in both rural and urban areas.[7] Rape, according to LeMaire's findings, occurs most frequently on Saturdays and Sundays, between the hours of midnight and six o'clock in the morning, among persons 15 to 19 years of age, the unmarried, and persons in low status rural occupations. Rapists were rarely psychotic or mentally deficient, and alcohol was considered a dominant factor in only 22 per cent of the cases. Unfortunately, LeMaire was unable to make any observations concerning the victims of rape.[8]

MAJOR FINDINGS OF THE PRESENT STUDY

Before proceeding to the derivations and tests of hypotheses, a concise description of the data collected in our study will be given in terms of time, place, people involved, violence used, and some characteristics of the victim and the offender.

Time, Place, and People. Our data are from the complete and original criminal records of 141 cases of rape and attempted rape coming before the court in Denmark in the years 1946 through 1958.[9] These cases constitute a nearly complete enumeration of the rape offenses brought before the criminal courts during the years 1956-1958 and a 50 per cent nonrandom sample for the preceding years. Comparison indicates that the sample may under-represent the milder offenses and cases of attempted rape, but it also shows that none of our major conclusions would be modified by a fuller coverage of cases.

Our data show that rape is predominantly, although not exclusively, a nocturnal crime. The hours from 12 to 2 o'clock in the morning have the greatest rape risk and exactly 2-3 of all rapes occurred between 10 in the evening and 4 in the morning. Saturday through Monday as well as Wednesday have higher than average incidence. Sunday is the day of maximum incidence and rapes occur then with about twice the frequency observed for Tuesday, the day of minimum incidence (25:13). Furthermore, there is a confirmation of the so-called "thermic law of crime" in as much as the four lowest figures occur for December through March. Rape is in most cases an open-air event.

We may list the place and frequency of occurrence as follows:

Place of Offense	*Per Cent of Cases*
Out-doors, Isolated place	48
In densely populated area	24
In-doors, Isolated house	11
In densely populated area	13
In automobile	4
Not ascertained	1
Total	101
	(N=141)

Most rapes are pair events, i.e., the rapist approaches his victim alone. However, both the constellation two males—one female, and the constellation three males—one female occurs. There were no cases where more than one victim was involved. We have:

Group Constellation	*Per Cent of Cases*
One male, one female	84
Two males, one female	10
Three males, one female	6
	100
	(N=141)

Amount of Violence. Even a casual reading of the police reports on rape reveals that rapists vary quite widely in the amount and seriousness of violence used.

It should be mentioned that in our sample there were no cases in which violence resulted in the death of the victim. The following ranking was developed and then tested by two outside criteria:

	Per Cent
Degree of Violence	*of Cases*
1. Interference with general body movement, disequilibration	35
2. Interference with vocalization	24
3. Interference with respiration	20
4. Producing traumas by beating or kicking[10]	21
	100
	(N=141)

The first three levels seem to function as a logical rank order considering the situation. The fourth category was empirically seen to be accompanied in most cases by either the second or the third, while it logically implies the first.

We may use as one criterion for this ranking the rapidity with which the police were alarmed (within 12 hours or later)

	Per Cent of Cases	
Police Notified with-	*Police Notified with-*	
Degree of Violence	*in 12 hours*	*N*
1 lowest	55	49
2	71	34
3	93	28
4 highest	87	30

Another possible criterion is leniency of social sanction. This comparison will be limited to cases of completed rape:

	Per Cent of Cases	
Offender Receiving 3	*Offender Receiving 3*	
Degree of Violence	*Years Prison or Less*	*N*
1	54	26
2	61	18
3	17	12
4	21	14

One interfering factor here is previous criminal record. In general similar crimes will be punished more severely on repetition than as first offense. On the whole, these comparisons suggest that there may be less difference between levels 3 and 4 on our scale than between the other levels.

One difficulty in a coitus situation is that what the stronger partner may perceive as bashful mockery the weaker partner may interpret as a maximum of resistance. Thus the medical analyst writes about one of our cases (21 years old, 6 feet tall, weight 190 pounds, skilled worker): "In his work as . . . he is used to handling (objects) weighing 140-150 pounds with ease and swiftness. It is therefore highly probable that a girl's resistance would not penetrate to his consciousness with the same strength as might have been the case, had he been weaker." He was actually acquitted in court. A contributing factor might be that the girl in question was described as "loose" by local authorities. (Violence level 1.)

The Victim.[11] The most likely victims of rapists seem to be those females who for some reason have to walk alone or go by bicycle alone to their home at a time of the day when most people are asleep.

The next most likely victims are those who on such occasions are accompanied by casual male acquaintances but still using the above modes of transportation. It is probably significant that no single case of rape in our data refers to females who used motorized vehicles.

Since the females with higher than average risk are mostly younger and unmarried persons returning home from visits, dances, restaurants, etc., it is a reasonable finding that about one half of all victims belonged to the age category 15 through 19 years, and 77 per cent were between 10 and 24 years of age, although the range spans from 8 to 77 years.[12] At least 85 per cent of the victims were single. Furthermore, at least in 37 per cent of the cases the rape experience is reported to be the victim's first sex experience.

The Rapist. The rapist is most likely to be a youth or young adult. Seventy-one per cent of our rapists were 15-29 years old, while another sixteen per cent were between 30 and 34.[13] As one might expect, the majority (70 per cent) are single or (5 per cent) previously married,[14] but still there is a surprisingly high remainder of married rapists (24 per cent). He is likely to possess some previous sex experience. He is neither taller nor shorter than the average male.

Intelligence tests on 87 persons of the group gave a median score of 88. When the unfavorable testing conditions are taken into account, as well as the fact that many of the supposedly more "normal-looking" were not tested, it is doubtful whether the group as a whole is less intelligent than the average male.[15]

Most rapists were examined by one or more psychiatrists. Serious mental deviation (insanity or imbecility) could only be documented in 11 cases. The modal psychiatric diagnosis was that of minor deviation from normality either in the form of mental retardation or in the form of some psychopathy. However, one third of the group was classified as normal and another 10 per cent were not examined.

The rapist is more often a man with a criminal background than a novice in deviant behavior. Only 33 percent had no previous criminal record, while 22 percent had received two or more prison sentences prior to the rape. His family background will be discussed below.

DERIVATION OF HYPOTHESES

Our major postulates are as follows:

1. A sex ratio for unmarried persons aged 15-49 years at or near 100 defines a condition of social equilibrium. Small departures from this equilibrium are relatively unimportant. However, larger departures, particularly those in the positive direction (male surplus), lead to social tensions which tend to find outlet in increasing efforts at securing efficient sexual approaches. Von Hentig is the major source for this postulate.[16]

2. The means by which males secure coitus outside of marriage depends on social status. With increasing male status the action potential of the male increases. In particular he can choose between many more social techniques in his sexual approach.[17]

3. Parallel with this correlation goes a differential attitude towards violence by social status. In the middle and upper classes violence is more readily delegated to police monopoly, and the use of violence is socially unacceptable under normal conditions. In the lower classes, by contrast, the use of violence, since it frequently appears to be the only method promising success, is not so readily dismissed.

A similar contention has recently been set forth by J.E.H. Williams, who writes: ". . . there is probably a sub-culture of violence among a certain portion of the lower socio-economic group, in which quick resort to physical aggression is a socially approved and expected concomitant of certain stimuli and in which violence has become a familiar but often deadly partner in life's struggles."[18]

4. Violence is more readily condoned in a solidary and highly interactive group than in a plurel of little or no interactivity.

The definition of "rape" used, is the following: *Rape (completed + attempted) is a successful or unsuccessful attempt at securing coitus by the method of more or less violence, which in a society creates sufficient disturbance to be reported to the police and brought before a law court.*

From the above postulates, we derive the following hypotheses to be tested by our data:

1. Rape will be more frequent in communities with a large sex

ratio than in communities with a sex ratio of about 100, assuming that there are no important differences in class structure.

2. The rapist will most likely be a member of the lower social classes.[19]

3. The female victim will be most likely to belong to the upper or middle classes, because in these classes the negative evaluation of violence will be most likely to insure that the case be brought before the police.

4. Between a rapist and his victim anonymity or a condition of low interactivity prevailed prior to the event.

5. As a consequence of derivations 2 and 3, a rapist-rapee status matrix as compared with data for marital unions will reveal an abnormally high incidence in the cells designating lower male status as compared with female's status.

TESTS OF THE HYPOTHESES

The Sex Ratio. The regions with highest positive departures from equilibrium sex ratio (rural communities) have the highest relative rape incidence. Hence derivation 1 is confirmed.[20]

The great difference in the frequency of rapes in regions having roughly the same sex ratio, such as in the capital and in the provincial cities, indicates that the sex ratio is not a sufficient explanation. It seems likely that the higher availability of sex satisfaction on commercial terms (prostitution, call girls etc.) in the capital may help to explain the difference observed between the capital and the other Danish cities.

Table 1. Sex Ratio and Rape by Place of Occurrence

Place	Sex ratio among un- married persons 15-49, 1957	Number of rapists	Rapist ratio per million of all males 15-49, 1950
Capital	93	10	43
Provincial cities	91	35	130
Elsewhere in Denmark .	163	96	175

Social Status of Rapist. Using the stratification system described by Svalastoga,[21] and in particular placing vagabonds and persons imprisoned twice or more in the lowest stratum, we arrive at the following status distribution of rapists:

	Per Cent
Social Status of Offender (1 highest, 9 lowest)	*of Cases*
4 (upper middle)	.7

Continued on p. 273

Social Status of Offender	Per Cent of Cases
6 (small enterprisers white collar employees)	3.5
7 (skilled worker and apprentices)	6.4
8 (unskilled or rural workers)	58.9
9 (criminal repeaters and/or vagabonds)	30.5
	100.0
	(N = 141)

Reference to the status distribution of the Danish adult population in derivation 2 is amply confirmed (see footnote 21). It is true that part of the difference might be explained by the relative youthfulness of the rapists; but this is of no great importance in this connection because we deal with a group which to an exceptional degree is characterized by mobility handicaps.

The rapist is an underprivileged person in several respects. At least 80 per cent have only 7 years of schooling not even including training for any craft, and only 3 per cent possess an intermediate high school diploma (9 or 10 years).

A repeated theme in the reconstruction of the offender's childhood is his desire to engage in some kind of craft training (4 years apprenticeship with modest pay) and the frustration of this desire due to the poor family economy. Seventeen per cent of the group were born out of wedlock. Also characteristic is a large sibling group. Where the number was given its median value was 6, and no less than 20 per cent of 102 rapists with known sibling size stemmed from sibling groups numbering from 10 to 17 children.

The social and economic status of the parents or foster-parents was on the average very low. Only 11 per cent had a middle-class origin, while 85 per cent were workingclass people, mostly unskilled. Information is missing for the remaining 4 per cent.

Poverty, disorderly home, criminal or other deviant behavior among family members are frequent, although not invariable, childhood experience of the rapist.

It is hard to escape the conclusion that the violence of this group is a tool used by a category of people who have less chance than most people to learn more refined ways of social persuasion or to acquire the means whereby favors are bought and not taken by force.

The highest ranking rapist in our sample strikingly illustrates how a high status person intent on sexual adventures has other methods at his disposal, which are barred to the low status male.

The records reveal that this high ranking person several times utilized sexually females who were economically dependent on him, and how he (even if parents of the victim protest) was able to appease them with pay-offs which did not mean much to him. Furthermore, it appears that several of his victims avoided reports to the police or to other people because they pitied his wife or felt that a police report might completely ruin him and his family. In fact, when finally arrested on the basis of rumors becoming more and more loud in his town, he was immediately fired from his high ranking position.

Social Status of Victim. Derivation 3 fails to obtain support from the data as the following tabulation shows.

In contrast to the contention of derivation 3 most rape victims have a lower (working) class background. It is true that the method of classification is somewhat slanted against derivation 3 in so far as a classification of young females on the basis of their own occupation (where their social origin is unknown) leads to a higher proportion of low status females than a classification by parental occupation solely would have given. However, the data show that even if we limit comparison to cases where the latter classification is possible, we arrive at the same result: Derivation 3 is false.

Social Status of Victims[22]		*Number of Cases*	*Percentage of Cases*
	3	1	.7
Upper or middle	4	4	2.8
classes	5	5	3.5
	6	20	14.2
	7	30	21.3
Lower classes	8	77[23]	54.6
	9	4	2.8
		141	99.9

Prior Relationship. Derivation 4 does stand up (Table 2) but not as well as expected. In about one fifth of the sample, the rapist and his victim were in the long acquaintance+relatives category. Although this could not be definitely ascertained, it seemed that the rate of previous interaction, even in the long acquaintance category, had been modest in most cases.

Table 2. Degree of Acquaintance at Time of Offense and Time of Notifying Police

	Police notified within 12 hours N	%	Police notified later N	%	Total N (Base: 141)	%
No mutual acquaintance	66	86.8	10	13.2	76	54
Mutual acquaintance but brief, super- ficial or indirect............	24	82.8	5	17.2	29	21
Long acquaintance	9	45.0	11	55.0	20	14
Relatives	2	18.2	9	81.8	11	8
N.A.	2	40.0	3	60.0	5	4
Totals	103	73.0	38	27.0	141	101

An indirect indication tending to support derivation 4 appears when we consider the correlation between acquaintance level and speed of alarming the police (Table 2). It appears that in most cases where the partners do not know each other, the offense is reported to the police within 12 hours, whereas this is rarely done where the partners are relatives.

In addition incestuous rapes are frequently reported to the police only several years after the event, and even then the report often occurs after some other event has caused a reduction in family solidarity.

One of our rape cases offers a remarkable illustration of the principles involved in hypothesis 4. The case concerns a female factory worker. She was surprised in her unlocked bedroom one night by an intruding male whom she did not recognize with certainty due to darkness. He proceeded to have coitus with her (violence degree 2). The following day (or possibly later) the female looked up the person with whom she last had willingly had coitus. She asked him whether he had been at her house the night of the enforced coitus, because she did not see the person. And she added that in case he was the person, "she would not report the case to the police." In fact, this is a case where no report was given to the police within the first 12 hours of the incident. The rapist proved, however, to be another person. He, too, was a long time acquaintance of the victim, but clearly not on the same level of intimacy as the person previously mentioned.

Rapist-Rape Status Relationship. Reference to Table 3 shows that derivation 5 is confirmed. The status-relationship between rapist and victim reveals an abnormally high frequency of cases where the female enjoys higher social status than the male.

Table 3. Comparison of the Social Status of Rapist and Victim

Social Status of Female Victim	Male Rapist Social Status						
	9	8	7	6	5	4 or 3	Total
3 or 4 (highest)	2	2	1				5
5	3	2					5
6	8	11		1			20
7	8	17	3	2			30
8	21	48	5	2		1	77
9 (lowest)	1	3					4
Totals	43	83	9	5	0	1	141

From Table 3, the following compilation comparing male and female status may be reported:

Female status is:	Observed %	Expected[23] %
Higher	51	19
Same	38	67
Lower	11	14
	100	100

$$N = 141$$

This finding is of course in part due to the fact that rapists are recruited so overwhelmingly from the lower social strata making a majority of all females their social superiors. However, even for constant social origin it can be shown that rapists are abnormally likely to seek their female partners far removed in social space.

To show this we shall limit our attention to the 90 per cent of the rapists who belong to the two lowest social strata. The other strata are so under represented that they do not have much evidential value treated in isolation.

Table 4. Social Status of Victim for Rapists in Stratum 8 or 9

Social status	Observed %	Expected[25] %
1-5	7.1	1.1
6	15.1	21.3
7	19.8	36.9
8, 9	57.9	40.7
Totals	99.9	100.0
	(N=126)	(N=263)

The author is not inclined to attribute any importance to the apparently lower upwards move to strata 7 and 6 among lower class rapists. It should be remembered that rapists are mostly to be found within the lower part of the two strata. They should therefore be expected to have fewer chances of contacts with females of higher status than most males in the strata mentioned.

It will be seen that among our five derivations four were confirmed while one, derivation 3, had to be rejected. This again means that there is something wrong with postulate 3 as stated above, which provided the basis for derivation 3.

It seems likely that the postulate exaggerates the working class-non-working class distinction. The chief distinction should perhaps be drawn further down the status scale. Another possibility is that since young females of working class background frequently have middle class employers the latter will in fact increase the probability of a rape against a working class female being reported to the police. Absence of relevant research makes it impossible at the present time to test the implications of these explanations. There is also the further possibility that derivation 3 should be reformulated to read as above, but with the addition "sex ratio in approximate equilibrium."

This explanation may be tested directly on our data by analyzing the urban material separately. Although the proportion of females of upper and middle class status thereby increases from 21.2 to 26.7 percent (N=45) still the majority of victims, even in an environment where the sex ratio is in approximate equilibrium, belong to the working classes.

Hence only further research can provide a more adequate axiomatization than was achieved in this study.

[1]J. S. Brown, "A Comparative Study of Deviations from Sexual Mores," *American Sociological Review*, 17 (April, 1952), pp. 135-146.

[2]We shall in this paper limit the concept to a consideration of the typical sex constellation—rapist: male, rapee: female.

[3]As an illustration we may cite the experience of a seventeen year old shop assistant from a small town who was raped in a nearby big town. She said that she had to leave the small town for some time because of public gossip—in the street, people would make hints about her "big town experiences."

[4]H. Zetterberg, *On Theory and Verification in Sociology*, Stockholm: Almquist and Wiksell, 1954.

[5]E. Wulffen, "Sexual Kriminalstatistik," in *Der Sexual Verbrecher*, Berlin, 1910, Chpt. 4. Compare also, S. Kaplan, "The Geography of Crime," in J. S. Roucek, *ed.*, *Sociology of Crime*, New York: Philosophical Library, 1961, pp. 160-192.

[6]Wulffen, *op. cit.*, pp. 293-296.

[7]The American crime rates for 1958 reveal that forcible rape is relatively more frequent in the rural than in the urban environment for all cities below 250,000. Above this size, the urban crime rate is higher and, considering cities alone, tends to increase with the size of the city. See, Kaplan, *op. cit.*

[8]L. LeMaire, *Legal Kastration*, Copenhagen, 1946. Mean age of rapists was given as 23 years in a Los Angeles report and as 26 years in a New York report (N=30). See, M. Guttmacher, *Sex Offenses*, New York, 1951, p. 67.

[9]The author is indebted to the Danish Ministry of Law for granting permission to use the original criminal records of each of the 141 cases. He also wishes to thank the Danish police represented by Kriminalkommisaer Bang, and the Danish Bureau of the Census, represented by sekretaer Rita Knudsen for their helpfulness. Preben Wolf gave valuable criminological advice with usual helpfulness.

[10]With one single exception no tools were used. The exception is represented by a 19 year old worker, a former butcher's assistant, who in the early night entered through the window, where he in the daytime had observed a young woman. He was equipped with a heavy iron hammer and directed two violent blows at the head of a young woman asleep in the room without any prior attempt at securing sexual privileges in other ways. He seems, however, to have been shocked by his own deed, because no traces of coitus could be determined. Although the female was severely hurt and remembered nothing of the event, she recovered later.

[11]A female is counted as one victim each time a new rapist approaches her. Hence there are somewhat below 141 different females in our data.

[12]Data from New York, 1937-1941, corroborate the tendency for rape victims to be young. See, H. Hentig, The Criminal and His Victim, New Haven, 1948, p. 402.

[13]Top risk: 20-24 years.

[14]Here including separated persons.

[15]For a different conclusion see Hentig, op. cit., p. 104.

[16]H. Hentig, "The Sex Ratio," Social Forces, 30 (May, 1951), pp. 443-449.

[17]Compare J. Thurber, Men, Women, and Dogs, New York, 1946.

[18]J.E.H. Williams in a review of M. Wolfgang, Patterns in Criminal Homicide, Philadelphia, 1958, in the British Journal of Sociology, 11 (1960), p. 95.

[19]In contrast to derivation 1 and postulate 1, which evolved in the course of the study, the rest of the postulates and derivations were developed prior to the study. It will be seen below that derivation 3 fails to receive support from our data.

[20]In fact, direct reference to the extreme sex-ratio is found in the court record of one of the cases here studied. This is also the single example of a case where rape is associated with homicide, the persons killed by the rapist being not the rape victim but her employers—a farmer and his wife who tried to help the rape victim. The day before the tragic event, the 18 year old future life prisoner was working in the hay fields with the later victim and a married female helper. These two women both asked the young boy, "what he sought here in Western Jutland, because here there were no girls." The young man responded that there had to be some. Whereupon the younger of the females said, "there is at most three."

[21]K. Svalastoga, Prestige, Class, Mobility, Copenhagen: Gyldendal, 1959.

[22]Based on the occupation of female's father or husband or in case of no data, on the occupatiion of the female herself.

[23]Includes three cases with incomplete information.

[24]From Svalastoga, op. cit., table 5.14, p. 388.

[25]Unpublished data from table relating social status of husbands at time of interview to social status of wife's father. Same nationwide sample as used in Svalastoga, op. cit.

Part VII

POPULATION AND ECOLOGY

The frog does not
Drink up
The pond in which
He lives.

An Indian Proverb

You will see, too, that modern natural history deals only incidentally with the identity of plants and animals, and only incidentally with their habits and behaviors. It deals principally with their relations to each other, their relation to the soil and water in which they grew, and their relations to the human beings who sing about "my country" but see little or nothing of its inner workings. This science of relationships is called ecology, but what we call it matters nothing. The question is, does the educated citizen know he is only a cog in an ecological mechanism? That if he will work with that mechanism his mental health and his material wealth can expand indefinitely? But that if he refuses to work with it, it will ultimately grind him to dust? If education does not teach us these things, then what is education for?

— Aldo Leopold,
"A Sand County Almanac"

Introduction to Part VII
(Population and Ecology)

The debate on population has become a popular topic in recent years. Although the demographic characteristics of any society are of fundamental importance, many issues remain to be resolved regarding population and environmental catastrophes.

An ecological consciousness will perhaps, in the long run, be

279

the difference between survival or extinction of the human species.

Professor Mayer's article, "U.S. Population Growth: Would Slower Be Better?" reviews the current demographic trends in this country. Over-population and its impact upon the individual and society with reference to future alternatives is the crux of his discussion.

Professor Mahmoudi's article on "Population Redistribution" examines the concern with over-population from a distribution perspective. A central tenet of this article is that rather than blame the numbers of people as causes of environmental and over-crowding problems, let us examine the patterns of population distribution more fully. Is *population* or its *redistribution* the problem? Here a case is made for the latter proposition.

Finally, Professor Hawley's article, "Ecology and Human Ecology," examines the fundamentals of the ecological perspective. The relationships between man and his social and natural environment are discussed in this last selection.

21.   U.S. POPULATION GROWTH: WOULD SLOWER BE BETTER?

Lawrence A. Mayer

Even with today's low birth rates, the population is growing fast enough to double in seventy-two years. Someday it will have to stabilize.

The movement to curb population growth in the U.S. has come into prominence, curiously enough, at a time when the birth rate is close to its all-time low. The actual low in the U.S. birth rate came in 1968, at 17.5 per thousand. While the rate rose a bit to 17.7 last year—the first increase in more than a decade—it was still lower than at any point during the great depression of the Thirties. And though the number of births last year was up 2 percent to 3,570,000, that total was about 700,000 below the all-time peak reached in 1957.

The U.S., then, appears to have already moved in the direction that proponents of population stability advocate. But it's not at stability yet. Even at the recent reduced birth rates, the population has been growing 1 percent a year, and that is enough to double it in a single lifetime of seventy-two years. Moreover, birth rates are now

Reprinted from *Fortune Magazine*, June 1970, by permission of the author and the publisher, Time, Inc.

*If this year's Census picked up the number of people thought to have been missed in the Census of 1960, the official figure for 1970 will finally be reported as about 210 million.

bound to go higher, at least for some years to come. One important reason has to do with the changing numbers of women aged twenty to thirty-four, who account for about three-quarters of all births. The size of this group remained practically constant at about 18 million between 1955 and 1965, but from 1965 to 1970 it grew by three million, and in the next fifteen years it will increase ten million more. This wave of younger women is the result, of course, of the baby boom that followed World War II.

While the number of young women began to increase markedly in the years following 1965, the number of births did not. The women who had reached at least the age of twenty-five by around 1965 had borne most of their children by that time, and births to them naturally slowed down drastically thereafter. At the same time, women who were then just moving into the childbearing ages delayed having children (see "Why the U.S. Population *Isn't* Exploding," FORTUNE, April, 1967). This delay should partly be made up at later ages, however, and meanwhile the ranks of the twenty- to thirty-four-year-olds will increase rapidly. These two factors virtually guarantee that there will be a rise in births during the years directly ahead.

> **A slowdown in growth** has already outdated the Census Bureau's high projection, only a few years old. Population is now following the bureau's low projection. The other curves shown were worked out by economist Stephen Enke of General Electric-TEMPO. The one labeled "recent family size" assumes that today's young women will have an average of 2.9 children, and that women will continue in that pattern. The "zero population growth" line assumes that, starting in 1975, the average per woman declines to 2.1 children—i.e., just enough for replacement. Because of the present age structure, growth would not reach zero for about sixty-five years. Both of Enke's projections assume some increase in life expectancies.

How boomy this baby boom will turn out to be is a question that perplexes demographers. Those at the Census Bureau who made four alternative population projections in 1967 have already discarded the highest as virtually impossible. What's more, it has become clear that the second highest is improbable. Up to this moment, it is the lowest that is on target with a figure of 205 million for 1970*. At any rate Census will soon issue a new, lower set of projections.

In the present era of changing mores and social upheavals, it is even more difficult than usual to forecast the probable course of U.S. population growth. Just about everything known, however, suggests to Census demographers that a range of projections for the year

2000 should at the outside be no higher than 325 million (the old Census high was 361 million). Even the 300 million people still commonly said to be inevitable by 2000 are no longer inevitable at all.

Some distance from zero

Population projections have to be built on many assumptions. One key assumption has to do with how large a family the average woman eventually will have. And nobody knows what that figure will be for the young women who will soon begin to bear children, or have recently begun. Surveys have shown that women expect what averages out as about 3.2 children. Demographers largely agree that at present it looks as if today's young women would have fewer children than that. But it would take a drop all the way down to an average of 2.1 children per woman (a bit more than 2.2 per married woman) to bring population growth to a halt. The 2.1 figure is sometimes referred to as the "zero population growth" rate. Obviously it takes two children to replace a set of parents. The extra 0.1 compensates for the girls who die before maturity and takes account of the fact that fewer girls than boys are born. (The 2.1 figure ignores net immigration, which has been contributing 0.2 percent a year to U.S. population growth.)

An important clue to future family size is the total fertility rate. This is the combined rate at which, in any particular year, women of all reproductive ages bear children. The figure for 1969 suggested women were building families at a rate that, if sustained, would give them an average of about 2.5 children by the end of their childbearing careers. This rate is very close to that underlying the present Census low projection. But the total fertility rate at any point in time may be an unreliable indicator. For example, the rate hit 3.7 per woman in the late 1950's, a figure demographers rightly suspected was too high to last. Many experts think the present 2.5 is too low to last.

Donald J. Bogue, a demographer at the University of Chicago, argues that the present fertility rate is *not* misleading. The rise in fertility that followed World War II, he believes, was merely a prolonged interruption of the decline in the U.S. birth rate that got started early in the nineteenth century. He thinks it quite significant that by 1968 white women were bearing children at a rate of only 2.37 per woman, 1.26 fewer than in 1957 and not so very far from the stability rate of 2.1. Childbearing by black women (who account for about 17 percent of all births) has come down by about the same proportion, and was at a rate of 3.2 per woman in 1968. Moreover, Bogue thinks the black rate may go below the white rate by the end of this century. He points out, for example, that the percentage of black women who bear five or more children has halved since 1957. Moreover, college-educated black women expect fewer children than college-educated white women expect.

Accordingly, Bogue sees comparatively moderate growth in the U.S. population by the year 2000. The low of about 280 million in the Census Bureau's 1967 projection is the top of Bogue's high range. Bogue's low goes down to 220 million.

The big little difference

A view quite different from Bogue's is advanced by Arthur A. Campbell, a widely respected government demographer now at the National Institutes of Health. He believes that the total fertility rate is probably giving off a false signal. He takes the depression years, when all measures of births were extremely low, as his bench mark. At that time, women born in 1909 were in their peak childbearing years. By age twenty-six (in 1935) they had given birth to but 1.05 children on average, and they finally produced the smallest American families on record, 2.23 children. By contrast, when women born in 1943 were twenty-six years old (in 1969), they had already averaged 1.57 children. It now looks as if these younger women would eventually have an average of close to three. Recent patterns suggest that 90 percent of today's young women will have at least one child; in contrast, nearly 25 percent of the women born in 1909 never had any children at all.

In short, Campbell believes that much of the recent decline in birth rates reflects a delay in childbearing by young women. And even though such delays tend to reduce the eventual size of families ("Later means less," demographers say), he still thinks current reproductive behavior is consistent with an average of 2.8 children per woman rather than 2.5. This seemingly insignificant difference has large implications. If sustained over thirty years to 2000, the higher figure would mean 25 million more Americans.

As surer means of birth control come into use, it becomes more important for demographers to know how many children people really want. One kind of information bearing on this question is what proportion of births represents unwanted children. In a recent paper, Professors Larry Bumpass of Wisconsin and Charles F. Westoff of Princeton maintain that 16 percent of the births to women who were nearing the end of their childbearing years in 1965—when the last national fertility survey was taken—were unwanted. They conclude that these women, on average, would have had only 2.5 children if they had been able to exercise perfect control over their fertility.

Variations on the Population Profile

These charts illustrate how changes in rates of population growth affect not only total numbers but also the age structure. The present profile reflects both the marked rise in births beginning in the 1940's and the leveling out and decline in births since 1957. If women continue to have families of present (or recent) size, the population will grow 50 percent by the year 2000 and will shift to a still younger age structure. But if family size declines to the "zero population growth" level by 1975, there will be similar numbers of people in all age brackets up to about fifty by the year 2000. (Data from Stephen Enke of G.E.-TEMPO.)

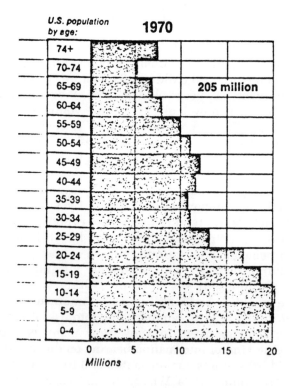

U.S. population by age: **1970**

205 million

2000—If present family-size pattern continues

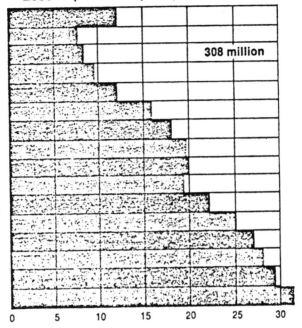

308 million

0   5   10   15   20   25   30

2000—"Zero population growth"

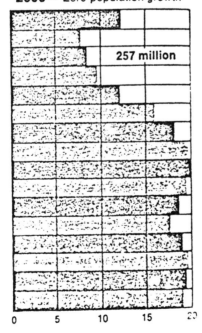

257 million

0   5   10   15   20

This is astounding, since whenever surveys have directly asked women how many children they wanted or expected, the average has always come out a little over three. Bumpass and Westoff, however, went back over the 1965 questionnaires to ascertain what parents said about wanting *each successive child*. In this way the two demographers arrived at their 2.5 figure. And this result could well be conservative. It can be imagined that parents find it difficult to describe children who may literally be sitting in the adjoining room as "unwanted."

By extending their analysis to the entire population, Bumpass and Westoff conclude that in the 1960's one-fifth of all births were unwanted—meaning about 700,000 annually in the past few years. The extra births are more widely spread among social classes than might be supposed. The poor and near-poor, of course, contributed more than their proportionate share, *but more than half* of the unwanted children were born to parents who were not considered poor. (A family of four that had an income of at least $4,000 in 1964 was classified as "nonpoor.")

The implications of these findings are quite far reaching. If the number of children that couples really want averages 2.5 rather than three or so, it might not require very extensive social alterations to attain population stability, assuming the availability of perfect contraception.

The population problem

A sense that population growth is becoming a burden rather than a boon has taken hold in the U.S. with surprising swiftness. Last July, only a year after President Johnson's restrained advocacy of family planning and his hesitant mention of "population change," President Nixon spoke out forthrightly about the "pressing problems" associated with population growth. In keeping with Mr. Nixon's request, Congress has established a Commission on Population Growth and the American Future.

All the attention to population has arisen from several interwoven concerns having to do with crowding, pollution, and deterioration of the environment. The U.S. is confronting a "popullution" problem, observes S. Fred Singer, Deputy Assistant Secretary of the Interior and director of that department's research on environmental quality. Also, it is disturbing to some that the U.S. is chewing up a disproportionate share of the earth's limited stock of natural resources.

Population growth, of course, is not the only villian in these matters. Under present arrangements, the nation's productive system provides high levels of consumption but also throws off inordinate amounts of pollution, waste, and discomfort. The uneven distribution of the population also affects the quality of life.

It is often said that the U.S. doesn't really have a population problem, because there are only fifty-five people per square mile (sixty-five excluding Alaska). Density in some European countries runs more than ten times as high. But the over-all density figure for the U.S. is misleading, because two-thirds of the population lives in metropolitan areas, where density is much greater. And nearly half of the people in metropolitan areas live in central cities, where the density averages around 7,000 per square mile (and a lot higher than that in city cores). It is true that these urban areas are becoming decentralized, but the continuing helter-skelter growth of suburbs is causing new problems of traffic, water supply, and pollution.

If the U.S. rationally altered the distribution of people, it is often contended, there would be no reason for concern about the size of the population. This is more easily proposed than done. Schemes to distribute the population differently are up against what appears to be an iron law of urbanization: in a technologically advancing society the bigger cities tend to grow in perpetuity. Public authorities have tried over the years to halt the growth of London, Paris, Tokyo, and Moscow. None has succeeded, not even the authoritarian government of the U.S.S.R.

Another often-mentioned possibility is to build new towns. Britain has carried out the largest endeavors along this line, having started twenty-seven new towns—new cities, really—since 1946. But they contain only about 1 percent of the total population. Most observers give Britain's new towns at least passing marks, in large part because they have preserved a lot of open space, especially around London. However, the towns have failed to improve conditions within London; the inferior housing that was evacuated filled up again with newcomers.

Only a few communities that really qualify as new towns have been built in the U.S., and those few are not very populous. Recently the federal government gave its first real support to a new town in more than thirty years by issuing a loan guarantee to Jonathan, about twenty miles from Minneapolis. The location of Jonathan supports those who contend that new towns can succeed only within the ambit of established cities. If that is true, then although new towns prevent haphazard development, they don't really do much redistributing. A number of experts think some redistribution could be accomplished if new towns were built around existing ones and used facilities already in place. They have in mind cities in the Middle West that could stand revival—cities with 20,000 to 40,000 people that have stopped growing or are losing population.

One way to try to get new cities built is for the federal government to grant tax incentives to business, an approach that a number of studies and some bills in Congress advocate. Other measures that Washington or local governments could try include selective placement of procurement contracts, provision of inter-area job information, and special channeling of assistance to home building. This spring the Nixon Administration was considering several alternative approaches to a new-town program.

Romantic nonsense

Many economists take a quite different approach to the problems of population distribution. Attempts to use subsidies and special assistance to get people and companies to relocate in less crowded parts of the country are "romantic nonsense," according to Dick Netzer, an urban-economics specialist at New York University. Of the many underlying reasons, perhaps the most important is that the key decisions about location are ordinarily not made by individuals seeking amenities, but by business organizations that cluster together in places they find economically advantageous.

The sensible way to change present patterns of distribution, Netzer and other economists maintain, is to make organizations and individuals pay the full costs of their activities. The argument is that if business, for one, was forced to pay for all the pollution, waste disposal, and traffic congestion resulting from its activities, and for all the benefits it gets from airports, highways, and other public facilities, the distribution of industry and people would be a lot different and the condition of the environment a lot better. In other words, the costs of producing and distributing goods and services should reflect the "externalities." The additional costs would, in many cases, be passed on to consumers. (See "The Economics of Environmental Quality," FORTUNE, February.)

Another way to reduce adverse effects of population growth on the environment is to reduce standards of consumption. It has been calculated that an attempt to get pollution in 1965 back to the levels of 1940 would have required reductions of 50 percent in the number of cars on the road, 50 percent in consumption of paper, 70 percent in generation of electric power, and 87 percent in the use of nitrogen fertilizer.

Still another set of troublesome questions connected with population has to do with the future adequacy of resources. The answers are by no means certain, though judging by the past alone there is nothing much to worry about. Important new materials such as petroleum and aluminum have been brought into use in the past century, and others, such as synthetic fibers and plastics, have emerged from laboratories. Additional reserves of minerals and fuels keep coming along. Better conservation methods have also added to supplies, as in the case of lumber. And improved technology has in some instances played an important role in holding down the consumption of materials. In 1968, electric utilities burned 480 million tons of fuel, measured in coal equivalents; Hans H. Landsberg of Resources for the Future calculates that 740 million tons would have been burned if the technology of 1940 had still been in use.

In principle there are only four real resources: the earth and its minerals, air, water, and fossil fuels. The first three can be constantly repurified or recycled in one way or another, maintains Roger Revelle of Harvard. But the fossil fuels—coal and petroleum—are irrecoverable once consumed, and are bound to run out within a few hundred years. However, most energy experts expect that, before the present century is over, breeder reactors to supply energy will be available, and some believe that controlled fusion will also prove feasible (see page 94).

The world, of course, is a long way from ideal utilization and recycling of materials. Moreover, if one extrapolates demand on the assumption that most or all countries will become industrially advanced, then it is possible to arrive at enormously large estimates of future global requirements for resources. Changes in technology and patterns of resource use will temper these requirements, but even so, demand for materials will certainly rise far above present levels.

The U.S. is already a large user and importer of a long string of raw materials from antimony to zinc. With only 6 percent of the world's population, the U.S. gobbles up about one-third of the world's materials. At present the high U.S. rate of imports helps provide underdeveloped countries with badly needed foreign exchange, but as they achieve a high degree of industrialization they may ration their exports of resources.

An eventual halt

It seems feasible, in theory at least, to mitigate problems arising from the distribution of population, environmental pollution, and scarcity of resources by altering government regulations, taxes, and subsidies, re-allocating costs, and adopting different technologies and life styles. But such measures, even if society is willing to accept the costs, will not enable the U.S. to postpone indefinitely facing questions about population growth. Eventually, growth will have to come to a halt. Though no one can formulate them with any precision, there must be limits to how many people the earth, or any nation, can hold. Accordingly, it might be wise to begin thinking now about ways to stabilize the population. If society waits until limitation becomes a matter of desperate urgency, it may be too late for humane, noncoercive policies, and in any event the quality of life will have been severely and perhaps irreparably impaired.

The economic and social consequences of population stability merit a great deal more research and thought than they have received. Still, it is possible now to foresee some of the effects. Whether the effects seem beneficial or not depends to some extent on individual values and tastes; at any rate, a lot of things would be different.

It was once believed by businessmen and by many economists that population growth was necessary to sustain national prosperity. Nowadays hardly any economist would argue in favor of that view. Despite a widely held assumption to the contrary, big business seems to have swung around too. A FORTUNE-Yankelovich survey of chief executives of the 500 largest corporations (February) showed that almost eight in ten favor some sort of effort that would curb further population growth.

The size of the gross national product would be smaller with population stability than with continued growth. More women would presumably go to work if there were fewer children, but once employment of women reached a ceiling there would be no further growth in the labor force. From then on the economy could grow only as fast as the average output per worker. This means that if productivity is still rising at 3 percent or so a year with the population stabilized, the economy's potential rate of growth would be 3 percent a year rather than the present rate of more than 4 percent.

The average standard of living is nevertheless likely to be higher with population stability. When population is rising, some proportion of national product must go to provide consumer goods and services

THE U.S. APPETITE FOR RESOURCES

U.S. Consumption as Percent of World Production

NATURAL GAS	67%	GYPSUM	29%
SILVER	58	MERCURY	28
MOLYBDENUM	50	CHROMIUM	28
SULPHUR	48	ANTIMONY	27
MAGNESIUM	43	ZINC	27
COBALT	41	CRUDE PETROLEUM	26
LEAD	37	TIN	26
PLATINUM	35	NICKEL	25
BAUXITE	30	COAL	21
COPPER	29	IRON ORE	21

and social overhead for additional people. With stability, the U.S. could use the freed resources to increase both private and public investment per capita. Because each member of the labor force would then be working with a larger or more advanced stock of capital, there would be more output and income *per worker*. And since workers would, on average, belong to smaller families, income *per person* would rise even faster. The income position of young families—with fewer children living at home than their counterparts of today—would benefit the most. It thus turns out that businessmen are confronted with a trade-off: a growing population would mean larger markets, and a stationary population would mean richer markets.

Markets would also be affected by the changed age composition of the population. By the year 2000, as the chart on page 285 shows, a population moving toward stability would have roughly the same number of people of each age up to about fifty. Several decades later, with population growth actually zero, all age groups except the very old would be approximately the same size. On the particular assumptions used to construct that chart, people under twenty-five would constitute one-third of the population compared to more than 45 percent at present, and the median age would be thirty-eight compared to twenty-eight. The market would thus be far more oriented toward older people and far less toward younger ones than is the case today. Apart from the different marketing strategies this implies, some industries would stand to gain, relatively, and others to lose.

With higher incomes and fewer children, young families could afford to spend more for travel, recreation, adult clothing, and home goods. The businesses that, on the whole, would presumably do worst are those with a kind of fundamental dependence on growth in numbers of people. Purveyors of goods and services for infants, producers of staple foods such as bread, sugar, and canned goods, bottlers of beer and soft drinks, construction, building-supply, and real-estate companies; and manufacturers of such tobacco products as are still being sold—all these could very well be stuck with relatively stagnant markets.

Population stability would also bring with it a somewhat less flexible economy, though it would not necessarily be less efficient. A growing population makes it easier to maintain opportunities for members of all occupations, and for business to make adjustments to changing tastes and technologies. Because markets grow faster, marginal investments are more likely to succeed and obsolete industries to hold on.

Stability is not likely to entail higher production costs. The U.S. market is already large enough to make it possible for most industries to enjoy maximum economies of scale, or it certainly will be by the time population growth levels out. At least one burden would grow, however. Social-security taxes and pension costs are bound to go up as stable population conditions are reached, because of the increase in the ratio of people receiving benefits to those paying.

Will youth be disserved?

Among the social benefits of population stability would be some reduction in poverty because there would be few large families. And smaller families would make for more education per child. That, in turn, implies a more highly skilled labor force and enhanced ability to innovate or to cope with advanced technology. The less the population grows, the less the need for increases in governmental expenditures in such areas as education, health, recreation, and water supply. Indeed, there would be less need for government regulation or intervention of many kinds. With relatively fewer young people around, there would presumably be less juvenile delinquency. With fewer drivers on the road, control of traffic would be less onerous. With fewer families looking for homes, there would be less pressure to alter the zoning of land.

Some people who have considered the matter maintain that population stability would bring some social disadvantages. Ansley

Coale of Princeton has pointed out that when there are about as many older as younger people, the average age of those who run things will be greater, and advancement in business, in politics, or in any other form of organized activity will perforce be slower, a situation that will be frustrating to oncoming generations. Things might not work out quite that way, however: a relatively smaller demand for the services of young people would be partially balanced by a relatively smaller supply. In general, it may be misleading to project today's attitudes into tomorrow's world. A changed population structure would have many interacting consequences that might affect the morale and outlook of both young people and their elders in ways difficult to foresee. At any rate, it is not certain that youth would be served any less well in a stable population than it is now.

The most sweeping attack on population stability comes from the pen of Alfred Sauvy. This distinguished French demographer's textbook has finally been published in English (*General Theory of Population*, Basic Books), and may well play an important role in future debate about population. Sauvy presents a long catalogue of social, cultural, and economic ailments that France has experienced from early in the nineteenth century to the present, and he attributes them largely or exclusively to the virtual stagnation of the population during most of that time. The argument is long and rich, but cause and effect are scarcely ever conclusively demonstrated, and there is a noticeable absence of the statistical analysis one might expect. Sauvy's main explanation is that when population stops growing, society loses a sort of creative pressure that stimulates and adds healthy ferment to all of its aspects. This sort of generalization is perhaps more persuasive to French readers than to others, for concern over slow population growth is widespread in France and has been of long-standing concern to the government. Surely there are other reasons for difficulties that the French are bothered about. Coale likes to point out, for example, that just as the Industrial Revolution in England was getting under way, France, under Napoleon, was undertaking a series of ultimately unproductive military adventures.

Assigned to motherhood

A society that wants to stabilize its population runs up against the puzzle of how to go about doing it. One difficulty is that little is known in any systematic way about the psychological and social motivations that impel people to become parents or to have large

families. For example, to what degree are decisions to have children
consciously arrived at and to what degree are they subconscious?
Knowledge about such matters may be an important prerequisite for
devising a population policy that would work.

Of course, if Bogue is correct that the U.S. is already moving
toward a halt in population growth, there isn't any puzzle to solve.
Or if Bumpass and Westoff are correct that the number of children
women really want averages out to around 2.5, then perhaps a
reasonably uncontroversial program might be able to reduce that
number to 2.1. Such a program would include an educational campaign about the long-run consequences of continued population
growth; a system for making means of contraception available to all
women; elimination of obstacles to abortion; and greatly intensified
research efforts to discover more reliable and acceptable contracep-
tive methods. (At the moment, research is under way on some three
dozen or so.) These steps would amount to a broadening and inten-
sification of present family planning. Complete freedom of choice
would be left to the individual.

But suppose Bumpass and Westoff are wrong, and people really
still want three children? Then intensified family planning, though
helpful, would be insufficient. Family planning in the U.S. has traditionally been put forward as a way of widening individual options,
not of implementing a population policy. Some claim that family
planning is incapable of fulfilling the latter role. The heart of the
argument is that what demographers call "pro-natalist" influences
are far too strong and deeply embedded to be counteracted solely
by voluntary family planning.

Government tax and subsidy policies are at least implicitly pro-
natalist. The examples that come to mind most easily are tax exemptions for children and, because of the split-income provision, higher
tax rates for single than for married people. FHA and VA assistance
to buyers of single-family homes has done a great deal to encourage
the growth of all those child-centered suburbs. In many ways, customs and social arrangements operate to favor motherhood—a situation that some women are now vigorously protesting. Many people
who advocate smaller families maintain that childbearing cannot be
reduced substantially until women have real and satisfying alternatives to motherhood as a primary role. Perhaps nothing would do
more to ensure the prevalence of small families than widespread success for the "women's liberation movement."

It will, of course, be somewhat easier to make a go of any
limitationist policy once biologists learn just how to predetermine

the sex of a child. In the U.S., as well as in other countries, many couples with one or more daughters decide to have additional children in the hope of having a son. However, if choosing the sex of children were to bring an appreciable change in the ratio of male to female births, that would not only enormously complicate population policy, but would also have other far-reaching social consequences.

A problem never faced before

There is some question whether a government can deliberately curtail a nation's population growth. Official approval apparently contributed to the postwar decline in Japan's population growth, but otherwise there is no direct evidence that government policies work. And the indirect evidence is negative. Some countries have consciously tried *pro*-natalist policies—France for the past thirty years, Germany under Hitler, Italy under Mussolini—with little success.

A great many proposed methods, some of them quite fanciful, have been put forward. Bernard Berelson, president of the Population Council, has listed twenty-nine different proposals to limit population growth apart from family planning. (Some really apply only to underdeveloped countries.) They include adding temporary sterilants—as yet undevised—to water-supply systems; licensing childbearing through permits that could be bought and sold on the open market, raising the legal age of marriage, and, of course, changing the tax system. The difficulty is to devise programs that are both feasible and effective. Measures that rank high on ethics, such as educational campaigns, might not be very effective. Deliberate changes in social institutions might eventually work, but they could have unforeseen side effects and would be hard to bring about.

Everyone who thinks about these matters is groping for answers to a problem that no democratic society has squarely faced before. The root question is how to reconcile long-run collective interest in limiting the growth of population with the desires of those who want to have more than two children. Uncomfortable choices will be involved if at some point society decides that it is desirable to curtail freedom to reproduce in order to preserve other freedoms or to preserve valued amenities.

Until recently almost all Americans took it for granted that the right to have as many children as one wants should not be abridged in any way. The number of people who openly disagree is a lot larger now than it was a few years ago, as is evidenced by the sudden emergence of the Zero Population Growth movement. The right to have children is not absolute, argues Judith Blake Davis, chairman of the department of demography at the University of California. She points out that much of the cost of the satisfaction enjoyed by families with many children is willy-nilly subsidized by others who must pay for the additional schooling and public services. The freedom to have children, she says, does not exist in a vacuum but in a context where the tax laws, the status of women, and various other social arrangements have a pro-natalist bias.

Symbolic commitment

It seems obvious that any population policy would have to meet certain ethical criteria. It should permit a maximum of individual freedom and diversity. It should not in any way impair the welfare of "extra" children. Also, it should not be used to practice selective coercion against any special group within the population.

The history and ways of Americans suggest that the fiscal system, which is impersonal and has long been used to accomplish social and economic ends, would come into play early in any effort to limit population growth. For example, there might be some form of bonus for not having more than a specified number of children. Or various kinds of tax disincentives might be enacted.

A proposal along these lines has been introduced in Congress by Senator Robert Packwood of Oregon. The bill would take effect in 1973 and would provide exemptions of $750 each for a family's first two children and none for any subsequent children. (Those born before the effective date of the act would not fall under this limitation, nor would adopted children.) Under tax provisions that were enacted last year and will take full effect in 1973, a family of four will get exemptions of $3,000 and a standard deduction of at least $1,000, so families below the poverty line won't be paying federal taxes anyway. The Packwood bill would therefore have no impact on large families among the poor. Nor would it have much impact on the well-to-do. The effect on people in middle-income brackets is uncertain, and Packwood, among others, suspects it wouldn't be great. "I don't regard a tax incentive per se as a key to population stabilization," he declares. "The important thing is that a tax-incentive bill, if passed, is a government commitment to make an effort to achieve stabilization. It would be symbolic."

Whatever the time or the circumstances, any policy of deliberately limiting population growth should be suffused with respect for the quality of individual life. This view was well expressed by Catherine S. Chilman, dean of the faculty at Hood College, in a paper recently presented at the New York Academy of Sciences. "We must care as a society," she said, "about the fulfillment and well-being of individuals as whole people, not just as potential reproducers. . . . While a humane population policy would recognize the need to motivate people to have no or very few children, it would lead from a social and psychological base rather than one that is exclusively material and technological. It would emphasize that there are many ways of being a respected, successful person other than having a large family; that there are many benefits, other than economic ones, alone, to be gained from controlling family size. It would build on and enhance the human need to love, cherish, nurture, and protect."

2. POPULATION REDISTRIBUTION

KOOROS M. MAHMOUDI

Introduction

One of the important things in the world is people. People, you and I included, are often viewed as being a problem. The terms population and problem have become synonymous. Although a relationship does indeed exist, it is rather simplistic to treat population alone as a source for any problem(s).

Sensational and catchy statements such as "population explosion," "population bomb," and "over-population" seem to imply that too many people are the cause of many social and environmental problems.

To understand certain basic facts about population, we should view the growth of human numbers in an historical context. The alarmist notions of population explosion, and the like, can best be understood by reviewing the demographic transition model. The demographic transition implies a shift from high fertility and high mortality (which was the case during most of human history) to low fertility and mortality. During the transition, because the mortality rates declined first (a function of technology) and fertility rates stayed high for a period, the growth of population increased manifold.

This transition can be illustrated in the following way.

The Demographic Transition*

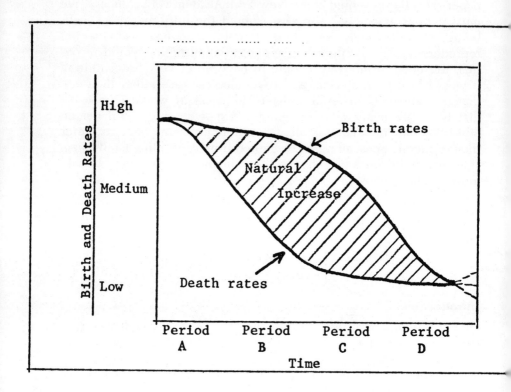

*Adopted from Ralph Thomlinson, *Population Dynamics*. New York: Random House, 1964. p. 18.

Period A (high fertility and mortality) demonstrates mankind's experience up until recent times. The growth of population during this period was almost nil. Period B (high fertility, but rapidly declining mortality rates) demonstrates the so-called population explosion period. Because of such rapid reduction in death rates, especially infant deaths, caused by breakthroughs in man's knowledge of medicine and, of course, technological gains, more people survived than ever before. This phenomenon first occurred in the Western world during the Seventeenth Century and only recently in the developing nations. Period C marks the reduction in fertility rates, thus bringing about a new balance. Here again, the rate of population growth is small and the transition from a high fertility and mortality to low fertility and mortality has taken place. The demographic transition, by and large, has been the experience of Western European nations and the United States. Most Asian, African, and South American countries are currently in Period B. Period D is what lies ahead. We do not know, with any degree of certainty, what the future patterns of fertility and mortality will be.

Based upon the observed patterns, what is, then, the nature of population problems of the Western world and particularly the United States? And how do such problems affect us as individuals?

I believe that the answer lies in the distribution of population and not the number of people per se. The fact of the matter is that during the transitional stage (Period B), industrialization and urbanization, concomitant with technological advancements, produced concentrations of people in relatively small geographic units: the development of the modern urban areas through the process of *urbanization*.

The underlying process, then, is not only the growth of human population but also the *distribution* of population.

It is my intent here to demonstrate the significance of understanding the contemporary community and its most important variable, people, by gaining insights into the nature of population redistribution.

Population Redistribution

Since the time of the first census of the United States in 1790, the rural areas of the country have proportionately lost population to the urban areas. Certainly, the relative growth of the cities within the processes of industrialization and urbanization are observable facts. The growth of the cities has been as much a consequence of internal migration as that of reproductive growth. In an historical perspective, the movement of population has tended to benefit the concentration of population and thus urbanization. As Shryock points out:

> The regions that have been experiencing net out-migration are characteristically agricultural whereas the regions with net immigration are more industrialized and urbanized. Furthermore, even within the gaining regions, there tends to be shifts of population from rural to urban areas.[1]

This process of population redistribution was first studied by a number of historians and geographers who tended to observe the trends in generalities. More recently, a number of economists and demographers have become more concerned with the effects of such redistribution basically from an economic point of view. For example, the most elaborate and encompassing of such studies which was presented in three volumes is that of *Population Redistribution and Economic Growth, United States, 1870-1950.*[2] The study is primarily concerned with methodological developments to measure population redistribution and also to correlate the changes in population with indices of economic growth as stimulants to population redistribution.

Another more recent study of economic growth and its relation to population is that of R.A. Easterlin. The primary objective of that study in the author's words is

> To seek an explanation of the causes and economic effects of the observed demographic swings and thereby to derive new insights into recent as well as possible implications for the future.[3]

The studies cited above are representative of the type of research undertaken by students of population redistribution in recent years.

Population Redistribution and Community Transformation

The demographic and economic changes through population redistribution, to be more meaningful, need to be analyzed in the context of the community from a sociological perspective.

Inherent in the process of population redistribution is migration. What seems to be a significant sociological factor is the transplantation of the community members through migration. The migrant finding himself in a new community differs from the indigenous population. It should be added at this point that population redistribution has been an important process in the United States. Changes in residence from one geographic unit to another are more common in this country than most.[4] Urban growth has been the rule in the United States through population redistribution. The significance of this can be seen in the following table.

Percent distribution of population of the United States in urban and rural areas: 1790-1970

year	total all classes	urban	rural
1970	100.0	73.5	26.5
1960	100.0	69.9	30.1
1950	100.0	64.0	36.0
1940	100.0	56.5	43.5
1930	100.0	56.2	43.8

Continued on p. 301

year	total all classes	urban	rural
1920	100.0	51.2	48.8
1910	100.0	45.7	54.3
1900	100.0	39.7	60.3
1890	100.0	35.1	64.9
1880	100.0	28.2	71.8
1870	100.0	25.7	74.3
1860	100.0	19.8	80.2
1850	100.0	15.3	84.7
1840	100.0	10.8	89.2
1830	100.0	8.8	91.2
1820	100.0	7.2	92.8
1810	100.0	7.3	92.7
1800	100.0	6.1	93.9
1790	100.0	5.1	94.9

SOURCE: U.S. Bureau of the Census, U.S. Census of population: 1970, General Population Characteristics. United States Summary, PC (1)-LB, P 10148; General Social and Economic Characteristics, United States Summary, PC (1)-IC, P. 1-199.

Students of population redistribution agree that the rates of internal migration were quite important in the process of urbanization as seen in the above table. Although the rate of migration has proportionately decreased in recent years, yet it is agreed that as much as 35% of urban and metropolitan growth can be attributed to internal migration.[5]

With an increasingly larger proportion of population in the urban areas, patterns of metropolitan growth and dominance have come to play an important part in this country's socio-economic organization.

Considering the rather significant proportion of migrants to the urban areas, certain patterns of "nomadism" seem to emerge. But this modern-day nomadism is not the same as the movements of the nomadic groups of the previous centuries. The nomadic tribes of the past always moved as communities. They took with them the same patterns of social organization, their culture, institutions, and also their basic community functions. However, the high rates of mobility in the United States are not of the same nature. "Individual" nomadism seems to be the rule at the present. It is not groups that migrate collectively, as was the case earlier, but rather families or individuals. By the same token, as migration takes place it is more of an individual decision. The mover, although taking his beliefs and experiences with him, confronts a new community upon his arrival. This pattern seems to weaken the community ties, at least in so far as the migrants are concerned. From a theoretical frame of reference, the transition from a gemeinschaft type to gesellschaft pattern of interaction will certainly have to be attributed to the migrating population in the process of population redistribution.

This uprooting process has latent consequences for the migrant. The mover from a rural community, where patterns of interaction are more personal and primary, finds himself in an impersonal world upon arrival in the urban area.

Those who have experienced rural life and urban residence will have no difficulty in understanding the diverse milieu of the respective areas.

Consequences of Population Redistribution

I believe the impact of population redistribution upon the individuals has been a negative one. A feeling of community loss underlies the anomia of modern city life. The relevant question seems to be: What made urban living a desirable end? Why such high rates of migration to the urban areas? I believe the answer can be found in the technological and economic order of the American Society. The modern day nomadism discussed above is induced by the nature of the labor force and the classical *push* and *pull* factors. The pull principle refers to attractive (economic) conditions which stimulate in-migration. The *push* principle refers to undesirable conditions which sort of force people to out-migrate from such areas.

I submit that the process of urbanization has been a forced process so far as the individual is concerned. Given the technological level of food production (primary economic activity), the small farmers who constituted the bulk of the U.S. population prior to 1920 could no longer maintain a livelihood in agriculture. This pattern is still evident in the United States even now. This is the essence of the push factor, forcing people to leave the country behind and seek a better life in some other locality. The alternative for many people was, of course, the city life. Not only were the employment opportunities attractive there (pull factor), but one was to find the "good life" in the gold-paved streets of the city.

The important factor in this process was *technology*. Mobility and migration became easier with the development of automobile and other modes of transportation. Economic production, thanks to technological advancements, made it possible for large numbers of people to find employment in manufacturing (secondary type economic activity). As more and more people came to the city, it became evident that services were required to take care of such concentration of population (tertiary type of economic activity). Today most Americans who live in the cities make their living by being a part of the service activities, i.e., education, communication, entertainment, etc. But what do the evidenced patterns of population redistribution mean to the average man? In answering this question, we can see why so much has been written recently regarding the problems of population. In the first place, population redistribution has meant concentration of population in small geographic units. This means that population density has increased. In other words, our contemporary urban environments are crowded with too many people. There are not very many good reasons for such concentration of population. On the contrary, high population density can be regarded as having a detrimental effect upon the patterns of societal organization.

The magnitude of the population concentration can best be illustrated by stating that 70% of the U.S. population (about 147 million people) reside on 2% of the land area. Between 40 and 50 percent of us live in 28 large cities with population of more than 1 million in each.[6] New York City has a population density of 25,000 per square mile. In certain areas of the city, Manhattan Island, the density is over 90,000 per square mile.

An elaborate study of Manhattan by behavioral scientists entitled *Mental Health in the Metropolis*, demonstrated that 18.5% of the 1660 cases interviewed were by definition healthy. The rest had neurotic and psychotic symptoms. Moreover

> Peptic ulcers, and coronary attacks are understandably more common in the city and probably have psychosomatic aspects. Lung cancer among non-smokers is eleven times more common in an urban environment than in a rural one.[7]

One could list numerous such problems that seem to surface as population density increases. I believe this is a heavy price which we pay to live in an urban environment. Yet we go on and rationalize the present situation in hopes of solving the urban problems.

The present situation of population density was created by the industrialists and the need for labor. A primary reason for urban in-migration is the availability of employment opportunities. In a recent study of population redistribution in Utah, I was able to demonstrate a high correlation between in-migration and economic opportunities in the metropolitan areas of that state.[8] The same pattern holds true for most metropolitan areas in the United States.

Conclusion

The objective of this paper was to demonstrate the impact of the population redistribution which is caused by economic reasons upon the individual. I consider the population problems to stem not from the numbers of people per se, but rather the irregular distribution of population which is induced by the nature of economic activity. The consequences of such population redistribution in forms of individual costs (both physical and psychological), plus the factors of air, water, and noise pollution, and of course, overcrowding should be warning signals to us.

Based upon the previous research, I believe it is high time that we made a case for decentralization of the population as a guideline for future patterns of population redistribution.

In sum, let us not confuse the economic problems and population problems of distribution with that of "population problems" per se. As Steve Weissman suggested recently:

> Simply, fighting this war on people with a people's war will not eliminate the need for each nation to determine how best to balance resources and population. But where there is greater economic security, national participation, elimination of gross class division, liberation of women, and respected leadership, humane and successful population programs are at least possible. Without these conditions, genocide is nicely mashed by the welfare imperialism of the West. In the lands of the self-seeking, humanitarianism is the most terrifying ism of all.[9]

1. Henry S. Shryock, Jr., *Population Mobility Within the United States*, Chicago: University of Chicago, 1964. p. 63.
2. Everett S. Lee, Ann R. Miller, Carol P. Brainerd, Richard A. Easterlin; *Population Redistribution and Economic Growth, United States, 1870-1950*, Philadelphia, Pa.: American Philosophical Society, Vol. I: "Methodological Considerations & Reference Tables". Also Kuznets, Miller, and Easterlin, Vol. II. "Analysis of Economic Change". Also, Eldridge & Thomas, Vol. III, "Demographic Analysis & Interrelation".
3. Richard A. Easterlin, *Population, Labor Force, and Long Swings in Economic Growth*, New York: Columbia University Press, 1968. p. 5.
4. Henry S. Shryock, Jr., *Population Mobility* . . . op. cit. pp. 63-116.
5. Everett Lee, et. al. *Population Redistribution* . . . op. cit., Also H.S. Shryock, Jr. *Population Mobility*. op. cit. pp. 70-100.
6. David M. Kiefer, "Population" in *Society and Environment: The Coming Collision*, ed. by Campbell and Wade, Boston: Allyn & Bacon, Inc. 1972. p. 236.
7. Marston Bates, "Crowded People" in *The American Population Debate*, edited by D. Callahan. New York: Doubleday & Company, 1971. p. 78.
8. Kooros M. Mahmoudi, "Net Migration As a Factor Affecting Metropolitan Growth in Utah: 1950-1970." Ph.D. dissertation, Logan, Utah: Utah State University Library, 1973.
9. Steve Weissman, "Why the Population Bomb Is a Rockefeller Baby." in *Eco-Catastrophe*, by the Editors of Rampart. San Francisco: Canfield Press. pp. 40-41.

23. ECOLOGY AND HUMAN ECOLOGY

Amos H. Hawley

Human ecology, from its inception to a comparatively recent date, is reminiscent of Alice's curious experience in the rabbit hole when she, after consuming the pretty little cake, opened out "like the largest telescope that ever was." Emerging abruptly in the early 1920's, human ecology quickly became, as an otherwise unkind commentator puts it, "one of the most definite and influential schools in American sociology . . ."[1]

It is now beginning to appear, however, that the period of burgeoning growth has given way to a second phase in which sober criticism rather than feverish application is the prevailing note. Reexamination and reappraisal are the order of the day.[2] This cannot be anything but welcome, for it is a necessary preface to the sorely needed reconstruction of human ecological thought. Hence the addition of still another voice to the developing symposium may not be amiss.[2a]

Perhaps it is to be expected that the sudden ascent to popularity of an innovation in scientific thought should be accompanied by a certain amount of confusion as to its specific connotation. If so, human ecology has satisfied expectations, for after twenty years it remains a somewhat crude and ambiguous conception. A perusal of the literature that has accumulated under the name can hardly fail to produce bewilderment. One finds it variously argued that the study deals essentially with "sub-social" phenomena, with the effects of competition, with spatial distributions, with the influence of geographic factors, and with still other more or less intelligibly delineated aspects of human behavior. There are some writers who would have human ecology encompass the whole field of social science, and there are others who prefer to relegate it to the status of a mere sociological research technique. Between these wide extremes the subject can be found identified in turn with biology, economics, human geography, sociology, and, as if not to overlook a possibility, it is sometimes described as marginal to all other life sciences.[3] Indeed, the sole point of agreement among the many diverse conceptions of human ecology seems to be that it pertains to some phase of man's relation to his physical universe. This, unfortunately, is no distinction, since most of the sciences of man may be characterized in the same manner.

Whatever may be said regarding the confusion as to the nature

Reprinted from *Social Forces*, Vol. 22, (1943-44), pp. 398-405, by permission of the publisher, Alpha Kappa Delta-National Sociology Honor Society.

of the study, it cannot be charged to a lack at the outset of careful attempts at systematic theoretical formulation. The success of human ecology in attracting and holding the large share of attention it has enjoyed is largely a result of the ingeniousness, simplicity, and utility of the early definitive statement.[4] But these seem to have been accepted as dogmas rather than, as intended, as suggestions of the possibilities of an ecological approach to the study of human social life. Subsequent work in the field, with very few exceptions, was not aimed at exploring the full implication of ecology as applied to man. Instead there was a wholesale application of a little understood point of view and in consequence the theoretical development of the discipline received scarcely any attention. In fact, most so-called ecological studies have been occupied with incidentals and by-products of the approach, and not a few are totally irrelevant to the caption under which they appear in print.

But to be more specific, responsibility for the existing chaos in human ecology, it seems to me, rests upon certain aberrant intellectual tendencies which have dominated most of the work that has been done. The more significant of these may be described as: (1) the failure to maintain a close working relationship between human ecology and general or bioecology; (2) an undue preoccupation with the concept of competition; and (3) the persistence in definitions of the subject of a misplaced emphasis on "spatial relations." Whether such habits of thought originated from one source or another is unimportant. What is important is that they have consistently confused the issue thereby hampering the progress of the discipline. The purpose of the present paper is to indicate the deficiencies of these elements of human ecological thought and thus to aid in clearing the way for a reorganization of the subject.

Probably most of the difficulties which beset human ecology may be traced to the isolation of the subject from the mainstream of ecological thought. Although it seems almost too elementary to mention, the only conceivable justification for a human ecology must derive from the intrinsic utility of ecological theory as such. Obvious as this may seem, it is not a fact that is generally taken seriously. Exponents of human ecology, despite their steadfast adherence to the name, tend to view with indifference or regret the fact that their subject has any connection with the parent discipline. This is indeed a paradox. If a person chooses to call this work ecology, it would appear reasonable to assume that his studies are intended to parallel, at least in some particulars, those of others working under the same general title. However, very few persons who regard themselves as human ecologists indicate an awareness that they are logically committed to follow out in the study of man the implications of ecology.

In general, students are divided into two camps with respect to the relation of human to general ecology. One group, taking the position that ecology offers an essentially biological approach to the study of the human community, has recognized a close association between the two.[5] But while this admission has been accompanied by a relatively free borrowing of terminology, it has yielded very little in the way of theoretical unity. The second group expresses a somewhat reactionary viewpoint. Its representatives strongly oppose even a suggestion of similarity between the two phases of the discipline on the ground that any assumption of analogy as between social and biological phenomena is invalid and impractical.[6] Human ecology, according to this view, should be developed independent of other branches of ecology.

Without entering into a detailed consideration of either of these positions, it will be sufficient to point out that the conception of ecology contained therein is actually a misconception. The widespread belief that ecology is a biologism, as it were, has no logical support, not even in the conventional academic distinction between sociology and biology. That ecology is basically a social science has long been clear to most serious students of the subject.[7] It is apparent, moreover, in almost every aspect of the discipline: in the root of the term ecology; in the historical details of the subject's development; in the large place given to sociological concepts such as community, society, niche, commensalism, symbiosis, dominance, succession, etc.; and in the manner in which problems for investigation are stated. But all of this appears to have escaped the majority of so-called human ecologists; they have proceeded without benefit from the theoretical position they believe themselves to have adopted. Evidently it is for such reasons that the concept competition and the interest in spatial analysis have absorbed so much of the energies of students of the subject.

The assignment of the concept competition to a key role in human ecology is, in fact, premised largely on the biological interpretation of the subject. The steps which lead to this inference may be simply stated. Struggle, of which competition is but a refined expression, is the law of biological nature and the circumstance out of which all order arises. Competition is therefore a biological phenomenon. Moreover, since competition is definable as a process in which individuals or other units affect one another through affecting a common limited supply of sustenance materials, it does not

presuppose consciousness or social consensus in the units concerned,[8] and what is not social must therefore be biological. Hence,
it is concluded, to base human ecology on the concept competition
is to carry through to the study of man the distinctive ecological
approach. Thus has competition come to be regarded as the necessary hypothesis of the study—as the efficient cause, so to speak,
in the development of ecological phenomena. "Human ecology,"
writes one author, in what may be considered a representative statement, "deals with society in its biological and symbiotic aspects that
is, those aspects brought about by competition and by struggle of
individuals, in any social order, to survive and to perpetuate
themselves."[9]

The defects in this line of reasoning are manifold. The desire
on the part of human ecologists to achieve a thorough-going natural
science treatment of human behavior undoubtedly lies at the roots
of their theorizing relative to competition. But the question as to
whether the struggle for existence is categorically a natural, in the
sense of biological, phenomenon is seldom considered. To insist that
it is, for no other reason than that the conception was first extensively
used in connection with a biological problem and later became recognized as a part of the language of biology, would appear to indicate
a stronger addiction to words than to thoughts. As a matter of fact,
a cogent argument can be made in favor of the inherent sociological
quality of the idea of struggle. Unless I am mistaken, "struggle for
existence" pertains primarily to the behavior of organisms relative
to one another.[10] If this be the province of biology, then *ipso facto*
all social science resolves itself into biology.

Further difficulty in this respect arises from the belief, not
limited to human ecologists, that a natural science must seek causa-
tion outside the sphere of consciousness. Competition, because of
its essentially unconsciousness or asocial character, is assumed to
provide a definitely natural science, i.e., objective and impersonal,
avenue of approach.[11] Why the natural and the conscious should be
regarded as mutually exclusive categories it is impossible to say.
Surely it is as natural for man to think and act accordingly as for
a squirrel to store nuts or for a rock, when loosened, to roll down
the mountain slope.

However, and more to the point, the distinction between conscious and unconscious activity is difficult if not impossible to maintain in practice. It presents problems of observation for which there
is no yardstick. Whether competition does or does not include conscious elements is a matter of definition and therefore subject to

individual opinion. What is important, if true, is that individuals do affect one another through affecting the available supply of required materials. This is all that need concern the ecologist. In any event, as economists, anthropologists and others have amply shown, an objective or so-called natural science approach does not stand or fall on an exclusive use of unconscious behavior as data.

The application of competition as an hypothesis also involves a number of serious problems. For example, it presupposes a knowledge—not always at hand—of the intrinsic qualities of the individuals or other units concerned, i.e., in regard to homogeneity or similarity of life requirements. Frequently individuals who at first glance might be considered competitors turn out to be so differentiated, through the operation of genetic processes and early conditioning, as not to be competitors at all. Braun-Blanquet states: "It has further been said that certain species [of plants] are in general confined to certain soils, but when they come into competition one wins on calcareous soil, the other on siliceous soil." But, he continues, "the life requirements of these pairs of species are so different that the question of competition cannot arise."[12] This illustrates the ecologist's need for an adequate taxonomy, a need which has been sadly neglected in the social sciences. The utility of competition as an explanatory tool will remain in doubt until a fuller knowledge of functional or social types is developed.

A related problem exists with regard to the observability of the operation of competition. The specific sequence of changes by which a homogeneous aggregate is converted into a differentiated and interdependent population has not been described in detail. Consequently it is almost impossible to indicate what to look for in order to see competition in action. The situation is not improved by pointing out that the process is a type of interaction, that is, a process of mutual internal modification. Ecologists, unfortunately, lack the technique for the observation of internal phenomena. Defined in terms of competitive interaction, ecology amounts to little more than the contemplation of a concept.[13] This, parenthetically, seems to be the net result of interactional theory in general so far as its use by sociologists is concerned. It would appear that psychologists are better equipped to deal with such a matter.

There would be no cause to mention this problem had human ecologists actually treated competition as an hypothesis to be tested and demonstrated. However, in no instance, so far as I am aware, has a student of the subject applied himself to such a task. The truth of the matter is that the concept serves in practice as a *post hoc* interpretation. This being the case, the question whether the concept describes what it is supposed to describe remains unanswered. Doubt will linger on this point until the prerequisites for observation have been fulfilled.

It has been fairly well established, however, that the competitive hypothesis is a gross over-simplification of what is involved in the development of pattern, structure, or other manifestation of organization. As a matter of fact, the customary interpretation of the Darwinian "struggle for existence" to mean that the primary and dominant relationship in animate nature is opposition whether clamorous combat or the more subtle competition, forms one of the neatest illustrations of the "fallacy of misplaced concreteness" that may anywhere be found. Darwin used the phrase in "a large and metaphorical sense,"[14] subsuming under it all expenditures of effort to maintain and expand life. Combination and cooperation as well as competition and conflict are embraced in the concept. That mutual aid is just as fundamental and universal as opposition has been abundantly shown in numerous field and laboratory studies by students of plants and animals.[15] There seems to be no reason to assume that human collective life is any more amenable to monistic explanation.

These remarks should not be taken to imply that competition has no place in ecological thought. The criticism is directed solely at the loose and extravagant use of the concept which enabled it to become accepted as the basic theoretical element in human ecology. The significance of competition may better serve as a topic for a separate discussion and hence will not be taken up here. Certainly competition is not the pivotal conception of ecology; in fact, it is possible to describe the subject without even an allusion to competition.

Another persistent inconsistency in human ecology, which also reflects the failure of the discipline to develop in close relation to general ecology, exists in the emphasis put upon spatial relations or spatial aspects of human interdependencies. The origin of this peculiarity may be found in early definitions of the subject, such as, human ecology is "a study of the spatial and temporal relations of human beings as affected by the selective, distributive, and accommodative forces of the environment."[16] While such a statement has the advantage of concreteness and was highly useful in the "absence of any precedent," it seemed to indicate a subordination of interest in symbiotic relations to a concern for the spatial pattern in which such relations are expressed. Thus it permitted human ecology to be construed as merely the description of distributions of social phenomena.

Accordingly, much of the research identified as human ecology has consisted in compiling inventories of the observable characteristics of community life and in plotting their distributions on maps. It is sometimes difficult to understand why this kind of work should be called anything other than geography, except possibly—out of deference to the geographers—because of the inferior cartographic skill which is often exhibited. The mapping of phenomena, however, is usually a first step in the establishing of correlations between crime, delinquency, domestic discord, mental disorders, etc., on the one hand, and housing conditions, recreational facilities, proximity to city center, and other physical features, on the other hand.[17] But so far as the determination of the degree of correlation is the sole aim of the study, which seems to be the rule rather than the exception, it is not ecological; it is rather more in the nature of a statistical study in psychological behaviorism. The prevalence of the use of the word ecology in connection with such work as this has been so great that it has come to be regarded, in some quarters, as a "method" to be compared and contrasted with so-called statistical, case-study, and historical methods.[18] In other words, one of the techniques employed in ecological research—mapping—has been mistaken for the discipline itself.

That space and time are merely convenient abstractions by which to measure activities and relationships has been rather consistently overlooked. To contend that human behavior is bound by such dimensions is but to insist that it occurs in an experiential universe and is therefore subject to observation and measurement. This is what is meant, fundamentally, when it is asserted that human ecology is a natural science. But it is important to note that every enterprise which may be called science is a natural science in at least this sense of the term. Every science, that is, must deal with the spatial and temporal aspects of its own subject-matter. The differences between scientific disciplines arise not in respect to method but rather in respect to problems. And in the case of human ecology as elsewhere the problem is the distinguishing feature. Spatial and temporal considerations are incidental to the investigation of the ecological problem.

Now it may be asked: What remains of human ecology, if its usual mainstays—the concept competition and spatial analysis—are removed to positions of minor importance? Before entering into a discussion of this question, it may be well to give some thought to the matter of preference of one definition or another for a given study. By what prerogative may one say that human ecology is this or that? The answer, of course, depends on how the criteria of appropriateness of a discipline happen to be regarded. Probably few will deny, however, that the problem with which a study is to be concerned must not only be significant but must also be a problem that is not already preempted by other disciplines. It is no easier to defend a needless duplication of effort than it is a preoccupation with irrelevant issues. Unless human ecology has a problem of its own, then, it is nothing and may as well be forgotten. But just as urgent is the necessity that a discipline be coherent within itself and consistent with the point of view it pretends to represent. There is no basis, in other words, for calling a study human ecology, if it is not ecological. Both of these considerations should be kept in the foreground in any definition or redefinition of the nature and scope of a subject for study. It is desirable, then, in returning to the original question, to begin with a review of the rudiments of general ecology.

Briefly stated, ecology is concerned with the elemental problem of how growing, multiplying beings maintain themselves in a constantly changing but ever restricted environment.[19] It is based on the fundamental assumption that life is a continuous struggle for adjustment of organism to environment. However, the manifest interrelatedness of living forms, which leads students to speak of the "web of life," suggests that adjustment, far from being the action of independent organisms, is a mutual or collective phenomenon. Drawing together the relevant facts, it seems that the inevitable crowding of living forms upon limited resources produces a complex action and reaction of organism with environment and organism with organism in the course of which individuals become related to one another in ways conducive to a more effective utilization of the habitat. As the division of labor which thus develops approaches equilibrium, such that the number of organisms engaged in each of the several activities is sufficient to provide all the needs that are represented, the aggregate of associated individuals assumes the aspect of a compact viable entity, a superorganism, in fact. The (biotic) community, as such a functionally or symbiotically[20] integrated population may properly be called, is in effect a collective response to the habitat; it constitutes the adjustment, in the fullest sense of the term, of organism to environment.

The subject of ecological inquiry then is the community, the form and development of which are studied with particular reference to the limiting and supporting factors of the environment.[21] Ecology, in other words, is a study of the morphology of collective life in both its static and its dynamic aspects. It attempts to determine the nature of community structure in general, the types of communities that appear in different habitats, and the specific sequence of change in community development.

Two elements, one implicit and the other explicit, in the conception as outlined here merit special emphasis. Not immediately evident perhaps, though nevertheless of basic importance, is the fact that the units of observation, *i.e.*, the data, are neither physiological processes nor anatomical structures but are rather the activities of organisms. Taxonomic characteristics are relevant only so far as they serve as indexes of behavior traits.[22] "When an ecologist says 'there goes a badger,'" writes Elton, "he should include in his thoughts some definite idea of the animal's place in the community to which it belongs, just as if he had said 'there goes the vicar.'"[23] Thus if the term species and species designations recur frequently in ecological discussion, it is simply because that is the most convenient way of referring to the expected or observed occupations of the organisms denoted.

Secondly, as already indicated, life viewed ecologically is an aggregate rather than an individual phenomenon. The individual enters into ecological theory as a postulate and into ecological investigation as a unit of measurement; but as an object of special study he belongs to other disciplines, *e.g.*, physiology, genetics, psychology, etc. The focus of attention in ecology is upon the population which is either organized or in process of becoming organized. This cannot be too strongly emphasized, for it places ecology squarely in the category of social science.

Human ecology, like plant and animal ecology, represents a special application of the general viewpoint to a particular class of living things. It involves both a recognition of the fundamental unity of animate nature and an awareness that there is differentiation within that unity. Man is an organism and as such he is dependent on the same resources, confronted with the same elementary problems, and displays in essential outline the same mode of response to life conditions as is observed in other forms of life. Thus the extension of patterns of thought and techniques of investigation developed in the study of man is a logical consummation of the ecological point of view. One important qualification is necessary, however; the extraordinary degree of flexibility of human behavior makes for a complexity and a dynamics in the human community without counterpart elsewhere in the organic world. It is this that sets man apart as an object of special inquiry and gives rise to a human as distinct from a general ecology.

While to reason from "pismires to parliaments" would do violence to the facts, it is nevertheless necessary to keep the phenomenon of culture in proper perspective. When man by virtue of his culture-producing capacity is regarded as an entirely unique type of organism the distortion is no less acute than if this quality were completely ignored. Human behavior, in all its complexity and variability, is but further evidence of the tremendous potential for adjustment inherent in life. Culture is nothing more than a way of referring to the prevailing techniques by which a population maintains itself in its habitat. The component parts of human culture are therefore identical in principle with the appetency of the bee for honey, the nest-building activities of birds, and the hunting habits of carnivora. To argue that the latter are instinctive while the former are not is to beg the question. Ecology is concerned less now with how habits are acquired, than with the functions they serve and the relationships they involve.

Thus despite the great difference between the behavior of men and that of lower forms of life—a difference which appears to be of degree rather of kind, the approach described as general ecology may be applied to the study of man without radical alteration. In simplest terms, human ecology is the descriptive study of the adjustment of human populations to the conditions of their respective physical environments. The necessity that life be lived in a specific place and time, operating upon man as it does upon other organisms, produces an inescapable compulsion to adjustment which increases as population increases or as the opportunities for life decrease. And out of the adaptive strivings of aggregated individuals there develops, consciously or unconsciously, an organization of interdependencies which constitutes the population a coherent functional entity. The human community, in other words, is basically an adaptive mechanism; it is the means whereby a population utilizes and maintains itself in its habitat. Human ecology, then, may be defined more fully as the study of the development and the form of communal structure as it occurs in varying environmental contexts.

The human community, of course, is more than just an organization of symbiotic relationships and to that extent there are limitations to the scope of human ecology. Man's collective life involves, in greater or less degree, a psychological and a moral as well as a symbiotic integration. But these, so far as they are distinguishable, should be regarded as complementing aspects of the same thing rather than as separate phases or segments of the community. Sustenance activities and interrelations are inextricably interwoven with sentiments, value systems, and other ideational constructs. Human ecology is restricted in scope then not by any real or assumed qualitative differences in behavior but simply by the manner in which its problem is stated. The question of how men relate themselves to one another in order to live in their habitat yields a description of communal structure in terms of its overt and visible features. It does not, however, provide explanations of all the many ramifications of human interrelationships. The external and descriptive approach of ecology is ill-suited to the direct study of the psychological counterpart of symbiosis, although it may serve as a fruitful source of hypotheses concerning that aspect of the community.

It may be helpful to call attention to the fact that the problems of human ecology, and ecology in general, are basically population problems. The broad question, as previously indicated, concerns the adjustment of population to the resources and other physical conditions of the habitat. This resolves itself into a number of related problems such as: (1) the succession of changes by which an aggregate passes from a mere polyp-like formation into a community of interdependencies; (2) the ways in which the developing community is affected by the size, composition, and rate of growth or decline of the population; (3) the significance of migration for both the development of the community and the maintenance of community stability; and (4) the relative numbers in the various functions composing the communal structure, together with the factors which make for change in the existing equilibrium and the ways in which such change occurs.

Clearly, human ecology has much in common with every other social science. The problem with which it deals underlies that of each of the several specialized studies of human social life. Its data are drawn from the same sources and it employs many of the same techniques of investigation. The point of convergence are, in fact, too numerous to detail in this paper.[24] There is no basis therefore to conclude from what has been said that human ecology is an autonomous social science: it is quite unlikely that there is any autonomy in science. The distinctive feature of the study lies in the conception of the adjustment of man to habitat as a process of community development. Whereas this may be an implicit assumption in most social science disciplines, it is for human ecology the principal working hypothesis. Thus human ecology might well be regarded as the basic social science.

[1]M.A. Alihan, *Social Ecology, A Critical Analysis* (New York, 1938), p. xi.

[2]M.A. Alihan, *ibid.*; J.A. Quinn, "Human Ecology and Interactional Ecology," *Amer. Sociol. Rev.*, V (Oct., 1940), 713-22; and W.E. Gettys, "Human Ecology and Social Theory," *Social Forces*, XVIII (1940), 469-76.

[2a]I am indebted to the late Professor R.D. McKenzie for most of the ideas set forth in this paper, but responsibility for their statement here is entirely mine.

[3]For a more exhaustive discussion of the variety of points of view in human ecology see J.A.Quinn, "Tropical Summary of Current Literature in Human Ecology," *Amer. J. Sociol.*, XLVI (Sept., 1940), 191-226.

[4]See R.D. McKenzie, "The Ecological Approach to the Study of the Human Community," in R.E. Park, E.W. Burgess, and R.D. McKenzie (eds.), *The City* (Chicago, 1925), pp. 63-79; R.E. Park, "The Urban Community as a Spatial Pattern and a Moral Order," E.W. Burgess (ed.), *The Urban Community* (Chicago, 1926), pp. 3-18; and R.D. McKenzie, "The Scope of Human Ecology," *The Urban Community*, pp. 167-82.

[5]See, R.E. Park, "Human Ecology," *Amer. J. Sociol.*, XLII (July, 1936), 1-15; and A.B. Hollingshead, "Human Ecology," in R.E. Park (ed.), *An Outline of the Principles of Sociology*, (New York, 1939), pp. 65-74.

[6]See W.E. Gettys, *loc. cit.*, pp. 470-71.

[7]See C.C. Adams, "The Relation of General Ecology to Human Ecology," *Ecology*, XVI (July, 1935), 316-35; J. Braun-Blanquet, *Plant Sociology*, trans. by G.D. Fuller and H.S. Conrad (New York, 1932); F.E. Clements and V.E. Shelford, *Bio-Ecology* (New York, 1939), p. 24 ff.; J. Arthur Thomson, *Darwinism and Human Life* (New York, 1911), pp. 72 ff.; H.G. Wells, Julian S. Huxley, and G.P. Wells, *The Science of Life* (New York, 1934), pp. 961-62.

[8]R.E. Park and E.W. Burgess, *An Introduction to the Science of Sociology* (Chicago, 1929), p. 506.

[9]A.B. Hollingshead, *loc. cit.*, p. 70.

[10]Cf. Charles Darwin, *Origin of Species* (New York, 1925), Chap. III. One exception exists in the fact that struggle may occur between an organism and the physical and mechanical conditions of the environment. But this, in the ecological point of view, is a major stimulus to inter-organic behavior.

[11]Cf. C.A. Dawson and W.E. Gettys, *An Introduction to Sociology* (New York, 1935), p. 122.

[12]J. Braun-Blanquet, *Plant Sociology*, Trans. by G.D. Fuller and H.S. Conrad (New York, 1932), pp. 15-16 (Parentheses mine). See also Gardner Murphy, Lois B. Murphy, and T.M. Newcomb, *Experimental Social Psychology* (New York, 1937), p. 339.

[13]Cf. James A. Quinn, "Human Ecology and Interactional Ecology," *Amer. Sociol. Rev.*, V (Oct., 1940), 21-22.

[14]*Origin of Species* (New York, 1925), p. 78.

[15]For a brief but excellent summary of this literature see W.C. Alee, *The Social Life of Animals* (New York, 1937), chap. III. See also M.L. McAtee, "The Malthusian Principle in Nature," *The Scientific Monthly*, 42 (May, 1936), 453 ff.

[16]R.D. McKenzie, "The Ecological Approach to the Study of the Human Community," *loc. cit.*, pp. 63-64.

[17]E.g., A.W. Lind, "Some Ecological Patterns of Community Disorganization in Honolulu," *Amer. J. Sociol.*, XXXVI (Sept., 1930), 206-20; E.S. Longmoor and E.F. Young, "Ecological Interrelationships of Juvenile Delinquency, Dependency, and Population Mobility," *Amer. J. Sociol.*, XLI (March, 1936), 598-610; and Stuart A. Queen, "The Ecological Study of Mental Disorders," *Amer. Sociol. Rev.*, 5 (April, 1940), 201-10.

[18]Calvin F. Schmid, "The Ecological Method in Social Research," in P.V. Young, *Scientific Social Surveys and Research* (New York, 1939), chap. XIL

[19]Environment, as used here, pertains to the physical and mechanical conditions of the habitat. It includes everything but the behavior of the organisms themselves.

[20]Symbiosis may be defined as the mutually beneficial living together of unlike forms.

[21]This definition differs but slightly from others. For example: (1) Ecology is the science of "the correlations between all organisms living together in one and the same locality and their adaptations to their surroundings." (Ernest Haeckel, *The History of Creation, II*, New York, 1896, p. 354); (2) "Ecology is the science of the relation of organisms to their surroundings, living as well as non-living; it is the science of the domestic economy' of plants and animals." (R. Hesse, W.C. Allee, and K.P. Schmidt, *Ecological Animal Geography*, New York, 1937, p. 6); (3) ". . . the essence of ecology lies in its giving the fullest possible value to the habitat as cause and the community as effect, the two constituting the basic phases of a unit process." (F.E. Clements and V.E. Shelford, *Bio-Ecology*, New York, 1939, p. 30); and (4) "The descriptive study of the interrelations between co-existing species, and, more generally, their environment, is the province of ecology." (A.J. Lotka, "Contact Points of Population Study with Related Branches of Science," *Proceedings of the American Philosophical Society*, 80, Feb., 1939, p. 611).

[22]Cf. H.C. Cowles, "An Ecological Aspect of the Conception of Species," *The American Naturalist*, XLII (1905), 265-71.

[23]Charles Elton, *Animal Ecology* (New York, 1927), p. 64.

[24]See R.D. McKenzie, "Demography, Human Geography, and Human Ecology," in L.L. Bernard (ed.), *The Fields and Methods of Sociology* (New York, 1934), pp. 52-66; and A.J. Lotka, *loc. cit.*

Part VIII

THE FUTURE OF MASS SOCIETY

"Once they are up who cares where they come down:
That's not my department." Says Werner Von Braun.

Tom Lehrer

All the lonely people. Where do they all come from?

Lennon and McCartny

Introduction to Part VIII
(The Future of Mass Society)

This last set of selections examines some of the important social processes of contemporary society. In sum, these articles provide us with some clues to the future of mass society. If the reader detects a certain pessimism in reading these selections, it is because the editors have been importantly influenced by the pessimism of a variety of scholars of society. Durkheim's observations on societal transition emphasize the anomie which inevitably accompanies structural differentiation, and Weber's concern for the restriction of individual freedom and alienation resulting from increasing bureaucratization are two such examples.

Some of the consequences of participation in our consumption-oriented society for the individual are considered in Professor Cohen's article. For Cohen, the impact of our social structure which emphasizes competitiveness, deferred gratification, and consumption results in a paradox. Whether one "succeeds" or "fails" in our society matters little. The outcome is the same for both. Anomie, loneliness, and despair are the rewards for those who "succeed" or "fail" in the context of the American social structure. Professor Blauner demonstrates that even in death one cannot escape the increasing bureaucratization which characterizes societal transition.

319

24. THE ANOMIA OF SUCCESS AND THE ANOMIA OF FAILURE: A STUDY OF SIMILARITIES IN OPPOSITES†

HARRY COHEN*

INTRODUCTION

Many years ago Emile Durkheim specified a condition of society where norms lose their prior meaning and value and where people as a result lose their place in the social structure and life. This he called *anomie*.[1] This concept has been frequently used in this form. Many years later Robert MacIver specified a type of personal behaviour which derived from and added to the societal problem of anomie. This he called *anomy*.[2] Still later the concept was further refined and the common spelling was changed to *anomia*.[3]

Anomie is a social or societal condition. *It may be seen as a 'sickness' of society in which norms are rapidly changing or where there are conflicting norms of what is right, good, proper and so on.* People do not share common values and goals and have little sense of cohesion to others and to the society. Clearer yet, according to Robert Merton, anomie refers to a breakdown of social standards governing behaviour and thus also signifies little social cohesion. When a condition of extensive anomie exists the rules of society lose their force; the populace no longer sees them as legitimate. A sense of *gemeinschaft*—trust, sense of 'community', relatedness and understanding—are lost, as is a widely shared sense of 'what goes and what does not go, of what is justly allowed by way of behaviour and of what is justly prohibited, of what may be legitimately expected of people in the course of social interaction.'[4]

Anomia refers to the confused, lonely state of mind of the unattached individual who may well derive his confusion and malaise from the characteristics of an anomic society which confuse his personal and mental well-being. He loses his 'bearings' as is said in popular parlance and his attachment to others and to society is weak. He suffers a condition where he loses a sense of 'belonging' to the group and rejects the norms or values of society.[5] It is, as Robert MacIver wrote a classic and sharp analysis of anomia (anomy), 'a state of mind in which the individual's sense of social cohesion—the

*Harry Cohen B.B.A. M.A. PH.D. Associate Professor, Department of Sociology and Anthropology, Iowa State University, Ames, U.S.A.

†This paper is a 'spin-off' of work partially sponsored by a Manpower Institutional Grant to the Industrial Relations Center of Iowa State University, provided by the United States Department of Labor.

Reprinted from *The British Journal of Sociology*, Vol. XXIII, No. 3, September 1972, by permission of the author and the publisher, Routledge and Kegan Paul Ltd.

mainspring of his morale—is broken or fatally weakened.'[6] Life is often seen as meaningless and a sense of aim, purpose or direction is limited or lacking.

Anomia takes many forms. One such type is the anomia of success. Without using these words Emile Durkheim really discussed this when he wrote of rapidly changing societies and their people on the upward swing toward affluence:

> From top to bottom of the ladder, greed is aroused without knowing where to find ultimate foothold. Nothing can calm it, since its goal is far beyond all it can attain. Reality seems valueless by comparison with the dreams of fevered imaginations; reality is therefore abandoned, but so too is possibility abandoned when it in turn becomes reality. *A thirst arises for novelties, unfamiliar pleasures, nameless sensations, all of which lose their savor once known.* Henceforth one has no strength to endure the least reverse. The whole fever subsides and the sterility of all the tumult is apparent, and it is seen that all these new sensations in their infinite quantity cannot form a solid foundation of happiness to support one during days of trial. The wise man, knowing how to enjoy achieved results without having constantly to replace them with others, finds in them an attachment to life in the hour of difficulty. *But the man who has always pinned all his hopes on the future and lived with his eyes fixed upon it, has nothing in the past as a comfort against the present's afflictions, for the past was nothing to him but a series of hastily experienced stages.* What blinded him to himself was his expectation always to find further on the happiness he had so far missed. Now he is stopped in his tracks; from now on nothing remains behind or ahead of him to fix his gaze upon. Weariness alone, moreover, is enough to bring disillusionment, for he cannot in the end escape the futility of an endless pursuit.[7]

In the anomic drive for power, prestige, money and the materialistic things that these can buy, in the drive for jobs that pay well and promotions that pay better, there is no end, no ultimate satisfaction, *for these are but means to ends* but which are transferred into ends in themselves by the anomic. There is never enough because the accumulation of wealth is external, and the rewards are not internal in terms of deeper personal and personality gratification and such. In addition, wealth is always relative; there is always more to be had. The wealth or other success attained is not enjoyed by the anomic; he sees only more ahead, and keeps running, never reaching his goal.

Anomic people do not know why they strive so, why they still miss something when they are richer and richer, their houses bigger and their earnings better. They rush around at a hectic pace to accumulate wealth of all kinds, but life remains truly meaningless; it is not *really* living as is commonly said. The anomic student rushes through courses and accumulates grades and little else; he gets his degree and is successful. Then he is shocked at the realization that it is an empty symbol, a piece of paper with little behind it except numbers of grades and wasted years. He gets the prestigeful job and realizes eventually with a jolt that it too is meaningless, that he is not really attached to the work, the firm, the people with whom he works; that he only goes through empty motions and has money only to show for all those years of life. He accumulates the money, the cars, the house in the suburbs, and realizes that he has wasted away his years always expecting the *next* stage, the next promotion, the next raise in pay, the next purchase, to give him what he really wants. These never become ends in themselves; he strives after means and once achieved these are like water in his hands which drips away, non-solid, with little possibility of attachment. He starts to search for more again, dissatisfied, unfulfilled. Instead of searching for ends such as creative work and relationships, the meeting of deep self-needs, he makes money, power and materialistic goods into ends. But these are means only; which sends him searching for more, hoping to find in the future the gratification for which he really searches. He lives for and with means, achieves them, is dissatisfied, and runs for means again; truly is there no end in the running, no end in and to his confusion, no end to the climbing. All he has are means to ends, water or sand in his hands, 'goods' to his life, but with no good in it. When finally he has what he thinks he wants, he looks up and the ladder is higher still. He must climb for more money. There is never enough because of the lack of fulfilment of his true wants; his true needs of self remain to be filled and this he can do in the only way he knows *how*, by more emphasis on means such as money and power to fill the void of empty ends, or unfilfilled ends, or unknown ends, unknown because he has never thought out the ends to life, to existence, to himself, to his deep self-needs. He may be successful but there is never enough. He becomes disillusioned, weary of the search for real happiness and fulfilment which he never finds despite the riches and other success-symbols accumulated. Hence he is prone to manifestations of anomia, including suicide. *This is one form of the anomia of success.*

Robert Merton adds to this picture of the anomia of success when he writes that oddly enough psychiatrists see many cases where businessmen fall into despair after a financial success, or where writers become suicidal soon after their books are acclaimed as the work of genius by the world, or where scientists suffer psychic collapse after making an important discovery. While there seem to be no statistics on the matter, Professor Merton writes that such occurrences have been remarked upon through the years, perhaps because paradoxical behaviour attracts notice. Such occurrences, illustrations of what is called the anomia of success, are 'statistically rare but theoretically significant.'[8] This type of anomia appears as a response to the discovery that *the attainment of a sought-after goal does not bring peace and contentment*; it is not a stable stopping point. Professor Merton, like Durkheim of so many years earlier, indicates that success, which appears from the bottom of the ladder to be the end of the hard road, becomes in actuality *only another way station, only another rung, without depth, only a means, but no end.* Colleagues and the public see each accomplishment as only the prelude to new and further successes. These social pressures keep the success stewing in his own cooker. People do not allow the success to remain in a place; there is no rest for the weary. It is not only that their own aspirations escalate, becoming wildly unlimited and insatiable, and so, even when achieved, bringing them no nearer to the top of the ladder of success, but it is also that more and more seems to be expected of the successful by others and this in itself is stressful. 'Less often than one might believe, is there room for repose at the top.'[9]

The anomia resulting from shifting norms and constant struggling on the way up the endless ladder of success is one type; another results from the slide downward too. This is called the *anomia of failure.*

It is the purpose of this paper to trace further the conditions inherent in both the anomia of success and failure, to hypothesize reasons explaining why success and failure both in modern society can lead to anomia, and to trace relationships between success and failure which lead to anomia in any case. Under certain conditions in modern Western culture success *and* failure have within them conditions in common. This is not commonly understood by societal leaders, lay population, and perhaps even by some sociologists too. This leads to surprise, unnecessary when one understands the conditions and processes involved, at symptoms of anomie and anomia in 'successful' peoples and groups, such as riot, strife, increasing suicide, crime and delinquency, often spoken of as 'senseless' because one does not understand the common 'sicknesses' inherent in both certain types of success and failure. People are more ready to accept the crime, suicide and other such personally and socially disruptive behaviour patterns of the failure; it comes as a shock to see the 'successful' suburbanite or his children, and others like them, fall into similar states of mind and behaviour. Perhaps a better understanding of the factors involved in both success and failure, and the comparable factors in anomia of success and failure can help people to overcome this confusion.

Under certain conditions success is a failure. The person who climbs the ladder of success on his knees, as Jonathan Swift said,[10] can be said to be a failure of a kind when he reaches the top. The person passing him downward, in the other direction, but on his two feet, may be seen, cultural evaluations notwithstanding, as a success, when evaluated by higher or even by more self-oriented standards. This paper will trace such processes.

ANALYSIS

Success may be evaluated in several ways: one is success on a personal level, having met one's own creative and productive 'self' needs and conscience; another is by accumulation of wealth, or other externals such as material possessions, prestige, power, high grades at school, and the like. Where a person becomes successful in reaching the culturally evaluated high goals he *thinks* he too wants (and he does on one level), but does not meet his deeper needs for self-respect, creativity and such, something still is left empty in the success. Here the person buys outward success by 'selling his soul,' as is commonly said. *Thus success of one type can really be a failure of another. The person gets still more confused when he thinks he should be happy but is not really so with his success.* He loses understanding of his own self. Even his lack of contentment in success confuses him; the culture teaches that materialistic success should make one happy, but he is not. Wherever he turns, he finds confusion, in the changes in his life wrought by success, in cultural pressures for 'more' without a stable stopping point, in the removal of a life-organizing goal toward success which has been achieved, and in his own self which remains malcontented instead of happy as the cultural picture says he should be.

Such 'culturally evaluated' success is often based on externals: the getting of money and such, but the deeper pleasures of self-fulfilment are often neglected. Furthermore, a person is taught in the striving for success to focus his attention on the future, instead of living in the present too. Each step in life becomes only a means; anomic people rarely see anything as pleasant as an end in itself. The elevating of means, such as money, to ends, is never enough since these are always empty in the means which they really are. These then become means to further ends, an endless ladder. For example, education becomes a place to earn grades instead of an end

in itself of pleasant interactions, creative fulfilment, and the contentment involved in learning the wisdom of the world. This is unfulfilling so *the grades become a means to attain a job which again is
not seen as an end in itself to meet creative self-needs, to enjoy the
pleasure of helping others in productive work, but as a means of
earning money to buy things to which one is again unattached and
cannot enjoy as beautiful, useful objects, made by creative people.*
This is the picture of the directionless anomic, and of those who may
be said to be alienated from things which they only accumulate and
own, but without unique or idiosyncratic attachment or understanding or appreciation, or even deep-seated pleasure. The job is unfulfilling so money becomes the goal and not productive work. This too
is unfulfilling because money is only a means, so this becomes a
means to another end, more money to buy more products and so on.
As Aristotle said in his now commonly neglected wisdom of the past:
'The life of money-making is a life of constraint; and wealth is obviously not the good of which we are in quest; for it is useful merely
as a means to something else.'[11] Truly this rushing after means without end or ends is an endless ladder as Emile Durkheim indicated
in the quotation presented earlier. With the eye on the future the
present wastes away unlived. Little is enjoyed *now*. The future
comes. With it culturally evaluated success may come but the anomia
persists; in fact it becomes worse, because while pushing on toward
the goal at least there was some drive as a cover-up and filler of
the inner emptiness, if only superficially. And when the goal is
reached, the drive melts. The emptiness of anomia remains overwhelming and pervasive.

People look for success to bring the contentment they really
want. Little do they realize that money and fame do not buy deep
relations of *gemeinschaft*-type, often not even fulfilment either
which they need to live as sane people. While they strive for success
they temporarily delude themselves into thinking that their loneliness, lack of sense of belonging and such will be cured in the future
when they become 'successful' in school, in the corporation world,
in Hollywood, in investments or whatnot. But when the success
comes they are miserably disappointed; they are no more content
than they were before. People do not love and understand them
more than before, they are not used the less and in fact are often
used the more, they are not satisfied and fulfilled with what they
have any more than before, and they are not content either despite
the attainment of the success. Worse yet, the person looks back to
the foul things he might have done, the empty years wasted, the

people he hurt, all in the drive for his success. A terrible depression sets in and he turns towards suicide or other manifestations of anomia, even in the days of his long-sought 'glory.'

The 'successful' but empty person does not have internal depth and cannot transfer his now satisfied success-drive to the beauty of life in general, to contemplation, to relationships with deep, satisfying people or to another re-creating task. This, in all his constant striving for sand-like means, he never learned; it is not part of his person, his life-view. Such a person now realizes that he must join the 'rat-race' again to avoid 'cracking' as is commonly said; there is no end to the search for ends confounded by opting for means. Indeed, to play on words, there is no end to it. An overwhelming discouragement sets in because the goals reached leave him empty; worse yet, he may realize that the goals reached are not his, are not deep or satisfying. The result is not joy but despair, and again tendencies towards manifestations of anomia such as suicide.

Even where the goal reached was a deep, socially-useful and self-satisfying and gratifying goal, success might well lead to anomia. This is because of anomie pervasive in society. People in such an anomic society have caught the 'disease' and everywhere they turn they see an endless greed, an endless running, more and more effort expended for more and more trappings of success in the forms of power, prestige, money and materialistic goods. Such people seeing a man himself reach even a deep goal cannot understand him and cannot bear to see him self-satisfied and gratified. They do not let him live to enjoy his success, but they egg him on. They push him, slander him, and press him to greater 'heights.' Because they themselves have found no ultimate foothold, they cannot understand a man who has. Under the persistent pressures of those around him, his family, his critics, his colleagues, and others, he is pushed toward further, often empty goals, as he realizes that people will not accept him as he is, successful and content to rest in fulfilling leisure or needing time to think of new directions to take in work or life. Hence, in order to maintain a sense of self that is dependent upon the sense of gemeinschaft with and good-will of others, he starts to run again, realizing finally that there is no end to it save death. He expected a sense of belonging when he finally reached his goal but others show him it is not enough: the wife presses for more money, his colleagues for more discoveries. If they have not reached their goals he must strive on too for they cannot stand to see a man fulfilled and satisfied when they are not. This is what Professor Merton refers to as this anomia of success which 'appears as a response to the personal discovery that the attainment of a long sought-after goal is no stable stopping point,' because 'associates and larger relevant publics hold each accomplishment to be only the prelude to new and further success.'[12] Thus the anomie of society can 'infect' even a successful man with deep goals which he has reached, now expecting to enjoy his success, needing months or years to build new goals upon that success, but pushed into running again too soon. The anomic goad him to the same behaviour as they themselves exhibit, for they cannot understand the man who wants little and is satisfied. This is only one example of how anomie can lead to anomia of the formerly 'uninfected.'

Worse yet, as much as people push a man to greater heights and do not let him rest in his success, they still envy him. Since in modern society people often rank themselves against others, the success of one man they know makes them feel lower; their sense of self is not based on inner strength, knowledge and abilities, but on external, quantifiable successes, such as in money terms and such. One man's richness or other successes thus makes others feel inferior. They may play up to him in the hope that he will throw some bones to them, or that some of his prestige will rub off on them, but basically, with all their 'friendliness' to him they burn with envy and feelings of inferiority, as well as degradation, because they prostitute themselves to be with him when they actually cannot stand and envy him. Thus the man who is successful may seem to gain in popularity, but he becomes more and more lonely; he senses the deceit, envy and hatred of his closest colleagues and others but cannot label these for certain, nor can he determine what it is that he has done to make people truly hostile to him, despite their external 'friendliness.' People may push him onward only because they share in the limelight. And they may push him onward because of their deep hatred for him which makes them want him to be miserable. They do not want him to rest, but they want him to suffer in his success. This he often does.

In addition, many people have the constant need for running and climbing higher and higher toward success built into their own mentality. The need for perpetual success in the form of more of anything and everything is taught as a valid goal by parents, schools and the mass media. These do not teach a person to be satisfied at some point with a sufficient amount of money, products, and such but to shine to the limits of his own individual uniqueness and creativity instead. Hence a person is under even internal strain to continue to compete and to succeed because he has internalized the message of the anomic society. There comes a point when this leads not to more ambition, but to despair at the endless ladder; hence anomia which cannot in an anomic society easily be thrown off by a transfer of drive to deeper satisfactions such as love, appreciation of beauty, or even thought over months and years which could lead to the next success but slowly, in time with his own expanding self and abilities.

Success may also require the rapid learning of new ways of life to meet the demands of a new subculture into which success has thrown a person such as a higher class level, or living in the public eye. This too can disorient a person and can make for the anomia of success.

Finally, success often gives a man more responsibility and more power to dispense favours. More 'phonies' then can latch on to him not for relationships with him as a person but to use him for their own ends. These untrustworthy people consistently disillusion him which pushes him into anomia and alienation. In an anomic society few can trust others; few know what to expect from them either. With increased responsibility for his actions the success finds that he is left more and more isolated in essence, despite all the people around him. He takes final responsibility but cannot easily delegate authority to others for advice or help for fear that they might do a low quality job, or use him, or cheat him. He is alone at the top with heavy burdens but without trust in the others around him upon whom he is dependent. Success of this type becomes a misery, not a pleasure, and the successful man suffers.

Emphasis on means which become empty ends, analysed in terms of the anomia of success, can also lead to the reverse, the *anomia of failure*. The person who lives a gratifying life, related closely in *gemeinschaft* with a closely knit group of people can withstand a sudden reverse of his materialistic fortunes. Certainly he is sad at his financial losses, but since the money, prestige and power were for him truly, and with full knowledge, only secondary means relegated to secondary place, and not mistakenly sought after as ends in themselves, and since he holds deep satisfactions as final ends in other areas of life, he can still continue with a fulfilled, stable life, albeit under hard times. The person whose sense of value was in the dignity of his own self, and in a love for people more than for things, whose self stood with head high and not bolstered in its anomic emptiness with materialistic trappings, money, or power that became a false part of self, can withstand the shock of loss of these because he thereby does not lose his relatedness to self, to people, or to life. And if such a person is surrounded by friends and relatives who love him for what he is in essence rather than only for his wealth, power, prestige and former successes, then they will stand behind him even when he is a financial or other failure, because he still remains a personal success, since the success is rooted in his essence as a human being rather than in what he owns or buys or achieves. However, the anomic who has little behind him or in him in terms of *gemeinschaft* and meaning and purpose to his life, and who bolstered his anomic, empty self with quantifiable, materialistic symbols and trappings of success, loses all when he loses his job, or when his investments fail, or when he loses his money. He has nothing to fall back on and is prone to suicide. In the American economic depression where the rich society abruptly changed to a poor one, one business failure after the other jumped from the Wall Street Towers of Mammon; life became unbearable without the money, power, prestige, etc. William Barrett aptly analyzes such feelings under the stress of loss, whether it be of money or a sweetheart or anything else:

> The unbearable loss is not really in itself unbearable; what we cannot bear is that in being stripped of an external object we stand denuded and see the intolerable abyss of the self yawn at our feet.[13]

If the self is an empty self, if a person has no real friends to fall back on, if he now stands denuded of the external object to which he was clinging, he now stands not only nude but like a ghost without even an inner substance at which to hold and grasp. Since his death-alive, his living emptiness now becomes evident, he feels an intolerable despair and may in his anomia take the next step of killing all through suicide to end the horror of the living death. In success a person is also thrown back upon his empty self because he has reached the goal that provided at least an externally organizing principle to life; hence tendencies again to suicide and related manifestations of despair. The retirement doldrums can also be analyzed this way. The man who for years waited for retirement from work lives to see the day of his success, retirement, come; then he may be left with total emptiness. His success is really a failure and he declines to any of the manifestations of anomia.

A person who has failed in an anomic society finds that his entire selfhood fails with the failure. He is crushed. Such a person, furthermore, likely has brought friends and surrounded himself with those like him. Likely he evaluates people in terms of 'What can he do for me?' and 'What can he buy?' His 'friends' evaluate him in the same way. Without his money or other success his 'friends' desert him for bigger and brighter pastures. Martha the maid, whom he has been fond of calling a member of his family, packs up and quits when he can no longer pay her the usual pittance. Doormen, waiters, bellhops, easy women, business associates, all of whom have been buzzing around him as insects around a shining bulb at night, one by one desert him when the attraction of his fame and money runs out, as they fly off to other still shining lights. His wife may change in her affections. His children may lose respect for him, for to them, as he taught them, he is less a man, less a father closely related in essence of *gemeinschaft* with them, but a moneybags with whom they have lost a true sense of attachment. As he has bought their love, so have they become used to evaluating him as such. When his moneybags dry up, so does their superficial respect.

One such case example: I was once invited to the home of one of my students for dinner. The man of the house, with obvious great pride, asked his teen-age son to play a piece on the piano for his guests, of which I was one. The son refused. Shortly thereafter his friends came to call for him for a night out on the town. When he asked for money, the father took a bill from his wallet, dangled it in front of his son, but pulled it out of reach as soon as he tried to take it. 'Play a piece on the piano for our valued guests,' ordered the father, and the son complied for the money, not for the sake of the gratification that his father and the guests might have received thereby from his skill at the piano, but he played without 'heart', evidenced by a rapid, lustreless performance, after which he grabbed at the bill. 'But dad, that's only a dollar,' he exclaimed in amazement when he saw the denomination. 'You can't go anywhere or do anything on a dollar here. You know that.' The father very calmly and coldly took another bill from his wallet, and coolly dangled it before his son. 'Now play another piece for me and for your guests, and this time slower and better,' and his son, with contempt in his eyes, did so.

Such a man who loses his money thereby loses his little control over his son who evidently cares more for the money than for the man. Such a man who loses his money loses more than that; he loses his entire status as man of the house. He loses the 'love' of his children too. In fact he loses control over his whole destiny which was arranged through and by money, and not through essence of self.[14]

Such a failure finds his sense of loss intolerable; not only the loss of money, which is bad enough, but his whole essence, his life, is lost. This he perceives now in its true emptiness. Drink, and perhaps suicide, or the transfer to a new type of rationalization or bolstering for his anomic existence become his fate.

Emile Durkheim noted that in economic disasters a type of declassification occurs which abruptly throws certain people into a social state lower than their previous one. Under this constraint they must change their whole way of living by scaling down in every area of life. The advantages of social position and influence are suddenly lost and they must start a new social education. But they cannot easily adjust to a new style of life in which repression of desires is necessary. They are not adjusted to the new condition forced upon them and they thus remain in a state of intolerable agony and confusion; for this reason their suffering 'detaches them from a reduced existence even before they have made a trial of it.'[15] The same declassification can occur in the rapid move upward too; hence manifestations of anomia in both cases, moving upward as well as sliding downward.

A sudden shift of fortunes upward or downward can lead even the formerly non-anomic into a brief period of anomia in which any of the characteristics of the 'disease' may be manifested until such a point that the now anomic can 'get his bearings,' 'get hold of himself,' and 'find himself' as we say it in popular parlance. However, the anomic person who covered up and rationalized away his anomia through his fortunes has nothing to hold onto when he loses them; he is inclined toward a more severe anomia. In short, it is not a time of trouble that causes anomia, although this can be the case for a temporary period of adjustment until the afflicted can 'come to himself' again, as is commonly said by even the layman (really by thinking through the meaning of his existence, developing a new direction, realizing the need others have for him, etc.). Peoples who have suffered much, but who have *gemeinschaft*, a sense of belonging, a sense of purpose, religious or otherwise, show a remarkable absence of indicators of anomia and anomie. For example, poorer nations have a lower suicide rate than richer. A nation at war against a clearly defined, commonly despised enemy also shows a low incidence of anomia and anomie and a low incidence of suicide and other indicators of the 'diseases.' A crisis (such as a natural disaster) that abruptly gives people a sense of *gemeinschaft* and of direction in the common tasks of survival also will lower all rates of anomia, precisely because anomia is a *lack* of sense of direction by definition. But times of trouble hitting the anomic who has rationalized away his loss might knock away the rationalization too under the stress. The true nature of his empty, wasted life becomes clear. He has nothing to fall back upon, especially if his 'friends' desert him. He is sick indeed and is quite prone to suicide and other extreme anomic symptons.

The person who has filled-in his void by money and loses that money is doubly anomic; first, in his confusion of means and ends; second, having even lost that, albeit anomic grasp on life. Where a person's social state, as identified with social influence, social position, wealth and the like, determines also his personal state with self, with family, and with friends, then most certainly does the loss of social influence, as Durkheim explains, make a man more than sad, it throws him into the mental depression as severe personally as the economic depression is to the society that has put all eggs into one monetary basket, that leaves nothing for people to hold onto in a time of trouble. When that money and such are lost so is everything else.

In addition, those who had little money or other external trappings of success to lose in the first place (e.g., the poverty-stricken) are relatively unaffected by economic or other dislocations and are less prone to anomia as a result. A depression leaves them in the same position as before; there is no need for adjustment. If their condition does not ever change upward for the better such people are not afflicted with the anomia of success caused by the rapid need to change a style of life with new norms which can throw such people's lives into disarray. As Confucius so aptly stated, 'He who makes his bed close to the ground does not have far to fall.'[16] However, poor people whose desires for a better life are stimulated by the mass media or through other means find their deprivation once accepted as the normal state of affairs now to be intolerable. Their hold on life is also lost and they become anomic and eventually embittered by (and alienated from) a social system that offers the advertised Good Life to others but not to them. They become disenchanted with their steady-state, and they demand more.

This analysis of the anomia of failure can now add to the analysis of the anomia of success too. Durkheim tells us that:

> It is the same [as economic disaster] if the source of the crisis is an abrupt growth of power and wealth. Then, truly, as the conditions of life are changed, the standard according to which needs were regulated can no longer remain the same. . . .[17]

Rapid changes in either direction, success or failure, can throw a person or society into an anomic state with an increase in symptoms and effects of anomia and anomie, including a high suicide rate, as these temporarily or permanently lose the sense of direction. A person has trouble adjusting to his new place in life. Modern society is one which itself changes rapidly, giving people no chance to 'gain hold of themselves,' as is commonly said. It should now be understood why rich societies and peoples and those rapidly on the way up or down suffer higher rates of anomie and anomia than poorer and relatively stable societies and people.

Another similarity between the anomia of success and that of failure is worth reiterating here. The anomic who has propped himself with crutches of monetary success and the like is left with nothing when the failure comes and he suffers the anomia of failure. The anomic who has propped himself with crutches of hard work defined as 'good' socially, but not meeting his real self-needs, the anomic who temporarily forgets while spending long hours at various tasks, might find himself confronted with success, the final attainment of his supposed life-goal. Yet, since he himself has nothing deep within him, he falls ill with the anomia of success. Actually, his success is really a failure to self. To this may be added the pressures of success discussed earlier. Everything is mixed up in his mind. He is anomic. Thus anomia of success and of failure, opposites, still share characteristics in common. This is why they both evidence comparable manifestations, such as suicide.

CONCLUSIONS

One of the most unchanging factors in modern society and life is change. This confuses people, who in mind and nature seem, with all their rushing to and fro, more like feudal man in relatively slow change, than modern mass man, forced to accept and adjust to many rapid social, technological and personal changes, some of which conflict with older norms and personal styles and conceptions of life. This confusion may be seen as a 'sickness,' and 'infection' deriving from a rapidly changing society. Such societal confusion is called anomie, which may be likened to a germ, a virus of the body politic. Vulnerable people, sometimes even the strong, succumb to the epidemic and fall into states of personal disarray, sometimes tending toward alcoholism, aggressive behaviour, crime or even suicide. Such people may be seen as 'ill' with what is called anomia.

Failure in an affluent society, or failure when once successful can, under certain conditions, lead to anomia. However, success can also lead to anomia, especially if the success is only culturally defined rather than inherently a personal success of the deeper self too. Other factors, discussed, can also lead to the anomia of success. The two forms of anomia frequently discussed in the literature, the anomia of success and failure, in analysis, seem to share characteristics in common. Under certain conditions, such as going down the ladder of success on one's two feet, with head high, what seems to be a failure really is also a success of the self in maintaining oneself, one's uniqueness and integrity. Under certain conditions, such as in climbing the ladder of success on one's knees, such a success can be a failure of self. A success that is not deep leads to the drive for more; the endless ladder fatigues, and the top finally is seen as the bottom, a bottomless pit of endless means and empty striving. Such a success is also a failure.

Men who are propelled by spacecraft to the moon are going up from the earth. From the vantage point of the moon they are coming down. Friedrich Nietzsche, philosopher, states the belief that by going under one can go over and become the *Ubermensch*, the over-man or the superman.[18] What Nietzsche meant is that by failure, by suffering, one can become deeper, more creative in sublimation, less flabby and flaccid, and better in many ways. Opposites are contained in one another. The success of cities in attracting a larger population eventually leads to failures of democracy, as Plato, Aristotle and others saw so long ago, and even of technology, as we notice in the technological crises (e.g., telephone inefficiencies, electrical power failures and shortages) and social crises (rising crime rates and such) in some American cities and elsewhere. Success yields failure and vice versa, one of the principles of ecological balance.

In the same way the anomia of success and the anomia of failure, seeming opposites, share, like success and failure themselves, many elements in common. Both certain forms of success and failure can yield anomia, and, on closer inspection yield it for the same reasons. We should no longer evidence surprise that success can bring with it anomia and anomic effects. Perhaps people ought to be helped to understand that success can be failure, and that failure is not a disaster, because, it can, in the going under, lead to higher people, as Nietzsche so well and so beautifully explained. And, in addition, people might be taught that under certain conditions, for example, failing because one refused to climb the ladder of success on the knees, failure is a personal triumph or success.

A subject such as anomia, which brings with it so many personal and societal miseries, is well worth the effort of further studies of many types.

NOTES

1. See Durkheim's book *Suicide*, Glencoe, Ill.: Free Press, 1951. First published in 1897. The English version cited was translated by John A. Spaulding and George Simpson and was edited by George Simpson. Also see Durkheim's, *The Division of Labour in Society*, Glencoe, Ill.: Free Press, 1947. First published in 1893.
2. See MacIver's *The Ramparts We Guard*, New York: Macmillan, 1950, ch. 10 and briefly elsewhere.

3. See Marshall B. Clinard, 'The Theoretical Implications of Anomie and Deviant Behavior,' and elsewhere in Clinard (ed.), *Anomie and Deviant Behavior*, New York: The Free Press of Glencoe, 1964, for a tracing of the development of the concept.
4. Robert K. Merton, 'Anomie, Anomia, and Social Interaction: Contexts of Deviant Behaviour' in Clinard, *Anomie and Deviant Behavior* (Ibid.), p. 226.
5. Edgar A. Schuler, Duane L. Gibson, Maude L. Fiero, and Wilbur B. Brookover (eds.), *Outside Readings in Sociology*, New York: Thomas Y. Crowell, 1953, p. 782. This definition of anomia (loss of sense of belonging and rejection of norms or values of society) is provided by the authors in a one paragraph introduction to a selection from the book by Robert MacIver, op. cit.
6. MacIver, op. cit., p. 85.
7. Durkheim, *Suicide*, op. cit., p. 256.
8. Merton, in Clinard, op. cit., p. 220.
9. Ibid., p. 221. Also see Rollo May, *Man's Search For Himself*, New York: Norton, 1953, pp. 169ff., for a discussion of suicide related to success, and to the desire for success.
10. Ambition often puts men upon doing the meanest offices: so climbing is performed in the same posture with creeping.' Cited in John P. Marquand, *Point of No Return*, Boston: Little, Brown, 1949, p. 219.
11. In his *Nicomachean Ethics*, Book I, ch. 3.
12. Merton in Clinard, op. cit., p. 221.
13. William Barrett, *Irrational Man: A Study in Existential Philosophy*, Garden City, New York: Doubleday Anchor, 1962, p. 169.
14. Mirra Komarovsky provides insight into effects such as these in her book, *The Unemployed Man and His Family*, New York: Dryden Press, 1940.
15. Durkheim, *Suicide*, op. cit., p. 252.
16. Cited in Ephraim Harold Mizruchi 'Alienation and Anomie: Theoretical and Empirical Perspectives' in Irving Louis Horowitz, *The New Sociology*, New York: Galaxy; Oxford University Press, 1965, p. 266.
17. Durkheim, *Suicide*, op. cit., p. 252.
18. See the writings of Nietzsche, especially *Thus Spoke Zarathustra*.

25.

Death and Social Structure†

ROBERT BLAUNER*

Death is a biological and existential fact of life that affects every human society. Since mortality tends to disrupt the ongoing life of social groups and relationships, all societies must develop some forms of containing its impact. Mortuary institutions are addressed to the specific problems of the disposal of the dead and the rituals of transition from life to death. In addition, fertility practices, family and kinship systems, and religion take their shape partly in response to the pressure of mortality and serve to limit death's disorienting

Reprinted from *Psychiatry*, Vol. 29, 1966, pp. 378-394, by special permission of the author and the publisher, The William Alanson White Psychiatric Foundation, Inc. Copyright is held by the Foundation.

*B.A. 48, M.A. 50, Univ. of Chicago; Ph.D. Univ. of Calif. 52. Asst. Prof. of Sociology, San Francisco State College 61-62; Asst. Prof. of Sociology, Univ. of Chicago 62-63; Asst. Prof. of Sociology, Univ. of Calif. 63- . Member, Amer. Sociol. Assn.

†I am grateful to the Equitable Life Assurance Society and its Director of Social Research, John W. Riley, Jr., for support of this project. Aid was also provided by the Institute of Social Science, University of California, Berkeley. I thank Fred Deyo for his research assistance, and David Matza, Norman Ryder, and Sheldon Messinger for their especially helpful comments.

possibilities. In this paper I shall be concerned with the social arrangements by which the impact of mortality is contained and with the ways in which these arrangements are related to the demographic characteristics of a society. In particular, I hope to throw some light on the social and cultural consequences of modern society's organization of death. Because of the abstractness of these questions and the inadequacy of the empirical data on which I draw, many of my statements should be read as speculative hypotheses rather than as established facts.

Mortality and its impact are not constants. In general, the demographic structure of preindustrial societies results in an exposure to death that appears enormous by the standards of modern Western life. Malinowski, writing of the Trobriand Islanders and other natives of Eastern New Guinea, states that "death . . . causes a great and permanent disturbance in the equilibrium of tribal life."[1] The great impact of mortality and the vividness of death as a theme in life emerge clearly from Goody's account of the LoDagaa of West Africa.[2] Jules Henry's study of the Kaingang "Jungle People" of the Brazil highlands depicts a tribe whose members are in daily contact with death and greatly obsessed with it.[3] Kingsley Davis speculates that many characteristics of Indian life, such as the high birth rate, the stress on kinship and joint households, and the religious emphasis, may be attributed to the nearness to death that follows from the conditions of thatsubcontinent.[4] The relatively small scale of communities in most pre-industrial societies compounds death's impact. Its regular occurrence—especially through the not infrequent catastrophes of war, famine, and epidemics—involves more serious losses to a society of small scale, a point that has been made forcibly by Krzywicki:

Let us take, for instance, one of the average Australian tribes (usually numbering 300-600 members). The simultaneous loss of 10 persons is there an event which quantitatively considered, would have the same significance as the simultaneous death of from 630,000 to 860,000 inhabitants in the present Polish state. And such catastrophes, diminishing an Australian tribe by some 10 persons, might, of course, occur not infrequently. An unfortunate war-expedition, a victorious night attack by an enemy, a sudden flood, or any of a host of other events might easily cause the death of such a number of tribesmen: in addition, there were famines, such as that which forced the Birria, for instance, to devour all their children, or the epidemics which probably occurred from time to time even in primitive communities. And, what is most important, conditions of primitive life sometimes created such situations that there was a simultaneous loss of about a dozen or a score of persons of the same sex and approximately the same age. Then such a misfortune affecting a community assumed the dimensions of a tribal disaster.[5]

This is not to suggest that a continuous encounter with mortality is equally prevalent in all preindustrial societies. Variations among primitive and peasant societies are as impressive as common patterns; I simply want to make the point that *many* nonmodern societies must organize themselves around death's recurrent presence. Modern societies, on the other hand, have largely succeeded in containing mortality and its social disruptiveness. Yet the impact of mortality on a society is not a simple matter of such demographic considerations as death rates and the size of the group. Also central is the manner in which a society is organized, the way it manages the death crisis, and how its death practices and mortuary institutions are linked to the social structure.

LIFE-EXPECTANCY, ENGAGEMENT, AND THE SOCIAL RELEVANCE OF THE DEAD

Death disrupts the dynamic equilibrium of social life because a number of its actual or potential consequences create problems for a society. One of these potential consequences is a social vacuum. A member of society and its constituent groups and relationships is lost, and some kind of gap in institutional functioning results. The extent of this vacuum depends upon how deeply engaged the deceased has been in the life of the society and its groups. The system is more disrupted by the death of a leader than by that of a common man; families and work groups are typically more affected by the loss of those in middle years than by the death of children or old people. Thus a key determinant of the impact of mortality is the age and social situation of those who die, since death will be more disruptive when it frequently strikes those who are most relevant for the functional activities and the moral outlook of the social order.

In modern Western societies, mortality statistics are more and more made up of the very old. The causes are obvious: The virtual elimination of infant and child mortality and the increasing control over the diseases of youth and middle life. Almost one million American males died in 1960. Eight percent were younger than 15 years. Fifty-five percent were 65 or older (29 percent were past 75), and another 18 percent were between 55 and 64. The middle years, between 15 and 54, claimed the remaining 19 percent of the deaths.[6] As death in modern society becomes increasingly a phenomenon of the old, who are usually retired from work and finished with their parental responsibilities, mortality in modern society rarely interrupts the business of life. Death is uncommon during the highly engaged middle years, and the elderly are more and more segregated into communities and institutions for their age group.

Although accurate vital statistics for contemporary preindustrial societies are rare, the available data indicate that the primary concentration of death is at the opposite end of the life-span, in the years of infancy and childhood. For example, among the Sakai of the Malay Peninsula, approximately 50 percent of the babies born die before the age of three; among the Kurnai tribe of Australia 40 to 50 percent die before the age of 10.[7] Fifty-nine percent of the 1956 male deaths in Nigeria among the "indigenous" blacks were children who had not reached their fifth birthday. Thirty-five percent of an Indian male cohort born in the 1940's died before the age of 10.[8] The same concentration of mortality in the early years was apparently also true of historical preindustrial societies.

Aside from this high infant and child mortality, there is no common pattern in the age composition of death in preindustrial societies. In some, there appears to be a secondary concentration in old age, suggesting that when mortality in the early years is very high, the majority of those who survive may be hardy enough to withstand the perils of middle life and reach old age. This seems to be the situation with the Tikopia, according to the limited demographic data. Thirty-six percent of the deaths in one period studied were those of people over 58, almost equaling the proportion who died in the first seven years.[9]

Table 1.   Number of Deaths During Specified Year
Age Per 1,000 Males Alive at Beginning
of Age Period*

Country	20-25	25-30	30-35	35-40	40-45
Congo, 1950-52	54	49	68	82	96
Mexico, 1940	46	53	62	71	84
U.S.A., 1959	9	9	10	14	23
Canada, 1950-52	2	2	2	2	3

*From United Nations, *Demographic Yearbook* 13th Edition; New York, Department of Economic and Social Affairs, 1961; p. 360. Decimals have been rounded off to the nearest integer.

In other societies and historical periods, conditions are such that mortality remains heavy in the middle years, and few people reach the end of a normal lifespan. Thus calculations of age at death taken from gravestones erected during the early Roman empire (this method is notoriously unreliable, but the figures are suggestive) typically find that 30 to 40 percent of the deceased were in their twenties and thirties; the proportion who died past the age of 50 was only about 20 percent.[10] The life-table of the primitive Cocos also illustrates this pattern. Only 16 percent of the deaths are in the old-age group (past 55 years), since mortality continues high for that minority of the population which survives childhood.[11] The contrast in death frequency during the middle years is suggested by the data shown in Table 1 on mortality rates for specific age periods for four countries.

The demographic pattern where mortality is high in the middle years probably results in the most disruption of ongoing life. Procedures for the reallocation of the socially necessary roles, rights, and responsibilities of the deceased must be institutionalized. This is most essential when the roles and responsibilities are deemed important and when there is a right integration of the society's groups and institutions. Such is the situation among the LoDagaa of West Africa, where many men die who are young and middle-aged. Since the kinship structure is highly elaborated, these deaths implicate the whole community, particularly the kinship group of the bereaved spouses. The future rights to these now unattached women, still sexually active and capable of child-bearing, emerge as an issue which must be worked out in the funeral ceremonies through a transfer to new husbands.[12] In contrast, in modern Western societies, the death of a husband typically involves only the fragmented conjugal family; from the point of view of the social order as a whole, it makes little difference whether a widow replaces her deceased husband, because of the loose integration of the nuclear family into wider kinship, economic, and political spheres.

Another way of containing the impact of mortality is to reduce the real or ideal importance of those who die. Primitive societies, hard hit by infant and child mortality, characteristically do not recognize infants and children as people; until a certain age they are considered as still belonging to the spirit world from which they came, and therefore their death is often not accorded ritual recognition—no funeral is held.[13] Aries has noted that French children were neither valued nor recognized in terms of their individuality during the long period of high infant mortality:

> No one thought of keeping a picture of a child if that child had . . . died in infancy . . . it was thought that the little thing which had disappeared so soon in life was not worthy of remembrance . . . Nobody thought, as we ordinarily think today, that every child already contained a man's personality. Too many of them died.[14]

One of the consequences of the devaluation of the old in modern society is the minimization of the disruption and moral shock death ordinarily brings about.

But when people die who are engaged in the vital functions of society—socializing the young, producing sustenance, and maintaining ceremonies and rituals—their importance cannot be easily reduced. Dying before they have done their full complement of work and before they have seen their children off toward adulthood and their own parenthood, they die with *unfinished business.* I suggest that the almost universal belief in ghosts in preindustrial societies[15] can be understood as an effect of this demographic pattern on systems of interpersonal interaction, and not simply as a function of naive, magical, and other "unsophisticated" world views. Ghosts are reifications of this unfinished business, and belief in their existence may permit some continuation of relationships broken off before their natural terminus. Perhaps the primitive Manus have constructed the most elaborate belief system which illustrates this point:

> Each man worships a spirit who is called the Sir-Ghost, usually the spirit of his father, though sometimes it may be the son, or brother, or one who stood in the mother's brother-sister's relationship. The concrete manifestation of this Sir-Ghost is the dead person's skull which is placed in a bowl above the inside of the front entry of the house. Any male can speak to his Sir-Ghost and receive communications from him. The Sir-Ghost acts as a ward, protecting his son from accidents, supervising his morals, and hopefully bringing him wealth. The relationship between the Sir-Ghost and his ward is a close parallel to that between father and son. With some changed emphases, it continues the relationship that existed in life and was broken by death. Since Manus die early, the tenure of a Sir-Ghost is typically only one generation. When the ward, the son, dies, this is seen as proof of the ghost's ineffectiveness, and the son's son casts him out, installing his own newly deceased father as Sir-Ghost. The same spirit, however, is not a Sir-Ghost to other families, but only a regular ghost and as such thought to be malicious.[16]

More common in primitive societies is an ambivalent attitude toward the ghost. Fear exists because of the belief that the dead man, frustrated in his exclusion from a life in which he was recently involved, wants back in, and, failing this, may attempt to restore his former personal ties by taking others along with him on his journey to the spirit world. The elaborate, ritually appropriate funeral is believed to keep the spirit of the dead away from the haunts of the living,[17] and the feasts and gifts given for the dead are attempts to appease them through partial inclusion in their life. It would appear that the dead who were most engaged in the life of society have the strongest motives for restoring their ties and the most feared ghosts tend to be those whose business has been the least completed. Ghosts of the murdered, the suicide, and others who have met a violent end are especially feared because they have generally died young, with considerable strength and energy remaining.

Ghosts of women dying in childbirth and of the unmarried and child-less are considered particularly malignant because these souls have been robbed of life's major purpose; at the funeral the unmarried are often given mock marriages to other dead souls. Ghosts of dead husbands or wives are dangerous to their spouses, especially when the latter have remarried.[18] The spirit of the grandparent who has seen his children grow up and procreate is, on the other hand, the least feared; among the LoDagaa only the grandparent's death is con-ceded to be a natural rather than a magical or malignant event, and in many societies there is only a perfunctory funeral for grandpar-ents, since their spirits are not considered to be in conflict with the living.[19]

The relative absence of ghosts in modern society is not simply a result of the routing of superstition by science and rational thought, but also reflects the disengaged social situation of the majority of the deceased. In a society where the young and middle-aged have largely liberated themselves from the authority of and emotional dependence upon old people by the time of the latters' death, there is little social-psychological need for a vivid community of the dead. Whereas in high-mortality societies, the person who dies often liter-ally abandons children, spouses, and other relatives to whom he is owing affection and care, the deceased in advanced societies has typi-cally completed his obligations to the living; he does not owe any-thing. Rather, the death is more likely to remind survivors of the social and psychological debts they have incurred toward him—debts that they may have been intending to pay in the coins of attention, affection, care, appreciation, or achievement. In modern societies the living use the funeral and sometimes a memorial to attempt to "make up for" some of these debts that can no longer be paid in terms of the ordinary give and take of social life.

The disengagement of the aged in modern societies enhances the continuous functioning of social institutions and is a corollary of social structure and mortality patterns. Disengagement, the tran-sition period between the end of institutional functioning and death, permits the changeover of personnel in a planned and careful manner, without the inevitably disruptive crises of disorganization and succession that would occur if people worked to the end and died on the job. The unsettling character of the Kennedy assassina-tion for our nation suggests the chaos that would exist if a bureau-cratic social structure were combined with high mortality in the middle years.[20]

For the older person, disengagement may bring on great psychological stress if his ties to work and family are severed more abruptly and completely than he desires. Yet it may also have positive consequences. As Robert Butler has described, isolation and unoccupied time during the later years permit reviewing one's past life.[21] There is at least the potential (not always realized) to better integrate the manifold achievements and disappointments of a lifetime, and doing so, to die better. Under favorable circumstances, disengagement can permit a person to complete his unfinished business before death: To right old wrongs, to reconcile longstanding hostile relations with relatives or former friends; to take the trip, write the play, or paint the picture that he was always planning. Of course, often the finances and health of the aged do not permit such a course, and it is also possible that the general status of the aged in a secular, youth-and-life oriented society is a basic obstacle to a firm sense of identity and self-worth during the terminal years.

BUREAUCRATIZATION OF MODERN DEATH CONTROL

Since there is no death without a body—except in mystery thrillers—the corpse is another consequence of mortality that contributes to its disruptiveness, tending to produce fear, generalized anxiety, and disgust.[22] Since families and work groups must eventually return to some kind of normal life, the time they are exposed to corpses must be limited. Some form of disposal (earth or sea burial, cremation, exposure to the elements) is the core of mortuary institutions everywhere. A disaster that brings about massive and unregulated exposure to the dead, such as that experienced by the survivors of Hiroshima and also at various times by survivors of great plagues, famines, and death-camps, appears to produce a profound identification with the dead and a consequent depressive state.[23]

The disruptive impact of a death is greater to the extent that its consequences spill over onto the larger social territory and affect large numbers of people. This depends not only on the frequency and massiveness of mortality, but also on the physical and social settings of death. These vary in different societies, as do also the specialization of responsibility for the care of the dying and the preparation of the body for disposal. In premodern societies, many deaths take place amid the hubbub of life, in the central social territory of the tribe, clan, or other familial group. In modern societies, where the majority of deaths are now predictably in the older age brackets, disengagement from family and economic function has permitted the segregation of death settings from the more workaday social territory. Probably in small towns and rural communities, more people die at home than do so in urban areas. But the proportion of people who die at home, on the job, and in public places must have declined consistently over the past generations with the growing importance of specialized dying institutions—hospitals, old people's homes, and nursing homes.[24]

Modern societies control death through bureaucratization, our characteristic form of social structure. Max Weber has described how bureaucratization in the West proceeded by removing social functions from the family and the household and implanting them in specialized institutions autonomous of kinship considerations. Early manufacturing and entrepreneurship took place in or close to the home; modern industry and corporate bureaucracies are based on the separation of the workplace from the household.[25] Similarly, only a few generations ago most people in the United States either died at home, or were brought into the home if they had died elsewhere. It was the responsibility of the family to lay out the corpse—that is, to prepare the body for the funeral.[26] Today, of course, the hospital cares for the terminally ill and manages the crisis of dying; the mortuary industry (whose establishments are usually called "homes" in deference to past tradition) prepares the body for burial and makes many of the funeral arrangements. A study in Philadelphia found that about ninety percent of funerals started out from the funeral parlor, rather than from the home, as was customary in the past.[27] This separation of the handling of illness and death from the family minimizes the average person's exposure to death and its disruption of the social process. When the dying are segregated among specialists for whom contact with death has become routine and even somewhat impersonal, neither their presence while alive nor as corpses interferes greatly with the mainstream of life.

Another principle of bureaucracy is the ordering of regularly occurring as well as extraordinary events into predictable and routinized procedures. In addition to treating the ill and isolating them from the rest of society, the modern hospital as an organization is committed to the routinization of the handling of death. Its distinctive competence is to contain through isolation, and reduce through orderly procedures, the disturbance and disruption that are associated with the death crisis. The decline in the authority of religion as well as shifts in the functions of the family underlies this fact. With the growth of the secular and rational outlook, hegemony in the affairs of death has been transferred from the church to science and its representatives, the medical profession and the rationally organized hospital.

Death in the modern hospital has been the subject of two recent sociological studies: Sudnow has focused on the handling of death and the dead in a county hospital catering to charity patients; and Glaser and Strauss have concentrated on the dying situation in a number of hospitals of varying status.[28] The county hospital well illustrates various trends in modern death. Three-quarters of its patients are over 60 years old. Of the 250 deaths Sudnow observed, only a handful involved people younger than 40.[29] This hospital is a setting for the concentration of death. There are 1,000 deaths a year; thus approximately three die daily, of the 330 patients typically in residence. But death is even more concentrated in the four wards of the critically ill; here roughly 75 percent of all mortality occurs, and one in 25 persons will die each day.[30]

Hospitals are organized to hide the facts of dying and death from patients as well as visitors. Sudnow quotes a major text in hospital administration: "The hospital morgue is best located on the ground floor and placed in an area inaccessible to the general public. It is important that the unit have a suitable exit leading onto a private loading platform which is concealed from hospital patients and the public."[31] Personnel in the high-mortality wards use a number of techniques to render death invisible. To protect relatives, bodies are not to be removed during visiting hours. To protect other inmates, the patient is moved to a private room when the end is foreseen. But some deaths are unexpected and may be noticed by roommates before the hospital staff is aware of them. These are considered troublesome because elaborate procedures are required to remove the corpse without offending the living.

The rationalization of death in the hospital takes place through standard procedures of covering the corpse, removing the body, identifying the deceased, informing relatives, and completing the death certificate and autopsy permit. Within the value hierarchy of the hospital, handling the corpse is "dirty work," and when possible attendants will leave a body to be processed by the next work shift. As with so many of the unpleasant jobs in our society, hospital morgue attendants and orderlies are often Negroes. Personnel become routinized to death and are easily able to pass from mention of the daily toll to other topics; new staff members stop counting after the first half-dozen deaths witnessed.[32]

Standard operating procedures have even routinized the most charismatic and personal of relations, that between the priest and the dying patient. It is not that the church neglects charity patients. The chaplain at the county hospital daily goes through a file of the critically ill for the names of all known Catholic patients, then enters their rooms and administers extreme unction. After completing his round on each ward, he stamps the index card of the patient with a rubber stamp which reads: "Last Rites Administered. Date

———— Clergyman ————." Each day he consults the files to see if new patients have been admitted or put on the critical list. As Sudnow notes, this rubber stamp prevents him from performing the rites twice on the same patient.[33] This example highlights the trend toward the depersonalization of modern death, and is certainly the antithesis of the historic Catholic notion of "the good death."

In the hospitals studied by Glaser and Strauss, depersonalization is less advanced. Fewer of the dying are comatose, and as paying patients with higher social status they are in a better position to negotiate certain aspects of their terminal situation. Yet nurses and doctors view death as an inconvenience, and manage interaction so as to minimize emotional reactions and fuss. They attempt to avoid announcing unexpected deaths because relatives break down too emotionally; they prefer to let the family members know that the patient has taken "a turn for the worse," so that they will be able to modulate their response in keeping with the hospital's need for order.[34] And drugs are sometimes administered to a dying patient to minimize the disruptiveness of his passing—even when there is no reason for this in terms of treatment or the reduction of pain.

The dying patient in the hospital is subject to the kinds of alienation experienced by persons in other situations in bureaucratic organizations. Because doctors avoid the terminally ill, and nurses and relatives are rarely able to talk about death, he suffers psychic isolation.[35] He experiences a sense of meaninglessness because he is typically kept unaware of the course of his disease and his impending fate, and is not in a position to understand the medical and other routines carried out in his behalf.[36] He is powerless in that the medical staff and the hospital organization tend to program his death in keeping with their organizational and professional needs; control over one's death seems to be even more difficult to achieve than control over one's life in our society.[37] Thus the modern hospital, devoted to the preservation of life and the reduction of pain, tends to become a "mass reduction" system, undermining the subjecthood of its dying patients.

The rationalization of modern death control cannot be fully achieved, however, because of an inevitable tension between death —as an event, a crisis, an experience laden with great emotionality—and bureaucracy, which must deal with routines rather than events and is committed to the smoothing out of affect and emotion. Although there was almost no interaction between dying patients and the staff in the county hospital studied by Sudnow, many nurses in the other hospitals became personally involved with their patients and experienced grief when they died. Despite these limits to the general trend, our society has gone far in containing the disruptive possibilities of mortality through its bureaucratized death control.

THE DECLINE OF THE FUNERAL IN MODERN SOCIETY

Death creates a further problem because of the contradiction between society's need to push the dead away, and its need "to keep the dead alive".[38] The social distance between the living and the dead must be increased after death, so that the group first, and the most affected grievers later, can reestablish their normal activity without a paralyzing attachment to the corpse. Yet the deceased cannot simply be buried as a dead body: The prospect of total exclusion from the social world would be too anxiety-laden for the living, aware of their own eventual fate. The need to keep the dead alive directs societies to construct rituals that celebrate and insure a transition to a new social status, that of spirit, a being now believed to participate in a different realm.[39] Thus, a funeral that combines this status transformation with the act of physical disposal is universal to all societies, and has justly been considered one of the crucial *rites de passage*.[40]

Because the funeral has been typically employed to handle death's manifold disruptions, its character, importance, and frequency may be viewed as indicators of the place of mortality in society. The contrasting impact of death in primitive and modern societies, and the diversity in their modes of control, is suggested by the striking difference in the centrality of mortuary ceremonies in the collective life. Because death is so disruptive in simple societies, much "work" must be done to restore the social system's functioning. Funerals are not "mere rituals," but significant adaptive structures, as can be seen by considering the tasks that make up the funeral work among the LoDagaa of West Africa. The dead body must be buried with the appropriate ritual so as to give the dead man a new status that separates him from the living; he must be given the material goods and symbolic invocations that will help guarantee his safe journey to the final destination and at the same time protect the survivors against his potentially dangerous intervention in their affairs (such as appearing in dreams, "walking," or attempting to drag others with him); his qualities, lifework, and accomplishments must be summed up and given appropriate recognition; his property, roles, rights, and privileges must be distributed so that social and economic life can continue; and, finally, the social units—family, clan, and community as a whole—whose very existence and functioning his death has threatened, must have a chance to vigorously reaffirm their identity and solidarity through participation in ritual cermony.[41]

Such complicated readjustments take time, and therefore the death of a mature person in many primitive societies is followed by not one, but a series of funerals (usually two or three) that may take place over a period ranging from a few months to two years, and in which the entire society, rather than just relatives and friends, participates.[42] The duration of the funeral and the fine elaboration of its ceremonies suggest the great destructive possibilities of death in these societies. Mortuary institutions loom large in the daily life of the community, and the frequent occurrence of funerals may be no small element in maintaining societal continuity under the precarious conditions of high mortality.[43]

In Western antiquity and the middle ages, funerals were important events in the life of city-states and rural communities.[44] Though not so central as in high-mortality and sacred primitive cultures (reductions in mortality rates and secularism both antedate the industrial revolution in the West), they were still frequent and meaningful ceremonies in the life of small-town, agrarian America several generations ago. But in the modern context they have become relatively unimportant events for the life of the larger society. Formal mortuary observances are completed in a short time. Because of the segregation and disengagement of the aged and the gap between generations, much of the social distance to which funerals generally contribute has already been created before death. The deceased rarely have important roles or rights that the society must be concerned about allocating, and the transfer of property has become the responsibility of individuals in cooperation with legal functionaries. With the weakening of beliefs in the existence and malignancy of ghosts, the absence of "realistic" concern about the dead man's trials in his initiation to spirithood, and the lowered intensity of conventional beliefs in an afterlife, there is less demand for both magical precaution and religious ritual. In a society where disbelief or doubt is more common than a firm acceptance of the reality of a life after death,[45] the funeral's classic function of status transformation becomes attenuated.

The recent attacks on modern funeral practices by social critics focus on alleged commercial exploitation by the mortuary industry and the vulgar ostentatiousness of its service. But at bottom this criticism reflects this crisis in the function of the funeral as a social institution. On the one hand, the religious and ritual meanings of the ceremony have lost significance for many people. But the crisis is not only due to the erosion of the sacred spirit by rational, scientific world views.[46] The social substructure of the funeral is weakened when those who die tend to be irrelevant for the ongoing social life of the community and when the disruptive potentials of death are already controlled by compartmentalization into isolated spheres where bureaucratic routinization is the rule. Thus participation and interest in funerals are restricted to family members and friends rather than involving the larger community, unless an important leader has died.[47] Since only individuals and families are affected, adaptation and bereavement have become their private responsibility, and there is little need for a transition period to permit society as a whole to adjust to the fact of a single death. Karl Marx was proved wrong about "the withering away of the state," but with the near disappearance of death as a public event in modern society, the withering away of the funeral may become a reality.

In modern societies, the bereaved person suffers from a paucity of ritualistic conventions in the mourning period. He experiences grief less frequently, but more intensely, since his emotional involvements are not diffused over an entire community, but are usually concentrated on one or a few people.[48] Since mourning and a sense of loss are not widely shared, as in premodern communities, the individualization and deritualization of bereavement make for serious problems in adjustment. There are many who never fully recover and "get back to normal," in contrast to the frequently observed capacity of the bereaved in primitive societies to smile, laugh, and go about their ordinary pursuits the moment the official mourning period is ended.[49] The lack of conventionalized stages in the mourning process results in an ambiguity as to when the bereaved person has grieved enough and thus can legitimately and guiltlessly feel free for new attachments and interests.[50] Thus at the same time that death becomes less disruptive to the society, its prospects and consequences become more serious for the bereaved individual.

SOME CONSEQUENCES OF MODERN DEATH CONTROL

I shall now consider some larger consequences that appear to follow from the demographic, organizational, and cultural trends in modern society that have diminished the presence of death in public life and have reduced most persons' experience of mortality to a minimum through the middle years.[51]

The Place of the Dead in Modern Society

With the diminished visibility of death, the perceived reality and the effective status and power of the dead have also declined in modern societies. A central factor here is the rise of science: Eissler suggests that "the intensity of service to the dead and the proneness for scientific discovery are in reverse proportion."[52] But the weakening of religious imagery is not the sole cause; there is again a functional sociological basis. When those who die are not important to the life of society, the dead as a collective category will not be of major significance in the concerns of the living.

Compare the situation in high-mortality primitive and peasant societies. The living have not liberated themselves emotionally from many of the recently deceased and therefore need to maintain symbolic interpersonal relations with them. This can take place only when the life of the spirits and their world is conceived in well-structured form, and so, as Goode has phrased it, "practically every primitive religious system imputes both power and interest to the dead."[53]

Their spheres of influence in preindustrial societies are many: Spirits watch over and guide economic activities and may determine the fate of trading exchanges, hunting and fishing expeditions, and harvests. Their most important realm of authority is probably that of social control: They are concerned with the general morality of society and the specfic actions of individuals (usually kin or clansmen) under their jurisdiction. It is generally believed that the dead have the power to bring about both economic and personal misfortunes (including illness and death) to serve their own interests, to express their general capriciousness, or to specifically punish the sins and errors of the living. The fact that a man as spirit often receives more deference from, and exerts greater power over, people than while living may explain the apparent absence of the fear of death that has been observed in some primitive and ancestor-worship societies.[54]

In modern societies the influence of the dead is indirect and is rarely experienced in personified form. Every cultural heritage is in the main the contribution of dead generations to the present society,[55] and the living are confronted with problems that come from the sins of the past (for example, our heritage of Negro slavery). There are people who extend their control over others after death through wills, trust funds, and other arrangements. Certain exceptional figures such as John Kennedy and Malcolm X become legendary or almost sainted and retain influence as national symbols or role models. But, for the most part, the dead have little status or power in modern society, and the living tend to be liberated from their direct, personified influence.[56] We do not attribute to the dead the range of material and ideal interests that adheres to their symbolic existence in other societies, such as property and possessions, the desire to recreate networks of close personal relationships, the concern for tradition and the morality of the society. Our concept of the inner life of spirits is most shadowy. In primitive societies a full range of attitudes and feelings is imputed to them, whereas a scientific culture has emptied out specific mental and emotional contents from its vague image of spirit life.[57]

Generational Continuity and the Status of the Aged

The decline in the authority of the dead, and the widening social distance between them and the living, are both conditions and consequences of the youthful orientation, receptivity to innovation, and dynamic social change that characterize modern society. In most preindustrial societies, symbolic contacts with the spirits and ghosts of the dead were frequent, intimate, and often long-lasting. Such communion in modern society is associated with spiritualism and other deviant belief-systems; "normal" relations with the dead seem to have come under increasing discipline and control. Except for observing Catholics perhaps, contact is limited to very specific spatial boundaries, primarily cemeteries, and is restricted to a brief time period following a death and possible a periodic memorial.[58] Otherwise the dead and their concerns are simply not relevant to the living in a society that feels liberated from the authority of the past and orients its energies toward immediate preoccupations and future possibilities.

Perhaps it is the irrelevance of the dead that is the clue to the status of old people in modern industrial societies. In a low-mortality society, most deaths occur in old age, and since the aged predominate among those who die, the association between old age and death is intensified.[59] Industrial societies value people in terms of their present functions and their future prospects; the aged have not only become disengaged from significant family, economic, and community responsibilities in the present, but their future status (politely never referred to in our humane culture) is among the company of the powerless, anonymous, and virtually ignored dead.[60] In societies where the dead continue to play an influential role in the community of the living, there is no period of the lifespan that marks the end of a person's connection to society, and the aged before death begin to receive some of the awe and authority that is conferred on the spirit world.

The social costs of these developments fall most heavily on our old people, but they also affect the integrity of the larger culture and the interests of the young and middle-aged. The traditional values that the dead and older generations represent lose significance, and the result is a fragmentation of each generation from a sense of belonging to and identity with a lineal stream of kinship and community. In modern societies where mobility and social change have eliminated the age-old sense of closeness to "roots," this alienation from the past—expressed in the distance between living and dead generations—may be an important source of tenuous personal identities.

These tendencies help to produce another contradiction. The very society that has so greatly controlled death has made it more difficult to die with dignity. The irrelevance of the dead, as well as other social and cultural trends, brings about a crisis in our sense of what is an appropriate death. Most societies, including our own past, have a notion of the ideal conditions under which the good man leaves the life of this world: For some primitives it is the influential grandfather; for classical antiquity, the hero's death in battle; in the middle ages, the Catholic idea of "holy dying." There is a clear relationship between the notion of appropriate death and the basic value emphases of the society, whether familial, warlike, or religious. I suggest that American culture is faced with a crisis of death because the changed demographic and structural conditions do not fit the traditional concepts of appropriate death, and no new ideal has arisen to take their place. Our nineteenth-century ideal was that of the patriarch, dying in his own home in ripe old age but in the full possession of his faculties, surrounded by family, heirs, and material symbols of a life of hard work and acquisition. Death was additionally appropriate because of the power of religious belief, which did not regard the event as a final ending. Today people characteristically die at an age when their physical, social, and mental powers are at an ebb, or even absent, typically in the hospital, and often separated from family and other meaningful surroundings. Thus "dying alone" is not only a symbolic theme of existential philosophers; it more and more epitomizes the inappropriateness of how people die under modern conditions.

I have said little about another modern prototype of mortality, mass violence. Despite its statistical infrequency in "normal times," violent death cannot be dismissed as an unimportant theme, since it looms so large in our recent past and in our anxieties about the future. The major forms, prosaic and bizarre, in which violent death occurs, or has occurred, in the present period are: (1) Automobile and airplane accidents; (2) the concentration camp; and (3) nuclear disaster. All these expressions of modern violence result in a most inappropriate way of dying. In a brilliant treatment of the preponderance of death of violence in modern literature, Frederick Hoffman points out its inherent ambiguities. The fact that many people die at once, in most of these situations makes it impossible to mitigate the effects on the survivors through ceremonies of respect. While these deaths are caused by human agents, the impersonality of the assailant, and the distance between him and his victim, makes it impossible to assign responsibility to understandable causes. Because of the suddenness of impact, the death that is died cannot be fitted into the life that has been lived. And finally, society experiences a crisis of meaning when the threat of death pervades the atmosphere, yet cannot be incorporated into a religious or philosophical context.[61]

A Final Theoretical Note: Death and Social Institutions

Mortality implies that population is in a constant (though usually a gradual) state of turnover. Society's groups are fractured by the deaths of their members and must therefore maintain their identities through symbols that are external to and outlast individual persons. The social roles through which the functions of major societal institutions are carried out cannot be limited to particular individuals and their unique interpretations of the needs of social action; they must partake of general and transferable prescriptions and expectations. The order and stability required by a social system are threatened by the eventual deaths of members of small units such as families, as well as political, religious, and economic leaders. There is, therefore, a need for more permanent institutions embedding "impersonal" social roles, universal norms, and transcendent values.

The frequent presence of death in high-mortality societies is important in shaping their characteristic institutional structure. To the extent that death imperils the continuity of a society, its major institutions will be occupied with providing that sense of identity and integrity made precarious by its severity. In societies with high death rates, the kinship system and religion tend to be the major social institutions.

Kinship systems organized around the clan or the extended family are well suited to high-mortality societies because they provide a relative permanence and stability lacking in the smaller nuclear group. Both the totem of the clan and the extended family's ties to the past and the future are institutionalized representations of continuity. Thus, the differential impact of mortality on social structure explains the apparent paradox that the smaller the scale of a community, the larger in general is its ideal family unit.[62] The very size of these kinship units provides a protection against the disintegrating potential of mortality, making possible within the family the varied resources in relational ties, age-statuses, and cultural experience that guarantee the socialization of all its young, even if their natural parents should die before they have become adults.

In primitive and peasant societies the centrality of magic and religion are related to the dominant presence of death. If the extended family provides for the society's physical survival, magic and counter-magic are weapons used by individuals to protect themselves from death's uncontrolled and erratic occurrence. And religion makes possible the moral survival of the society and the individual in an environment fraught with fear, anxiety, and uncertainty. As Malinowski and others have shown, religion owes its persistence and power (if not necessarily its origin) to its unique capacity to solve the societal and personal problems that death calls forth.[63] Its rituals and beliefs impart to the funeral ceremonies those qualities of the sacred and the serious that help the stricken group reestablish and reintegrate itself through the collective reaffirmation of shared cultural assumptions. In all known societies it serves to reassure the individual against possible anxieties concerning destruction, nonbeing, and finitude by providing beliefs that make death meaningful, afterlife plausible, and the miseries and injustices of earthly existence endurable.

In complex modern societies there is a proliferation and differentiation of social institutions that have become autonomous in relationship to kinship and religion, as Durkheim pointed out.[64] In a sense these institutions take on a permanence and autonomy that makes them effectively independent of the individuals who carry out the roles within them. The economic corporation is the prototype of a modern institution. Sociologically it is a bureaucracy and therefore relatively unconnected to family and kinship; constitutionally it has been graced with the legal fiction of immortality. Thus the major agencies that organize productive work (as well as other activities) are relatively invulnerable to the depletion of their personnel by death, for their offices and functions are impersonal and transferable from one role-incumbent to another. The situation is very different in traditional societies. There family ties and kinship groups tend to be the basis of economic, religious, and other activities; social institutions interpenetrate one another around the kinship core. Deaths that strike the family therefore reverberate through the entire social structure. This type of social integration (which Durkheim termed "mechanical solidarity,") makes premodern societies additionally vulnerable to death's disruptive potential—regardless of its quantitative frequency and age distribution.

On the broadest level, the relationship between death and society is a dialectic one. Mortality threatens the continuity of society and in so doing contributes to the strengthening of social structure and the development of culture. Death weakens the social group and calls forth personal anxieties; in response, members of a society cling closer together. Specific deaths disrupt the functioning of the social system and thereby encourage responses in the group that restore social equilibrium and become customary practices that strengthen the social fabric. Death's sword in time cuts down each individual, but with respect to the social order it is double-edged. The very sharpness of its disintegrating potential demands adaptations that can bring higher levels of cohesion and continuity. In the developmental course of an individual life, death always conquers; but, as I have attempted to demonstrate throughout this essay, the social system seems to have greatly contained mortality in the broad span of societal and historical development.

[1]Bronislaw Malinowski, *Argonauts of the Western Pacific*; London, Routledge, 1922; p. 490; cited in Lucien Levy-Bruhl, *The "Soul" of the Primitive*; London, Allen and Unwin, 1928; p. 226.

[2]Jack Goody, *Death, Property and the Ancestors*; Stanford, Stanford Univ. Press, 1962. This is the most thorough investigation in the literature of the relationships between the mortuary institutions of a society and its social structure; I am indebted to Goody for many ideas and insights.

[3]Jules Henry, *Jungle People*; Richmond, Va., William Byrd Press, 1941.

[4]Kingsley Davis, *The Population of India and Pakistan*; Princeton, Princeton Univ. Press, 1951, p. 64.

[5]Ludwik Krzywicki, *Primitive Society and Its Vital Statistics*; London, Macmillan, 1934; p. 292. The very scale of modern societies is thus an important element of their control of mortality; unlike the situation in a remote village of India or the jungle highlands of Brazil, it would require the ultimate in catastrophic mortality, all-out nuclear war, for death to threaten societal survival.

[6]United Nations, *Demographic Yearbook*, 1961, 13th Edition; New York, Department of Economic and Social Affairs, 1961; see Table 15. A very similar age distribution results when a cohort of 100,000 born in 1929 is tabulated in terms of the proportions who die in each age period. See Louis I. Dublin and Alfred J. Lotka, *Length of Life*; New York, Ronald, 1936; p. 12. The outlook for the future is suggested by a more recent life-table for females in Canada. Of 100,000 babies born in the late 1950's, only 15 percent will die before age 60. Seventy percent will be 70 years old or more at death; 42 percent will die past 80. See United Nations, *Demographic Yearbook*; pp. 622-676.

[7]See footnote 5; pp. 148, 271. A more recent demographic study of the Cocos-Keeling Islands in the Malay Peninsula found that 59 percent die before age five. See T. E. Smith, "The Cocos-Keeling Islands: A Demographic Laboratory," *Population Studies* (1960) 14: 94-130. Among 89 deaths recorded in 1952-1953 among the Tikopia, 39 percent were of infants and children below age eight. See W. D. Borrie, Raymond Firth, and James Spillius, "The Population of Tikopia, 1929 and 1952," *Population Studies* (1957) 10: 229-252. The Rungus Dusun, "a primitive, pagan agricultural" village community in North Borneo, lose 20 percent of their females in the first year of life, and another 50 percent die between the first birthday and motherhood. See P. J. Koblenzer and N. H. Carrier, "The Fertility, Mortality and Nuptiality of the Rungus Dusun," *Population Studies* (1960) 13:266-277.

[8]See United Nations, *Demographic Yearbook*, in footnote 6; pp. 622-676.

[9]See Borrie, Firth, and Spillius, in footnote 7; p. 238.

[10]Calculated from tables in J. C. Russell, "Late Ancient and Medieval Population," *Transactions of the Amer. Philosophical Soc.*, Vol. 48,wPart 3, pp. 25-29.

[11]See Smith, in footnote 7. In Nigeria during 1956, only 13 percent of male deaths recorded were of men older than 55 years. Twenty-eight percent occurred among males between 5 and 54. Similarly in Algeria during the same year, 30 percent of all male deaths among the Moslem population took people during the middle years of life (between 15 and 49). Only 13 percent were old men past 60. See United Nations, *Demographic Yearbook*, in footnote 6; Table 15.

[12]See Goody, in footnote 2; pp. 30, 73 ff. In some high-mortality societies, such as traditional India, remarriage is not prescribed for the affected widows. Perhaps this difference may be related to the much greater population density of India as compared to West Africa.

[13]Robert Hertz, "The Collective Representation of Death," in Hertz, *Death and the Right Hand*, translated by Rodney and Claudia Needham; Aberdeen, Cohen and West, 1960; pp. 84-85. See also Goody, in footnote 2; pp. 208 ff.

[14]Phillipe Aries, *Centuries of Childhood: A Social History of Family Life*, translated by Robert Baldick; New York, Knopf, 1962; pp. 38 ff.

[15]After studying 71 tribes from the human area files, Leo Simmons generalizes that the belief in ghosts is "about as universal in primitive societies as any trait could be." See Simmons, *The Role of the Aged in Primitive Society*; New Haven, Yale Univ. Press, 1945; pp. 223 ff. Another student of death customs reports that "the fear of a malignant ghost governs much of the activity of primitive tribes." See Norman L. Egger, "Contrasting Attitudes Toward Death Among Veterans With and Without Battle Experience and Non-Veterans," unpublished M.A. Thesis, Dept. of Psychology, Univ. of Calif., Berkeley, 1948; p. 33.

[16]Adapted from William Goode, *Religion Among the Primitives*; Glencoe, Ill., Free Press, 1951; pp. 64 ff., 194 ff. The former Sir-Ghost, neglected after his forced retirement, is thought to wander on the sea between the villages, endangering sea voyages.

Eventually he becomes a sea-slug. A similar phenomenon is reported with respect to the shades of ancient Rome; a deceased husband began as a shade with a distinct personality, but was degraded to the rank of the undifferentiated shades that haunt the world of the dead after time passed and the widow remarried. Thus the unfinished business had been completed by someone else. See James H. Leuba, *The Belief in God and Immortality*; Boston, Sherman, French, 1916; pp. 95-96.

[17]The most complete materials on ambivalence toward ghosts are found in James G. Frazer, *The Fear of the Dead in Primitive Religion*, 3 vols.; London, Macmillan, 1933, 1934, and 1936. Volume II is devoted to various methods of keeping dead spirits away.

The connection between the ambivalent attitude toward the ghost and the neomort's uncompleted working out of his obligations on earth is clear in Henry's description of the Kaingang: "The ghost-soul loves and pities the living whom it has deserted, but the latter fear and abhor the ghost-soul. The ghost-soul longs for those it has left behind, but they remain cold to its longings. 'One pities one's children, and therefore goes with them (that is, takes them when one dies). One loves (literally, lives in) one's children, and dies and goes with one's children, and one (the child) dies.' The dead pity those they have left alone with no one to care for them. They have left behind parts of themselves, for their children are those 'in whom they live.' But to the pity, love and longing of the ghost-soul, the children return a cry of 'Mother, leave me and go!' as she lies on the funeral pyre. The Kaingang oscillate between a feeling of attachment for the dead and a desire never to see them again." See Henry, in footnote 3; p. 67.

Eissler suggests that an envy of the living who continue on is one of the universal pains of dying. Such an attitude would be understandably stronger for those who die in middle life. See Kurt R. Eisslr, *The Psychiatrist and the Dying Patient*; New York, Internat. Univ. Press, 1955; pp. 149-150.

[18]See Frazer, in footnote 17; Vol. III, pp. 103-260.

[19]See Goody, in footnote 2, pp. 208-209; Levy-Bruhl, in footnote 1, p. 219; and Hertz, in footnote 13, p. 84.

[20]See Elaine Cumming and William E. Henry, *Growing Old* (New York, Basic Books, 1961) for a theoretical discussion and empirical data on the disengagement of the old in American society. In a more recent statement, Cumming notes that disengagement "frees the old to die without disrupting vital affairs," and that "the depth and breadth of a man's engagement can be measured by the degree of potential disruption that would follow his sudden death." See "New Thoughts on the Theory of Disengagement," in *New Thoughts on Old Age*, edited by Robert Kastenbaum; New York, Springer, 1964; pp. 11, 4.

[21]Robert N. Butler, "The Life Review: An Interpretation of Reminiscence in the Aged," PSYCHIATRY (1963), 26:65-76; see p. 67.

[22]Many early anthropologists, including Malinowski, attributed human funerary customs to an alleged instinctive aversion to the corpse. Although there is no evidence for such an instinct, aversion to the corpse remains a widespread, if not universal, human reaction. See the extended discussion of the early theories in Goody, in footnote 2; pp. 20-30; and for some exceptions to the general rule, Robert W. Habenstein, "The Social Organization of Death," *International Encyclopedia of the Social Sciences*, forthcoming.

[23]Robert J. Lifton, "Psychological Effects of the Atomic Bomb in Hiroshima: The Theme of Death," *Daedalus* (1963), 92: 462-497. Among other things, the dead body is too stark a reminder of man's mortal condition. Although man is the one species that knows he will eventually die, most people in most societies cannot live too successfully when constantly reminded of this truth. On the other hand, the exposure to the corpse has positive consequences for psychic functiong, as it contributes to the acceptance of the reality of a death on the part of the survivors. A study of deaths in military action during World War II found that the bereaved kin had particularly great difficulty in believing in and accepting the reality of their loss because they did not see the body and witness its disposal. T. D. Eliot, "Of the Shadow of Death," *Annals Amer. Academy of Political and Social Science* (1943), 229:87-99.

[24]Statistics on the settings of death are not readily available. Robert Fulton reports that 53 percent of all deaths in the United States takes place in hospitals, but he does not give any source for this figure. See Fulton, *Death and Identity*; New York, Wiley, 1965; pp. 81-82. Two recent English studies are also suggestive. In the case of the deaths of 72 working-class husbands, primarily in the middle years, 46 died in the hospital; 22 at home; and 4 at work or in the street. See Peter Marris, *Widows and Their Families*; London. Routledge and Kegan Paul, 1958; p. 146. Of 359 Britishers who had experienced a recent bereavement, 50 percent report that the death took place in a hospital; 44 percent at home; and 6 percent elsewhere. See Geoffrey Gorer, *Death, Grief, and Mourning*; London, Cresset, 1965; p. 149.

[25]Max Weber, *Essays in Sociology*, translated and edited by H. H. Gerth and C. Wright Mills; New York Oxford Univ. Press, 1953; pp. 196-198. See also Max Weber, *General Economic History*, translated by Frank H. Knight; Glencoe, Ill., Free Press, 1950.

[26]Leroy Bowman reports that aversion to the corpse made this preparation an unpleasant task. Although sometimes farmed out to experienced relatives or neighbors, the task was still considered the family's responsibility. See Bowman, *The American Funeral: A Study in Guilt, Extravagance and Sublimity*; Washington, D.C., Public Affairs Press, 1959; p. 71.

[27]William K. Kephart, "Status After Death," *Amer. Sociol. Review* (1950), 15:635-643.

[28]David N. Sudnow, "Passing On: The Social Organization of Dying in the County Hospital," unpublished Ph.D. Thesis, Univ. of Calif., Berkeley, 1965. Sudnow also includes comparative materials from a more well-to-do Jewish-sponsored hospital where he did additional fieldwork, but most of his statements are based on the county institution. Barney G. Glaser and Anselm L. Strauss, *Awareness of Dying*; Chicago, Aldine, 1965.

[29]See Sudnow, in footnote 28; pp. 107, 109. This is even fewer than would be expected by the age-composition of mortality, because children's and teaching hospitals in the city were likely to care for many terminally ill children and younger adults.

[30]See Sudnow, in footnote 28; pp. 49, 50.

[31] J. K. Owen, *Modern Concepts of Hospital Administration*; Philadelphia, Saunders, 1962; p. 304; cited in Sudnow, in footnote 28; p. 80. Such practice attests to the accuracy of Edgar Morin's rather melodramatic statement: "Man hides his death as he hides his sex, as he hides his excrements." See E. Morin, *L'Homme et La Mort dans L'Histoire*; Paris, Correa, 1951; p. 331.

[32]See Sudnow, in footnote 28; pp. 20-40, 49-50.

[33]See Sudnow, in footnote 28; p. 114.

[34]See Glaser and Strauss, in footnote 28; pp. 142-143, 151-152.

[35]On the doctor's attitudes toward death and the dying, see August M. Kasper, "The Doctor and Death," pp. 259-270, in *The Meaning of Death*, edited by Herman Feifel; New York, McGraw-Hill, 1959. Many writers have commented on the tendency of relatives to avoid the subject of death with the terminally ill; see, for example, Herman Feifel's "Attitudes toward Death in Some Normal and Mentally Ill Populations," pp. 114-132 in *The Meaning of Death*.

[36]The most favorable situation for reducing isolation and meaninglessness would seem to be "where personnel and patient both are aware that he is dying, and where they act on this awareness relatively openly." This atmosphere, which Glaser and Strauss term an "open awareness context," did not typically predominate in the hospitals they studied. More common were one of three other awareness contexts they distinguished: "the situation where the patient does not recognize his inpending death even though everyone else does" (closed awareness); "the situation where the patient suspects what the others know and therefore attempts to confirm or invalidate his suspicion" (suspected awareness); and "the situation where each party defines the patient as dying, but each pretends that the other has not done so" (mutual pretense awareness). See Glaser and Strauss, in footnote 28; p. 11.

[37]See Glaser and Strauss, in footnote 28; p. 129. Some patients, however, put up a struggle to control the pace and style of their dying, and some prefer to leave the

hospital and end their days at home for this reason (see Glaser and Strauss, in footnote 28; pp. 95, 181-183). For a classic and moving account of a cancer victim who struggled to achieve control over the conditions of his death, see Lael T. Wertenbaker, *Death of a Man*; New York, Random House, 1957.

For discussions of isolation, meaninglessness, and powerlessness as dimensions of alienation, see Melvin Seeman, "On the Meaning of Alienation," *Amer. Sociol. Review* (1959), 24:783-791; and Robert Blauner, *Alienation and Freedom: The Factory Worker and His Industry*; Chicago, Univ. of Chicago Press, 1964.

[38]Franz Borkenau, "The Concept of Death," *The Twentieth Century* (1955), 157:313-329; reprinted in *Death and Identity*, pp. 42-56 (see footnote 24).

[39] The need to redefine the status of the departed is intensified because of tendencies to act toward him as if he were still alive. There is a status discongruity inherent in the often abrupt change from a more or less responsive person to an inactive, non-responding one. This confusion makes it difficult for the living to shift their mode of interaction toward the neomort. Glaser and Strauss report that relatives in the hospital often speak to the newly deceased and caress him as if he were alive; they act as if he knows what they are saying and doing. Nurses who had become emotionally involved with the patient sometimes back away from postmortem care because of a "mystic illusion" that the deceased is still sentient. See Glaser and Strauss, in footnote 28; pp. 113-114. We are all familiar with the expression of "doing the right thing" *for the deceased*, probably the most common conscious motivation underlying the bereaved's funeral preparations. This whole situation is sensitively depicted in Jules Romain's novel, *The Death of a Nobody*; New York, Knopf, 1944.

[40]Arnold Van Gennep, *The Rites of Passage*; London, Routledge and Kegan Paul, 1960 (first published in 1909). See also W. L. Warner, *The Living and the Dead*; New Haven, Yale Univ. Press, 1959; especially Chapter 9; and Habenstein, in footnote 22, for a discussion of funerals as "dramas of disposal."

[41]See Goody, in footnote 2, for the specific material on the LoDagaa. For the general theoretical treatment, see Hertz, in footnote 13, and also Emile Durkheim, *The Elementary Forms of the Religious Life*; Glencoe, Ill., Free Press, 1947; especially p. 447.

[42]Hertz (see footnote 13) took the multiple funerals of primitive societies as the strategic starting point for his analysis of mortality and social structure. See Goody (in footnote 2) for a discussion of Hertz (pp. 26-27), and the entire book for an investigation of multiple funerals among the LoDagaa.

[43]I have been unable to locate precise statistics on the comparative frequency of funerals. The following data are suggestive. In a year and a half, Goody attended 30 among the LoDagaa, a people numbering some 4,000 (see footnote 2). Of the Barra people, a Roman Catholic peasant folk culture in the Scottish Outer Hebrides, it is reported that "most men and women participate in some ten to fifteen funerals in their neighborhood every year." See D. Mandelbaum, "Social Uses of Funeral Rites," in *The Meaning of Death*, in footnote 35; p. 206.
Considering the life-expectancy in our society today, it is probable that only a minority of people would attend one funeral or more per year. Probably most people during the first 40 (or even 50) years of life attend only one or two funerals a decade. In old age, the deaths of the spouse, collateral relations, and friends become more common; thus funeral attendance in modern societies tends to become more age-specific. For a discussion of the loss of intimates in later years, see J. Moreno, "The Social Atom and Death," pp. 62-66, in *The Sociometry Reader*, edited by J. Moreno; Glencoe, Ill., Free Press, 1960.

[44]For a discussion of funerals among the Romans and early Christians, see Alfred C. Rush, *Death and Burial in Christian Antiquity*; Washington, D.C., Catholic Univ. of America Press, 1941; especially Part III, pp. 187-273. On funerals in the medieval and preindustrial West, see Bertram S. Puckle, *Funeral Customs*; London, T. Werner Laurie, 1926.

[45]See Eissler, in footnote 17; p. 144: "The religion dogma is, with relatively rare exceptions, not an essential help to the psychiatrist since the belief in the immortality of the soul, although deeply rooted in man's unconscious, is only rarely encountered nowadays as a well-integrated idea from which the ego could draw strength." On the basis of a sociological survey, Gorer confirms the phychiatrist's judgment: ". . . how

small a role dogmatic Christian beliefs play . . ." (see Gorer, in footnote 24; p. 39). Forty-nine percent of his sample affirmed a belief in an afterlife: twenty-five percent disbelieved; twenty-six percent were uncertain or would not answer (see Gorer; p. 166).

[46]The problem of sacred institutions in an essentially secular society has been well analyzed by Robert Fulton. See Fulton and Gilbert Geis, "Death and Social Values," pp. 67-75, and Fulton, "The Sacred and the Secular," pp. 89-105, in *Death and Identity*, footnote 24.

[47]LeRoy Bowman interprets the decline of the American funeral primarily in terms of urbanization. When communities were made up of closely knit, geographically isolated groups of families, the death of an individual was a deprivation of the customary social give and take, a distinctly felt diminution of the total community. It made sense for the community as a whole to participate in a funeral. But in cities, individual families are in a much more limited relationship to other families, and the population loses its unity of social and religious ideals. For ethical and religious reasons, Bowman is unwilling to accept "a bitter deduction from this line of thought. . .that the death of one person is not so important as once it would have been, at least to the community in which he as lived." But that is the logical implication of his perceptive sociological analysis. See Bowman, in footnote 26; pp. 9, 113-115, 126-128.

[48]Edmund Volkart, "Bereavement and Mental Health," pp. 281-307, in *Explorations in Social Psychiatry*, edited by Alexander H. Leighton, John A. Clausen, and Robert N. Wilson; New York, Basic Books, 1957. Volkart suggests that bereavement is a greater crisis in modern American society than in similar cultures because our family system develops selves in which people relate to others as persons rather than in terms of roles (see pp. 293-295).

[49]In a study of bereavement reactions in England, Geoffrey Gorer found that 30 of a group of 80 persons who had lost a close relative were mourning in a style he characterized as *unlimited*. He attributes the inability to get over one's grief "to the absence of any ritual, either individual or social, lay or religious, to guide them and the people they come in contact with." The study also attests to the virtual disappearance of traditional mourning conventions. See Gorer, in footnote 24; pp. 78-83.

[50]See Marris, in footnote 24; pp. 39-40.

[51]Irwin W. Goffman suggests that "a decline in the significance of death has occurred in our recent history." See "Suicide Motives and Categorization of the Living and the Dead in the United States"; Syracuse, N.Y., Mental Health Research Unit, Feb., 1966, unpublished manuscript; p. 140.

[52]See Eissler, in footnote 17; p. 44.

[53]See Goode, in footnote 16; p. 185. Perhaps the fullest treatment is by Frazer; see footnote 17, especially Vol. I.

[54]See Simmons, in footnote 15; pp. 223-224. See also Effie Bendann, *Death Customs*; New York, Knopf, 1930; p. 180. However, there are primitive societies, such as the Hopi, that attribute little power and authority to dead spirits; in some cultures, the period of the dead man's influence is relatively limited; and in other cases only a minority of ghosts are reported to be the object of deference and awe. The general point holds despite these reservations.

[55]See Warner, in footnote 40; pp. 4-5.

[56]The novel, *Death of a Nobody* (see footnote 39) is a sensitive treatment of how its protagonist, Jacques Godard, affects people after his death; his influence is extremely short-lived, and his memory in the minds of the living vanishes after a brief period. Goffman suggests that "parents are much less likely today to tell stories of the dead, of their qualities, hardships, accomplishments and adventures than was true a hundred years ago." See footnote 51; p. 30.

[57]In an interesting treatment of the problem from a different theoretical framework, Goffman has concluded that the sense of contrast between what is living and what is dead in modern society has become attenuated, in large part because of the decline in exposure to death. He has assembled evidence on social differences within our society: for example, women, lower-class people, and Catholics tend to have closer and more frequent contact with death or images of the dead than men, middle-class persons, and Protestants. (See footnote 51.)

The question of what is the representative American imagery of afterlife existence would be a fruitful one for research. Clear and well-developed imageries are probably typical only among Catholics, fundamentalists, and certain ethnic groups. The dominant attitude (if there is one) is likely quite nebulous. For some, the dead may be remembered as an "absent presence," never to be seen again; for others as "a loved one with whom I expect (or hope) to be reunited in some form someday." Yet the background of afterlife existence is only vaguely sketched, and expectation and belief probably alternate with hope, doubt, and fear in a striking ambiguity about the prospect and context of reunion.

58In primitive societies ghosts and spirits of the dead range over the entire social territory or occupy central areas of the group's social space. In ancestor-worship civilizations such as Rome and China, spirits dwell in shrines that are located in the homes or family burial plots. In these preindustrial societies symbolic contact with the dead may be a daily occurrence.

Likewise, in the middle ages, cemeteries were not on the periphery of the societal terrain but were central institutions in the community; regularly visited, they were even the sites for feasts and other celebrations, since it was believed that the dead were gladdened by sounds of merry-making. (See Puckle, in footnote 44; pp. 145-146.) The most trenchant analysis of the cemetery as a spatial territory marking the social boundaries between the "sacred dead and the secular world of the profane living" in a small modern community is found in Warner, in footnote 40; Chapter 9. Yet Warner also notes that people tend to disregard cemeteries as a "collective representation" in rapidly changing and growing communities, in contrast to the situation in small, stable communities. Goffman (see footnote 51; p. 29) notes that "increasingly the remains of the dead are to be found in huge distant cemeteries that are not passed or frequented as part of everyday routines. . .[or] in cities in which our very mobile population *used* to live."

59Feifel has suggested that American society's rejection of (and even revulsion to) the old may be because they remind us unconsciously of death. See footnote 35; p. 122.

60According to Kastenbaum, the tendency of psychiatrists to eschew psychotherapy with the aged and to treat them, if at all, with supportive (rather than more prestigious depth) techniques may be a reflection of our society's future orientation, which results in an implicit devaluing of old people because of their limited time prospects. See Kastenbaum, "The Reluctant Therapist," pp. 139-145, in *New Thoughts on Old Age*, in footnote 20. The research of Butler, a psychiatrist who presents evidence for significant personality change in old age despite the common contrary assumption, would seem to support Kastenbaum's view. (See footnote 21.)

Sudnow contributes additional evidence of the devaluation of old people. Ambulance drivers bringing critical or "dead-on-arrival" cases to the county hospital's emergency entrance blow their horns more furiously and act more frantic when the patient is young than when he is old. A certain proportion of "dead-on-arrival" cases can be saved through mouth-to-mouth resuscitation, heart massages, or other unusual efforts. These measures were attempted with children and young people but not with the old; one intern admitted being repulsed by the idea of such close contact with them. See Sudnow, in footnote 28; pp. 160-163.

61Frederick J. Hoffman, *The Mortal No: Death and the Modern Imagination*; Princeton, Princeton Univ. Press, 1964; see especially Part II. In a second paper on Hiroshima, Robert J. Lifton also notes the tendency for the threat of mass death to undermine the meaning systems of society, and the absence of a clear sense of appropriate death in modern cultures. See "On Death and Death Symbolism: The Hiroshima Disaster," PSYCHIATRY (1964), 27:191-210. Gorer has argued that our culture's repression of death as a natural event is the cause of the obsessive focus on fantasies of violence that are so prominent in the mass media. See Geoffrey Gorer, "The Pornography of Death," pp. 402-407, in *Identity and Anxiety*, edited by Maurice Stein and Arthur Vidich; Glencoe, Ill., Free Press, 1960; also reprinted in Gorer's *Death, Grief, and Mourning* (see footnote 24).

The inappropriateness inherent in the automobile accident, in which a man dies outside a communal and religious setting, is poignantly captured in the verse and chorus of the Country and Western song, "Wreck on the Highway," popularized by Roy Acuff. "Who did you say it was, brother?/Who was it fell by the way?/When whiskey and blood run together,/Did you hear anyone pray?"

Chorus: "I didn't hear nobody pray, dear brother/I didn't hear nobody pray./I heard the crash on the highway,/But I didn't hear nobody pray."

[62]The important distinction between ideal family structures and actual patterns of size of household, kinship composition, and authority relations has been stressed recently by William Goode in *World Revolution and Family Patterns*; New York, Free Press of Glencoe, 1963; and by Marion Levy, "Aspects of the Analysis of Family Structure," pp. 1-63, in A. J. Coale and Marion Levy, *Aspects of the Analysis of Family Structure*; Princeton, Princeton Univ. Press, 1965.

[63]Bronislaw Malinowski, *Magic, Science and Religion*; Garden City, N.Y., Doubleday Anchor, 1955; see pp. 47-53.

[64]Emile Durkheim, *Division of Labor*; Glencoe, Ill., The Free Press, 1949.